MICHIGAN BUSINESS STUDIES

Volume 2   Number 1
          New Series

THE DEVELOPMENT OF ECONOMIC POLICY

Financial Institution Reform

Sidney L. Jones

Division of Research
Graduate School of Business Administration
The University of Michigan
Ann Arbor, Michigan

Printed in the United States of America
All rights reserved

Library of Congress Cataloging in Publication Data

Jones, Sidney Lewis.
 The development of economic policy.

 (Michigan business studies; v. 2, no. 1)
 Bibliography: p.
 Includes index.
 1. Financial institutions—United States.
I. Title. II. Series.
HG181.J59   332.1'0973   79-22964
ISBN 0-87712-197-4

CONTENTS

ILLUSTRATIONS

Tables

Figures

FOREWORD

This is an important book.

It is important because continued economic progress depends upon our ability to make financial markets more efficient and responsive to the dynamic and changing patterns of both flows of savings and demands for financing. Historically, we can see a recurring pattern in which financial institutions, because of the way they have been structured, have been plagued by inundating inflows of dollars, followed by hemorrhaging outflows as market interest rates pierce regulated ceilings. Various institutions, though providing customers with essentially similar services, have been subjected to differing regulations, thus impeding the healthy competition that makes for both efficiency and innovation in our economic system. By the late sixties, recognition of the need for rationalization of our kaleidoscopic financial landscape was widespread, and Dr. Jones here lays out with care the problems that needed attention.

The book is important for another reason as well. As a biography of the whole reform effort, written by one with broad experience in government and there at the time, the book provides an education in the processes of public policy generally. In the political arena, it is not enough that "something clearly needs to be done." Institutions adapt to and become comfortable with rules and regulatory processes, even if they are in some objective sense irrational; and proposed changes will be opposed even by those whose institutions might thereby become more dynamic and efficient. Empires in government—both in Congress and in the executive branch—emerge and prosper in the administration of this structure, and they do not take kindly to change.

For those with more general interest in the processes of public policy, this book details the political impediments that lie between proposals that would serve the general welfare and the actions necessary to implement them.

Dr. Jone's book, therefore, will be read with interest and profit not only by those with specific concerns about our financial system, but by citizens generally who would like to know more about the way the processes of public policy actually operate in the world of government. For them, this is a choice seat on the fifty-yard line.

PAUL W. McCRACKEN

Ann Arbor, Michigan
June 1979

PREFACE

The strategy of *The Development of Economic Policy: Financial Institution Reform* is to review an example of the government's decision-making process as a framework within which to analyze the development of national economic policy. The analysis of the selected case examines the role of special interest groups, academic experts, public commissions and consultants, executive branch task forces, and congressional committees. The conclusions are not novel, but they are substantiated by the case example, which describes the failure to accomplish comprehensive reform of financial institutions because of internal procedural breakdowns and the divisive efforts of key special interest groups. Representative government provides many benefits, but it is vulnerable to stonewalling tactics.

Chapter 1 presents an overview of the process of institutional reform and a summary of the case study upon which the discussion in this book is based. The role of financial institutions in the economic system and the competitive pressures affecting the patterns of financial disintermediation when funds move out of savings-oriented institutions are summarized in Chapter 2. The regulatory response to the competitive structure of financial institutions is discussed in Chapter 3, and Chapter 4 reviews the activities and recommendations of the President's Commission on Financial Structure and Regulation. Chapters 5 through 8 summarize the development of the Financial Institutions Act of 1973 and the revised version submitted in 1975, and analyze the diverse views of the many witnesses. Chapters 9 and 10 review the activities and recommendations of the FINE Study and the Financial Reform Act of 1976, and discuss the outlook for future reform initiatives.

The first ten chapters thus present a specific case as an example of how economic policy decisions are made; the final four chapters discuss the policy implications of these experiences in reform. Among the major policy issues that are discussed are the role of presidential advisers, both outside commissions and internal interagency committees; the contributions of congressional hearings; the choice of strategies in submitting piecemeal or comprehensive legislation; and the realities of the marketplace as a substitute for legislative change in developing economic policy.

The book was written during my tenure as a Fellow at the Woodrow Wilson International Center for Scholars, an organ of the Smithsonian Institution. My interest in the subject of financial institutions comes from my experiences in teaching and writing as a Professor of Finance at the University of Michigan, as well as from my association with the Council of Economic Advisers in the late 1960s, when the Hunt Commission was formed, and with the Treasury Department as Assistant Secretary for Economic Policy during the period of legislative analysis. The policy conclusions in the final chapters and the evaluation of historical events are my personal views and should not be interpreted as representing any organizational dogma or the opinions of my former colleagues in the government.

While a single example may not be representative of the entire system of government, financial institution reform was selected for analysis because it combines the key elements of policy making involving the Executive Office, Congress, academic experts, regulatory officials, and a variety of interest groups in the private sector. The summary of experiences and conclusions that follows represents the distilled observations of almost eight years in government service and the personal review of more than one hundred books, monographs, and articles, as well as more than ten thousand pages of congressional testimony. This combination of experiences and study convinces me that governments can—and must—improve their economic policies if the general public's disillusionment about the quality, efficiency, and objectivity of legislative and administrative actions is to be replaced by a spirit of trust and support.

SIDNEY L. JONES

Washington, D.C.
May 1979

1

BACKGROUND OF INSTITUTIONAL REFORM

The most difficult challenge facing governments is to rationalize competing interests while developing policies that are adaptable to changing conditions. Aversion to change is natural: people are reluctant to relinquish established claims and accept the uncertainties of future adjustments. But pressures for change are continual because those with fewer advantages desire equality, and equals prefer superiority. Government institutions therefore become the focal point of both new initiatives for and organized resistance to change.

Those familiar with the processes of government are increasingly concerned about the viability of the institutions and procedures for making policy decisions. Such concerns are based on the complexity of problems confronting modern governments, the intensity of pressures created by special interest groups, the overwhelming organizational difficulties of developing collective decisions and then administering the resulting compromises, the obvious human limitations of officials responsible for action, and the apparent acceleration of change which rapidly makes established rules and processes obsolete. In general, there is increasing skepticism about the interest of governments in responding to individual problems and their capacity to do so in a society that is dominated by groups and collective solutions.

The American system is based on the assumption that lawmakers, bureaucrats, technicians, and the judiciary will somehow arrive at prudent decisions in adapting to change. While this faith in the ultimate effectiveness of the system is necessary, it provides less than adequate support at present, when the performance of most governments is severely criticized. Economic instability has increased. Social dissatisfaction continues. Public esteem for political leaders has declined sharply. Concealed and open evasion of laws

1

and regulations has become commonplace as the general public reacts to increased intervention in daily life. At a time when government decisions have become more important in shaping the economic and social environment of this unusually large and complex nation, there is extensive disillusionment about the quality, efficiency, and objectivity of legislative and administrative actions. Increased public understanding and confidence are required, and public officials must become more accountable for their policy decisions, if the American system is to endure.

The basic issues are these: Can governments formulate and administer policies adaptable to changing conditions and thus earn the uncoerced support of the societies they serve? Can they identify problems that are pervasive enough to affect a significant number of people, organize expert opinion, develop rigorous and objective analysis, prepare and gain approval for constructive legislation, and effectively apply and enforce the resulting laws and regulations? Can the collective approach to policy making overcome human failings and the debilitating effects of necessary compromises? Can the "art of the possible," as expressed in the political process, be adapted to create the technical rules necessary for directing the complex affairs of a modern society? In short, can the democratic decision-making system be made to work better in the future?

Although the process of making decisions has long been a favorite topic for research, many scholarly studies are abstract descriptions of what should be rather than what is. In contrast, the writings of experienced officials are frequently only anecdotal reviews of their own careers. The point of view here is that each decision is clearly unique because the possible combinations of issues, personalities, options, information, external constraints, time frames, historical precedents, and so on, are infinite. Nevertheless, certain underlying human and procedural patterns are repeated when governments make decisions, and the outcome of these should be guidelines for improvement. For example, occasional committee meetings provide a forum in which serious analysis by informed officials can take place, along with strenuous debate, selection and ranking of decisions about what to do, about the timing and sequence of actions, and about how to monitor and evaluate the interim and final results. Most senior government officials, however, are appalled by the amount of time they spend in daily committee meetings which are generally used for the inefficient verbal exchange of information pegged to the level of the least informed member of the group.

A classic example occurred August 17, 1971, when the economic leaders of the premier economy in the world—the Secretary of the Treasury, the Director of the Office of Management and Budget, the Chairman of the Council of Economic Advisers, the Chairman of the Federal Reserve Board of Governors, numerous Cabinet Secretaries, and an array of Under and Assistant Secretaries—crammed themselves into the Roosevelt Room of the West Wing of the White House two days after wage and price controls were announced and devoted over four hours to discussing in excruciating detail such policy issues as whether or not the price of tree stumps should be controlled. While this ludicrous example is not typical of every meeting, more leadership time and energy are probably wasted in such meetings than are committed to substantive decisions. Nevertheless, each administration perpetuates the same interagency procedures with little improvement in the preparation or conduct of such sessions. Only the personalities and organization charts change with time.

Although such examples are familiar to experienced officials, and suspected by everyone else, procedural improvement does not occur. The purpose of this study is to analyze a specific example as a basis for discussing the general approach to developing economic policies, using the example as the hook on which the general discussion will hang. This approach, it is hoped, will exert some discipline to keep the study from being merely a collection of anecdotes by one more former government official. The recommendations in the last four chapters, reflecting my personal experiences and reading of published materials, attempt to focus on the chronic decision-making problems that confront every government. The case description is meant to be of technical interest to some readers, and it does involve a fundamental factor in the operation of the economy. The generalizations that follow will cover broader issues.

This case study concerns the extensive effort to reform the legislative and regulatory environment for financial institutions—commercial banks, savings and loan associations, mutual savings banks, and credit unions—which serve as intermediaries for collecting savings and matching the funds with demands for loans and investments. This financial system is expected to provide: (1) an effective payments mechanism; (2) a safe and efficient means of collecting and allocating savings; (3) convenient, low-cost savings and lending programs; and (4) basic controls consistent with established national economic stabilization and social objectives. All of these goals are supposed to be achieved within an environment of constant change and intense competition and without eroding the basic confidence of savers and borrowers.

Unfortunately the operating and regulatory realities have not always matched these noble aspirations. At various times severe cyclical swings in interest rates have created "credit crunches," disintermediation of savings away from deposit institutions, volatile earnings and even failures, disruption of housing markets, and general uncertainty. On rare occasions the entire system has been shaken by widespread panics, such as the bank closings during the Great Depression of the early 1930s. Even during relatively stable periods a number of controversial issues persist in relation to portfolio lending and investment powers, competition for funds, diversification of services, international expansion, the safety of deposits, regulatory supervision and chartering, and merger and branching policies. Much of the consequent tension results from the simple fact that the legislative and regulatory framework created during times of crisis, particularly in the Great Depression, could not take into account the environment of the 1970s with its new institutions, electronic transfers of funds, increased use of retail credit, and the distorting effects of intense inflation.

For all of these reasons many analysts have long argued in favor of a comprehensive reform of the entire system rather than the ad hoc approach of patching up specific problems during periods of severe strain. The difficulty has always been to design legislation that would be politically acceptable.

The accumulation of problems could no longer be ignored after the financial distortions in 1966 and 1969–70, when savings were rapidly drained out of deposit institutions into marketable securities offering higher yields. The federal government reacted in 1966 by expanding, on the model of regulation Q, controls over the level of interest payments on deposits to restrict the competition for savings among different financial institutions. But that expedient action did not solve the fundamental problems of disintermediation, and it also discriminated against savers with small accounts who cannot shift their funds into higher-yield marketable securities. Most important, the general expansion of government controls did not provide the necessary flexibility in the marketplace to match changing conditions. What was needed was a system of free markets and intensified competition that would not erode the basic confidence of the general public or disrupt the achievement of social goals such as the growth of housing construction. By the end of the 1960s it was generally recognized that the distortions caused by periodic financial

strains and the confusing maze of regulations had created the necessary support for an integrated approach to general reform. The history of that effort provides the case example used in this study.

Reform Efforts, 1961–75

Comprehensive efforts to modify the structure of financial institutions began in 1961 when the private Commission on Money and
Credit published a series of monographs urging widespread reform. Although there was no broad legislative response, several
piecemeal changes took place during the 1960s. The severe distortions created by financial disintermediation, as savings moved out
of depository institutions into other investments in 1966 and 1969–
70, renewed the pressures for comprehensive reform, particularly
when the politically powerful housing industry was disrupted. The
Economic Report of the President, published in February 1970, announced the appointment of a President's Commission on Financial
Structure and Regulation, and formal operations began in June
1970.[1] That group of experts, which came to be known as the Hunt
Commission, approached the assignment—developing specific legislative proposals—with a philosophical commitment to create more
flexibility and competition in the financial system by granting increased lending and investment powers, expanding services, removing regulatory restrictions on the payment of interest on deposits, modifying chartering guidelines, and revising the regulatory
functions. Its basic recommendation was that narrow institutional
specialization mandated by statutes and regulations should be
eliminated so as to "move as far as possible toward freedom of
financial markets and equip all institutions with the powers necessary to compete. . . . Markets will work more efficiently in the
allocation of funds and total savings will expand to meet private
and public needs."[2]

Following the completion of the Hunt Commission Report in December 1971 an interagency committee chaired by the Treasury Department was formed. Extensive discussion within the administration and with private groups culminated in a presidential message to
Congress on August 3, 1973, and submission of the Financial Institu-

---

1. Council of Economic Advisors, *Economic Report of the President* (Washington, D.C.:
   Government Printing Office, Feb. 1970), p. 104.
2. U.S., *Report of the President's Commission on Financial Structure and Regulation,* Dec.
   1971, p.9.

tions Act (FIA 1973) in October 1973.[3] The administration's recommendations were divided into seven major sections: (1) payment of interest on time and savings deposit accounts, including the phasing out of regulation Q, which regulates such payments; (2) expanded deposit liability powers and reserves; (3) expanded lending and investment powers; (4) modified chartering regulations for thrift institutions; (5) expanded powers for credit unions; (6) removal of interest rate ceilings on mortgage loans insured by the Federal Housing Administration and guaranteed by the Veterans Administration; and (7) introduction of a new mortgage interest tax credit as a trade-off for eliminating the special treatment of reserves for losses on bad debts granted to thrift institutions. These proposals generally followed the Hunt Commission's recommendations, although no reference was made to reforming the regulatory agencies. The administration also strongly emphasized the importance of considering FIA 1973 as a "comprehensive package" for legislative purposes.

Congressional hearings before the Subcommittee on Financial Institutions of the Senate Committee on Banking, Housing, and Urban Affairs, chaired by Senator McIntyre of New Hampshire, began in November 1973. From the beginning the hearings were understood to be for "informational purposes" and actual legislation was not expected for at least one year. Nevertheless, extensive testimony was received from the administration, academic experts, representatives from financial institutions, and other interest groups. Sharply differing views were immediately apparent, and these disputes ultimately prevented successful completion of comprehensive reform in subsequent hearings. The major points of controversy included: (1) the strong rejection by thrift institutions and small banks of any proposal to alter the provisions of regulation Q under which interest payments on deposits are controlled; (2) the equally intense pressure from thrift institutions to restore their advantageous interest rate differential for payments on deposits to at least one-half of 1 percent; (3) major criticism from the savings and loan industry, labor, and housing interests that the expanded lending and investment powers for thrift institutions would result in a massive diversion of funds away from mortgage markets leading to a serious decline in housing activity as well as a probable "destruction" of thrift institutions; (4) persistent doubt among many witnesses, particularly those representing the

3. U.S., Department of the Treasury, *Recommendations for Change in the U.S. Financial System*, Aug. 3, 1973, pp. 1–34.

savings and loan industry and housing interests, that the expanded powers would enable thrift institutions to compete effectively against aggressive commercial banks; (5) widespread skepticism that the proposed mortgage interest tax credit would effectively stimulate mortgage lending or provide a reasonable trade-off for the potential loss of special treatment for thrift institutions in the use of bad debt reserves for tax relief; (6) the strong resentment of credit unions about their alleged exclusion from the Hunt Commission and planning sessions for FIA 1973, and their claim that the administration's proposals would not adequately meet their long list of specific legislative goals; and (7) the division of interest between the small and large commercial banks.

In submitting the omnibus legislative package the administration originally hoped that the expanded powers and reforms would create an acceptable trade-off for the potential loss of regulation Q interest rate controls and the rate differential favoring thrift institutions. In fact, every interest group could find something in the bill to oppose, and the positive incentives were not strong enough to create universal support. Each group claimed that it would be relatively worse off in a competitive sense even though some of the individual recommendations for reform might provide desirable benefits. The familiar process of wars of attrition between interest groups occurred, and FIA 1973 was not reported out by the Senate subcommittee.

These initial hearings and subsequent meetings with various interest groups formed the basis of revised legislation, which the administration submitted on March 19, 1975. In presenting the new Financial Institutions Act of 1975 the administration attempted to forestall opposition by emphasizing that, according to several academic studies, housing activity would actually benefit from diversification of lending and investment powers, and it also solicited the support of powerful consumer groups. Specifically FIA 1975 changed the technical language of the 1973 version in several sections; it compromised on the regulation Q issue by calling for a complete review of the situation at the end of the phasing-out period before finally eliminating the controls; and it offered the thrift institutions the option of continuing to use their existing procedures regarding bad debt reserves until 1979, when the tax credit approach to mortgage interest would become mandatory. However, the main thrust of increasing institutional flexibility and competition to improve the overall allocation of resources in the economy continued to be emphasized.

At this point in the evolution of the reform effort the action shifted to the Congress, the ultimate authority on legislative issues, and to the private markets, where actual events were rapidly overtaking the recommendations. The interesting juxtaposition of the formal legislative process, increasingly disrupted by interest group pressures, and the rapidly changing financial institutions as they responded to the realities of the marketplace is a central feature of this study.

When the Senate subcommittee hearings resumed in May 1975, Treasury and other administration officials again emphasized the need to approve an integrated set of reforms. The industry interest groups largely repeated their previous testimony calling for specific portfolio powers and new services as well as continuation of existing regulatory procedures. Despite the presentation of several econometric simulations of the financial system by which academic economists demonstrated that the housing sector would probably benefit from the proposed reforms, the private sector was even more intransigent in opposing changes of the competitive structure, and each industry interest group pushed for piecemeal legislation to achieve its own specific goals. Underlying the formal presentations, however, was a growing recognition that dramatic changes were occurring in the marketplace—in particular, the imminent reality of an electronic funds transfer system that would revolutionize the process of third-party payments and competition for savings.

The growing awareness of competitive realities, the effective leadership of Senator McIntyre of New Hampshire, and a strong lobbying effort by the Treasury Department eventually led to approval of FIA 1975 in the Senate on December 11, 1975, by a vote of 79 to 14. However, the favorable vote was somewhat misleading because the bill as passed required action by the House Ways and Means Committee and the Senate Finance Committee to approve the mortgage interest tax credit. Even more important was the obvious point that the Senate vote would be meaningless unless the House of Representatives also acted favorably on comprehensive reform legislation. The various interest groups were very much aware of this crucial fact.

The House Committee on Banking, Currency, and Housing, under the new leadership of Congressman Reuss of Wisconsin, began its consideration of financial institution reform by rejecting the proposals sponsored by the Republican administration as being too narrow and insensitive to the needs of the housing industry. To broaden the scope and shift the orientation of the proposed legislation, Congressman Reuss announced on April 24, 1975, the initiation of a massive study of the entire financial system. The resulting study, known as the Financial Institutions and the Nation's Economy (FINE) project, produced several volumes of academic studies and committee staff papers.

House hearings on the FINE study began in December 1975 under the jurisdiction of the Subcommittee on Financial Institutions Supervision, Regulation, and Insurance, chaired by Congressman St Germain of Rhode Island. In March 1976 the House subcommittee held extensive hearings on the resulting legislation, titled the Financial Reform Act of 1976 (FRA 1976), which was intended to cover six broad topics: (1) restructuring of the regulatory agencies; (2) depository institutions (the subject considered in FIA 1975); (3) housing; (4) bank holding companies; (5) reform of the Federal Reserve System; and (6) international banking.

Once again, extensive testimony was collected from the administration, the academic community, and the financial industry. Broad support for FRA 1976 could not be developed, however, because of various disruptive pressures, particularly the unwillingness of each interest group to accept the compromises necessary in any integrated package of changes, the political tensions created by the rapidly approaching national elections scheduled in November 1976, and internal disagreements among subcommittee members about legislative strategy.

When it became apparent that the omnibus legislation recommended in FRA 1976 could not be reported out favorably, the broad bill was split into three self-contained parts relating to: (1) depository institutions; (2) governing authority for the Federal Reserve System; and (3) international banking. Even with this major adjustment it was clear that the administration preferred the Senate-passed FIA 1975, and that political realities in the House of Representatives would prevent any action before the national election. When the second session of the 94th Congress closed at the end of 1976 pending legislation automatically died, including the favorable Senate vote on FIA 1975.

At the beginning of the 95th Congress the credit unions succeeded in obtaining rapid approval of their own legislative package of detailed reforms, despite the objections of competing financial institutions, and the regulation Q controls over interest rates paid on deposits were easily extended. No legislation for comprehensive reform of financial institutions was introduced for consideration by the Senate or the House of Representatives in 1977.

In writing an epitaph for such comprehensive reform several

months before its actual demise, one critic observed that, although the reforms had a strong case,

> By the time all the debris has fallen from the collapse of the reform effort it should be crystal clear that there is no loud and active political constituency for financial reform. Yet the reform was addressed to a real problem posed by the marketplace, and blocking it has created an impasse. Sooner or later Congress will have to face what it will duck this year.[4]

Despite the disappointing failure of comprehensive financial reform initiatives the overall experience does provide insights into the process of developing economic policy. The complexity of the issues and the challenging organizational problems highlight both the difficulty and the great importance of policy formulation. There are both strengths and weaknesses in the procedures now used and it is hoped that this study will be useful in the continuous efforts to improve the process.

4. Stanley Wilson, "Housing Lobby Wrecks Financial Reform," p. 36.

2

COMPETITIVE STRUCTURE OF FINANCIAL
INSTITUTIONS

Economic development demands an efficient financial system to accomodate savers interested in minimal risks, personal liquidity, diversification of investments, different savings instruments, convenience of deposit and withdrawal, various personal financial services, and a reasonable rate of return; borrowers want stable sources of funds at reasonable costs and terms. Our system of depository institutions—commercial banks, savings and loan associations, mutual savings banks, and credit unions—serves well in this intermediary function by allocating the accumulated savings among various borrowers. Since the average saver does not have the time, skill, or large amount of money needed to invest directly in the open market this intermediary service is beneficial. Similarly, borrowers can find centralized sources of funds and thus reduce the uncertainties and costs of arranging necessary financing.

This complex system includes a variety of both general-purpose and highly specialized institutions, ranging from giant multibillion-dollar commercial banks serving customers around the world to small credit unions operating in borrowed rooms and using part-time help. This extreme diversity exists because the evolving needs of savers and borrowers have continually required new types of financial institutions and readjustments by existing organizations. As of December 31, 1976, there were 14,671 commercial banks with assets of $1.031 trillion; 4,821 savings and loan associations with assets of $392 billion; 473 mutual savings banks with assets of $135 billion; and 22,608 credit unions with assets of $45 billion. The combined financial resources of $1.6 trillion at the end of 1976 constituted a strong basis for the entire U.S. economic system.

Depository Financial Institutions as Intermediaries

Commercial banks

Commercial banks actually serve a dual role in the financial system. First, they are the only institutions authorized to "create" money by extending loans based on fractional reserves. Second, they are the largest and most diversified of the various financial intermediaries responsible for accumulating savings and allocating them to various borrowers.

Measured in terms of size and diversity of services to both savers and borrowers, commercial banks differ greatly from the so-called thrift institutions—savings and loan associations and mutual savings banks—and credit unions. Because of the overlapping competition for savings deposits among all four of these institutions, however, and the role of commercial banks in all branches of of the financial system, including real estate finance, they are included in this brief review of institutional characteristics. In even more pragmatic terms, it is impossible to discuss any reform initiatives for financial intermediaries without including commercial banks because of their central role and powerful competitive capabilities.

At the end of 1976 the approximately 14,700 commercial banks in America held assets totaling over $1 trillion. As would be expected, the industry included a diverse range of banks, differing in size, lending and investment policies, consumer savings and lending activities, and geographical concentration of operations. The larger banks offer a broad array of services to both national and international customers, including business loans, state and local government security investments, trust services, personal loans, real estate financing, and a long list of related activities permitted under the laws governing bank holding companies. On the liability side of the balance sheet, commercial banks attract not only demand deposits used for unlimited checking accounts but the same types of savings and time accounts that the other deposit institutions compete for. The distribution of commercial bank assets and liabilities is summarized in Table 1.

The crucial point in understanding the role of commercial banks in the following discussion of financial institution reform is that their wide array of banking services straddles many fields of interest, creating both competitive advantages and tremendous needs for funds. At the same time, commercial banks are generally granted considerable freedom to participate in these various markets. Because of this com-

Table 1

COMMERCIAL BANKS, ASSETS AND LIABILITIES,
DECEMBER 1976
(In Billions of Dollars)

Assets	
Loans, gross	$ 594.9
U.S. Treasury securities	102.5
Other investments	148.9
Currency and coin	12.1
Reserves with Federal Reserve banks	26.1
Balances with banks	49.6
Cash items in collection	48.4
Total assets	$1,030.7
Liabilities	
Demand deposits	$ 336.8
Time deposits	501.4
Borrowings	80.2
Total capital accounts	78.1
Total liabilities and capital	$1,030.7

Source: Federal Reserve System.
Note: Totals include items not shown separately.

petitive flexibility, the goals of savings and loan associations, mutual savings banks, and credit unions are directly linked to the activities of commercial banks, even though institutions from one group may be competing against the others in only narrow parts of the financial markets. The flexibility and diversity of commercial banks, with all their competitive advantages as well as their heavy responsibilities in serving so many basic economic needs, create a difficult problem for Congress and government agencies charged with regulating the financial system. They must balance the general interests served by the diversified commercial banks against the specific interests of real estate and consumer finance and the more specialized financial institutions that serve those markets. The necessity to rationalize these sometimes conflicting interests explains the complexity of the legislative and regulatory efforts.

Savings and loan associations

Savings and loan associations comprise the second largest deposit intermediary and the largest mortgage financing institution. Along with mutual savings banks, they have provided a large pool of funds to support the rapid expansion of housing. Although the two are not identical, they are frequently lumped together under the general heading of thrift institutions, reflecting their similar functions of accumulating savings deposits and then allocating them to borrowers, particularly for residential mortgages in the case of savings and loan associations.

The Oxford Provident Building Association founded in Philadelphia in 1831 was the beginning of the savings and loan industry in America. The purpose of the early "building societies" was to pool the funds of a relatively few individuals to make rotating housing loans to the associated members. As the demand for housing increased, the intermediary function of matching general savings and mortgage credit needs evolved; but growth was slow until the 1940s, when the end of World War II created a tremendous boom in housing. The operating policies of the savings and loan industry were revolutionized at that time to meet the exploding demand for housing, and the results were good for both the associations and the general public. Savers were generally paid a differential of three-fourths to 1 percent above the return permitted on savings accounts at commercial banks to attract savings, and an unusually aggressive advertising and sales program helped to make more funds available for lending. The savings and loan industry increased its total assets from $17 billion in 1950 to $130 billion by 1965. Assets continued to grow, although at a somewhat slower and more erratic pace, reaching $392 billion at the end of 1976. During this period of rapid change the savings and loan institutions truly became the nation's housing finance specialists, and at the end of 1976 they held $261 billion of the total outstanding one- to four-family residential mortgage debt of $556 billion.

Much of the specialization of savings and loan associations has resulted from managements' preferences in filling the tremendous demand for housing credit. However, government regulations have also been an important cause of the unusual degree of specialization, which in turn created a concentration of association holdings of mortgage loans amounting to over 82 percent of total assets in 1976. Tax laws were carefully written so that special additions to a reserve for losses on loans could be deducted from gross income as a means of improving the after-tax profits of mortgage loans.

To be eligible for this special reserve deduction, an institution must invest 60 percent of its assets in qualifying real property loans. To get the maximum deduction permitted, a minimum of 82 percent of total assets must be committed to real property loans. Accordingly, national policies have clearly supported the intense specialization of savings and loan associations, the purpose being to achieve our housing goals. Certain competitive risks have been created in mandating this specialization. Nevertheless, this financial intermediary has continued to grow and support housing finance. In recent years there has been some diversification into apartment building loans and mobile home financing, but approximately 80 percent of the total mortgage portfolio is still one- to four-family residences. Other innovations have included the extension of education loans and the new authority to make third party payments by federally chartered associations. On the liability side, increased use of certificates of deposit with different maturities and yields has developed. Savings and loan associations nevertheless remain basically a financial intermediary accumulating personal savings to finance residential real estate transactions. The assets and liabilities of the industry are summarized in Table 2.

Associations may be chartered by individual states or receive a federal charter from the Federal Home Loan Bank Board (FHLBB). At the end of 1976 approximately 42 percent of those associations holding 58 percent of the industry's total assets were federally chartered. The government authority that grants the charter is also responsible for regulation and supervision, but there is some overlap in authority because the Federal Savings and Loan Insurance Corporation (FSLIC) provides deposit insurance for 84 percent of the individual associations holding almost 98 percent of the industry's assets. All federally chartered associations are insured, and until 1976 they were permitted to use only the mutual form of organization (in the first year nine federal associations switched to the stock form). At the end of 1976 there were 4,126 mutual associations holding $305 billion of assets, compared to 732 capital stock associations with assets of $87 billion, or 22 percent of the savings and loan industry's total assets.

Mutual savings banks

Mutual savings banks were formed in the early nineteenth century to promote thrift among industrial workers by providing a safe and convenient place for their savings at a time when commercial banks were not interested in such deposits. The mutual savings banks clearly filled a vacuum and have subsequently become a major part of the financial intermediary system in those areas where state charters are available. Many mutual savings banks are now multibillion-dollar institutions operating, with highly competitive policies, in the major financial centers of the Northeast.

Table 2

SAVINGS AND LOAN ASSOCIATIONS,
ASSETS AND LIABILITIES, DECEMBER 1976
(In Millions of Dollars)

Assets	
Mortgage loans	$323,005
Cash, investments, and securities	35,724
Real estate owned	1,930
Federal Home Loan Bank stock	2,800
Other assets	28,448
Total	$391,907
Liabilities	
Savings deposits	$335,912
Federal Home Loan Bank advances	15,862
Other borrowed funds	3,221
Loans in process	6,840
Other liabilities	8,074
Net worth	21,998
Total	$391,907

Source: Federal Home Loan Bank Board; United States League of Savings
    Associations.
Note: Totals affected by rounding.

The mutual form of organization is still consistent with the semi-charitable goals of the original savings banks. Savings banks are now operating in seventeen states, but the major institutions are still concentrated in New York, New Jersey, Pennsylvania, and New England. In those states mutual savings banks have attracted one half or more of all savings deposits and compete aggressively with commercial banks and savings and loan associations. The growth of mutual savings banks has been curtailed, however, by the geographical restrictions, the postwar economic difficulties of New England, and the increasing competition for savings from other deposit institutions. At the same time, the differential interest rate historically paid on their deposits has narrowed as a result of competitive and regulatory changes.

The mutual savings bank industry has long pushed for federal chartering of new institutions, a development that would open up new geographical areas and provide the flexibility of dual chartering systems already available to commercial banks, savings and loan associations, and credit unions. Legislation permitting federal charters was first submitted in 1957 and has been proposed on numerous occasions since then. Strong opposition of other financial institutions has repeatedly prevented favorable congressional action, however, even though most studies of the financial system, including those prepared by the Commission on Money and Credit and the President's Commission on Financial Structure and Regulation, supported this regulatory change.

The major distinguishing characteristic of mutual savings banks is the degree of asset diversification that they permit. Throughout the postwar period they have become major sources of long-term mortgage loans, and these commitments now represent approximately two-thirds of their total assets. But they also invest in corporate bonds, government securities, and other types of loans, and they even hold small amounts of corporate stocks. This flexibility in investment is a great advantage to mutual savings banks which they have used effectively to improve their profitability and liquidity, but they have also played a major role in housing finance. Another important innovation in recent years has been the introduction of third party payment systems—effectively representing checking plans, known as NOW accounts—in New Hampshire and Massachusetts, eventually to extend to all six New England states. This innovation has been well received by the public, and other areas are now increasing the competitive powers of mutual savings banks. The distribution of assets and liabilities is summarized in Table 3.

The major contribution of mutual savings banks to housing finance has caused them to be classified with savings and loan associations as thrift institutions specializing in mortgage lending. This definition does reflect the basic savings orientation of mutual savings institutions, but it exaggerates the degree of investment specialization. While it is true that mutual savings banks have shifted the balance of their investment portfolios into mortgages and away from the government securities accumulated during World War II, they retain the flexibility to diversify their asset holdings according to private institutional preferences and in response to developments in the marketplace. This added flexibility and the excellent liquidity and solvency of mutual savings banks in the past should be carefully considered in evaluating the proposed reforms for the financial intermediary system.

Credit unions

Credit unions are cooperative nonprofit organizations of individual members with a common bond based on occupation, group membership, or residence. They were originally formed in the early

Table 3

MUTUAL SAVINGS BANKS, ASSETS AND LIABILITIES,
DECEMBER 1976

Assets	
Loans	
Mortgages	$ 81,630
Other	5,183
Investments	
U.S. government	5,840
State and local	2,417
Corporate and other	33,793
Cash	2,355
Other assets	3,593
Total	$134,812
Liabilities	
Deposits	$122,877
Other liabilities	2,884
General reserve accounts	9,052
Total	$134,812

Source: National Association of Mutual Savings Banks.
Note: Totals may not add due to rounding.

1900s to promote thrift, personal financial education, and cooperative borrowing programs. Although modern credit unions have changed in size and popularity, they are still oriented to consumers and continue to have close relations with their members. Like other financial institutions, the range of sizes and operating policies includes not only very large organizations providing a variety of sophisticated services at major government facilities and private companies but also very small units serving only a limited clientele. They remain the most rapidly growing deposit institutions, and in recent years they have become strong competitors for savings flows, providing approximately 15 percent of the massive expansion of consumer credit.

Members' deposits have been technically defined as shares, indicating ownership interest in the credit union, and all accounts have received the same dividend rate. Recent diversification into regular deposit accounts and certificates of deposit should expand the services to savers. Credit union assets consist largely of personal and consumer installment loans to enable members to acquire consumer durables or pay personal bills, although some organizations have started offering home mortgage loans. Other assets may include limited amounts of government securities and a few miscellaneous

Table 4

CREDIT UNIONS, ASSETS AND LIABILITIES, DECEMBER 1976
(In Millions of Dollars)

Assets	
Loans outstanding	$34,107
Other assets including cash	10,753
Total	$44,861
Liabilities	
Savings (shares and deposits)	$39,124
Reserves	2,290
Other liabilities	3,446
Total	$44,861

Source: Credit Union National Association.

loans and deposits at other financial institutions. The distribution of assets and liabilities is summarized in Table 4.

Sponsoring agencies often provide free physical facilities and operating services, including payroll deductions, and most officials are unpaid volunteers elected by their fellow members. The resulting low operating costs have enabled credit unions to offer attractive yields to member savers and advantageous consumer credit charges to member borrowers. Credit unions are also exempt from income taxes on retained earnings—a major advantage. Technically, their services are limited to members eligible under the common bond requirements.

Federal charters have been used by approximately 60 percent of the credit unions, making them subject to the National Credit Union Administration. State charters and supervision are also now available in most states. The phenomenal growth of credit unions indicates that they have filled an important need in the financial system, and they have rapidly evolved into a very strong and competitive intermediary.

Specialization and Competitive Overlap

The four depository institutions described above are only part of the total financial system, which includes life insurance companies, fire and casualty insurance companies, investment funds, mortgage companies, pension funds, venture capital firms, investment bankers, business and consumer finance companies, trust managers, factoring firms, leasing companies, real estate investment trusts, state and local government financial agencies, small business investment companies, and over one hundred federal credit programs. Nevertheless, the depository institutions are a central part of the entire system and have provided approximately two-thirds of the total funds advanced to the nonfinancial sectors of the economy since 1960. This basic importance justified the establishment of the Presidential Commission on Financial Structure and Regulation and the legislation considered by Congress.

The four depository institutions are similar in that their liabilities consist largely of savings deposits (sometimes called share accounts) and their assets are basically loans and investments. But there are important differences: for example, the relative size of deposits in each institutional category varies (see Table 5).

The rapid growth of deposits throughout the system, particularly in savings and loan associations during the postwar housing boom, is also varied, as indicated in Table 6. Two particular points should be emphasized in Table 6: the specific slowdown in savings inflows in 1966, 1968–69, and 1973–74; and the increased flows to commercial banks during the third episode, at the same time that thrift institutions were suffering seriously reduced savings inflows—or disintermediation.

A third difference involves the range of services each institution offers savers and borrowers in the extremely competitive financial markets. Commercial banks have traditionally enjoyed a competitive edge because of their more diversified lending and investment practices and their more comprehensive array of saving options and financial services. At the other extreme, credit unions have offered only one type of savings account and restricted their loans to short-term consumer credit to members. Savings and loan associations specialized in mortgage loans and limited their savings and service programs until the growing competitive pressures forced them to reconsider their prospects under existing legislative and regulatory restrictions. Mutual savings banks have concentrated on mortgage loans but have also diversified in answer to other investment opportunities; and they have continued to compete strongly with commercial banks in those states where charters are available.

In this general environment the competitive pressures escalated rapidly in the 1960s, when commercial banks moved into retail-consumer financial markets after concentrating on wholesale commercial interests during most of their history. The blurring of familiar competitive relations included a sharp expansion of new banking services aimed at the consumer as both a saver and bor-

Table 5

TOTAL OVER-THE-COUNTER SAVINGS AT DEPOSITORY FINANCIAL INSTITUTIONS, 1950–76
(In Billions of Dollars)

Year	Total	Commercial Banks*	Savings and Loan Assns.†	Mutual Savings Banks‡	Credit Unions§
1950	$ 69.8	$ 34.9	$ 14.0	$ 20.0	$ 0.9
1955	108.7	46.0	32.1	28.1	2.4
1960	170.5	67.1	62.1	36.3	5.0
1965	302.8	130.8	110.4	52.4	9.2
1970	439.2	205.8	146.4	71.6	15.4
1975	822.0	393.4	285.7	109.9	33.0
1976	933.3	435.1	335.9	122.9	39.2

Source: Federal Home Loan Bank Board; Federal Reserve System, Board of Governors.
Note: Totals may not add due to rounding.
*Time and savings deposits of individuals, partnerships, and corporations.
†All types of savings.
‡Regular and special savings accounts.
§Shares and members' deposits.

Table 6

ANNUAL CHANGE IN FINANCIAL ASSETS OF HOUSEHOLDS,* 1965–76
(In Billions of Dollars)

Year	Total	Commercial Banks	Savings and Loan Assns.	Mutual Savings Banks	Credit Unions	Life Insurance Reserves	Pension Fund Reserves	Credit and Equity Instruments
1965	$ 47.7	$14.9	$ 8.5	$ 3.6	$1.0	$4.8	$12.1	$ 2.8
1966	54.8	11.9	3.6	2.6	1.0	4.7	14.5	16.5
1967	52.9	18.7	10.6	5.1	0.9	5.1	14.0	–1.5
1968	56.3	18.1	7.5	4.2	1.3	4.6	15.6	5.0
1969	57.6	0.7	4.1	2.6	1.7	5.0	16.3	27.2
1970	66.2	27.0	11.0	4.4	1.2	5.2	19.2	–1.8
1971	91.3	28.1	28.0	9.9	1.7	6.2	21.1	–3.7
1972	108.2	25.6	32.7	10.2	2.5	6.6	22.6	8.0
1973	124.8	39.3	20.2	4.7	3.6	7.4	25.6	24.0
1974	130.7	35.4	16.1	3.1	2.6	6.5	29.6	37.4
1975	150.6	25.4	42.8	11.2	5.4	5.4	37.4	23.0
1976	173.6	39.7	50.6	13.0	5.5	7.0	46.4	11.4

Source: Federal Home Loan Bank Board; Federal Reserve System, Board of Governors.
*Time and savings deposits at institutions, investments in life insurance and pension plans, and purchases of direct market instruments such as stocks and bonds.

rower, new physical facilities, increased advertising and sales pro-
motions, and aggressive diversification into new activities under
the broad umbrella of holding company reorganizations.

Thrift institutions attempted to respond by seeking specific legislative changes permitting them to diversify lending practices and customer services to become "family financial centers" and thus fill a
gap that commercial banks had previously left open. Despite the
obvious direction of market developments, however, the historical
specialization of these institutions on both sides of the balance sheet
continued. In the future, institutions should be allowed to be more
responsive to changing conditions and to diversify or specialize according to the interests of savers and all types of borrowers, rather
than the goals of government regulatory agencies and specific private pressure groups.

Finally, there are major differences in the regulatory environment
affecting portfolio policies, chartering and branching rules, liquidity
requirements, deposit interest rate rules and general operating policies. These will be briefly reviewed in the next chapter.

Disintermediation in the Financial Markets

Specialization by thrift institutions has provided the bulk of
funds required by the rapidly expanding residential mortgage markets, created economies of scale and management expertise, and
encouraged widespread thrift and home ownership in America.
However, the system of real estate finance that has evolved has
serious structural problems: (1) a mismatch between the short-term
maturities of relatively small personal savings accounts and the
long-term maturities of relatively large mortgage loans; (2) the risks
created by "borrowing at the margin" and "lending at the average"; and (3) the shifting term structure of interest rates over time.
The periodic financial strains since the mid-1960s have raised serious questions about the long-term viability of the existing system
of financial intermediaries.

The first problem involves the mismatch in the time profile of assets
and liabilities. The liabilities, represented by savings and time accounts, are generally considered by savers to be highly liquid. Passbook savings accounts have effectively permitted immediate withdrawal even though legal technicalities may require prior notification.
Such accounts are fixed-dollar obligations which cannot be adjusted
to reflect external economic conditions or the individual institution's
liquidity position. Efforts have been made to attract savings by offer-

ing savings certificates with fixed maturities; but the average length is still relatively short, and most accounts are still subject to sudden and unexpected withdrawal.[1] The assets of thrift institutions and many small commercial banks are committed to long-term residential loans or fixed maturity bonds. Mortgage loans typically have maturities ranging from twenty to thirty years, although the average is much shorter because borrowers frequently change homes and must then make full payment of the outstanding balance.[2] Nevertheless, a number of years are required to roll over a portfolio of home mortgages. This imbalance in the timing of loan outlays and collections and the fluctuating pattern of savings deposits and withdrawals create flow-of-funds problems. Fortunately these strains can usually be absorbed, or at least moderated, by relying on accumulated liquid reserves and temporary assistance provided by various federal agencies to improve liquidity, as long as economic conditions are normal and interest rates remain relatively stable.

The term "borrowing at the margin" refers to the return that financial institutions must offer to most savers to attract their deposits. The crucial point is that when interest rates throughout the financial system shift, the rates paid to passbook savings must be adjusted to remain competitive. In other words, to prevent savers from moving their funds to other savings institutions offering higher returns or into open-market financial instruments with higher yields, the marginal rate must be paid on all savings not covered by fixed maturity agreements. Savers continue to consider many circumstances that affect their decisions, including risk, convenience, diversification, other services, and the size and probable duration of the yield gap; but they are increasingly sensitive to changes in the marginal interest rate. At the same time, the return to the financial institutions that are lending money is the "average rate" charged on

1. Savings certificates issued in varying denominations and maturities increased to approximately one-third of total deposits of mutual savings banks and to more than one-half of the savings at savings and loan associations by the end of 1973. This development did moderate the short-run sensitivity of savings accounts to external pressures, but the higher yields required to attract savers created serious earnings problems and the risk that a substantial volume of such certificates might mature at a time when financial conditions might cause withdrawals. Even the certificate savings can usually be withdrawn prior to the fixed maturity if a yield penalty is accepted.

2. In the early 1960s the average life of residential mortgage loans declined to approximately $6\frac{1}{2}$ years; by 1970 the average life had increased to almost 11 years before declining to a level of 8 years in the mid-1970s.

individual mortgages with fixed interest payments over an extended period. Since the "average lending rate" is a cumulative figure, it changes very slowly even though the "marginal" rate charged on new loans may be significantly different from the "average" return on the entire portfolio.

During the last twenty-five years, particularly since 1965, the trend of interest rates has been upward. Accordingly, the fixed interest rates charged on mortgage loans in prior years have pulled down the overall earnings of mortgage-oriented financial institutions. A crunch occurs whenever general interest rates increase sharply and thus cause savers to demand a higher current return on their deposits, even though the average return on the total portfolio of mortgage loans is only gradually improved as new loans are made at the higher interest rates prevailing in the financial markets. Reforms have been recommended allowing thrift institutions to diversify their loan portfolios and in this way to improve their flow of funds during such periods of strain, but opposition by housing interests along with the management preferences of many of the thrift institutions have prevented this change. Similarly, some have suggested the use of "variable rate" mortgage contracts so that current returns to lenders can more quickly adjust to fluctuating interest rates in the financial markets. But this approach has not attracted enough support because critics claim that borrowers will object strongly to paying higher rates whenever the general level of interest charges moves upward. Once again, this imbalance can generally be absorbed by financial institutions as long as economic conditions and interest rates remain relatively stable.

A third structural problem affecting mortgage lenders involves the underlying pattern of interest rates over time. Following World War II, yields on home mortgages were substantially higher than comparable returns on corporate and government bonds. At the same time, short-term interest payments on open-market instruments and savings deposits were exceptionally low. This upward sloping yield curve—that is, low short-term rates with increasing returns as maturities lengthened—was ideal for thrift institutions because they could easily attract large inflows of savings at minimal costs and could then use the funds to fill the booming demand for home mortgage loans at relatively higher interest rates. It was a good time to be borrowing short and lending long and the "marginal" cost of savings acquired was well below the "average" return on the portfolio of residential mortgage loans made after the war.

This favorable structure began to shift in the mid-1960s, however, as monetary policies reacted to economic problems caused by accelerating inflation, and short-term interest rates increased sharply, including the yields paid on savings deposits. The yield differential available on home mortgages compared to long-term bonds also narrowed from 2 percentage points to parity by 1970.

Since 1970 the return on mortgage loans has frequently been lower than comparable yields on high grade long-term corporate securities, making it increasingly difficult for mortgage-oriented thrift institutions to attract savings in the financial markets without seriously restricting their earnings prospects. In this environment the risks of the intermediary institutions in balancing short-term interest costs against long-term interest returns made it a bad arrangement to be borrowing short and lending long because the fixed returns on mortgage contracts could not be adjusted.

The structural problems described above have frequently caused flow-of-funds difficulties for depository institutions, but the distortions were generally manageable until the mid-1960s, when the federal government's loss of control over its fiscal policies created a decade of stop-and-go economic performance with periods of accelerated growth followed by serious recessions. From fiscal 1966 through fiscal 1976, the federal budget increased from $135 billion to $366 billion, or 172 percent. During that decade federal budget deficits were reported in nine years and totaled $211 billion; "net" borrowings by various federally sponsored agencies, and obligations issued by federal agencies involving loan guarantee and insurance programs which are excluded from the budget figures, totaled another $189 billion. During the ten years from 1966 to 1976 the narrowly defined money supply—currency and demand deposits—increased at an annual rate of 5.7 percent, compared to a yearly pace of 2.5 percent from 1956 to 1966. And during the same period the consumer price index increased at an annual rate of 5.8 percent, compared to a yearly pace of 1.8 percent from 1956 to 1966. (The historical annual average rate from 1890 to 1970 was also 1.8 percent.) The stability of economic activity and the intensity of inflation pressures clearly changed in the mid-1960s, with profound effects throughout the financial system.

Because political expediency prevented the effective coordination of fiscal and monetary policies that was needed to stabilize the economy and moderate the accelerating inflation, the Federal Reserve System was left with the exceedingly unpopular responsibility of fighting inflation with only its monetary tools. While it was helpful to have some responsible institution playing goalie in the economic system, the devastating effects of general instability and excessive inflation during the last decade are clearly demonstrated by the financial distortions that occurred in 1966, 1969–70, and 1973–74. As inflation accelerated and output boomed the application of monetary restraint periodically led to rising interest rates and disproportionate disruptions in residential construction. The sharp increase in interest rates unfortunately forced the mortgage-oriented thrift institutions into the structural traps described above. As the rates paid to savers increased to, or beyond, the average return on the total portfolios of outstanding mortgage loans, the competitive position of thrift institutions was severely damaged.

The federal government attempted to relieve the distortions created by commercial banks' competition for savings by establishing maximum deposit interest rate ceilings, but this resort to expediency did not solve the basic problem of unstable economic conditions and accelerating inflation, nor did it alleviate the competitive pressures from other sectors of the financial system. Whenever interest rates on open-market financial instruments—short-term government securities and private obligations, including the new money market funds—increase rapidly, many savers react by withdrawing their deposits in savings institutions to invest them directly. The process of bypassing the intermediary savings institutions to invest directly in open-market instruments has been given the technical name *disintermediation*. The massive withdrawals of savings that occur during periods of disintermediation have become the most disruptive force affecting depository institutions during the last decade.

Specific Examples of Disintermediation

The historical patterns of disintermediation can be easily traced by identifying fluctuations in economic activity and inflation pressures. Economic disturbances were relatively mild during the years immediately after World War II, and the favorable mix of low short-term interest rates and advantageous yields on mortgage loans kept costs down and earnings up for thrift institutions. Commercial banks usually concentrated on attracting demand deposits that were paid little if any return, and there was very little competition for personal savings. For example, in 1950 savings and loan associations paid an average return on deposits of 2.52 percent; the comparable figure for commercial banks was 0.94 percent. On the asset side, commercial banks had little interest in mortgage lending, partly because of government regulations, or in consumer loans. As a result the financial markets were largely compartmentalized and disintermediation remained only a theoretical concept.

The first signals of approaching distress occurred in the late 1950s, when short-term interest rates increased sharply, causing the overall interest-yield curve to flatten and thus eliminating the advantage of borrowing short and lending long. As the use of monetary policies increased to combat economic distortions and brief flurries of inflation, open-market interest rates became more volatile with resulting fluctuations in the flows of savings. An ominous sign occurred in October 1959, when the Treasury sold its famous Magic Fives (government securities offering a 5 percent yield) and savings flowed out of financial institutions located in money centers where savers had become sensitive to interest rate differentials. Commercial banks also became more aggressive in competing for deposits to support the rapid growth of loans. A major policy shift involved their issue of certificates of deposit in large denominations to attract funds from business customers and to prevent the further diversion of short-term funds away from demand deposits into various open-market instruments. Banks later offered small-denomination certificates to compete for personal savings. By 1960 commercial banks were paying an average return of 2.56 percent on savings and time deposits, compared to the 3.86 percent paid by savings and loan associations. They also aggressively exploited their "one-stop banking" group of personal financial services and moved into consumer loans on a selective basis, concentrating on the more profitable financing of automobiles and major appliances. The relaxing of government rules controlling the maximum payments that commercial banks could offer for savings and time accounts helped the banks to extend even further their consumer activities.

As these basic adjustments continued, economic conditions in the United States were also becoming more volatile. A relatively severe recession occurred in 1958 and a milder version followed in 1960. As external economic conditions became more difficult, the narrow specialization of savings and loan associations in local residential mortgage loans made them particularly vulnerable both to the erosion of earnings on their total assets as the postwar housing boom moderated and to increasing costs as they competed for the deposits needed for continued growth. Mutual savings banks fared somewhat better because of their policies calling for more diversified portfolio investment, and because they had established savings positions in key money markets in the Northeast. The signs of approaching change were clear, however, and serious discussions about reforming the existing system of financial intermediaries were initiated.

By 1965 conditions were rapidly changing as the risks of investing in long-term mortgage contracts with fixed returns that relied mainly on over-the-counter savings subject to immediate withdrawal caused widespread concerns about the basic stability of the system. Commercial bank competition intensified; the overall level of interest rates increased; cyclical fluctuations in mortgage financing and residential construction also increased; and the historical yield differential on thrift institution deposits over commercial bank savings and time accounts narrowed from three-fourths of 1 percent to only one-half of 1 percent. When the federal government rapidly increased its spending to cover simultaneously the costs of the expanding military operations in Vietnam and the domestic social programs, the Federal Reserve System restrained the growth of the money supply to combat the inflation pressures. The resulting "credit crunch" in 1966 caused short-term interest rates to rise above the level of long-term rates. The double-barreled impact on financial institutions was predictable and disastrous. Earnings of financial intermediaries were whiplashed by the rising costs caused by competition for funds. In September 1966 Congress enacted enabling legislation giving the Federal Home Loan Bank Board (FHLBB) and the Federal Deposit Insurance Corporation (FDIC) authority to join with the Federal Reserve Board in controlling the maximum amounts of interest paid on all intermediary deposit accounts.[3] This action also formalized the one-half of 1 percent interest rate differentials historically paid by thrift institutions relative to commercial bank payments, and that gap was maintained until July 1973. Very little could be done, however, to improve the earnings on long-term mortgage loans, and the thrift institutions experienced a severe earnings squeeze and liquidity strains. Both economic realities and federal regulations prevented the deposit institutions from raising their deposit payments to match the rising short-term yields available from open-market instruments. As savers discovered the disparities in earnings from their savings a massive diversion of funds into open-market investments created the first major disintermediation experience. In turn, the availability of real estate financing tightened and new housing starts declined 26 percent in 1966. This experience did not mean that the overall pace of savings was reduced but there

3. The Federal Reserve System already controlled the maximum interest payments on commercial bank savings and time account deposits, having done so since 1933.

was a shift—a disintermediation—away from the financial depository institutions to other types of commitments.

As summarized in Table 6, household savings inflows in 1966 compared to 1965 declined from $14.9 to $11.9 billion for commercial banks, from $8.5 to $3.6 billion for savings and loan associations, and from $3.6 to $2.6 billion for mutual savings banks. Credit unions also experienced a leveling off of savings inflows. With housing starts falling, interest rates on new mortgage loans rising, disintermediation disrupting the depository institutions, and general unhappiness among labor groups, housing contractors and individual home buyers, the reactions of Congress were also predictable: more government spending, including the expansion of federal housing programs; and more government regulation to patch the holes created by competitive pressures in the marketplace.

After 1965 commercial banks acted to diversify their services by creating one-bank holding companies, and they continued expanding into consumer markets and personal savings accounts. New types of deposit accounts were developed, and other sources of funds were used, as the parent holding companies issued commercial paper and subordinated debenture bonds in the open market, and large banks tapped the emerging Eurodollar market. The controversy generated by such diversification was finally resolved by Congress when it decided that all bank holding companies, regardless of the number of banks in the system, should be allowed to engage in businesses "closely related" to banking, under the following guidelines:

> The Board of Governors of the Federal Reserve System was empowered to identify the types of businesses permitted under this definition. With these powers, the Board has determined that industrial banking, mortgage banking, servicing loans, performing fiducial activities, acting as investment advisor, leasing personal property, investing in community welfare projects, providing bookkeeping and data processing services and, within limits, selling insurance [are] functions appropriate for holding company subsidiaries. Moreover, holding companies can tap money and capital markets in ways which are prohibited to banks, thus broadening the ability of the total enterprise to attract funds. The activities of non-bank subsidiaries are not restricted to the state in which the bank subsidiary is chartered.[4]

As these competitive pressures developed, the thrift institutions also attempted to gain new powers that would strengthen their com-

---

4. U.S., Congress, Senate, Committee on Banking, Currency, and Urban Affairs, *Reform of Financial Institutions: 1973*, p. 223.

petitive position; but their legislative initiatives were largely unsuccessful. Thrift institutions were still locked into somewhat narrowly specialized operations when the next financial disruption occurred in 1969. As indicated in Table 6, the slowdown in the rate of savings inflows to financial depositories actually began in 1968, but the full crunch hit in 1969 when the flow of savings for intermediary institutions turned negative, causing more sophisticated savers to shift their funds into Treasury bills and other open-market investments.

By that time commercial banks had narrowed even further the gap between the returns paid on savings and time accounts, but all three major deposit institutions suffered disintermediation in 1969; open-market interest rates moved as much as 2 percent above the maximum yields available on deposits, and only credit unions reported an increase in the pace of savings inflows. Once again housing starts declined, and pressures increased for more congressional aid to the real estate markets as well as for more regulation. The seriousness of the situation was then further complicated by the unexpected financial collapse of the large Penn Central railroad holding company in June 1970.

As usual, the calls for financial institution reform were easily ignored when the total household savings inflow to thrift institutions and commercial banks was jumping from an increase of only $7.4 billion in 1969 to a gain of $42.4 in 1970 and $68.5 billion by 1972, and while new housing starts were rising from 1.4 million units in 1970 to a record 2.4 million units in 1972. The turnaround did not last, however, and the next wave of disintermediation was under way by mid-1973, when rapid economic growth and rampant inflation again disrupted the economy and forced monetary policy actions.[5]

In addition to the usual shifts in the structure of interest rates, several regulatory policy changes on July 5, 1973, significantly altered the pattern of savings. Anticipating another round of disintermediation, regulatory authorities allowed the deposit payment differential on passbook savings to narrow to one-fourth of 1 percent by increasing the commercial bank ceiling to 5 percent and completely removing the maximum rate limits on 4-year certificates. During the next four months, before Congress reimposed maximum limits of $7\frac{1}{2}$ percent for thrift institutions and $7\frac{1}{4}$ percent for com-

---

5. The year-over-year rates of inflation as measured by the consumer price index were (percentage increases): 1965, 1.7; 1966, 2.9; 1967, 2.9; 1968, 4.2; 1969, 5.4; 1970, 5.9; 1971, 4.3; 1972, 3.3; 1973, 6.2; 1974, 11.0; 1975, 9.1; and 1976, 5.8.

mercial banks, these "wild card" certificates created two basic changes. First, depositors quickly began shifting their funds into the new 4-year certificates and the pace of passbook savings inflows slowed down. During the four months in which the no-ceiling certificates were permitted, it is estimated that over 80 percent of the increase in time accounts in commercial banks was accounted for by the "wild card" certificates and that without this new instrument "there would have been an absolute decline in the volume of consumer-type time and passbook accounts."[6] At savings and loan associations the new 4-year certificate deposits increased to $13 billion outstanding, while total deposits rose only $1½ billion.

Second, the "wild card" certificates moderated the overall amount of disintermediation by narrowing the gap between yields on open-market instruments to 1 percent or less. There was a sharp divergence, however, in what each type of deposit institution experienced in 1973 as summarized in Table 6. Commercial banks used the temporary power to issue no-ceiling "wild card" certificates in denominations as low as $1,000. They also made use of their new authority to pay a "full 5 percent" on regular passbook accounts to increase their rate of savings inflows in 1973, and again in 1974 as the long-term competitive balance seemed to shift. During the eighteen months after July 5, 1973, commercial banks gained 68 percent of the total increase in household savings in savings and time accounts, compared to 46 percent in the preceding eighteen months. Between the second and third quarters of 1973, the "wild card" period, the annual rate of deposit inflows at commercial banks surged 42 percent from $33.1 to $47.0 billion. Savings and loan associations and mutual savings banks experienced the exact opposite: their rate of savings inflows declined in 1973 and 1974 (Table 6). At savings and loan associations the seasonally adjusted annual rate of household savings growth dropped from $20.1 billion during the second quarter of 1973 to $7.1 billion in the third quarter.[7] Many leaders in the thrift institution industry considered that this decline provided overwhelming evidence of commercial banks' competitive advantages in attracting deposits, and they argued for more, not less, government protection during the congressional hearings on reform proposals.

6. U.S., Congress, Senate, Committee on Banking, Housing, and Urban Affairs, *Financial Institutions Act of 1975*, May 14, 1975, p. 142.

7. U.S., Congress, Senate, Committee on Banking, Housing, and Urban Affairs, *Financial Institutions Act, 1973*, p. 876.

The familiar pattern of declining housing starts (down from 2.4 million new units in 1972 to 1.2 million starts in 1975), rising mortgage interest rates, and unhappy interest groups once again created pressure for Congress to expand the government's role in the construction and financing of housing and the regulation of real estate markets. Not even the record return flows of savings into financial intermediaries in 1975 and 1976 and the recovery of new housing starts to an annual rate of just under 2 million units by the end of 1976 could erase the bitter memory of three severe occurrences of disintermediation in nine years.

The savings inflows at commercial banks and thrift institutions following the severe disintermediation of 1973–74 are shown in Figure 1. The sharp alleviation of inflation pressures from 1974 to 1976 and the reduction in money market interest rates compared to the yields on deposits restored the savings inflows as indicated. When inflation accelerated in 1977 and Treasury borrowing needs increased, money market interest rates again moved above the maximum passbook returns permitted on deposits at financial institutions. Short-term interest rates on 3-month Treasury bills moved up from a low of 4.41 percent in 1977 to a level of 8.17 percent by October 11, 1978; federal funds jumped from 4.47 percent to 8.71 percent; and commercial paper notes with 90–119 day maturities rose from 4.63 to 8.83 percent during the same period.

As money market rates increased above the controlled returns permitted for savings deposits, concern about another round of unwanted financial disintermediation was again evident. During the first five months of 1978 the net inflows of savings to savings and loan associations totaled $10.09 billion, a reduction of 41 percent from the comparable period in 1977. A repetition of the 1973–74 experience did not occur, however; savings inflows stabilized during the summer months and then improved later in 1978. Mortgage funds remained generally available to home buyers willing to pay the higher mortgage interest rates demanded. Primary market interest rates on conventional home mortgages, as reported by the Federal Home Loan Bank Bank Board, increased from 8.94 percent in April 1977 to 9.69 percent by August 1978. Other mortgage interest rates showed similar increases; and in some local lending markets double-digit rates were once again reported, along with some tightening of rules governing loan maturities and down-payment requirements.

Despite the increases in money market interest rates from 1977 lows to 1978 highs, the heavy disintermediation of savings was

When money market interest rates climb sharply above passbook rates . . .

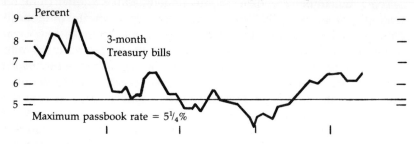

average noncompetitive bids at weekly Treasury bill auctions rise . . .

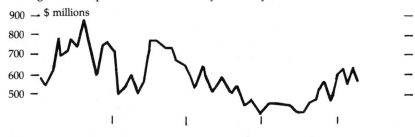

and savings inflows at commercial banks and thrift institutions are sharply curtailed.

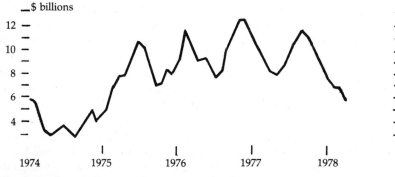

Fig. 1. Savings inflows and money market interest rates.
Source: Morgan Guaranty Survey, June 1978, p. 3.
Note: The maximum passbook rate for commercial banks is $1/4$ point lower than the maximum for thrift institutions plotted above. Savings flows are seasonally adjusted changes in combined average monthly deposits, excluding large CDs.

avoided—at least through October 1978—because of the supportive actions of the Federal Home Loan Bank Board and other agencies involved in the secondary mortgage markets. Innovative regulatory changes permitted the issue of new 26-week certificates of deposit offering an interest return approximately equal to the yield on 6-month Treasury bills, and a new 8-year certificate of deposit offered a relatively high yield for savers willing to make long-term commitments. The initial response to the 26-week certificates indicated that deposits can be retained if the return is competitive with other money market instruments. There are serious problems, however, because the higher deposit returns squeeze the profits of the financial institutions involved, and an increased risk of deposit volatility is created by emphasizing the 26-week maturities if market interest rates fluctuate. At this time it is impossible to predict the longer-term results of these innovative adjustments, but it is significant that the regulatory agencies continue to search for ideas that will help reduce the severe distortions caused by financial disintermediation. Until meaningful progress is made in stabilizing the entire economy through sustained fiscal and monetary policies this search will evidently have to be continued.

Summary Results of Disintermediation

The preceding account of the recent experiences of financial intermediary institutions clearly indicates the importance of basic economic and inflation factors. Since 1965 the economic environment has become more unstable with waves of disintermediation recurring as a consequence. The causes have been: (1) the upward trend of interest rates and volatile shifts in the pattern of short- and long-term yields; (2) the adjustment of interest rates to reflect both the overall acceleration of inflation and the uncertainties caused by wide swings in price pressures; (3) competitive changes in the private financial markets; (4) regulatory changes; and (5) the growing sensitivity of savers to differences in the yields available from various deposit accounts and open-market financial instruments. These changes have dramatically affected the competitive environment.

For individual institutions disintermediation creates a whiplash effect that disrupts their profitability, liquidity, solvency, and competitive performance, that is, their ability to satisfy the interests of savers and borrowers. Profits are squeezed by disintermediation pressures as rising short-term interest rates push up the costs of holding and attracting deposits, while earnings from longer-term loans and investments remain relatively fixed. For example, at the end of the 1974 financial distortion the average effective rate paid on deposits by mutual savings banks was 5.76 percent; the average rate of return on their portfolios of mortgage loans was 6.98 percent. The gross spread of 1.22 percent had to cover all operating expenses and additions to reserves before any possible net benefits could be realized. Financial intermediaries operating on such thin margins are obviously very vulnerable to changing costs. Similarly, the slow turnover of long-term assets creates ominous liquidity strains when deposit flows are volatile. Most commercial banks are able to adjust to unexpected deposit flows because their loans and investments have relatively short maturities, but thrift institutions must often turn to external sources for help in maintaining liquidity. If these strains on profit and liquidity continue long enough, the underlying solvency of individual institutions is threatened and mergers, or even liquidations, must be arranged. Finally, the distortions caused by disintermediation lead to stop-and-go lending and investment practices which prevent financial institutions from developing stable saving and borrowing relations with customers.

At the national level the fluctuations in housing credit have contributed to the boom-and-recession pattern of housing starts, thus precluding the stability needed to create an efficient construction industry. Since people change homes for a variety of reasons, often unrelated to economic conditions, the erratic pattern of mortgage financing resulting from disintermediation creates serious hardships for the many families who may be unable to obtain necessary loans or may have to accept interest rates and terms that are disadvantageous.

Congress cannot ignore serious problems affecting the housing industry because of the basic social importance of national legislative goals for this sector and the very effective lobbying by important private interest groups. As a result, the periodic breakdowns in real estate financing, along with related inefficiencies, have led to a growing role for government agencies in the housing industry. The Federal National Mortgage Association (FNMA), the Government National Mortgage Association (GNMA), the Federal Home Loan Mortgage Corporation (FHLMC), the Federal Home Loan Bank Board (FHLBB), and the Federal Housing Administration (FHA) have all been assigned important roles in the attempt to increase and stabilize the availability of mortgage financing, particularly for low- and medium-income families. Direct involvement through an array of Housing and Urban Development Department (HUD) programs has also increased the government's role. There is irony in this expanded government involvement, however, even beyond the debates about the proper allocation of responsibilities between the private and public sectors; the federal agencies listed above must frequently sell bonds in the open market to raise the funds needed to support the mortgage markets. In the process of tapping the capital markets, these specific bond issues compete against depository institutions for the funds available for saving and investment. There is no precise way of measuring the amount of overlapping competition, but at least part of the disintermediation that occurs results from such sales of government agency securities. The stop-and-go pattern of real estate activity, including residential construction, also seriously complicates the government's economic stabilization efforts, particularly the timing of adjustments in monetary policy. The Federal Reserve System must be constantly aware of the potential impact of its policies on the housing sector because of this sector's fundamental social importance and preferred position in Congress.

The ideal solution would be to create more stable economic conditions and to moderate inflation pressures to match the environment subsequent to World War II, when mortgage lending was advantageous and policies did not create large swings of interest rates, leading to periodic disintermediation. However, since economic instability and rates of inflation well above the historical average are likely to characterize the U.S. economy for the foreseeable future, the search for more specific solutions to the problems of fluctuating real estate financing, volatile housing construction and turnover rates for existing homes, and periodic disintermediation appears likely to continue.

Most academic economists recommend that the financial intermediary system be made more competitive and flexible to give it the strength necessary to overcome disintermediation pressures. Specific interest groups typically advocate a different approach, calling for more powers for their particular institutions in relation to asset and liability management, but at the same time asking for continued, or even broadened, government regulation to protect against unwanted competitive pressures that may hurt profitability, liquidity, solvency, and the stability of saving flows and investment and lending efforts.

3

GOVERNMENT REGULATION AND FINANCIAL INTERMEDIARIES

The United States depends upon a complex mix of financial institutions to match the flows of funds between the sources and users of capital and thus contribute to the efficient allocation of resources. We have relied chiefly on competition to regulate that process; but free markets may not always produce the desired results, particularly adequate credit for housing and consumer goods and services. The economic failure or gross mismanagement of financial institutions may also create broad social disruption. Recognizing this high degree of public interest, the government has historically regulated financial institutions, and its direct involvement was rapidly increased during the severe economic depression suffered in the early 1930s. The principal question that has faced public officials for several years is whether the present framework of regulations, largely developed forty years ago, is still the appropriate arrangement for the 1970s and beyond, given the likelihood that economic growth, disruptive inflation, and dynamic technological changes will dominate the financial markets.

The use of government regulations to control private markets has several major goals: (1) promoting efficient competition by restricting monopoly distortions and unfair business practices; (2) protecting public health and safety; (3) maintaining public confidence in the system; (4) allocating and protecting scarce resources; and (5) promoting equal opportunities.[1] In the financial markets, government regulations attempt to strike a proper balance between competition and innovation on the one side and the safety and soundness of the

---

1. Domestic Council Review Group on Regulatory Reform, *The Challenge of Regulatory Reform* (Washington, D.C.: The White House, Jan. 1977), pp. 2–3.

system on the other. Actual results have favored the protection of savers and borrowers to prevent institutional failures, unwanted concentration of financial resources, and repetition of the serious liquidity strains which restrict growth and periodically cause financial panics. More recently government intervention has also attempted to influence the allocation of national resources and the cost of credit to specific sectors of the economy to achieve congressional mandates.

Unfortunately the patchwork of regulations developed over the last forty years has also created many problems, and the confusing puzzle of overlapping rules has caused Arthur F. Burns, the highly esteemed former Chairman of the Board of Governors of the Federal Reserve System, to describe the present bank regulatory system as "a jurisdictional tangle that boggles the mind," creating sometimes conflicting jurisdictions and policies that result in a "competition in laxity" among the regulators.[2]

Regulatory Functions and Institutions

Basic regulatory functions include the chartering, supervision, and insuring of financial institutions. Hundreds of specific rules enable regulatory agencies to carry out these functions. In particular they control: (1) granting of charters to new institutions; (2) guidelines for mergers; (3) insurance of deposits; (4) rules for branching; (5) liquidity reserve requirements; (6) capital investment standards and the sale of notes and subordinated bonds; (7) maximum ceilings for interest payments on deposits; (8) foreign operations; (9) types of allowable loans and investments; (10) types of deposit accounts and other services offered to customers; (11) permissible ancillary activities; and (12) the form and timing of reports that must be submitted to the supervisory offices. In addition, regulatory authorities frequently exert a strong moral compulsion, using the various regulatory tools as a lever—or occasionally as a club—to force financial institutions to conform to expected standards of behavior.

A major feature of the financial regulatory system is its great emphasis on maintaining a dual approach to chartering and supervision by which commercial banks, savings and loan associations, and credit unions can operate under the direction of state authorities

---

2. Arthur F. Burns, "Maintaining the Soundness of Our Banking System," (Paper delivered at the 1974 American Bankers Association Convention, Honolulu, Hawaii, Oct. 21, 1974), p. 18.

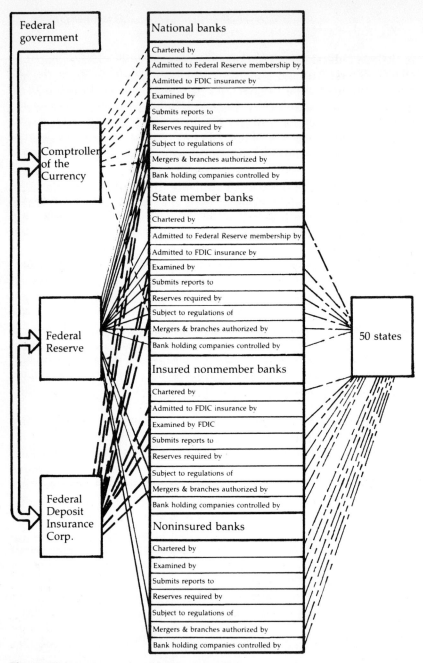

Fig. 2. The tangled web of bank regulation.

Source: Hearings on Financial Structure and Regulation before the Subcomm. on Financial Institutions of the Senate Comm. on Banking, Housing and Urban Affairs, 93d Cong., 1st sess. 619 (1973).

or various federal agencies. Only mutual savings banks are limited to state charters, and no provision has been made to grant federal charters to stock-type savings and loan associations. Proponents of the dual system of authority argue that centralization of supervision would stifle innovation and freedom of entry by eliminating the competition between regulatory jurisdictions. This claim is the basis of an overwhelming commitment to the dual system, and there is little likelihood that the confusion caused by redundant regulatory arrangements and the oddities of applying different laws to the same kinds of financial institutions in each state will lead to any major changes in the current arrangement. The distribution of federal and state institutions at the end of 1975 is summarized in Table 7.

The key to understanding the diffusion of regulatory powers is to recognize that the agency issuing the charter is also usually responsible for direct supervision. For example, national commercial banks are chartered only by the Comptroller of the Currency and are supervised by that office. Since all national banks are required to be members of the Federal Reserve System and have their deposit accounts insured by the Federal Deposit Insurance Corporation, they must also obey the rules established by those national agencies. However, national banks are not subject to individual state laws except for conformance to branching rules. A commercial bank

Table 7

TYPE OF FINANCIAL INTERMEDIARY INSTITUTIONS
BY NUMBER AND TOTAL ASSETS, DECEMBER 31, 1976
(In percentages)

	Source of Charter		
	State	Federal	Total
Number of institutions			
Commercial banks	68	32	100
Savings and loan associations	58	42	100
Mutual savings banks	100	0	100
Credit unions	44	56	100
Share of total assets			
Commercial banks	43	57	100
Savings and loan associations	42	58	100
Mutual savings banks	100	0	100
Credit unions	46	54	100

Source: Federal Reserve System, Federal Home Loan Bank Board, and National Credit Union Administration.

chartered by a state is supervised by the Federal Reserve System if it is a member, or by the Federal Deposit Insurance Corporation if it is not a member of the Federal Reserve System but does have its deposits insured. A fourth category includes a small number of state banks that are not members of the Federal Reserve System and do not have federal deposit insurance. The last three categories of banks are all subject to state supervision.

The same division of responsibilities—depending upon the source of their charter, membership in the Federal Home Loan Bank System, and the use of federal insurance for deposits—applies to savings and loan associations. Credit unions have a similar set of choices. Only mutual savings banks are limited to state supervision, although individual institutions that belong to the Federal Reserve System or the Federal Home Loan Bank System must conform to their regulations. It should also be noted that state-chartered financial institutions do not have the same powers or obligations as those operating in the same state under federal charters. In short, there are opportunities to experiment with different financial regulations and compare operating results. Since there are fifty different state jurisdictions, the scope and quality of regulation of financial institutions vary widely; but most public officials, academic experts, and financial intermediary managers evidently believe that the dual system is an essential feature of any future financial market and that fundamental change is unlikely.

At the federal level several different agencies are involved in regulating the financial system. Three basic regulatory agencies are responsible for commercial banks: the Comptroller of the Currency, the Federal Deposit Insurance Corporation, and the Federal Reserve System.

The *Comptroller of the Currency* charters and supervises all national banks. This office is attached to the Treasury Department.

The *Federal Deposit Insurance Corporation (FDIC)* insures the deposits of all national banks and of each state bank that decides to belong to the Federal Reserve System. It also supervises those state banks that arrange for the deposit insurance but do not belong to the Federal Reserve System. This procedure effectively spreads some form of federal jurisdiction over almost all commercial banks. The original level of insurance on individual accounts, beginning January 1, 1934, was $5,000. This figure has increased over the years to $40,000. The protection thus provided has strengthened the public's confidence in the banking system, following the trauma caused by the widespread bank failures in the 1920s and early 1930s, and it has enabled the FDIC to deal effectively with the relatively few commercial bank failures that have occurred in recent years.

The *Federal Reserve System (FRS)*, created in 1913, is probably best known for its central bank functions in carrying out national monetary policies, but it also has several important regulatory functions. For example, all state banks belonging to the FRS are subject to its supervision. Its Board of Governors is also responsible for regulations concerning international banking activities, bank mergers, branching by state banks that are members of the system, deposit reserve requirements, maximum limits on the interest paid on savings and time deposits, and the specific supervision of one-bank holding companies which have been used to diversify into related business activities.

Various proposals have been made to centralize all federal regulatory responsibilities in the FRS in an attempt to simplify the overlapping jurisdictions and correct the gaps in coverage, but Congress has never acted on these proposals. An alternative approach calls for the creation of a new Federal Banking Commission, which would absorb the regulatory functions of the FRS, the FDIC, and the Comptroller of the Currency. This has been considered by Congress, but the present separation of responsibilities has continued without change.

The Board of Governors has attempted to overcome some of the problems of enforcing its monetary policies within the fragmented regulatory system by asking Congress to require uniform deposit reserve requirements for all commercial banks, but even this modest adjustment of the status quo raises a storm of protest based on the sanctity of the dual banking system of national and state banks.

The irony of the current competitive environment is that few new state banks are joining the FRS, and during the last ten years 551 banks have withdrawn from formal membership. In 1977 the erosion of members accelerated: 69 banks left the FRS, including 5 bank holding companies with total deposits of over $2 billion. From 1960 to date, membership in the FRS has declined from 51 percent to less than 40 percent of the number of banks, and the proportion of total commercial bank deposits held by member banks has been reduced from 87 percent to about 72 percent. On July 10, 1978, the Board of Governors of the FRS sent to Congress a plan to halt the erosion of members. A key element of their proposal was that all financial depository institutions should be required to maintain reserves with the FRS on transaction accounts over $5 million. In addition to the universal reserve requirement the plan also proposed consideration of new charges for some of the services provided by the FRS and the possible payment of compensation to institutions for the required reserves deposited. These issues are controversial and will require considerable review by Congress.

Insured state banks that do not belong to the FRS are still subject to the supervision of the FDIC, but many analysts believe that the central banking functions of the Board of Governors are being eroded. Issues involving regulatory jurisdictions are extremely sensitive, and a committee-of-regulators approach has been substituted for the missing consolidation of powers needed to coordinate the entire system of financial intermediaries. The form of separation of powers appears to override the substance of the many complex problems that exist.

In issuing federal charters and regulating the savings and loan associations in the system, as well as in supervising the approximately 70 mutual savings banks that are members, the Federal Home Loan Bank System (FHLBS) performs the same functions as the Federal Reserve System does for commercial banks. Its subsidiary, the Federal Savings and Loan Insurance Corporation (FSLIC) also provides deposit insurance similar to the FDIC coverage of commercial bank deposits. In addition to exercising supervisory authority over the operating policies of members, the Federal Home Loan Bank Board (FHLBB) serves as a central credit facility to provide secondary liquidity to members affected by heavy withdrawals of deposits. In recent years advances to members to strengthen their liquidity, particularly during the recurring waves of disintermediation, have been a major factor in government efforts to preserve the flows of mortgage credit. At the end of 1976 advances to members totaled $15.9 billion, following substantial net repayments of $6 billion during 1975 and 1976 as savings flows to thrift institutions accelerated.

To acquire the funds necessary to provide these advances to members the FHLBS sells consolidated debt obligations in the open markets. Since the buyers of these attractive securities may well be diverting part of their deposits away from savings in thrift institutions, this is somewhat like chasing one's tail, that is, the pressures of disintermediation are probably increased by direct sales of FHLB debt instruments to assist the mortgage markets indirectly by making advances to members. It is difficult to estimate the actual amount of funds so diverted, but the existing system is firmly established and will continue.

Credit unions have adopted the same type of system with a National Credit Union Administration, established in 1970, to charter and regulate federal credit unions, state-chartered organizations being supervised by individual states. A federal credit union insurance program is also provided and a central liquidity fund is available to assist members temporarily in difficulty.

This very brief review of the functions and institutions involved in the regulation of financial intermediaries cannot cover the many complex issues or evaluate the various proposals for reform. Even so, it indicates many puzzling characteristics in the existing system of special regulatory offices and parallel federal and state jurisdictions. Since the dual system of allowing both federal and state charters and supervision is apparently untouchable, the regulatory authorities are left with the challenging assignment of improving procedures and coordinating their efforts from the inside. Unfortunately, overlapping efforts as well as gaps in coverage seem to be closer to what actually happens than the glowing descriptions of how a dual system creates a cooperative group of regulators intent on fostering innovation and efficiency to benefit the general public as well as special interest groups.

In most cases the ingenuity of private financial institutions and the competitive pressures of the marketplace are enough to overcome, or at least minimize, the frustrations of the regulatory process. One crucial supervisory function, however, involving the manipulation of maximum limits governing the returns paid on deposits at financial intermediaries, has significantly affected the competition for funds and the ability of those institutions to fulfill their basic saving and lending functions.

Government Response to Financial Disintermediation

As summarized in Chapter 2, disintermediation occurs when household savings are invested directly in open-market instruments rather than through financial intermediaries. The flow of funds in the marketplace is sensitive to interest rate differentials, and wide swings have occurred since the mid-1960s. Public policies have tried to restrict the competition among financial intermediaries for savings, with the intention of limiting the destabilizing forces, but it has not been possible to insulate thrift institutions against outside pressures. These government actions have directly influenced the competitive environment for savers and borrowers and have become the central issue in the various reform proposals.

Specific efforts to restrict the competition for household savings deposits resulted from the financial chaos created by the Great Depression of the early 1930s. The Banking Act of 1933 included two

relevant provisions: (1) commercial banks were prohibited from paying any interest on demand deposits; and (2) the Board of Governors
of the Federal Reserve System was authorized to regulate the rates
of return paid by member banks on savings and time accounts.[3] The
board used its administrative authority to issue regulation Q, which
established interest rate ceilings on savings and time accounts paid
by member commercial banks at 3 percent as of November 1, 1933.
The ceiling figure was reduced to $2\frac{1}{2}$ percent on February 1, 1935,
and then remained in effect until the 3 percent maximum limit was
restored on January 1, 1957. Throughout most of this period the
deposit interest rate controls had no substantive impact because the
market rates available elsewhere were usually well below the maximum deposit yields that were permitted.

The minor adjustment in 1957 actually signaled a new era of commercial bank competition for deposits and a reaction to increasingly
volatile economic conditions, including inflation and interest rates,
which ultimately created disintermediation pressures. The ceiling
was next increased to 4 percent on January 1, 1962, for deposits held
twelve months or more, and additional tinkering affecting the payments on time accounts with maturities of less than twelve months
occurred in 1963. Finally, on November 24, 1964, the limits for savings and time accounts were split, the maximum rate for time accounts of more than ninety days moving up to $4\frac{1}{2}$ percent.

The severe disintermediation experienced in 1966 resulted in the
first major change in deposit interest rate controls since the 1930s:
the Federal Home Loan Bank Board was given the authority to
regulate the returns paid on deposits by its members, and the
Federal Deposit Insurance Corporation was authorized to set maximum rates for commercial banks not belonging to the Federal Reserve System. All three regulatory bodies were directed to coordinate their actions, and an integrated set of controls was developed
using the administrative authority granted to each agency. An advantageous yield differential favoring thrift institutions, originally
set at three-fourths of 1 percent and later narrowed to one-half of 1
percent, was specified, and the new provisions also permitted in-

---

3. Demand deposits are the familiar checking accounts used to make third party
payments. Savings accounts do not require any obligation to leave the funds on
deposit for specific periods or to give written notice of intended withdrawal
(banks may technically require 30 days notice, but rarely do so) but such accounts
cannot be used for payments by check. Time accounts require the deposits to be
left for a specified period and may require prior notice of withdrawal, but they
also may not be used for third party payments.

creased flexibility for setting maximum rates based on different maturities on time accounts and on the size of deposit accounts. The rate differential provided for thrift institutions was in answer to the argument that they require a competitive advantage to survive against "full service" commercial banks. Strong pressure was also applied to the Treasury Department to stop issuing government securities in small denominations (under $10,000). The intention was to discourage direct investment in Treasury bills and other securities; the sale of open-market instruments by banks and other private corporations was discouraged. Even more important, the extension of rate controls to thrift institutions marked a major initiative by the federal government to extend its control over the entire financial intermediary system, to shelter nonbank institutions, and to influence the costs and allocation of credit in the private markets. Following the basic decision, regulatory agencies were continually involved in an effort to maintain a competitive balance between aggressive commercial banks that provide a full range of financial services, including checking accounts, and the more specialized mortgage-oriented thrift institutions and rapidly growing credit unions.

Following the extension of deposit interest rate controls in 1966 the competitive environment in the financial markets continued to change rapidly. Many commercial banks adopted a growth philosophy which depended upon aggressive "liability management" techniques to attract the funds needed for supporting the expansion of loans and investments, foreign operations, and numerous new banking activities operating under the umbrella of one-bank holding companies. As part of their emphasis on growth, many banks sold large denomination certificates of deposit and various open-market instruments such as commercial paper and subordinated debenture bonds.

The various regulatory authorities tried to respond to the rapid pace of change, but the difficulty of applying general guidelines to every innovation was readily apparent. For example, by 1970 deposit rate controls clearly could not prevent the disintermediation of large accounts, so the maximum ceiling on short-term time deposits of $100,000 or more was eliminated. It also appears that at least some of the regulators recognized the dilemma of constantly reacting to innovations in the private sector and that they preferred to emphasize general fiscal and monetary policies to achieve economic goals while relying on private markets to determine interest rates and the allocation of capital. Nevertheless the web of regulatory controls once begun generally tends to grow larger, and by the 1970s an amazing array of detailed arithmetic guidelines had been developed to control every type of savings and time accounts created by private financial institutions (Table 8).

The increasing difficulty of maintaining a viable program of controls over deposit interest rates in a period of changing financial markets and volatile economic and inflation conditions culminated in an intense debate over the future of regulation Q controls and the interest differential advantage granted to thrift institutions. The study prepared by the President's Commission on Financial Structure and Regulation as well as the legislative proposals considered by Congress focused on this basic issue. The dispute became particularly strong in July 1973 when regulations were changed to permit the removal of interest ceilings on new 4-year certificates and to narrow the differential further to one-fourth of 1 percent. After four months of shifting flows of funds among financial intermediaries and widespread uncertainty about competitive imbalances, Congress restored maximum limits on the new "wild card" accounts, as indicated in Table 8. Since that adjustment the debate has continued; meanwhile existing deposit controls were extended by Congress in April and again in November of 1977.

The original Banking Act of 1933 was intended to prevent the use of excessive interest payments on deposits in order to attract funds. The widespread bank failures of the 1920s and early 1930s were believed to be the direct result of banks' being forced to make more risky loans to cover the higher deposit costs. It was also believed that cutthroat competition for funds had attracted deposits away from country banks to money market centers, particularly New York City, for speculation in the stock market. For the most part, scholarly historical studies have rejected this explanation of bank failures in that era, but the argument was emphasized by Senator Glass during the debate on the legislation:

> We confide to the Federal Reserve Board authority which it does not now possess in this connection to regulate interest on time deposits in order to put a stop to the competition between banks in payment of interest, which frequently induces banks to pay excessive interest on time deposits and has many times over again brought banks into serious trouble.[4]

Whatever the original concerns, the basic motive for controlling deposit interest payments by the mid-1960s had shifted; instead of emphasizing the soundness of the commercial banking system, the

4. U.S., Congress, Senate, *Congressional Record*, 73d Cong., 1st sess., 1933, 77, pt. 4:3729.

Table 8

INTEREST RATE CEILINGS ON SAVINGS
AT FHLB MEMBER SAVINGS ASSOCIATIONS
(In Percentages)

Type of Account	Sept. 1966	Dec. 1969	Jan. 1970	May 1973	July 1973	Nov. 1973	Dec. 1974‡
Regular passbook	4.75	4.75	5.00	5.00	5.25	5.25	5.25
90-day notice	*	5.00	5.25	5.25	5.75	5.75	5.75‡
Certificate:							
30 to 89 days:							
No minimum	*	*	*	*	5.25	*	*‡
90 to 179 days:							
No minimum	*	*	5.25	5.25	5.25	5.75	5.75
$1,000 minimum	*	*	5.25	5.25	5.75	5.75	5.75
180 to 364 days:							
No minimum	*	*	*	*	5.25	5.75	5.75
$1,000 minimum	5.25	5.25	5.25	5.25	5.75	5.75	5.75
1 but less than 2 years:							
No minimum	*	*	*	*	5.25	5.75	*
$1,000 minimum	5.25	5.25	5.75	5.75	6.50	6.50	6.50
2 but less than 2½ years:							
No minimum	*	*	*	*	5.25	5.75	*
$1,000 minimum	5.25	5.25	5.75	5.75	5.75	6.50	6.50
$5,000 minimum	5.25	5.25	6.00	6.00	6.50	6.50	6.50
$10,000 minimum	5.25	6.00†	6.00	6.00	6.50	6.50	6.50
2½ but less than 4 years:							
No minimum	*	*	*	*	5.25	5.75	*
$1,000 minimum	5.25	5.25	5.75	5.75	5.75	6.75	6.75
$5,000 minimum	5.25	5.25	6.00	6.00	6.75	6.75	6.75
$10,000 minimum	5.25	6.00†	6.00	6.00	6.75	6.75	6.75
4 but less than 6 years:							
No minimum	*	*	*	*	6.75	*	*
$1,000 minimum	5.25	5.25	5.75	5.75	none	7.50	7.50
$5,000 minimum	5.25	5.25	6.00	6.00	none	7.50	7.50
$10,000 minimum	5.25	6.00†	6.00	6.00	none	7.50	7.50
6 or more years:							
No minimum	*	*	*	*	6.75	*	*
$1,000 minimum	5.25	5.25	5.75	5.75	none	7.50	7.75
$5,000 minimum	5.25	5.25	6.00	6.00	none	7.50	7.75
$10,000 minimum	5.25	6.00†	6.00	6.00	none	7.50	7.75
$100,000 minimum:							
30- to 59-day maturity	*	*	*	*	none	none	none
60- to 89-day maturity	*	*	6.50	none	none	none	none

(continues)

Table 8 (*continued*)

90- to 179-day maturity ...	*	*	6.75	none	none	none	none
180- to 364-day maturity ..	5.25	5.25	7.00	none	none	none	none
1-year or more maturity ..	5.25	5.25	7.50	none	none	none	none

Source: Federal Home Loan Bank Board
Note: Certain details of a technical nature, and rate ceilings prevailing only
      for a short time or in limited geographic areas, have been omitted.
*Not authorized.
†Applicable only to certain certificate renewals.
‡Effective Nov. 27, 1974, associations may pay the maximum certificate rate
on all governmental unit certificate accounts with 30-day minimum terms
and balances less than $100,000, and on all governmental unit notice ac-
counts.

attempt has been to insulate thrift institutions and small banks from
the aggressive competition of larger banks. Many believe that the
efficient functioning of financial markets may not by itself create the
allocation of capital in the way best suited to certain social goals,
particularly satisfying the need for mortgages and consumer credit.
When market results and social goals are incompatible, Congress
often sets up regulatory guidelines ensuring that credit is allocated in
the preferred manner at interest rates which are kept below marketplace charges by direct or indirect government subsidies.

The various government programs created to assist housing and
mortgage financing are classic examples of congressional efforts to
help achieve the goal stated in the 1949 declaration of national
housing policy—to provide "a decent home and a suitable living
environment for every American family, thus contributing to the
development and redevelopment of communities and to the advancement of the growth, wealth, and security of the Nation." To
accomplish this goal Congress created the Federal Housing Administration to provide mortgage insurance, Veterans Administration
mortgage guarantees, the Federal Home Loan Bank System to assist mortgage-oriented financial institutions, Federal National Mortgage Association, Government National Mortgage Association, Federal Home Loan Mortgage Corporation, and a variety of direct
assistance programs for low-income families buying or renting
housing. Congress has also specified that mortgage interest payments may be deducted from taxable income in computing taxes
and has allowed special deductions from taxable income in the
form of bad debt reserves to be made by thrift institutions that
specialize in real estate mortgage loans.

In addition to these important government spending and tax programs to assist housing, Congress has also relied on regulation in an effort to protect those financial institutions that specialize in mortgage lending. A mutual dependence between Congress and the mortgage-lending specialists has thus developed over the years, and this relation must always be considered in proposals for structural and regulatory reform. It is unrealistic to expect Congress to ignore the plight of thrift institutions during periods of financial disintermediation which severely disrupt the flow of funds into mortgage markets to support the housing industry. In exchange for assuming the risks of "borrowing short and lending long," described in Chapter 2, mortgage specialists are given special protection even though the actual results of such government intervention do not prevent the disruptive effects of disintermediation.

Government policies are evidently based on the assumption that if competition is uncontrolled commercial banks will drive up deposit rates to the point where mortgage lenders will no longer be able to compete for savings. Even greater government intervention in the financial markets is a logical result, since additional controls must be created as the marketplace attempts to overcome or evade the restrictions created by the original controls. The basic role of rate controls is succinctly summarized in the following statement made by the Chairman of the Federal Home Loan Bank Board:

> We have attempted to shelter thrift institutions from sharp swings in monetary conditions through a system of rate control imposed upon thrift institutions and upon commercial banks with respect to their consumer savings and time accounts. The controls were designed to prevent destructive rate competition between commercial banks and thrift institutions that would divert funds from housing and threaten the solvency of thrift institutions. We certainly agree that, in the climate of 1966 and subsequent years, this was essential and the Board supported the extension of rate control on various occasions.[5]

Arguments in Favor of Deposit Interest Rate Controls

Some advocates of deposit interest controls still emphasize the risks of potential rate wars to attract savings. For example, the executive vice-president of the United States League of Savings Associations, a group representing 98 percent of the assets of the savings and loan industry, has testified that:

5. U.S., Congress, Senate, Committee on Banking, Housing, and Urban Affairs, *Financial Structure and Regulation*, p. 108. Statement of Thomas R. Bomar, chairman of the Federal Home Loan Bank Board.

Of course, some competition and the ability to innovate and structure new services and products is healthy, but taking all price restraints from the savings market would produce a chaotic situation that we do not believe is good for the country. Regulation Q type ceilings are absolutely needed to keep one aggressive institution from pursuing suicidal programs that could weaken all the financial institutions in a particular savings market.[6]

Others are more pragmatic and simply claim that controls have effectively prevented destructive rate wars between financial intermediaries, even though the maximum limits used have not prevented serious disintermediation during periods of high and rising interest rates in the financial markets.

In a very detailed statement before the Senate subcommittee responsible for legislative oversight, the National Association of Mutual Savings Banks argued that the system of differential ceilings on deposit interest rates was never intended to prevent disintermediation but was established to provide direct support for housing markets, to moderate the severity of short-term deposit outflows, and to alleviate the scarcity of housing credit caused when savings move to commercial banks.[7] Advocates of controls claim that this basic purpose has been achieved and that the experience with the no-ceiling, 4-year "wild card" certificates in July 1973 is a clear example of the competitive pressures that result if the regulations are relaxed or removed. This argument was evidently persuasive in Congress because deposit rate controls on the 4-year certificates were restored after four months.

A variation of this theme is that the thrift institutions do recognize the serious competitive problems created when temporary disintermediation causes deposits to flow into open-market instruments, but such periodic crises are a bearable risk compared with the constant pressures created when commercial banks enter the consumer markets. The testimony of the savings and loan industry executive quoted earlier effectively summarizes these considerations:

> What we are concerned about is an everyday proposition. That is the competition of the commercial banks and the competition of one savings and loan versus another, and one bank versus another in any one community.
>
> Now, the regulation Q ceiling at least keeps that kind of competition in

---

6. U.S., Congress, Senate, Committee on Banking, Housing, and Urban Affairs, *Financial Institutions Act, 1973*, p. 414. Statement of Norman Strunk, executive vice-president, United States League of Savings Associations.

7. Ibid., p. 963. Statement of the National Association of Mutual Savings Banks.

hand, so that when we do have periods of high market rates such as we have now, we haven't exhausted ourselves competing with each other in periods of low-interest rates.[8]

Some analysts also claim that removal of the differential rate control authority would "inevitably lead to the increasing domination of commercial banks in the financial system, and could ultimately result in the disappearance of independent, consumer-oriented thrift institutions."[9] This argument goes on to describe the possibility that widespread takeovers of thrift institutions by commercial banks would create a monopolistic environment, with the result of limiting future returns to savers and eroding necessary support for real estate financing. In summary, this argument claims that eliminating the ceilings or allowing them to increase beyond the thrift institutions' ability to pay would destroy the intermediary system because dog-eat-dog competition with commercial banks from day to day is the real risk, rather than the periodic competition from open-market instruments. Stated in its simplest form, "The principal competition of the savings and loan business generally is not the money market; it is the commercial banking business."[10]

Another major argument for continued maximum limits and differential rate authority is that thrift institutions suffer specific disadvantages regarding earnings, liquidity, and solvency in "borrowing short and lending long," and that these justify and require special competitive tools if such institutions are to remain viable specialists in mortgage financing. This point was made in the testimony of the president of the National Savings and Loan League:

> It isn't simply a matter of whether it's good economics to have free competitive market conditions relative to savings rates . . . in fact, there is a great deal of evidence to show that given the kind of interest rate cycles we have experienced in the past 7 or 8 years and which most people [say] we are going to continue to experience, there is no way for the holder of long-term fixed-rate mortgages to compete with the savings rate against assets that are short-term assets in commercial banks which often simply flow with the prime rate.[11]

Even if thrift institutions are allowed to diversify their loans and investments to strengthen profits and improve their liquidity position, according to their representatives, such changes would still not

8. Ibid., p. 382. Statement of the United States League of Savings Associations.

9. Ibid., pp. 68–69. Statement of the National Association of Mutual Savings Banks.

10. Ibid., p. 414. Statement of the United States League of Savings Associations.

11. U.S., Congress, Senate, Committee on Banking, Housing, and Urban Affairs, *Financial Institutions Act of 1975*, May 14–16 and June 11, 1975, p. 187.

create a competitive balance. Accordingly, they argue, controls should be retained to prevent both the slow erosion of their competitive position and the emergency pressures they experienced in the summer of 1973. To support their view that controls will be needed in the future, representatives of the thrift institutions included in their congressional testimonies quotations from two of America's most eminent economists. From a study by Professor Paul W. Samuelson, holder of the Nobel Prize in economics:

> Even if we were to move toward a time when ceilings become in effect inoperative, a strong pragmatic case can be made for maintaining the power to reinstate ceilings on a standby basis . . . . In time of emergency, it is easier to take a weapon off the shelf than to forge a new one. Therefore, standby powers to reimpose ceilings do make good sense.[12]

Professor James S. Duesenberry of Harvard University has written:

> There is a good case to be made for standby powers for the supervising agencies to set ceilings. Circumstances like those of 1966 may recur again; and in those circumstances, it would be irresponsible for the supervisory agencies to let free competition have its way.[13]

A fifth supportive argument for continued controls involves the important advantages of liquidity, low risk, and relatively good returns during most periods that thrift institutions provide for savers. Advocates of controls strongly deny the academic criticism that small and unsophisticated savers are discriminated against because deposit rate controls restrict their earnings during periods of rising open-market yields. To support their argument, thrift institutions claim that savers prefer the convenience and safety provided by deposit accounts, and that those who want to shift their funds may readily do so if they are willing to give up the advantages of passbook accounts. Extensive advertising has publicized the yield differences, and larger numbers of savers are shifting their funds directly into open-market instruments whenever interest rates rise. They also emphasize the longer-term benefits of enabling thrift institutions to remain strong enough to promote personal thrift and mortgage lending.

---

12. Paul W. Samuelson, "An Analytic Evaluation of Interest Rate Ceilings for Savings and Loan Associations and Competitive Institutions," in *Study of the Savings and Loan Industry,* prepared for the Federal Home Loan Bank Board by the Wharton School of Finance and Commerce, University of Pennsylvania, July 31, 1969, vol. 4, p. 1589.

13. James S. Duesenberry, "Appraisal of Selected Policy Instruments Affecting Savings and Loan Associations," ibid., p. 1603.

Finally, thrift institutions strongly reject the arguments against deposit interest rate controls, and they call for a restoration of the original interest rate differentials permitted on their accounts in order to strengthen competition. This viewpoint prevails even though the proponents recognize that disintermediation is not prevented. Ideally most disintermediation problems could be avoided if fiscal and monetary policies would stabilize the national economy and control inflation, but this favorable result is not likely in the near future. Most thrift institutions and small commercial banks therefore firmly support the continuation of maximum limits on deposit interest rates as the best way to satisfy the long-run interests of most savers and home mortgage borrowers.

Arguments against Deposit Interest Rate Controls

The basic arguments against controls are of two kinds: pragmatic criticisms of the actual results and general objections to government intervention in the private markets. Critics of controls also emphasize the long-term viability of thrift institutions and the goals of real estate finance, but they recommend the gradual elimination of restrictions to improve the competitive position of financial intermediaries. Since it is impossible to extend controls over the entire financial system in order to govern the costs and allocation of credit, the existing restrictions unfairly inhibit the competitive reactions of financial intermediaries. When the flow of savings into deposit institutions is shut off, mortgage lending quickly declines because thrift institutions are no longer able to transfer additional deposits directly into new mortgage loans, and other financial institutions with broader investment powers switch to open-market instruments. Critics therefore claim that regulation Q has not only failed to sustain the necessary flow of funds into mortgage financing, creating serious liquidity and profitability problems for specialist institutions, but that such controls have actually contributed to disintermediation by making it impossible for mortgage-oriented financial intermediaries to compete for funds in the broader markets. Since savings will ultimately flow to the financial instruments offering the best package of comparative yield, risk, and convenience, freezing the rates paid by thrift institutions and commercial banks at a given relationship does not solve the basic problem. Nor is it possible to substitute temporary premiums and special services to compensate savers for lower financial returns. Experience suggests that it is the small savers who suffer when deposit returns are artificially depressed below current market rates, and critics of controls emphasize the apparent inequity of limiting the returns to the small, less sophisticated savers while those with higher incomes and more experience are able to evade the regulatory restrictions by shifting their funds directly into open-market securities.

This paradox caused Congressman Henry S. Reuss, currently chairman of the powerful House Committee on Banking, Currency, and Housing, to comment critically: "Regulation Q is intellectually indefensible but politically damned near eternal."[14] Critics contend that this situation has developed because Congress has been more concerned about the cost of funds to mortgage borrowers than the rates of return paid to savers, but even this bias may be counter to the real interests of borrowers placed at a disadvantage by the periodic chaos in the mortgage markets as a result of disintermediation.

Critics also claim that each successive round of disintermediation has made all savers increasingly sensitive to differences in available yields, so that with each shift in interest rates the flows of savings into direct investments will be larger and the reaction time shorter, as people become educated by experience and widespread advertising. It is also obvious that financial institutions are becoming more imaginative in developing new instruments to avoid the restrictions of controls like regulation Q. The new certificates of deposit issued beginning June 1, 1978, by commercial banks and thrift institutions enabling them to offer flexible returns to savers linked to the discount yields on Treasury bills on new 6-month instruments and a high, fixed-rate yield on new 8-year certificates are a classic example of how the market adapts to new realities when the regulatory environment is reasonable. In this changing financial environment, rate controls eventually become self-defeating.

The philosophical argument against controls focuses attention on the increasing role of government in the private economy. While the proper degree of government involvement is still being argued, the role of regulatory controls has continued to increase. Critics claim that this expansion is contrary to the basic principles of the U.S. economy, which is supposed to be based on free markets and intense competition. They further claim that rate controls make thrift institutions, credit unions, and smaller commercial banks too dependent on government protection and reduce the competitive pressures that lead to increased efficiency and innovation. A protected system of financial institutions, they say, forces the government to

14. "What Went Wrong With Financial Reform," *Business Week*, Nov. 3, 1973, p. 84.

substitute controls for marketplace competition to protect institutions that are inefficient and unable to compete in open markets. Critics of controls contend that competition is a better taskmaster and that specific abuses, such as imprudent loans and investments and unreasonable deposit interest rate wars, are best handled individually by regulatory authorities. Finally, some critics complain that the preferred position granted to mortgage borrowers is unreasonable because it is a disservice to other borrowers. Housing is clearly a fundamental social issue that deserves public attention. But there are many other desirable social goals that may be shortchanged by tilting the allocation of credit to real estate finance at partially subsidized rates. Those advocating the allocation of resources in response to marketplace decisions in which the cost of resources is balanced against the benefits created at the margin argue that it would be better to help low-income families by direct subsidies for housing. The indirect approach to stimulating the housing industry through a complex maze of government spending programs and controls over the allocation and costs of credit has not created a stable housing industry or a satisfied public.

This issue remains one of the most controversial problems in our modern economy, and this brief chapter cannot comprehensively develop the many arguments, but it is important to note that at least some analysts would prefer to see the financial system more responsive to market forces, rather than to rely on government-imposed regulation. Empirical evidence demonstrates that controls like regulation Q do not work, and economic theory argues that national resources—including capital—should be allocated in competitive markets so that individuals, who are not only buyers of many different products and services but also workers interested in the growth of jobs through investment, can express their preferences—not depend on government officials to tell them what they should want.

Summary

The future role of regulation Q and other regulatory policies used to influence the flows of savings and the allocation of credit will undoubtedly remain one of the most controversial issues facing public officials. Part of the policy reactions will depend upon four marketplace variables: (1) the overall level of economic stability and inflation as a determining factor in the volatility and general level of interest rates; (2) the related demands for credit from consumers, businesses, federal, state, and local governments, and foreign borrowers; (3) the responses of financial institutions in developing new types of saving and investment instruments; and (4) the behavior of savers as they consider their future prospects and the outlook for inflation.

The decisions of public officials in adapting to these marketplace developments, or in trying to tilt the system to achieve goals mandated by governments, will be the other key factor. This brief review of the financial intermediary system and government regulation provides a background for understanding the reform efforts of recent years. The intense debate about the role of deposit interest rate controls and differential payments goes directly to the primary issue of institutional competition and innovation. Although the conflicting views of each interest group are clear, the realities of dynamic market forces and a prolonged legislative process have created a puzzling mixture of academic analyses and pragmatic arguments by interest groups. These issues are the subject of the following chapters.

4

COMPREHENSIVE REFORM BEGINS: THE PRESIDENT'S COMMISSION ON FINANCIAL STRUCTURE AND REGULATION

The complexity of national problems often causes presidents of the United States to supplement the effort of government officials by creating public advisory commissions, composed of eminent generalists, expert specialists, and representatives of interest groups, to prepare recommendations for legislative and administrative policies. Ideally their concerted efforts should rise above the special interests of individual members and help to achieve broad public goals. One authority has described the role of commissions in this way:

> Basically the creation of advisory committees marks a recognition of those "rules of the game" in the United States that prescribe that individuals and groups likely to be affected should be consulted before governmental action is taken. Such consultation is in most cases prerequisite to the action's being accepted as fair.[1]

Although presidential commissions have no direct authority, they do affect public policies in a variety of ways. First, commissions are used to study national issues and prepare recommendations for policy actions. They are expected to evaluate available information from public and private sources rapidly and with minimal new research, and to identify and rank policy options and develop consensus recommendations. They are meant to build on the expertise and analytical skills of the members, who are usually either widely respected leaders with broad backgrounds or technical specialists with unique knowledge and experience.[2]

1. David B. Truman, *The Governmental Process*, p. 458.
2. Thomas R. Wolanin, *Presidential Advisory Commissions*, p. 31. In his comprehensive analysis of the role of presidential commissions Wolanin cites the following

Commission studies are generally limited to available policy options, and a basic assumption seems to be that the government can and should do something to correct the problems that led to the creation of the commission. In some situations commissions are used as a substitute for internal staff analysis, despite the major disadvantages of having to wait for an outside committee's decisions, because the established government agencies lack credibility in preparing policy recommendations—the familiar problem of assigning the fox to guard the chickens—and also because the atmosphere of crisis that exists from day to day in most offices precludes such basic studies. After carefully analyzing the functions of presidential commissions Wolanin concluded:

> The real problem [in this period, 1945–72] was that though the White House was theoretically capable of doing the job of policy analysis, its staff was overwhelmed with routine program planning, administrative management, legislative liaison, [and] political and ceremonial tasks.[3]

Many national problems are complicated by genuine confusion about goals and actual conditions. In these situations the commission serves as a clearing house for ideas and information. Even when sources of empirical data and feasible policy options are readily identifiable, however, the conflicting demands of interest groups may be so intractable that commissions have difficulty finding basic points of agreement. Commissions usually try to develop comprehensive packages of recommendations, including trade-offs that offer compromise solutions, but this approach is extremely difficult and time consuming. Powerful interest groups usually prefer the familiar disadvantages of the status quo to the uncertainties of change. Hence such constituencies rarely reward their leaders for workable compromises but often severely reprimand them for agreeing to any loss of special advantage.

---

advantages of such groups: their ability to persuade Congress and the public; the quality of the members; their temporary existence; the fact that they do not have to worry about institutional maintenance and usually have a specific mandate; the limited scope of their studies; their isolation from daily operating crises; their group identity, mutual respect, and positive environment; the short but intense effort expected of them; their extensive exchange of information and feedback; their flexibility, originality, and quality of their staff; the explicit support of the White House for gaining cooperation; their access to governmental and private information from consultants and government agency staffs and materials.

3. Ibid., p. 52.

Many presidential commissions have also been created to validate the views of internal presidential advisers under the assumption that, acting independently or with some Executive Office guidance, they will develop the same recommendations. The prestige and credibility of the outside commissions can thus offer major advantages to the administration in dealing with the Congress and the general public. For each commission, variations will occur in the relative importance of motives for creating a fresh study of national issues, in the policy positions of special interest groups, and the intensity of their commitment, and in the need to create independent recommendations with improved credibility; but the basic function of policy analysis is universal.

A second way in which presidential commissions influence public policy is that commission reports often become guidelines for subsequent legislative and executive initiatives. Such studies are generally considered to be more objective and independent of the usual political pressures and of efforts by existing government agencies to increase their powers. No matter how carefully government officials prepare their recommendations, they are usually suspected of being self-serving, excessively optimistic, politically motivated, or much worse. This inherent handicap is partly overcome by creating a blue-ribbon group of eminent private citizens and representatives of interest groups to help educate and persuade possible critics. Such an approach creates a buffer for the President against the charge that internal staff recommendations are aimed more at expanding the power of the Executive Office and reelecting the incumbent than at attacking the national problems studied by the commissions.

Third, commissions serve as a damage-control device to help presidents maintain leadership in policy making. By appointing a new commission, the President gains some control over the timing of the report, the balance of members, the format of the study, and the response he will give to the recommendations—enthusiastic personal endorsement or undercutting it by releasing the report to the public on a Friday afternoon just before a long holiday weekend. From the viewpoint of the President, the public announcement of a newly appointed commission preempts the initiatives of others in the Congress or the private sector who might be planning a competing study that could threaten the power of the President.

In the modern political world where form often dominates substance and symbols are all-important, Presidents must always be out in front on key national issues. Appointing a commission is considered a sign of vigorous leadership, foresight, concern, and rigorous independence from any bias that might influence a less responsible leader. The image of a dynamic President forcefully taking charge in a crisis and hammering out a tough but fair solution that serves the entire electorate is part of the mythology of presidential leadership that much of the daily activity of senior advisers is devoted to developing. At the same time, the President can avoid getting too far out in front on controversial issues when he has referred the problem to a commission, because he must wait for the considered judgment of his personally appointed panel of outside advisers. The President can then use the commission's recommendations as a trial balloon to evaluate the political and public response before committing himself.

Fourth, commission reports are useful when the decision-making process gets down to the pushing and shoving stage of shaping legislative and administrative actions. The President has a powerful weapon against his opposition when he can refer to supportive recommendations made by an important group of acknowledged experts. It is even more useful if he can capture representatives of the potential opposition by drawing them into the general agreement created by the commission report. There is always the risk, of course, that a commission's report may support the opposition. That is why internal advisers refer to them as "unguided missiles." But that possibility can be partly controlled because the President determines the mandate and membership of the commission, the form and timing of the public report, and its subsequent application within the operating agencies of the government.

Fifth, the President can also use commissions to help control his own bureaucracy. Government agencies charged with administering a program are rarely in the vanguard of advocates of change. The major reasons why bureaucracies become entrenched lie in inertia, vested interests in existing programs, strong internal leadership, and commitments to outside interest groups. The President can use a commission to stimulate the bureaucracy to participate in the study, and the final report can become a lever to force internal change.

Sixth, commissions are sometimes used to delay decisions or to prevent any positive action. The natural internal dynamics of committees often work to postpone any meaningful response. In other situations there may be an explicit understanding that the commission is to be used as a holding action. This cynical view of commissions may be widespread among observers of the political system and the general public, but such a use is probably less common than is generally supposed. The very appointment of a commission arouses public interest and creates expectations among the interest groups, academic experts, the news media, and Congress. Most commissions are appointed to consider a real national problem; and unless the issue fortuitously disappears during the extended analysis some explicit response must eventually occur. Even if the President chooses to ignore the recommendations of his commission, the final report can be used by Congress and private interest groups to push for tangible action.

In reality, presidential commissions are usually created for all of the general reasons described and for many other specific purposes. In all cases their analysis is used to shape policy recommendations, to educate and persuade, to give the President control over the policy-making process, and occasionally to delay or even prevent any positive response.

They play an important part in the diversified process of developing national policies because they conform to the accepted rules of the game described by Truman. Most Americans want to believe that policies are determined only after a thorough and objective analysis of all available information and that every interested group can present its views to qualified experts—a presidential commission, the administration, the Congress, regulatory agencies, internal interagency committees, and so on—to ensure that a final decision will be based on fair and equitable compromises. The gap between this idealistic view and reality is discussed in detail in Chapters 9 through 12.

Background of the Commission on Financial Structure and Regulation

Public concern about complex financial affairs and the controversial aspects of structural and regulatory reform have given rise to many public and private commissions to study the financial system. One particularly comprehensive analysis began in 1958, when the Commission on Money and Credit was established by the Committee for Economic Development. The opening paragraph of that private study stated:

> Our monetary, credit and fiscal policies and the instruments and institutions through which they operate must be so designed that they can make an essential contribution in the decades ahead to the improvement of our standards of living through simultaneously achieving low levels of unemployment, an adequate rate of economic growth, and reasonable price stability.[4]

4. Commission on Money and Credit, *Money and Credit: Their Influence on Jobs, Prices and Growth* (Englewood Cliffs, N.J.: Prentice-Hall, 1961).

This paraphrasing of the familiar passage in the Employment Act of 1946, which summarizes national economic goals as "to promote maximum employment, production, and purchasing power," was meant to stress the basic role of the financial system in the total economy. While it is difficult to summarize briefly the numerous academic and private industry monographs that were prepared, the essential message was an appeal for greater equality in chartering, investment, branching, supervision, and taxation to achieve more competition. Despite the generally favorable reaction of the academic community to the detailed recommendations calling for increased flexibility regarding assets and liabilities and extensive regulatory reforms, the report did not lead to comprehensive legislation.

Nevertheless, the Commission on Money and Credit did provide a philosophical and descriptive foundation for subsequent reform efforts. The same topics were once again analyzed in 1963 by a high-level interagency group that included all of the senior economic officials in the government.[5] Even the support of that Cabinet group could not create a high enough priority to have the technical reform recommendations included in the package of presidential legislative initiatives.

One reform effort that was almost successful was the Federal Savings Institutions Act calling for broadened powers for thrift institutions (savings and loan associations and mutual savings banks), which was favorably reported by the House Banking and Currency Committee in December 1967. The committee report created controversy, however, by arguing that commercial banks had gained their growing competitive advantages at the expense of the thrift institutions by adjusting interest rates to attract deposits. The committee report stated: "This legislation would redress this growing competitive imbalance by strengthening savings institutions."[6] Although it had the administration's strong support and that of the mutual savings banks, savings and loan associations, and major groups representing housing, mortgage lending, and real estate, the bill was narrowly defeated in the House Rules Committee in 1968 by the vigorous lobbying of the commercial banking industry, which opposed structural changes in mortgage-oriented thrift institutions.

---

5. *The Report of the Committee on Financial Institutions to the President of the United States*, April 1963.

6. U.S., Congress, Senate, Committee on Banking, Housing, and Urban Affairs, *Financial Institutions Act, 1973*, p. 935.

Despite the lack of specific response to the 1961 report of the Commission on Money and Credit and to the 1963 Cabinet study, and despite the narrow defeat of the thrift institution legislation in 1968, irresistible pressures for change through adjustments in the marketplace continued to build. The unfortunate acceleration of inflation in the mid-1960s and the related sharp increases in interest rates to historically high levels led to severe distortions throughout the financial system which disrupted the entire economy. By the end of that decade there was widespread support for a complete review of the problems among the leaders of the financial industry, academic experts, members of congressional committees (particularly Senator William Proxmire, an active member of both the Joint Economic Committee and the Senate Committee on Banking, Housing, and Urban Affairs), and senior officials of the administration that assumed office in January 1969.

The first public announcement of the plans to form a presidential commission appeared in the *Economic Report of the President* released on February 2, 1970. The general goals of the administration were summarized by the Council of Economic Advisers:

> Our expanding and increasingly complex economy must have financial institutions reflecting the vitality that comes from vigorous innovation and competition. Financial services required by tomorrow's economy will differ in as yet undefinable ways from those appropriate today. The demands on our flow of national savings . . . will be heavy in the years ahead, and our financial institutions and financial structure must have the flexibility that will permit a sensitive response to changing demands. Thus the time has come for a thorough examination of needed changes in our financial institutions and our regulatory structure. This study will be carried out by a commission to be appointed by the President early this year.[7]

On April 22, 1970, Reed O. Hunt, the retiring chairman of the board of Crown Zellerbach Corporation, was designated chairman of the new commission, which was formally established on June 16, 1970. At that time a broad mandate was given to "review and study the structure, operation, and regulation of the private financial institutions in the United States, for the purpose of formulating recommendations that would improve the functioning of the pri-

---

7. Council of Economic Advisers, *Economic Report of the President* (Washington, D.C.: Government Printing Office, Feb. 1970), p. 104.

vate financial system."[8] The group took very seriously the charge to develop specific legislative proposals, and the influence of this constraint became a major strength in the commission's study and the chief cause of criticism from those who preferred more bold and sweeping recommendations. The commission also emphasized the need for flexibility in adjusting to changing conditions, particularly the severe distortions resulting from inflation, and the accelerating pace of technological change. However, as the study progressed, a more pragmatic approach dominated the efforts to devise proposals that could gain general acceptance. A series of integrated trade-offs of competitive factors was arranged among the different financial institutions. The ideal was a competitive framework of flexible institutions that would select operating policies according to the choices of managers rather than statutory requirements. Although this approach was conceptually attractive to most of the members, the recommendations that emerged did not meet the test of being what is called politically feasible, given the framework of government institutions and private interests within which economic policies are developed.

The Operations of the Hunt Commission

The members of the Hunt Commission were named according to the general pattern of including eminent generalists, expert specialists, and representatives of the interest groups involved (see the appendix to this chapter for a complete list of the commissioners). The group comprised six businessmen, four commercial bankers, two insurance company representatives, two savings and loan association executives, a mutual savings banker, one business economist, one state legislator, one senior official from organized labor, and two academic representatives. Congressman Wright Patman, the powerful Chairman of the House Committee on Banking, Currency, and Housing in 1970, strongly criticized the composition of the commission, saying that it was dominated by representatives of the financial community. They would of course argue for the traditional goals of that sector, he said, and hence any report issued by them would be merely a rehash of existing practices and viewpoints. Since any legislative recommendations resulting from the Hunt Commission's efforts would ultimately have to be considered by Congressman Patman's key committee, his comments sounded an early warning of the disappointing events that followed. Nevertheless, despite his harsh criticism, and other complaints about includ-

8. U.S., *Report of the President's Commission on Financial Structure and Regulation*, p. 1.

ing four commercial bankers in the group, the quality of the commission and its professional staff was widely respected, and the balance of interests was generally considered to be reasonable.

At the first meeting, held on June 27, 1970, it was decided that the commission would function as a committee-of-the-whole and would focus its attention on a limited number of structural and regulatory issues. Fourteen additional meetings were held during the next eighteen months, and the final report was submitted, as scheduled, on December 22, 1971. By all accounts the commission functioned efficiently, was provided with a competent professional staff, and invited and received hundreds of reports and personal statements from representatives of interest groups, the administration, and the financial regulatory commissions. The commission's report emphasized that it had been granted independence in selecting its staff and conducting the study.

In his foreword to the final report, Chairman Hunt commented that the final recommendations did not always represent the views of individual members but that the "report as a whole" did have the "broad support" of the members. One commissioner, however, Lane Kirkland, the Secretary-Treasurer of the AFL-CIO, refused to sign the report. In explaining his dissent, Mr. Kirkland said that "the basic thrust of these recommendations is designed to promote the interests of private financial institutions without any genuine regard for the most urgent problems and needs of the nation."

He then stated a number of objections: (1) The recommendations would not make financial institutions more responsive to social needs, and they failed to fulfill the responsibility "for seeing to it that a fair share of the financial resources are allocated to social priorities," even though the commission recognized "that free competition by itself does not allocate resources properly." (2) The commission "abdicates its responsibility" by merely recommending direct subsidies and tax incentives for housing to fulfill congressional goals, because such actions do not "adequately compensate for the tendency of the private financial structure to assign a higher priority to corporate enterprise and other preferred customers at the expense of programs and projects which are essential to meet the requirements of life in this country for the average citizen." (3) A National Development Bank should be created to make direct loans and to guarantee private loans for social projects. (4) Asset reserve requirements should be used for all financial institutions, so that they would have to funnel a given percentage of their resources into housing and other social investments deserving priority. (5) The commission's recommendations would act to "channel funds out of the housing market as well as to raise the cost of mortgage money—especially during a tight credit market." (6) The suggested diversification of lending and investment powers would hurt housing and make the thrift institutions more nearly like commercial banks. (7) Removal of FHA and VA mortgage interest ceilings would push up rates. (8) The Federal Reserve System's independence should be modified to make it more responsive to congressional policies. (9) Financial institutions should be regulated more closely to prevent conflicts of interest. (10) The Social Security system should be expanded, and the commission's recommendation for private tax-sheltered annuity plans is simply a "vehicle for the benefit of the wealthy." (11) The credit union recommendations are too restrictive and would push these institutions in the direction of becoming commercial banks. (12) "Financial institutions cannot be placed in the same category as other private businesses" and should not be judged by "whether they make a good profit or not" because "every financial institution must, in part at least, adopt its policies and practices to the attainment of broader public goals." But this will not occur because the "competition for capital and credit, the allocation of priorities as between corporate giants and such urgent needs as low-cost housing, medical aid and educational facilities, mass transit and state and local government needs, cannot safely or fairly be left to the sole discretion of the banking fraternity."[9]

Besides Kirkland's comprehensive rejection, two commissioners from the business sector submitted a specific dissent to the recommended use of a mortgage interest tax credit which they believed would "seriously distort normal credit flows and relationships among various types of credit instruments."[10] A third commissioner, the president of a residential construction firm, added his serious reservations about the potential effectiveness of the recommendations to provide for improvements in the mortgage markets.[11]

Although only one commissioner refused to sign the report, an indication at least of broad support for the compromises developed through the committee process, the comprehensive objections of Kirkland and the specific concerns about housing finance have been worth emphasizing because the same arguments influenced the later

9. U.S., *Report of the President's Commission on Financial Structure and Regulation*, pp. 129–33.

10. Ibid., p. 134.

11. Ibid., p. 135.

analysis of legislation in the Congress, when the administration's proposals, based largely upon the recommendations of the Hunt Commission, were submitted. Since the conflicting viewpoints could not be rationalized, the legislative proposals were not approved by the Congress.

Major Recommendations of the Commission

The principal theme of the commission's final report is that a stronger and more efficient financial system is needed that will contribute more to the national economic well-being than a highly fragmented and regulated arrangement. To accomplish this goal eighty-nine basic recommendations and twenty-seven more detailed suggestions were made under ten general headings.[12] The assumptions unifying these recommendations included the following:

1. Although constant change will characterize the future financial system, the adjustment process will be evolutionary rather than revolutionary. Accordingly, all of the suggestions are permissive, allowing the individual financial institutions to select their own policies.

2. Free market forces are more effective than any set of governmental procedures for achieving a stable and efficient financial system that provides maximum benefits to both savers and borrowers. This viewpoint is evident in the suggestions for removing unnecessary regulatory restraints and permitting increased flexibility for financial institutions that are willing to accept more competitive risks in exchange for more powers. It was recognized that a transition period would be required to phase in the new institutional arrangements.

3. All institutions competing in the same markets should do so on an equal basis. Equality refers to investment and lending powers, reserves, taxation, chartering, branching, and regulation. This does not mean that the future financial system should have only one type of intermediary institution. Specialization should continue, but the choice of policies and strategies should be given to the financial institutions. This increased freedom to compete creates many risks, and one can understand why many managers enjoying the protection of statutory and regulatory barriers to competition would not welcome such changes.

4. The commission attempted to anticipate the criticism that social goals might be slighted if more institutional flexibility and

12. Ibid., pp. 23–133.

competition were permitted by explicitly recommending "open and direct subsidies or, alternatively, the use of tax credits" whenever housing and other social needs were not being fulfilled. This preference for direct subsidies rather than portfolio controls and mandatory regulatory requirements was based on the following arguments:

The overriding advantages of the direct subsidy and tax credit methods are that they are efficient and that they make the cost of achieving social goals visible, both in absolute and relative terms. The value of programs can be assessed easily and promptly. Direct subsidy and tax-credit programs also avoid the "hidden tax" and inflationary effects of special regulations and special agency financing. Program financing parallels the allocation of real resources and permits better planning, management, and accounting.[13]

5. The Commission strongly urged that the recommendations be evaluated as a package. None of the individual recommendations was particularly new or unique, and hence the opposing arguments were familiar to public and private officials. The report explicitly recognized the bittersweet combination of gains and losses for each type of financial institution, but the risks involved in proposing a comprehensive package of changes were thought preferable to the problems arising from piecemeal adjustments that often increase the existing distortions. This approach is logical, given the interdependence of the entire financial system. Nevertheless political costs are incurred when special interest groups object to an integrated set of recommendations, and these hazards ultimately frustrated the legislative initiatives that followed the Hunt Commission report.

Although it is not appropriate to analyze all eighty-nine recommendations in this brief summary, it is useful to identify the major suggestions in order to explain the legislation proposed in 1973 by the administration.

Section A. Regulation of interest rate ceilings on deposits. The seven recommendations in Section A deal directly with the basic issue discussed in Chapter 2. The commission favored: (1) abolishing regulatory authority to stipulate deposit interest rate maximums on various accounts of $100,000 or more; (2) permitting the Board of Governors of the Federal Reserve System to continue to set ceilings on accounts of less than $100,000, using standby authority during periods of serious disintermediation; (3) allowing the Board to re-

13. Ibid., p. 118.

duce the $100,000 cutoff figure; (4) permitting the Board to phase out the interest rate differentials now permitted on different types of accounts; (5) requiring a uniform deposit interest rate ceiling after the phasing out of existing differentials; (6) eliminating the Board's standby authority to establish deposit interest rate ceilings after ten years; and (7) continuing to prohibit the payment of interest on demand deposits, even though changes in the marketplace are rapidly making this restriction obsolete. The commission argued that the additional powers granted to thrift institutions would make such regulation of competition unnecessary.

Section B. Functions of depository financial institutions. The principal suggestions for increasing institutional flexibility and competition are outlined in Section B. It was recommended that savings and loan associations and mutual savings banks receive increased lending and investment powers, including authority to make (1) mortgage loans on all types of residential and nonresidential properties; (2) construction loans; (3) mobile home loans; (4) direct real estate investments, including limited equity participations; (5) secured and unsecured consumer loans in amounts not to exceed 10 percent of total assets; (6) commitments in investment-grade U.S. government, state, municipal, and private debts; (7) and limited investments in equity securities. A "leeway provision" for investments in other financial institutions was also recommended.

The commission favored the further expansion of powers for thrift institutions as well, to permit them to: (1) diversify the types of deposit accounts offered to customers; (2) offer limited third-party payment services, including checking accounts and credit cards, to individuals and nonbusiness entities; (3) make limited equity investments in community rehabilitation and development corporations engaged in providing housing and employment opportunities for those with low and moderate incomes; (4) issue subordinated debt instruments of all maturities; (5) extend their lending powers geographically; (6) manage and sell mutual funds subject to proper regulation; and (7) engage in various fiduciary and insurance services for individuals and nonbusiness entities.

This wide range of additional powers was intended to strengthen the capabilities of thrift institutions in real estate finance "in ways that reflect market conditions and the particular abilities of the organizations themselves . . . restricted only by considerations of safety and soundness." The other major goal was to aid the evolution of thrift institutions into "family financial centers" by enabling them to offer a full range of time and savings accounts, and certificates of deposit with varying interest rates, withdrawal powers, and maturities, and by granting them more diversified lending powers to permit consumer loans, third-party payment systems, checking accounts, and a variety of personal and insurance services. The thrift institutions welcomed the expanded powers for real estate financing. Differences of opinion developed, however, about the relative merits of some recommendations and their effects on housing, particularly the recommendation to permit more diversified lending and investment practices and thus strengthen liquidity by improving earnings and stabilizing cash flows. Sharp controversy also arose over the requirements that as a "price of admission" the thrift institutions should pay for the expanded powers by accepting the same treatment as commercial banks with regard to taxation, ceilings on interest rates for deposits, reserve requirements, and regulatory supervision.

The commission's recommendations for commercial banks appear to be more technical than those relating to the other institutions. The major issues in the type of services offered by banks had already been thoroughly reviewed when the Bank Holding Company Act was being considered, before the Hunt Commission study, and the regulatory and legislative history of controlling the affairs of commercial banks apparently precluded any sweeping new recommendations. The few technical suggestions included in the report focused on: (1) allowing banks more flexibility in presenting various assets for discounting purposes at Federal Reserve Banks; (2) abolishing restrictions on bank real estate financing; (3) permitting equity investments in community rehabilitation and development corporations; (4) adding a "leeway provision" to allow limited diversification into any assets, excluding equity investments in any firms other than their own subsidiaries; (5) approving the use of subordinated debt instruments of all maturities, and increased use of acceptances; (6) authorizing commercial banks to manage and sell mutual funds and to underwrite certain municipal revenue bonds secured by revenues from essential public services; and (7) a catch-all provision approving participation in a variety of financial, fiduciary, or insurance functions consistent with the Bank Holding Company Act. The recommendations that chiefly interested commercial banks appear to relate to protection of their competitive position rather than acquisition of any new powers.

Finally, Section B made several major recommendations that would strengthen the competitive position of credit unions and greatly enlarge their role in the financial system. Specific suggestions included: (1) creation of a Central Discount Fund authorized to make temporary advances to credit unions to improve their liquidity; (2) expansion of their lending powers to include secured and unsecured consumer installment loans, educational loans, and residential and agricultural mortgage loans to members; (3) permission to invest in investment grade private and government debt instruments; (4) diversification of the types and terms of deposit accounts offered; (5) power to provide third-party payment mechanisms to members as part of an interest-bearing loan or line of credit agreement; and (6) diversification of the types of financial services offered to members.

Section C. Chartering and branching of depository financial institutions. For thrift institutions, the commission recommended three very important changes in Section C. These permitted: (1) federal charters for stock savings and loan associations and for mutual savings banks, including enabling legislation by states to allow state-chartered thrift institutions to convert voluntarily to federal charters; (2) the elimination of all statutory restrictions preventing statewide branching of thrift institutions either *de novo* or through mergers; and (3) development of procedures for allowing mutual institutions to convert to stock companies. At the time of the report all fifty states and other territories permitted the chartering of mutual savings and loan associations, but only twenty-one states allowed stock companies chartered by the state. Only eighteen states and Puerto Rico provided for the chartering of mutual savings banks. In this situation the commission's recommendation to create competition in the granting of charters and to establish more uniform regulation presented an unusually controversial issue that had already disrupted numerous reform attempts. The federal chartering of mutual savings banks had been a prime goal of that industry for many years, but disagreements about how reserve and surplus accounts should be treated when a mutual institution is converted to a stock company were so intense that Congress had finally declared a moratorium on such conversions. The topics covered by these specific recommendations continued to arouse extreme controversy during the subsequent congressional hearings.

The commission similarly recommended that state laws be changed to permit unrestricted statewide branching by commercial banks, and that federal charters be made available for creating mutual commercial banks. The question of limiting or expanding branch banking in individual states has also been bitterly debated from the beginning of the U.S. banking system. Recently the disputes have been intensified by the growing use of electronic transfer systems in locations other than the bank's offices. The commission's proposal to extend equality of treatment and competition to mutual commercial banks through federal chartering also triggered a sharp reaction from some bankers, who expressed concern about the emergence of unfair competition. As always, the reactions of specific interest groups depended upon whose ox was being gored.

The commission confronted an equally explosive issue by raising the tax status of credit unions and the trend toward liberalizing the required bonds of association which have been used to limit membership services. The commission was audacious enough to criticize the practice of extending the financial services of credit unions and modifying the membership bonds without reconsidering their exemption from federal income taxes. Recognizing the growth in the size and diversification of some credit unions, the commission recommended permitting a credit union to convert its charter into either a mutual savings bank, a mutual savings and loan association, or the proposed mutual commercial bank form of organization. Representatives of credit unions vigorously denounced this section of the report during their congressional hearings on the proposed legislation.

Section D. Deposit reserve requirements. The Hunt Commission continued its assault on controversial issues by recommending in Section D that all state-chartered commercial banks and all thrift institutions offering third-party payments be required to join the Federal Reserve System (all national banks are already members), and that the legally required deposit reserves against demand and similar deposits be the same for all institutions following a transition period. The commission also recommended that reserve requirements be the same for all members of the system regardless of their location and size, that legal reserve requirements on demand deposits be gradually reduced, and that reserves on time and savings accounts no longer be required.

These recommendations would favor the request of the Board of Governors of the Federal Reserve System to extend its requirements to all commercial banks, regardless of their membership status, in order to improve the functioning of monetary policies. But the suggestions met strong opposition from many state-chartered banks; they also created resentment among representatives of thrift institutions, who feared that they would now become subject to the Federal Reserve System, which they tend to associate with the commercial bank industry. Section D is another example of the intensity with which interest groups react when ideas that have been hotly debated for many years are included in an omnibus set of recommendations.

Section E. Taxation of financial institutions. In view of the expanded powers suggested for each type of financial institution, the commission recommended in Section E that Congress enact a uniform tax formula for all depository firms offering third-party payment services and that taxation be made uniform for all institutions competing in the same markets. The debate on this section led to the preparation of several conflicting studies attempting to prove the actual incidence of taxation for each category of institutions. As would be expected, the conclusions from each analysis depended largely on the definitions used.

For example, an analyst opposed to a uniform tax might cite the fact that commercial banks invest heavily in tax-exempt municipal bonds as evidence that tax avoidance is prevalent. A group of governors and mayors, on the other hand, would argue that such supportive bank investments are absolutely necessary to enable states and municipalities to raise money at advantageous interest rates. Since commercial banks have not had the same protection that thrift institutions have in the form of reserves for bad loans, the emphasis on tax-exempt bonds in their investment portfolios is a natural development. Tax reform has always been extremely difficult, and it is probably asking too much to expect sweeping legislative changes that will create competitive equality, given the fragmented nature of the financial system and the entrenched positions of the various interest groups.

Section F. Deposit insurance. The commission recommended in Section F the development of uniform methods of handling claims for deposit insurance payments in cases of institutional failure. The section also advised that the welfare of the community should be the dominant motive, rather than the avoidance of payouts from the insurance fund. The universal use of deposit insurance beginning in 1934 has greatly increased the safety of deposits, and this section involved largely procedural issues.

Section G. Housing and mortgage markets. The crucial role of housing and mortgage loans was evident in all of the commission's analyses and recommendations, even though its formal mandate did not include any direct reference to these problems. No attempt to change the structure and regulation of the financial system can succeed unless the Congress is satisfied that the powerful interests of the housing industry are recognized. Furthermore the availability and quality of housing are clearly such important public concerns that they have long received special emphasis in Congress, even though housing is only one of the fundamental needs shaping the quality of life in America.

The commission apparently anticipated that its comprehensive package of suggestions would have minimal chances for acceptance unless the housing and real estate interests could be satisfied. In Section G, therefore, the commission proposed eleven major actions which it hoped would directly aid the housing and mortgage markets enough to elicit support for financial institution reform, or at least to neutralize the opposition. Despite this special effort to cultivate support, critics attacked the Hunt Commission's ideas during the congressional hearings that followed by arguing that the changes would seriously hurt the housing situation and the thrift institutions that specialize in real estate finance.

Specifically, the commission made several major suggestions: (1) abolishing administrative or statutory interest rate ceilings on FHA-insured and VA-guaranteed mortgages; (2) authorizing variable rate mortgage interest options for FHA and VA loans, including guidelines for disclosing the terms to borrowers; (3) consideration of government insurance to cover the risks of portfolio losses resulting from rising interest rates for institutions holding long-term mortgages; (4) development of secondary markets for mortgages, including the variable rate types; (5) elimination of state usury laws limiting interest rates on mortgages, and of other state laws limiting the efficiency of real estate markets; (6) development of a special tax credit based on gross interest income from residential mortgages; and (7) direct subsidies to consumers if mortgage financing is not sufficient to fulfill national housing goals.

The proposal for a mortgage interest tax credit became a major part of the administration's legislative package along with several of the other suggestions by the commission. However, housing interests and key members of Congress were not convinced that the benefits claimed would adequately offset the loss of existing advantages, or that the incentives provided by the tax credit would significantly improve the financing of real estate. As a result, the widespread support needed to push the reforms through the legislative process did not develop.

Section H. Regulation and supervision of financial institutions. Section H contained a series of recommendations for the complete overhaul of the regulatory system. Over the years, considerable dissatisfaction has developed in the Congress and the financial system, and particularly among the regulators themselves, concerning the procedures used, the fragmented distribution of responsibilities, and the scope of regulatory authority, which is sometimes redundant and in other cases insufficient to meet modern requirements. Although this part of the report was very important, it was a self-contained section which could be separated from the rest of the recommendations without seriously restricting the other structural changes. The administration chose the simplified approach of separating the structural from the regulatory packages, the aim being to improve the prospects for favorable response by reducing some sources of controversy. The fourteen major regulatory reform suggestions in Section H, involving the formation of new agencies and the thorough realignment of responsibilities among existing public authorities, will therefore not be covered here despite their importance to the general subject of reforming the financial system and to the whole work of the Hunt Commission. Congress has frequently considered these controversial topics, and legislative proposals continue to be submitted to each session of Congress; but no comprehensive reform has been approved despite the thorough review presented in the Commission's report. Once again, regulatory reform demonstrates the complexity and sensitivity of financial issues and their controversial character.

Section I. Life insurance companies. The commission made only three technical recommendations for life insurance firms, and none of them relates directly to the problems of deposit institutions or housing issues. Section I recommended that: (1) state insurance laws be amended to allow life insurance companies to issue policies containing flexible interest rates on policy loans, with the object of controlling the outflow of funds during periods of high interest rates; (2) state taxes on life insurance companies be reviewed; and (3) a reasonable balance be sought between social insurance and private insurance to provide economic security. The last suggestion would require a separate study to sort through all the complex issues. The chief point of interest here is that the life insurance company's recommendations were not included in the administration's legislative package.

Section J. Trust department and pension funds. Section J contains a number of technical recommendations concerning the development of a federal "prudent man investment rule" to guide those with fiduciary responsibility for investments, and a list of detailed suggestions for operating a trust department and pension fund. Particularly stressed was the need for full disclosure of information to regulatory authorities. Once again, the technical suggestions did not cover the depository institutions or housing issues, and hence the administration did not include these topics in its legislative package submitted to Congress.

Reaction to the Hunt Commission Report

Unlike many presidential commissions' reports, the Hunt Commission's recommendations were not quickly filed away and forgotten. They provoked intense debate throughout the financial community and served as the basis for legislative packages submitted by the administration to Congress. Like the study by the Commission on Money and Credit, completed ten years earlier, the Hunt Commission's study became the benchmark reference for subsequent discussion of financial institution reform.

Critics of the report claimed that it merely reviewed an array of familiar topics that had been argued for years, without proposing any bold and innovative changes. Such criticism ignores the main goal of the commission: to develop an internally consistent set of recommendations that would both strengthen financial institutions operating in the current, more competitive, environment and present enough compromises to ensure the support necessary for political acceptance.

The Hunt Commission did not attempt to conduct any new research or to extend its recommendations beyond adjustments of the existing system. It never had any illusions about creating a new financial system but merely wanted to provide a more flexible environment in which financial institutions could evolve in the directions selected by the managers of those institutions.

Critics quickly condemned the compromises required to maintain any hopes for political survival; they were looking for dramatic changes and for promises that the problems of modern societies could be solved by government planning and spending. Nevertheless, pragmatism soon replaced general idealism as the commission reacted to the views of powerful interest groups and recognized the dominating influence of the housing interests. The Hunt Commission continued to hope that the increased powers recommended for each type of financial institution would be a sufficient trade-off for the sacrifices and risks associated with increased competition. As it turned out, the financial institutions were generally unwilling to accept even the relatively restricted recommendations for organized reform, although many of the specific changes were already occurring in the marketplace. Thus the pragmatists were disappointed by the unwillingness of interest groups to compromise, while the idealists claimed that not enough attention was given to the broader economic issues facing society.

From the beginning, widespread and enthusiastic support throughout the financial community, or at least among the four basic types of depository institutions, was seen to be necessary if the omnibus legislation based on the Commission's recommendations were to gain approval. Without such consolidated support, and in view of the lack of real awareness and support among the general public, it seemed unlikely that Congress would overcome its obvious preference to avoid controversy over an issue with little public appeal, especially just before the November 1972 elections. Individual members of Congress have little to gain and potentially much to lose if they become trapped in an acrimonious debate over a specific problem like financial institution reform. The administration, which had been counted on to provide not only enthusiastic support and publicity for the philosophy but specific recommendations as well, was in the same position, although it did begin the internal processes of preparing legislation.

It had been assumed that credit unions would be enthusiastic about the Hunt Commission report because it provided for a new central fund to meet liquidity strains and expanded their lending and investment authority. Credit unions did welcome these recommendations but remained skeptical of the omnibus approach to reform. One reason was their hope of obtaining expanded powers from Congress through their own legislative efforts, a hope that turned out to be well founded; another was their strong opposition to any changes in their bond of membership rules or tax exemption status.

Mutual savings banks were also expected to support the broad reforms because these included approval of federal charters and expanded powers. Their support was modified, however, by strong opposition to the removal of ceilings on deposit interest payments and the differential granted to thrift institutions in allowing them to pay higher returns to savers. The mutual savings bank industry also opposed the recommendations to permit conversions into stock organizations. Savings and loan associations were expected to have little enthusiasm for the comprehensive report and to oppose very strongly the removal of ceilings on deposit interest payments and the differentials.

Finally, the commercial bank sector had a split reaction to the report, reflecting the division between large and small banks. Since very few new powers were proposed for commercial banks in exchange for the possible encroachment of both the thrift institutions offering "family financial centers" and the aggressive credit unions, most smaller banks resisted the potential erosion of their protected position. The smaller banks also rejected the recommended removal of the regulation Q controls for limiting interest payments on deposits, although they did welcome the phasing out of the payment differentials. Large banks seemed to be more resigned to the increase in competition that might result from granting more powers, including the crucial third-party payment rights, to thrift institutions and from the improved position of credit unions. This public attitude was apparently based on an awareness that rapidly changing technology in the marketplace and regulatory adjustments were already leading to a more competitive environment. Accordingly, the large commercial banks tentatively approved the main intent of the Hunt Commission report, with one major proviso summarized in the comment of a banker who had served as a commissioner:

> If you believe there is a reasonable chance in a very short period of time for these specialized institutions to broaden their powers and become very near to what you are now, to cut the gap of competition between your package of services and theirs, then I think you have to say, we'd better find a way to do it and make certain that they pay the price of entry.[14]

The so-called price of admission for allowing thrift institutions to have checking account operations included: (1) equality of taxation; (2) uniform deposit interest ceilings, and eventually no ceilings; (3) equal supervisory burdens (after checking accounts reach 10 percent of total deposits for thrift institutions); and (4) membership in the Federal Reserve System and equality of reserve requirements, eventually at a low level. The reaction of the thrift institutions was that

14. American Bankers Association, *Summary and Interpretive Analysis of the President's Commission on Financial Structure and Regulation*, p. 15. Statement of Kenneth A. Randall, member of the Hunt Commission, President of United Virginia Bankshares, Incorporated, and former Chairman of the Federal Deposit Insurance Corporation.

they were already paying more taxes and that they needed expanded powers to preserve competition. In short, the reactions in the financial community ranged from strong antagonism to limited support contingent on adjustments that would maintain existing advantages. The consensus needed to push through the omnibus recommendations did not exist.

Given the fragmented reaction of financial institutions to the report, the housing interests became a dominant factor in the prospects for the Hunt Commission recommendations. The erratic flow of funds into the housing sector was naturally an important variable in the commission's analysis; however, the competitive structure of the financial system was thought to deserve prime consideration, and if an efficient financial system could not produce enough mortgage financing then direct subsidies to consumers should be used. The reaction of housing interests was strongly in favor of continuing, even expanding, the various regulatory and statutory practices in a way that would actually increase the flow of funds into housing. When the commission explicitly rejected proposals to restrict thrift institutions to the financing of housing and to force other financial institutions to commit more of their resources to real estate finance, the political future of the report was effectively determined.

The commission argued that requiring institutions to invest a specified percentage of their portfolios in particular types of investments is the equivalent of a special tax and would distort the proper allocation of funds. Nevertheless, housing interests were not satisfied with the commission's arguments that permitting the thrift institutions to diversify their portfolio of loans and investments would actually help firms to be stronger and more profitable and thus provide a more stable source of mortgage financing. Since this fundamental difference could not be resolved during the course of the commission's study, the report had to be issued without the supportive consensus within the financial community that would have allayed the strong opposition of the housing interests and served to persuade a skeptical Congress.

Appendix

Members of the President's Commission on Financial Structure and Regulation

Reed O. Hunt (Chairman)
Retired Chairman of the Board
Crown Zellerbach Corporation

Atherton Bean
Chairman of Executive Committee
International Multifoods Corporation

Morris D. Crawford, Jr.
Chairman of the Board
The Bowery Savings Bank

Morgan G. Earnest
President
Earnest Homes, Incorporated

J. Howard Edgerton
Chairman of the Board
California Federal Savings

Richard G. Gilbert
Chairman and President
Citizens Savings Association

Wiliam D. Grant
Chairman of the Board and President
Businessmen's Assurance Company

Alan Greenspan
President
Townsend-Greenspan and Company, Inc.

Walter S. Holmes, Jr.
President
C.I.T. Financial Corporation

Lane Kirkland
Secretary-Treasurer
AFL-CIO

Donald S. MacNaughton
Chairman of the Board and Chief
Executive Officer
The Prudential Insurance Company of America

Edward H. Malone
Vice-President of Trust Operations
General Electric Company

Rex J. Morthland
Chairman of the Board
The Peoples Bank and Trust Company

William H. Morton
President
American Express Company

Ellmore C. Patterson
Chairman of the Board
Morgan Guaranty Trust Company of New York

Kenneth A. Randall
President
United Virginia Bankshares, Inc.

Ralph S. Regula
Attorney and State Senator
State of Ohio

Ezra Solomon*
Former Dean Witter Distinguished
Professor of Finance
Stanford University

R. J. Saulnier
Professor of Economics
Barnard College, Columbia University

Robert H. Stewart, III
Chairman
First National Bank of Dallas

---

* Resigned September 1, 1971, to become a member of the Council of Economic Advisers.

5

THE FINANCIAL INSTITUTIONS ACT OF 1973

By the early 1970s competitive forces had clearly demonstrated the barriers to efficiency and innovation that existed in financial markets dominated by stop-and-go economic policies and severe inflation. The old rules no longer served the interests of savers and borrowers. Nevertheless, twenty-two months passed after submission of the Hunt Commission Report before the administration initiated legislation in October 1973. Meanwhile special interest groups prepared their public statements and marshaled their private lobbying efforts, professors continued to argue philosophical points and construct elaborate econometric models of the financial markets, and congressional staffs worked on the position papers that would be needed in the future hearings.

Within the administration a task force headed by Treasury officials collected detailed statements from interested Executive Office agencies as a basis for evaluating the Hunt Commission Report and drafting specific legislation. Treasury officials also talked with special interest groups to build support for the anticipated reforms and to neutralize potential opposition from real estate finance and construction interests. After the standard internal review that controls the Executive Office's legislative initiatives, the technical advisory board working with Treasury officials made three decisions: (1) the legislative proposals would focus on depository institutions and would not make any recommendations regarding insurance companies, trust departments, pension funds, the securities industry, or the proliferation of commercial banking activities by one-bank holding companies; (2) a comprehensive package of major structural changes would be recommended, rather than detailed changes for each financial intermediary; and (3) the reforms in the regulatory structure recommended by the Hunt Commission would not be included.

Despite these restrictions, the resulting proposals for financial intermediary reforms represented the most extensive effort since the 1930s to change the financial system, and the administration announced its proposals August 3, 1973, in a Presidential Statement to Congress and a detailed background discussion paper prepared by the Treasury Department.[1] As part of that announcement, the Hunt Commission's recommendations were recognized as being "of major assistance in our further deliberations concerning the best ways to correct the weaknesses in our financial system."[2] After some last minute efforts to clarify the mortgage interest tax credit to attract the support of housing interests and mortgage-oriented lenders, or at least to moderate their opposition, the legislative proposals prepared by the administration were submitted to Congress on October 18, 1973.

The Administration's Legislative Proposals

The Financial Institutions Act of 1973 was introduced on behalf of the President in the Senate Committee on Banking, Housing, and Urban Affairs and then assigned to its Subcommittee on Financial Institutions, chaired by Senator Thomas J. McIntyre of New Hampshire. Under Senator McIntyre's leadership and with help from two of the Senate's most able and experienced members, William Proxmire of Wisconsin and Wallace F. Bennett of Utah, the subcommittee effectively fulfilled its job of collecting and evaluating detailed statements from former members of the Hunt Commission, various administration officials, academic experts, and numerous representatives of financial institutions and housing interests during the four sets of extensive hearings that began in November 1973 and continued through December 1974.

In his opening statement Senator McIntyre emphasized the importance of broadening the competitive structure of financial institutions but admitted that the hearings would be long and complicated:

> This legislation, if enacted, will have a far reaching impact and substantially change existing rules and regulations presently governing savings and loan associations, credit unions, mutual savings banks, and commercial banks. In view of the substantial number of recommended changes contained in S.2591 and the resistance to these proposed changes . . .

1. U.S., Department of Treasury, *Recommendations for Change in the U.S. Financial System.*
2. Ibid., p. 2.

exhibited by several of the trade associations representing various types of financial institutions, I anticipate that the subcommittee's consideration of these proposals will require intensive and in depth hearings. As chairman of this subcommittee, I would like to make it clear to all interested parties that these hearings will not be an exercise in wasted motion. Structural change and reform at the legislative level is, in my opinion, necessary and will be made.[3]

Senator McIntyre rightly emphasized that it would take many months of formal hearings to develop a better understanding of the financial system and that the Senate would not be able to act on the legislation before late 1974 or early 1975. His guarded forecast about the prospective schedule reflected his concern about the complexity of the issues, the strong opposition of some interest groups, the skepticism in the Congress about the administration's decisions to limit the legislation to financial intermediaries and to delete the proposals for regulatory reform, and perhaps most important the recognition by Congress of the fundamental link between structural financial reform and housing interests. Senator Proxmire effectively summarized his own underlying concern in a concluding comment following statements by eminent academic economists calling for more competition and efficiency in the financial markets to improve the national allocation of resources.

> Gentlemen, I have great respect for all of you. You are all very distinguished economists and widely recognized. Of course, I know of your excellent work in my capacity as a member of the Joint Economic Committee, and I admire you greatly, but I must say I can see why this is called a dismal science. It was never more dismal in my view than the attitude you fellows have developed toward housing.
>
> Now, the Congress established a view in 1949 that a decent home and a suitable living environment for every American family should be our goal, and we quantified that in 1968, and maybe unwisely, by saying we were going to have 26 million housing starts over 10 years. We have fallen far below that. Perhaps it was unrealistically high, but it was a goal which I think had a very worthy social purpose.
>
> It is my belief, and it seems to be the belief of many people in the Congress and in the country, that it is not only desirable for people to have an opportunity to own their own home, but it has a very good effect on the family, on the children, and a sense of responsibility and the sense of community obligation. And for all these reasons, it seems to me it is not just a matter of figuring out the opportunity costs of money, or figuring out what is the most efficient way to organize the money mar-

---

3. U.S., Congress, Senate, Committee on Banking, Housing, and Urban Affairs, *Financial Structure and Regulation*, pp. 2–3.

kets. It is a matter of recognizing that some social goals maybe ought to take precedence here.[4]

The Philosophy behind the Administration's Recommendations

The administration's recommendations for financial reform were presented at the opening session of congressional hearings by William E. Simon, Deputy Secretary of the Treasury. His theme was the need for immediate restructuring of the system to make it more free and competitive and better able to avoid continuing waves of financial disintermediation and even more government intervention. Stated most generally, the basis of this approach is to allow interest rates on savings and mortgage loans to respond to market forces, and to rely on direct subsidies to achieve specified social goals. The ultimate elimination of regulation and similar controls is a necessary part of this strategy. Secretary Simon then outlined five major goals that he felt would be achieved by adopting the legislation proposed in the Financial Institutions Act of 1973.[5]

The first goal would be to create a "more efficient financial system" that recognizes the savers' interest in earning high rates of return and the borrowers' interest in minimizing the costs of borrowing. Since market conditions constantly change and each community's needs are different, it is important to develop flexibility in the financial system. This does not mean eliminating specialized financial intermediaries; these may well have unique comparative advantages in serving certain markets. What the act was intended to do was to move away from specialization necessitated by statutes or regulations so that managers of financial institutions could become more responsive to the interests of their customers.

Second, the financial system should serve a diversity of interests rather than be "designed around any one social objective," because such goals change with time and "should be taken care of with tailormade subsidies, which are aimed specifically at the problem to be addressed."

Third, the financial system should now become more oriented toward the consumer-saver, after concentrating on the needs of major borrowers for many years. The financial system should provide more services to consumers and allow the returns paid for deposits

4. U.S., Congress, Senate, Committee on Banking, Housing, and Urban Affairs, *Reform of Financial Institutions*, p. 13.

5. Senate, Committee on Banking, Housing, and Urban Affairs, *Financial Structure and Regulation*, p. 23. Statement of William E. Simon.

to reflect changing market conditions. In addition, loans for consumer purchases, personal needs, and mortgages should be available from more sources, and the resulting competition should help to minimize borrowing costs.

Fourth, the dependence of thrift institutions on the federal government should be reduced by allowing them to "bring their assets and liabilities into better balance by shortening the maturity of some of their loans and by stretching out the maturities of their deposits." Secretary Simon argued that the greater financial stability thus given to thrift institutions, combined with increased mortgage lending by commercial banks interested in the special tax advantages to be offered, would actually increase the flow of funds into housing.

Fifth, in addition to making more funds available for real estate financing a major goal should be to stabilize the annual pace of mortgage lending and break the feast-or-famine cycle that has badly disrupted the housing markets during the last decade.

The Treasury testimony was followed by statements from the Board of Governors of the Federal Reserve System, and representatives from the Federal Home Loan Bank Board, Comptroller of the Currency, Federal Deposit Insurance Corporation, and National Credit Union Administration. These government agencies had participated in the administration's interagency effort to prepare the Financial Institutions Act of 1973, and each statement strongly supported the general approach and most of the detailed recommendations reviewed below, except for some minor disagreements over timing and procedures. For example, in responding to a question from Senator Proxmire concerning an apparent disagreement, Governor Robert C. Holland, representing the Federal Reserve Board, expressed general support but indicated some reservations about the effect of changes on mortgage financing.

> We believe this proposal affords more flexibility and more freedom for all the depository financial institutions and that its time has come. Indeed, time is, in a sense, passing us by. . . . What I was trying to indicate in my statement is that we on the Board aren't sure that the sum total of all these effects is going to provide more housing finance. We think there is a chance they might provide less, or at least in some circumstances might provide less, and therefore it is wise to be careful as to how we proceed.
>
> We wouldn't say, "Don't do it." We think the changes involved here are too needed to be held back, but we would suggest we proceed gradually and with room for judgment.[6]

6. Senate, Committee on Banking, Housing, and Urban Affairs, *Financial Structure and Regulation*, pp. 154–56. Statement of Robert C. Holland.

Details of the Administration's Recommendations

The Financial Institutions Act of 1973 contained seven major sections which, the administration argued, should be considered only as one comprehensive proposal, since even greater distortions could be caused by piecemeal actions.[7]

Section 1: Payment of Interest on Deposit Accounts—(a) Interest rate ceilings on time and savings deposits to be eliminated after five and one-half years. Parity of interest ceiling between commercial banks and thrift institutions to be achieved by raising the rate permitted banks in four annual steps commencing 18 months after proposed legislation is enacted; (b) Continuation of prohibition against payment of interest on demand deposits; (c) All NOW [negotiable order of withdrawal] accounts to be subject to interest rate ceilings until the maximum limits are eliminated;[8] (d) Administrative decision on the actual levels of ceiling rates to be made by the appropriate regulatory authorities following joint consultations; and (e) A truth-in-savings provision giving full disclosure of the terms applying to savings deposits and certificates.

This section covers the extremely controversial issue of regulating interest rates on deposits and the differential advantage granted to thrift institutions that was reviewed in Chapter 3. Because of the long history of government controls and the difficulties anticipated in having thrift institutions adjust their asset portfolios to improve earnings and strengthen their competitive position, it was recognized that an extended transition period would be required and that deregulation could not begin unless the additional depository and asset diversification powers were granted to thrift institutions. The Federal Home Loan Bank Board (FHLBB) was particularly emphatic regarding the need to maintain the controls and favorable differential until the transition to a new competitive environment could be completed.

Governor Holland's statement for the Board of Governors of the Federal Reserve System went even further in recommending a gradual phasing out of existing controls to avoid unexpected competitive developments. This phase would then be followed by a continuation

---

7. Senate, Committee on Banking, Housing, and Urban Affairs, *Financial Structure and Regulation*, pp. 24–35.

8. A NOW account is a negotiable order of withdrawal. In reality, they are checks drawn on savings accounts at mutual savings banks, commercial banks, and savings and loan associations. They differ from demand deposits in that they bear interest and financial institutions may legally require a thirty-day delay in honoring withdrawal orders. Authority to experiment with these accounts in the early 1970s was granted in New Hampshire and Massachusetts.

of standby authority "to reimpose ceilings should it become clear that uncontrolled rates threaten to undermine the safety and soundness of depository institutions or to conflict with other public interest considerations."[9] While admitting that the temptation to restore controls by continuing standby authority would work against his philosophical preference for getting rid of interest rate ceilings on deposits, Governor Holland indicated that the unknown risks of changing the competitive environment and the volatile nature of deposits payable on demand make it prudent to have such power. This view was consistent with his general concern that the proposed asset diversification for thrift institutions might hurt housing prospects and that the regulatory agencies should retain the flexibility needed to accelerate or reduce the pace of change.

This section of the act highlights the usual disparities between philosophical preferences for free and competitive markets and the realities of governmental regulation. Experience indicates that once controls are used they are rarely removed, because of the uncertainties of returning to an uncontrolled market environment. Administration spokesmen argued that competitive equity justifies the removal of controls, but this viewpoint directly challenges the mutually satisfactory relation between Congress and thrift institutions working together to achieve the national housing goals mandated by the federal government as described in Chapter 2. This rapport was once again demonstrated when legislation extending the controls on deposit interest rates was easily passed early in 1977.

Section 2: Expanded Deposit Liability Power and Reserves—(a) For federal thrift institutions, checking accounts, third-party payment powers, credit cards, and NOW accounts will be available to all customers, individual and corporate; (b) For national banks, savings accounts and NOW accounts will be available to all customers, individual and corporate; (c) All federally-chartered institutions and all state-chartered institutions which are members of the Federal Reserve System or the Federal Home Loan Bank System will be required to maintain reserves against deposits in demand and NOW accounts in a form and amount prescribed by the Federal Reserve Board after consultation with the Federal Home Loan Bank Board; (d) State-chartered savings and loan associations insured by the Federal Savings and Loan Insurance Corporation (FSLIC) need not be members of the Federal Home Loan Bank System; (e) NOW deposits will be subject to the same range of reserves as demand deposits. However, the Federal Reserve Board, after consultation with the Federal Home Loan Bank Board, may establish a different level of required reserves for NOW

9. Senate, Committee on Banking, Housing, and Urban Affairs, *Financial Structure and Regulation*, p. 303. Statement of Robert C. Holland.

accounts; (f) Required reserves for demand deposits and NOW accounts will range from 1 to 22 percent. Those for savings accounts will range from 1 to 5 percent and those for time accounts will range from 1 to 10 percent.

Section 2 of the act attempted to provide flexibility on the liabilities side to match the new asset powers recommended in Section 3. In essence, it was the carrot in a trade-off granting added asset and liability powers in exchange for the loss of deposit interest rate controls and the adjustment of deposit reserves and tax rules. The key point was that such changes, particularly the new authority to provide checking accounts, would help thrift institutions achieve their goal of becoming family financial centers offering a broad array of consumer services.

Beginning in 1970 savings and loan associations were permitted to make third-party payments out of deposit accounts, using nonnegotiable orders, but the process was very limited and inconvenient. Prearranged transfer of funds to an approved list of businesses and individuals was another approach used to overcome the competitive disadvantage of being unable to offer checking accounts. Given the inconvenience and limited scope of these payment arrangements, the recommendation to allow thrift institutions to offer unlimited checking accounts and other third-party payment programs was a major change in the competitive balance.

A parallel suggestion was to permit national banks to offer NOW and savings accounts to individuals and corporations. The Federal Reserve System's Board of Governors objected to allowing corporations to have interest-bearing savings and NOW accounts because such action would effectively eliminate the historic distinction between demand deposits used for transactions and personal thrift accounts. Nevertheless, the recommendation was included in the administration's legislative proposal to provide greater competitive flexibility. The rapid development of electronic transfer systems and the simplicity of transferring account balances by telephone had already made the technical rules largely obsolete, and this change would merely have acknowledged a reality.

In exchange for the expansion of depository powers, the Board of Governors of the Federal Reserve System was to be granted authority to establish uniform reserve requirements on all transactions accounts (checking and other third-party payment deposits) for all financial institutions after consulting with the Federal Home Loan Bank Board. The extension of Federal Reserve authority to part of the deposits held by thrift institutions in order to fulfill their responsibilities for monetary control would have been another major change, even though the authority was specifically limited to checking and NOW accounts at savings and loan associations and mutual savings banks. Commercial banks have long argued that the reserve requirements should be based on the type of deposits rather than the identity of the financial institution, and hence this adjustment would have met one of their important goals. As it turned out, these changes were too revolutionary for Congress or the financial institutions to accept in one legislative proposal, but many of the recommended changes have been permitted in the private financial markets in recent years.

Section 3: Expanded Lending and Investment Powers—Federal savings and loan associations will be authorized to: (a) Make consumer loans not exceeding 10 percent of their total assets; (b) Make real estate loans under the same conditions as commercial banks; (c) Make construction loans not tied to permanent financing; i.e., interim construction financing as offered by banks; (d) Make community welfare and development investments on loans for, as well as direct investment in, residential and related properties, including participation in rental income or a share of capital gains on the sale of property, but with this so-called leeway authority not to exceed 3 percent of their total assets; (e) Acquire high quality commercial paper and private investment-grade corporate debt securities in accordance with approved-list and other guidelines established by the FHLBB. Such investments are not to exceed 10 percent of total assets, with the maximum limitation to be set at 2 percent in the first year and growing to 10 percent, at the rate of 2 percent per year, over a 5-year period; (f) Utilize for consumer loans the unused portions of authorized investments in private corporate debt, commercial paper and debt securities, and community welfare loans; and (g) Continue the acquisition of a full range of U.S. Government, State, and municipal securities.

National banks will be granted: (h) Powers to make real estate loans without present restrictions . . . ; and (i) A leeway authority, not to exceed 3 percent of total assets, for community welfare and development investments on the same conditions as thrift institutions. Finally, (j) regulatory agencies will be granted extended authority to assist member institutions experiencing liquidity strains.

The intent of Section 3 was to help thrift institutions diversify their investments and develop as "family finance centers" which would still specialize in mortgage lending but would be more competitive and have more stable flows of funds. Their two major competitive disadvantages would have been eliminated under the proposed legislation: the lack of checking account services and the restrictions on their authority to offer consumer loans and various types of savings accounts. Thrift institutions were already authorized to extend credit to depositors on the security of their account balances and to make loans for education, mobile homes, home improvements, and consumer durable goods purchased for the home. The proposed legislation would have granted authority to make any consumer loans in amounts up to 10 percent of total assets plus any unused amounts permitted for open-market investments and community development loans.

In addition to allowing a greater range of customer service, this policy change was expected to: (1) improve profitability, because the "net" yield on consumer loans is approximately 1 percent higher than the "net" return on residential mortgage loans; (2) provide new outlets for funds during periods of slack housing demand; (3) improve liquidity by adding loans and investments with shorter turnover periods; and (4) attract additional customers and deposits. It is estimated that one-half of all U.S. families and two-thirds of young families in the United States use consumer debt, so this diversification would expand the number of potential customers. It was also suggested that other consumer services be provided, including personal financial counseling, tax planning, trust services, estate planning, automatic investment programs, and special accounts for retirement, education, and other purposes. Finally, this section recommended greater powers for financial intermediaries in making loans for construction and home buying, the intent being to improve the availability of funds and promote competition.

Section 4: Charters for Thrift Institutions—(a) The FHLBB be empowered to charter stock thrift institutions, granting them powers identical to those enjoyed by mutual savings and loan institutions; (b) Newly empowered federally-chartered thrift institutions may be called either "Federal Savings and Loan Associations" or "Federal Savings Banks." (c) State-chartered mutual savings banks may convert to a federal charter and be granted all of the asset and liability powers available to all federally-chartered thrift institutions. In addition, they may grandfather their life insurance, equity investments and corporate bond investments. These equity and corporate investments may be no greater than levels determined by their average percent of assets for the 5-year period of January 1, 1968 through December 31, 1972.

Although Section 4 focuses on a technical regulatory issue, there were several controversial points which critics emphasized. First, mutual savings banks would finally be granted federal charters; these would have increased their opportunities for expansion. After almost twenty years of frustrated attempts to legislate this authority, only twenty-one states authorized the operation of mutual savings banks at the time that the Financial Institutions Act of 1973 was submitted to

Congress. This single issue would have been enough to create a fierce legislative struggle. Second, existing state-chartered mutual savings banks were to be allowed to convert to federal charters without giving up their existing investment powers. Third, the widest possible freedom would be granted in shifting from mutual to stock charters, or vice versa, and between state and federal charters. Extreme controversy over the conversion of mutual savings and loan associations into stock organizations had forced a congressional moratorium on such transfers, and federal charters have always been restricted to mutual savings and loan associations. These issues are confusing and of minor importance to most outsiders, but within the financial trade associations they are vigorously debated, and massive lobbying efforts are quickly mounted whenever Congress considers legislation affecting chartering powers.

Section 5: Credit Unions—(a) A Central Discount Fund will be established for insured (Federal or state) credit unions solely to provide funds to meet emergency, temporary liquidity problems. Capital for the funds will be obtained through subscriptions by credit unions wishing to join. The Fund is to be administered by the National Credit Union Administration (NCUA); (b) Principal loan terms of credit unions be lengthened from five to seven years in the case of unsecured loans and from ten to twelve years in the case of secured loans; (c) Lines of credit be permitted to account for different credit ratings and for individual circumstances of different members, thereby permitting more flexibility in the making of loans; (d) Authority be given to credit committees to offer preapproved credit programs or lines of credit; (e) Credit unions have authority to issue share certificates with varying dividend rates and varying maturities subject to regulations promulgated by the Administrator; (f) The Administrator of the NCUA be given authority to permit loans to be made at a rate of interest exceeding the maximum one percent per month; (g) Credit unions retain their tax-exempt status as long as they remain within the bounds of the existing tax law; (h) Credit unions that want to expand their services and assume the burdens of full service mutual thrift institutions be permitted to do so.

This section included a number of technical, but important, changes designed to help credit unions adapt to the new competitive environment. The key points involved the creation of a government facility to provide emergency liquidity assistance, the diversification of lending and deposit powers, and the reaffirmation of tax-exempt status for credit unions willing to limit their financial services to authorized members. Although the credit union trade associations expressed strong criticism of the financial reform efforts, most independent observers felt that such associations were particularly well treated by the administration's proposals.

Section 6: Federal Housing Authority (FHA) and Veterans Administration (VA) Interest Ceilings—(a) The National Housing Act be amended to remove statutory and administrative rate ceilings on all Housing and Urban Development insured mortgages. Interest rates for mortgages and loans insured under the Act would be at the rate agreed upon by the mortgagee and mortgagor. The mortgagee would be permitted to charge the mortgagor a one percent origination fee, but would not be permitted to charge any discount points to either the buyer or seller; (b) The authority of the Administrator of the Veterans Administration to set interest ceilings on VA guaranteed or insured loans be rescinded.

Experience has clearly demonstrated that federal efforts to hold down the interest rates on FHA-insured and VA-guaranteed mortgage loans have not worked. When the market rate for conventional mortgages is above the arbitrary level established by the Secretary of Housing and Urban Development and the Administrator of the Veterans Department, lenders have charged a fee, called "points," at the time of the loan in order to bring the actual return up to the current market rate. The charging of points ultimately increases the cost to the home buyer and creates great confusion. In some instances the actual flow of funds into FHA and VA mortgages may be reduced by setting the administrative rate below the competitive level required. The elimination of the artificial rate ceiling and the prohibition of points or fees would not make the effective interest costs on FHA or VA mortgage loans higher, but it would stabilize the flow of funds into such commitments and would also benefit home buyers by clarifying the real costs of borrowing and by allowing the deduction of interest charges for income tax purposes (discount points are not deductible). Most important, making FHA and VA mortgages more responsive to changing conditions in the marketplace would enable federal programs to focus on the real need of low-income families for direct subsidies.

Section 7: Taxes—(a) The special reserve provisions applicable to thrift institutions be eliminated and all thrift institutions compute reserve additions under methods similar to the ones applicable to commercial banks; (b) Thrift institutions be compensated for the tax benefit being eliminated by means of a new tax credit equal to a percentage of the interest earned from residential mortgages; (c) The tax credit be made available to all taxpayers.

Section 7 would have eliminated the special procedures used when thrift institutions holding at least 60 percent of their assets in real property loans calculate their reserves for bad debts, which are deducted from taxable income before determining income taxes. The proposed act called for thrift institutions to use a method based on experience, similar to the procedure used by commercial banks for calculating their future reserve deductions. To compensate thrift institutions for the loss of this special provision the administration proposed a new tax credit to be applied as a direct offset to mortgage interest income, and this would be made available to all taxpayers holding eligible mortgages. The details of this new tax credit were not specified in the August 1973 announcement by the administration, but the notice emphasized that it would be large enough to offset the loss of special bad debt reserve deductions. Treasury officials subsequently explained the mortgage interest tax credit as follows:

> The size of the credit has been calculated so as to give thrift institutions full compensation, in fact, overcompensation, for the tax benefit they would have received through deductions for additions to a reserve for losses on loans. . . For institutions which have invested over 70 percent of their assets in residential mortgage loans, a tax credit, not a deduction, equal to 3.5 percent of the residential mortgage interest income will be allowed. If less than 70 percent of the taxpayer's assets are in residential mortgages, the credit percentage will be reduced by one-thirtieth of 1 percentage point for each 1 percentage point below 70 percent. No credit will be available unless at least 10 percent of the taxpayer's assets are invested in residential mortgages. For example, institutions holding 55 percent of their assets in residential mortgages, the average for mutual savings banks, would receive a 3.0 percent tax credit; . . . Thus there is an ever-increasing incentive for higher investment in mortgages. Furthermore, if an institution has less than 10 percent of its assets devoted to mortgages, there is a tremendous incentive to reach the 10 percent level.[10]

The history of the mortgage interest tax credit is a fascinating example of how proposals must adapt to political realities. In the original August 1973 announcement the Treasury Department had emphasized that the tax credit was part of the "overall goal of reducing functional specialization among financial institutions." Hence a basic " 'tax neutrality' is sought, by providing that a given investment or activity will be subject to the same income tax provisions regardless of the functional type of financial institution making the investment or engaging in the activity."[11]

To anyone familiar with the Treasury Department's activities this states a common position held by the tax experts in the Office of Tax Policy. Like most of their recommendations, the statement makes excellent economic sense. But successful legislation must pass politi-

10. Senate, Committee on Banking, Housing, and Urban Affairs, *Financial Structure and Regulation*, p. 34.
11. Department of the Treasury, *Recommendations for Change*, p. 14.

cal rather than economic tests. The resulting storm of protests from special interest groups forced the administration to shift its emphasis from theoretical economic arguments to the more politically attractive position that the new tax credit would help stimulate mortgage lending and contribute to the achievement of national housing goals. Regardless of the economic merits of the proposal, the initial approach was wrong, and the administration spent the next three years trying to convince skeptical thrift institutions, housing interests, and key members of Congress that the tax credit would effectively aid the housing industry and adequately compensate for the loss of other regulatory and tax advantages. The irony in the situation is that the size and eligibility requirements of the proposed mortgage interest tax credit caused it to be rejected by critics as being "too little, too late," even though it was originally added to the proposed legislation in the hope that it would encourage acceptance of other changes in the existing competitive balance.

The Impact of the Financial Institutions Act of 1973 on Housing

The administration correctly anticipated that concern about the effect of financial reforms on the housing market would be a crucial factor in the ultimate legislative decision. Accordingly, a special section summarizing the administration's argument that housing would actually benefit from the proposed reforms was included in the August 3, 1973, general summary of recommendations.[12]

The demand for housing depends upon a variety of economic and demographic factors, including the pace of family formation, general economic conditions, inflation, government programs, and the availability and cost of mortgage funds. Most officials in the real estate industry and most economists believe that the supply of mortgage funds is the dominant variable, and most studies of short-term movements of mortgage credit and housing construction support their position. All of these also argue that the specialized financial institutions that have developed have supplied more mortgage credit at lower interest rates than would otherwise have occurred and that changing their characteristics would reduce the availability of funds and increase costs. The administration view, based on information from the Interagency Task Force Study on Housing, a group led by the Council of Economic Advisers, was that "the financial effects on housing production operate primarily

12. Department of the Treasury, *Recommendations for Change*, pp. 29–34.

through general credit conditions"; and even though "credit rationing may occur in the very short run . . . over any significant period of time it is the general level of interest rates, rather than the flow of mortgage credit which acts as the rationing instrument for housing and other durable assets."[13]

Whichever argument is correct, it is clear that strong financial intermediaries are essential to the supply of adequate mortgage credit. The legislative debate concentrated on this important point by attempting to determine the net impact of the proposed changes on the financial system. The recommendations had created conflicting forces, and which of the two would dominate was not clear. The diversification of lending and investment powers could reduce the percentage of assets committed to mortgage loans by thrift institutions. On the other hand, the general strengthening of the competitive position of financial intermediaries would increase their total assets and thus improve the availability of mortgage credit. Even more important, according to several administrative witnesses, the suggested reforms would provide a more stable source of mortgage financing by moderating the disruptive effects of disintermediation and increasing the profitability and liquidity of the key lenders. To the degree that deposit inflows could be sustained during periods of rising open-market interest rates and to the degree that the timing to match up deposits and assets could be improved, the availability of mortgage credit would be stabilized.

The administration argued that the net effects of the diversification of deposits and assets would be at least neutral and, one could hope, even favorable in influencing the flow of funds into mortgage credit. A further argument was that the addition of the mortgage interest tax credit to the total proposal would be an added stimulus to housing by making mortgages more profitable to present lenders and by attracting funds from other institutions, particularly commercial banks. An economic study of the possible impact of the Hunt Commission recommendations on housing finance, prepared by Professors Ray C. Fair and Dwight M. Jaffee for the Department of Housing and Urban Development, produced the following conclusions:

> Our results indicate that the housing market would probably, on net, gain under the Hunt Report, while the mortgage stock may gain or lose depending on the specific assumptions. In any case, the magnitudes

13. Ibid., p. 31.

involved are small relative to the current outstanding stocks of these assets.[14]

Judging by the analysis of its interagency committee and the expected results from including the mortgage interest tax credit in the legislative proposal, the administration hoped that it could persuade the housing interests to support the proposed law. As expressed in its opening testimony before Congress:

> Our in-depth studies conclude that even without any increased tax incentives for housing, there would be minimal, if any, adverse impact on housing finance from these recommendations. However, with the addition of a tax credit which will be available to all institutions and individuals, there can be little doubt that not only will there be more money available for housing finance but more importantly that such money will be more constant and predictable and that we will be less likely to have the stop-and-go of mortgage funds that we have witnessed three times in the past 7 years.[15]

Summary of Administration Proposals

The goal of the Financial Institutions Act of 1973 was to increase competition and stabilize financial conditions by expanding deposit flexibility and broadening the lending and investment powers of financial intermediaries without obstructing the attainment of important national housing objectives. The administration's proposals followed the philosophy and many of the specific recommendations of the President's Commission on Financial Structure and Regulation and the earlier private Commission on Money and Credit. The key assumption was that individual financial institutions could be persuaded to give up a certain degree of regulatory protection in exchange for considerably broadened operating powers, which would be made available but not forced upon any institution. In other words, individual financial intermediaries would be allowed increased discretion in lending and investing decisions by management and in selecting the types of deposit accounts and other services they offer customers. In exchange they would be expected to accept the increased rigors and risks of more open and competitive private financial markets. The explicit trade-off proposed that each type of financial intermediary give up something to obtain the advantages offered. The administration hoped that

---

14. Ray Fair and Dwight Jaffee, *An Empirical Study of the Implications of the Hunt Commission Report for the Mortgage and Housing Markets*, HUD Contract H 1781, April 1972, p. 2 of abstract.

15. Senate, Committee on Banking, Housing, and Urban Affairs, *Financial Structure and Regulation*, p. 37. Statement of William E. Simon.

the complete set of reforms would be considered balanced enough to justify the required compromises.

The direction of the complete proposal was consistent with the policy preferences of the Treasury Department and the other Executive Office agencies involved in preparing the Financial Institutions Act of 1973. Although these philosophical commitments to foster free and competitive markets are often ignored in specific government decisions that must gain widespread political acceptance, and the individual agencies were certainly not above pushing their own vested interests and protecting their existing regulatory powers, the administration's recommendations clearly favored reliance on competitive forces in the private marketplace.

The recommendations contained in the proposal also seemed to be consistent with the trend of technological developments and institutional changes already occurring. The resentment that suggestions for change always arouse was foreseen, and the administration attempted to minimize general controversy by limiting its proposals to financial intermediaries and by avoiding the regulatory reform issues. It also tried to anticipate the probable opposition of housing interests by preparing studies of the possible impact of the diversification of lending and investment powers and by advocating the new mortgage interest tax credit. Finally, the administration appealed for general support, arguing that the proposed legislation would promote efficiency, increase competition, result in more equitable regulation, and make institutions more responsive to changing conditions.

Unfortunately for the administration, economic arguments concerning efficiency, competition, regulatory reform, and responsiveness are not the dominant issues—in some cases they are not even the relevant issues—in a political decision on the relative status of financial institutions. The support that would induce Congress to respond favorably to the recommended legislative reforms required widespread agreement among the institutions combined with help from the housing interests. The entrenched position of each group of financial institutions and the skepticism of the housing interests made this impossible. Disappointing developments in the domestic economy and the notable erosion of presidential leadership in 1973 and 1974 while the proposed law was being considered by the Senate further complicated the situation. Most important, Congress was unwilling to act because it has purposely created an operating environment for financial institutions that helps achieve its mandated housing goals, and this point must always be recognized in considering the prospects for financial institution reform.

6

RESPONSES OF FINANCIAL INSTITUTIONS

Following the presentations of administration and regulatory officials in support of the Financial Institutions Act in November 1973, the representatives of various financial intermediary trade associations expressed their strong views in the second round of hearings held in May 1974. The common feature of the special interest groups' presentations was dissatisfaction with the existing competitive arrangements, particularly the disruptions caused by periodic waves of financial disintermediation. Beyond this similarity, however, each group strongly defended its own special advantages and criticized the other financial institutions, particularly the commercial banks. A reading of these individual testimonies clearly indicates the lack of widespread support for the comprehensive reforms recommended by the administration, and the unalterable opposition to specific proposals such as the removal of regulation Q and similar controls. Indeed, each group was clearly willing to forgo specific advantages provided by the proposal rather than give up certain existing benefits.

Even though senior representatives of commercial banks, savings and loan associations, and mutual savings banks participated in the President's Commission on Financial Structure and Regulation, which actually developed many of the recommendations included in the proposed legislation, the large trade associations representing the financial intermediaries were apparently unwilling to compromise on several key issues. There are two principal reasons for their negative reactions. First, each group preferred to work independently with Congress to push for its own specific set of legislative goals and to oppose unilaterally the legislative initiatives of competing financial intermediaries. Second, many industry and trade association representatives correctly recognized that continuous developments in the marketplace and individual regulatory rulings were already creating many of the changes proposed.

In that legislative environment, there was little incentive to compromise, and hence the Senate hearings on the Financial Institutions Act of 1973 became a forum for each group to recite its unique and numerous contributions to the nation's economic and social welfare and to review a long history of grievances based on the allegedly unfair competitive practices of other financial institutions. Unfortunately, these emotional statements and the frequent assertion that disruptive competitive developments occur unless the government directly controls private economic activities were rarely supported by theoretical arguments or empirical evidence, except for occasional references to friendly academic studies. Senator McIntyre, assisted by Senators Proxmire and Bennett, searched for possible compromises and rightly questioned the most exaggerated statements: for example, that entire groups of financial institutions would literally be destroyed if legislative changes were enacted. But the congressional hearings lasting through 1976 indicate that the prevailing arguments rested on the same familiar grounds, the need for unique advantages and protection from competition to prevent widespread failures of financial institutions.

Commercial Banks

The commercial banking industry is a highly diversified group of over 14,000 institutions ranging in size and activities from small unit banks serving local markets to multibillion dollar financial giants having offices around the world and providing national and foreign customers with a long list of financial services. Two major trade associations represent this wide range of interests: the American Bankers Association, whose members hold approximately 95 percent of the total assets of the industry; and the Independent Bankers Association of America, describing itself as the representative of "grass roots banking," since over one-half of its 7,200 members operate in communities with a population of less than 5,000 people (90 percent are located in communities of less than 30,000 people). Both organizations devoted considerable effort to arranging regional seminars and compiling detailed surveys among their members for use in preparing their principal statements to the Senate subcommittee on the Financial Institutions Act of 1973. The sharp divisions of opinion between these two major organizations offer a classic example of the complex legislative activities of special interest groups.

The creation of specialized groups within a single major industry, based in this case on the size and competitive characteristics of the member banks, indicates the sophistication required in dealing with Congress and with hundreds of government agencies. There are, of course, many situations in which their special interests overlap and reinforce rather than act against each other, leading to the formation of temporary alliances tailored to each new piece of legislation and administrative ruling.

Government officials must be alert to the changing composition of such alliances and know exactly which groups are being represented. For example, both the American Bankers Association and the Independent Bankers Association of America favored the elimination of the deposit interest rate differential granted to thrift institutions, but they disagreed on most of the other recommendations in the proposed legislation as indicated in the following summary of the American Bankers Association (ABA) and Independent Bankers Association of America (IBAA) statements.

Section 1. Payment of Interest on Deposit Accounts
ABA   (a) Favors free markets, but considers that the elimination of deposit interest ceilings is not appropriate until state usury laws are removed and thrift institutions receive expanded powers to test results; favors elimination of rate differentials two years after the legislation.
       (b) Takes no definitive position on paying interest on demand deposits but recommends a specific congressional decision.
       (c) Opposes negotiable order of withdrawal (NOW) accounts and recommends that expansion be delayed until Congress decides about the payment of interest on demand deposits.
       (d) Supports consultations among regulatory agencies and Treasury participation.
       (e) Supports principle of truth-in-savings provision but believes ample statutory authority already exists for issuing regulations.
IBAA   (a) Strongly opposes elimination of deposit interest ceilings because of destructive competition and higher costs; supports elimination of rate differentials.
       (b) Favors prohibition of interest payments on demand deposits.
       (c) Strongly opposes NOW accounts.
       (d) Opposition to NOW accounts makes interagency consultation unnecessary.
       (e) Supports truth-in-savings provision with modifications but prefers voluntary approach.

Section 2. Expanded Deposit Liability Powers and Reserves
ABA   (a) Does not oppose granting federal thrift institutions checking accounts, third-party payment powers, credit cards, and NOW accounts for individuals providing rate ceilings, taxes, reserve

requirements, and supervisory burdens are equalized, but opposes granting them to governments and corporations.

(b) Favors corporate savings accounts but opposes NOW accounts except as a defensive measure if other financial intermediaries have such powers, and recommends congressional decision on issues of paying interest on demand deposits.

(c) Favors uniform reserves as to percentage and nature for all institutions holding demand deposits and NOW accounts as determined by the Federal Reserve Board after consulting with the Federal Home Loan Bank Board.

(d) Supports exemption of state-chartered savings and loan associations from membership in Federal Home Loan Bank systems.

(e) Supports uniform reserves for NOW accounts, if permitted.

(f) Supports reduction of lower limit for legal reserves on all types of accounts to 1 percent and variable maximum requirements.

IBAA (a) Opposes use of NOW accounts which circumvent good banking practices and opposes checking accounts for thrift institutions.

(b) Opposes corporate savings accounts and NOW accounts for commercial banks because of threat to deposit system.

(c) through (f) Offers no comment in view of opposition to NOW accounts and payment of interest on demand deposits.

Section 3. Expanded Lending and Investing Powers

ABA (a) through (g) Supports expansion of powers of Federal Savings and Loan Associations to make limited consumer loans (10 percent of assets), unrestricted real estate loans, limited community welfare and development investments (3 percent), acquisition of high quality commercial paper and corporate debt (10 percent), purchase of government securities, and authority to increase consumer loans if community and corporate commitments are below the ceilings.

(h) and (i) Supports expanded powers for national banks to make unrestricted real estate loans and community welfare and development investment (3 percent).

(j) Supports increased flexibility for regulatory agencies providing liquidity aid.

IBAA (a) through (g) Opposes extension of powers as a diversion of funds away from housing, an undesirable shift of thrift institutions into commercial banking activities, and extension of unfair regulation.

(h) and (i) Takes the position that these recommendations are unnecessary because national banks were granted authority to increase housing and community commitments in omnibus housing legislation.

(j) Opposes increase in Federal Home Loan Bank Board powers.

Section 4. Charters for Thrift Institutions

ABA (a) through (e) Supports recommendations to permit federal chartering of stock thrift institutions to function as savings and loan associations or savings banks and continuation of certain investment powers with the limitations that "Federal Savings Banks" be limited to states that now charter savings banks and that the investment powers permitted be equalized.

IBAA   (a) through (e) Opposes recommendations as constituting an unnecessary creation of a third banking system and a negative factor leading to increased vulnerability of thrift institutions to takeovers and concentration of financial institution ownership.

Section 5. Credit Unions

ABA   (a) Supports creation of Central Discount Fund for credit unions to improve liquidity.

(b) through (j) Does not object to liberalization of rates and terms of loans at credit institutions other than questioning the advisability of lengthening the maturities of loans; further suggests that if credit unions receive third-party payment powers they should be treated like other mutual thrift institutions.

IBAA   Recommends a study by Congress to reassess the favored tax treatment applied to credit unions if their asset powers are extended.

Section 6. FHA and VA Interest Ceilings

ABA   Supports the recommendation that FHA and VA mortgage interest rate ceiling be abolished.

IBAA   Supports the recommendation but believes the issue is moot because of the actions of the Secretary of HUD.

Section 7. Taxes

ABA   (a) Supports the recommendation that commercial banks and thrift institutions use the same procedure in calculating their reserves for bad debts.

(b) and (c) Supports the concept of a tax credit applied to all types of housing loans and applied uniformly to all lenders at a rate established by regulation rather than by statute.

IBAA   Opposes the tax recommendations because they would not remove all differences in tax treatment and little incentive would be provided for commercial banks to expand residential mortgage loans.

After some initial uncertainty the American Bankers Association gave a carefully qualified endorsement to the general goals of the proposal, as indicated in the statement of Rex J. Morthland, President of the organization and a former member of the Hunt Commission.

We believe that there is growing consensus in our industry that, although a few proposals need special analysis and consideration in timing, the provisions in the Financial Institutions Act S.2591 represent the best vehicle for providing our financial system with the flexibility necessary to manage the changes we must inevitably face. The American Bankers Association is not opposed to granting nonbank thrift institutions broader powers which will allow them to serve the public better. However, the grant of additional powers must be tied to uniformity of treatment concerning deposit interest rates, taxes, and reserves if the entire financial system is to operate as effectively and economically as possible.[1]

Although the ABA statement appeared to damn with faint praise the key sections, and it established several important conditions as part of its contingent acceptance as well as seeming to waffle on the issue of removing regulation Q controls in deference to the views of many of its smaller member banks, it gave at least a qualified public endorsement of the proposed law, in contrast to the negative reactions of most financial intermediaries other than the National Association of Mutual Savings Banks, whose response is discussed in the next section.

However, even this tentative support was made directly contingent upon passage of a comprehensive act which would require the elimination of deposit interest rate ceilings and call for equality of treatment for all financial intermediaries with regard to reserves, taxes, and regulations. Since the thrift institutions vigorously oppose such changes and the credit unions are extremely protective of their present status, these expectations were unlikely from the beginning to be satisfied. The ABA stand regarding regulation Q was probably the most puzzling aspect of their statement because their position appears to change frequently. After strongly criticizing the way in which both the differential and rate ceilings had been administered in favor of thrift institutions, and emphasizing that controls had not prevented disintermediation and serious disadvantages for small savers, the ABA testimony seemed to suggest standby controls, or a gradual phasing out of controls on a state or regional basis, or at least a more flexible administration of the controls. However, a position paper issued by the ABA stated "we do not support the phasing out of regulation Q by legislative edict now, or in the foreseeable future."[2]

The ABA seemed to be caught in the same kind of crossfire regarding interest payments on demand deposits as an alternative to the very real costs of providing many free services, but that dilemma was evaded by calling for a congressional study. Since most bankers seem to believe that paying such interest would be a major disaster,

1. U.S., Congress, Senate, Committee on Banking, Housing, and Urban Affairs, *Financial Institutions Act of 1973*, p. 286. Statement of Rex J. Morthland.
2. Frank E. Bauder, "Statement of Position," *Report to the Second General Session of the 1973 Annual Convention of the American Bankers Association* (Chicago, Ill.: Oct. 9, 1973), p. 11.

the ABA was placed in a difficult position. In this context the ABA strongly objected to the proliferation of NOW accounts "unless and until Congress decides that interest should be permitted on demand deposits." It is interesting that these same controversial issues are still no closer to any legislative solution four years later.

The irony of this procedural breakdown is that the government projects itself into the private market with the good intention of accomplishing social goals but then has difficulty facing up to controversial economic issues which, because of the government controls, the markets can no longer solve directly. Most analysts agree that regulation Q is not working well; but the dependence of financial institutions on such artificial protective measures has evidently become too much for Congress and the regulatory agencies to change without serious political consequences after more than a decade of forcing the private markets to conform to limited competition. Once again, the process of adding new controls to make old controls function better is clearly demonstrated by the example of financial institution reform. The freedom to make future decisions is continuously eroded by this process.

The IBAA statement strongly rejected five of the seven major recommendations, and it ignored the credit union proposals except to ask for a politically sensitive congressional reassessment of the favored tax treatment. The only suggestion accepted was the relatively innocuous one that the interest rate ceilings on FHA and VA mortgages be abolished. The IBAA statement was unusually critical of the expansion of asset portfolio and deposit powers and the removal of regulation Q controls. These changes, they claimed, would increase costs and permit large banks to trigger destructive rate wars to attract deposits. In fact, the IBAA categorically rejected almost every proposal as being counterproductive or likely to create a group of competitive institutions which would duplicate the existing commercial banking system and thus cause unnecessary competitive pressures, increased inflation, greater risks in loans and investments, and a substantial diversion of funds away from housing.

The IBAA statement particularly objected to the recommendation to grant checking accounts, third-party payment powers, and NOW accounts to other financial intermediaries. In fact, 97.5 percent of the IBAA members had voted against this suggestion. The basis of their argument was that borrowers would suffer if deposit costs increased, and the diversification of payment powers would disrupt traditional banking practices. Their response to the idea of enlarging lending and investment powers was similar. As to the tax recommendations, the IBAA flatly rejected the proposal because it would not eliminate "all differences" in the treatment of different financial institutions, and because the proposed tax remedy would not attract more funds into housing mortgages. In his statement representing the IBAA views, President Embree K. Easterly emphasized that his organization was not trying merely to preserve the status quo but that the members had "grave doubts" that the proposed structural changes would produce the desired results. They attack "symptoms rather than causes," he said, and would seriously increase the risks of unwanted concentrations of financial power.[3] The IBAA also criticized administration officials for not giving them more opportunities to shape the recommendations and bitterly rejected the Treasury's request for help in August 1973.[4]

The guarded support of the ABA and the overwhelming criticism of the IBAA sharply reduced the chances that a comprehensive package of reforms would be accepted. In the minds of most financial managers the "devil we know" seemed preferable to the uncertain effects on competition created by structural and regulatory reform, even though the American economic system is allegedly based on free markets and competition. The reaction of the commercial banking representatives also signaled to the other financial intermediaries that regulation Q controls would not be a major issue. Thus they were able to concentrate their efforts on working directly with Congress to gain unilateral expansion of asset portfolio and depository powers rather than accepting the compromises required in the Financial Institutions Act of 1973.

Mutual Savings Banks

Among the major financial intermediaries, the National Association of Mutual Savings Banks was by far the strongest source of support for the proposed legislation. The leaders of the association believed that the legislation would enable them to achieve their two major institutional goals. It would give them access to federal charters, and so enable them to gain the regulatory and operating advantages of the dual system available to other financial intermediaries. It would also permit diversification of savings accounts, financial services, and asset portfolio powers, thus opening the way for them to become "family financial centers." These new benefits were

3. Senate, Committee on Banking, Housing, and Urban Affairs, *Financial Institutions Act of 1973*, p. 344. Statement of Embree K. Easterly.
4. Ibid.

considered so important that the association readily accepted all provisions of the comprehensive package except the proposal to eliminate the deposit interest rate ceilings and differentials and the
change in calculating the reserves for bad debts. Their official position was summarized by Morris D. Crawford, Jr., the Chairman of
the Bowery Savings Bank and a member of the Hunt Commission,
in an attachment to the association's statement:

> The position of the savings bank industry on structural change is long-
> standing and unequivocal: mutual savings banks must develop into full-
> service family banking institutions, capable of competing more effectively
> for savings over all stages of the business cycle, and of serving all of the
> changing financial needs of families over all stages of their economic life
> cycle. Our statement focuses, in particular, on the three essential require-
> ments for such a modernized family banking system:
> (1) A federal charter alternative for mutual savings banks, so that the
> progressive influence of the dual state-federal system of chartering and
> supervision long available to all other depository industries will be ex-
> tended to our industry;
> (2) A full range of financial services to consumers, including consumer
> loans, checking accounts, NOW accounts, credit card and other modern
> funds transfer services, and extension to thrift institutions of full partner-
> ship in the development of electronic funds transfer services; and
> (3) Flexible investment powers, including authority to invest in a wide
> range of federal, state, and local government and corporate debt and
> equity securities, as well as all types of mortgages.[5]

The response of the National Association of Mutual Savings Banks
is shown in the following summary of this group's statements.

Section 1. Payment of Interest on Deposit Accounts
  (a) Vigorously opposes elimination of permanent federal authority to es-
      tablish deposit interest rate ceilings and meaningful differentials for
      mortgage-oriented thrift institutions; may be able to rely on standby
      controls if inflation is controlled, if thrift institutions have completed
      structural adjustments of assets and deposit liabilities, and if interest
      costs are reduced to prevent a repetition of "wild-card" certificate
      experience of July 1973.
  (b) Takes no official position on payment of interest on demand deposits
      but believes Congress should delay action until thrift institutions have
      checking accounts.
  (c) Suggests that NOW accounts should have rate ceilings equal to pass-
      book account rates, but differential rates paid on deposits at thrift
      institutions and commercial banks should continue.

5. Senate, Committee on Banking, Housing, and Urban Affairs, *Financial Institutions
   Act of 1973*, p. 858. Statement of the National Association of Mutual Savings
   Banks.

(d) Favors formalizing consultation process and requiring concurrence of two regulatory agencies before changing rate controls.

(e) Supports principle of truth-in-savings but believes adequate authority exists.

Section 2. Expanded Deposit Liability Powers and Reserves

(a) Strongly supports checking accounts, third-party powers, and NOW accounts for federal thrift institutions and individual and corporate customers.

(b) Supports commercial bank savings accounts and NOW accounts for corporations.

(c) and (e) Takes position that states should set reserves for institutions not belonging to FRS or FHLBS.

(d) and (e) Takes no official position.

Section 3. Expanded Lending and Investing Powers

Supports recommendations (a) through (j) to grant expanded powers for consumer loans, unrestricted real estate loans, community welfare and development investments, corporate debt investments, purchase of government securities, and flexible liquidity assistance, except that portfolio percentage guidelines are not needed and once Congress grants authority regulatory agencies can set details.

Section 4. Charters for Thrift Institutions

(a) through (d) Strongly supports dual chartering system as means of acquiring federal charters to expand geographically and to select type of regulation desired, but is unalterably opposed to conversions of mutual institutions to stock form at state or federal level, so the moratorium on such changes should continue; objects to limitations placed on investment powers for federal thrift institutions.

Section 5. Credit Unions

Takes no official position on FIA 1973 recommendations.

Section 6. FHA and VA Interest Ceilings

Supports elimination of FHA and VA mortgage interest rate ceilings to stabilize the flow of funds.

Section 7. Taxes

Offers no direct comments on changing reserves for bad debts and proposed mortgage interest tax credit but states that no persuasive case has been made for changing the 1969 tax rules.

The basic arguments of the National Association of Mutual Savings Banks were presented in an unusually candid article written by Grover W. Ensley, the executive vice-president of the organization for many years, in which he described how greatly thrift institutions needed expanded powers to become full-service financial centers if they were to avoid obsolescence.[6] As a professional economist, Ensley further claimed that free markets best serve the general public and that competition would increase the amount and stability of mortgage credit flows. Finally, he cited five fundamental problems created by the existing structural and regulatory arrangements: (1) specialized lending institutions protected by legislative barriers contradict the concept of free competitive markets; (2) private thrift institutions have become a pawn of the government in attempts to attain legislative goals; (3) major revisions in the tax code in 1969 effectively eliminated the advantages possessed by thrift institutions; (4) regulation Q controls lead to financial disintermediation; and (5) housing subsidies create other risks. Although Ensley's article was written in 1971 during the Hunt Commission's deliberations, it correctly foresaw many of the issues that were debated during the congressional hearings several years later.

In their formal testimony on the Financial Institutions Act of 1973, the mutual savings banks enthusiastically supported sections 2, 3, 4, and 6; by expanding their investment and lending powers and consumer services these provisions would enable thrift institutions to compete more effectively with commercial banks on both a price and a functional basis. At the same time, the association categorically denied the criticism by housing interests that the supply and stability of mortgage credit would be reduced. Some of these expanded powers had already been granted to mutual savings banks by early 1974: Connecticut permitted consumer loans, and individual checking accounts were expected to be allowed in 1976; Massachusetts and New Hampshire permitted NOW accounts; and other states, such as Maryland, already granted mutual savings banks flexible powers approximately equal to those of commercial banks. The pattern was erratic, however, and the key financial state of New York, where 56 percent of total savings bank assets were concentrated, did not permit personal checking accounts or consumer loan powers at the time that the new legislation was proposed. The National Mutual Savings Bank Association firmly believed that survival of its members depended upon the liberalization of operating powers in existing markets and upon access to federal charters so that they could expand geographically and thus increase their deposits and improve their earnings under the same competitive advantages as full service commercial banks.

6. Grover W. Ensley, "Financial Institutions Should Be Modernized," *Commercial and Financial Chronicle* 213 (May 27, 1971), pp. 1604–5.

Despite their strong support for improved competitive powers for thrift institutions, the mutual savings banks vigorously defended the continuation of regulation Q controls to protect their access to household savings, basing their argument on the grounds that full service commercial banks "would continue to have an inherently greater ability than thrift institutions to raise earnings and deposit interest rates in inflationary periods of high and rising interest rates. These considerations underscore the need for continued deposit interest rate ceilings and differentials."[7]

In summary, mutual savings bank officials evidently saw no contradiction in simultaneously advocating increased powers for themselves to lend, invest, charter, and extend consumer services but continued controls for other financial institutions, because they believed that the structure and regulation of the financial markets must be weighted against the commercial banks to create fair competition. In arguing this view they pointed to the overwhelming number and the wide geographic distribution of commercial bank offices, their power to develop highly diversified asset portfolios and a variety of financial services for consumers, and their technological advantages in transferring funds. They also emphasized the strong shift in the flow of household savings and time deposits to all major depository institutions, particularly the growing share held by commercial banks: 1946–56, 30 percent; 1957–65, 42 percent; and 1966–74, 54 percent. The dramatic inflow of funds to commercial banks in the summer of 1973 when the "wild card" 4-year savings certificates with no interest rate ceilings were issued was constantly referred to by thrift institution officials. It was, they said, conclusive evidence of the need for deposit interest rate ceilings and differentials despite the resulting financial disintermediation; and they asserted that such restrictions are made obsolete as technological changes occur and savers become more experienced.

The differing institutional perceptions of the actual meaning of fair competition thus continued to create "a dialogue among the deaf," which frustrated the efforts toward comprehensive legislative reform of financial institutions. It was left to the marketplace to work out the necessary adjustments according to existing laws and regulatory practices until some financial crisis should occur or specific interest groups could persuade key members of Congress to support their proposals.

7. Senate, Committee on Banking, Housing, and Urban Affairs, *Financial Institutions Act of 1973*, p. 1086. Statement of the National Association of Mutual Savings Banks.

Savings and Loan Associations

Comprehensive statements on behalf of the savings and loan associations were submitted by two major trade associations, the United States League of Savings Associations (USLSA) and the National Savings and Loan League (NSLL). Hundreds of pages of testimony and background materials were prepared by spokesmen for these two powerful organizations. The clearest summary of the organizations' views is probably found in two impressively direct statements by Norman Strunk, the long-term executive vice-president of the U.S. League of Savings Associations. The first statement reviews the chief arguments.

> In general, therefore, we view this bill with limited enthusiasm. It does little for us in terms of asset diversification, does little for us in terms of liability diversification. It does little to increase the profitability of our institutions and, as a result, our ability to pay more for savings. Its basic recommendation—to remove interest rate controls on savings deposits— will place our institutions at the complete mercy of the competitive forces in the savings markets. While putting thrift institutions at the brink, the bill does not provide protection in terms of meaningful asset flexibility and flexible mortgage yields such as might be provided by a variable rate mortgage contract. In other words, this bill, if passed in its present form, would add greatly to the perils of the savings and loan business, yet really do very little for the business to protect it against chronic inflation and interest rate spirals—the reasons for which it was written.[8]

The second statement explains even better why the trade-off envisioned by Treasury officials was rejected.

> The Administration and the Treasury have insisted that this bill be taken on a "package" basis. As we see it, the "package" approach has little to commend it but it does have the potential of enormous and probably fatal harm. As now written, this bill is a death warrant for the savings and loan business. We do believe, of course, that some of the proposals in the bill have great merit and that parts of it should be approved. But our support of these individual sections of the bill is vastly outweighed by our concern over the proposal to phase out interest rate controls within 5½ years. The proposal for abolition of controls is, of course, the keystone of the Administration's proposal.[9]

While these comments indicate the underlying reasons for rejecting the administration's recommendations, the principal emphasis in the public statements of these groups, of course, focused on the close links between housing and thrift institutions in satisfying the

---

8. Senate, Committee on Banking, Housing, and Urban Affairs, *Financial Institutions Act of 1973*, p. 413. Statement of Norman Strunk.
9. Ibid.

intent of Congress. This triangular relationship was clearly deline-ated at the beginning of Strunk's testimony.

> Twenty-five years ago the Congress made a commitment to provide "a decent home and a suitable living environment for every American family." The savings and loan business has been a willing participant in this undertaking; we provide today the financing for more than half of the residential home purchases in our country. However, our business is poorly equipped to survive in economic conditions such as those we are now experiencing.
>
> Thus, in our view, the time has come for the Congress to face the tough decision: does it wish to continue to honor its 1949 commitment, or does it prefer to abandon the goal which has made America a nation of home owners?
>
> If the Congress still believes in this goal, there appear to be three choices: first, it could assign to Government agencies the task of providing adequate home finance. We submit that in the long run this is the most inefficient and expensive route to travel.
>
> Or the Congress could leave long-term mortgage finance to other more diversified financial institutions. But we have seen through the years that commercial banks, for example, are "fair weather friends" for residential finance: for several years, life insurance companies have been decreasing their mortgage originations and holdings.
>
> The third choice is to give the thrift institutions—which have specialized in mortgage finance—the tools they need to function in a climate of persistent inflation and these recurrent periods where short-term interest rates surpass long-term rates.[10]

Their argument was essentially that the changes proposed in the Financial Institutions Act would threaten the adequacy and stability of housing financing and lead inevitably to the "federalization" of the real estate markets.

> We think we have to be first-class savings and loan associations if there is to be any hope at all of preserving the private sector of the home financing business in this country.
>
> The alternative to keeping a viable savings and loan business for providing the bulk of the funds for home building and home purchase on a private enterprise basis is to turn the whole job of providing long-term credit for housing to the Federal National Mortgage Association and similar agencies.
>
> Unless thrift institutions are able to compete for the savings business of American families, the mortgage market will consist of the Government and quasi-Government agencies and our institutions will turn into a type of mortgage banking and brokerage firm—originating mortgages to be made, but then sold to one of the huge Federal mortgage banks.[11]

10. Ibid., p. 411.
11. Ibid., p. 393.

This same theme was advanced by Gilbert G. Roessner, president of the National Savings and Loan League, in his congressional testimony.

> Mr. Chairman, members of the subcommittee, this legislation if enacted in full as the administration has insisted, is going to eliminate the housing specialist for the United States. The savings and loan industry, if this legislation is enacted as a package, will become, we submit, a mini-commercial bank.
>
> Housing under this bill need not be served by the thrift industry any longer. Indeed, if that is what the Congress wants to do, then this bill should be enacted in full.
>
> The homebuyer will be bidding for his funds against such giant corporations as General Motors and American Telegraph. I do not need to tell you who will get his money first.[12]

These dire predictions, that a $300-billion financial intermediary system would be destroyed by the competition of commercial banks for savings deposits if the rate control and differential were both eliminated, caused the two trade organizations for savings and loan associations to reject the administration's proposals for comprehensive reform. As a substitute, each group suggested an evolutionary approach that would strengthen their existing powers and provide some added flexibility within the present framework. The U.S. League of Savings Associations argued that with only "minor changes" their members could continue to function as the major source of mortgage credit. Specifically they requested a revision of section 5(c) of the Home Owners' Loan Act to remove a number of burdens by permitting: (1) more freedom regarding the percentage of assets and dollar size of loans for residential mortgages; (2) collateral loans; (3) line-of-credit loans to builders; (4) general relief from first lien requirements; (5) authority to make equity investments in real estate; (6) flexibility for urban renewal loans; (7) removal of area limits on loans for acquisition and development of land; (8) development of new sources of funds; and (9) consideration of variable interest rate mortgages. The National Savings and Loan League similarly argued for an evolutionary approach based on: (1) continued rate controls and a one-half of 1 percent rate differential on their savings accounts; (2) tax incentives for exempting individual interest income on the first $750 of savings deposits; (3) a guarantee that savings and loan associations would participate in the developing electronic funds transfer systems; (4) unrestricted loan authority for any purpose up to $10,000; (5) federal chartering of stock associa-

12. Senate, Committee on Banking, Housing, and Urban Affairs, *Financial Institutions Act of 1973*, p. 440. Statement of Gilbert G. Roessner.

tions and conversion rights to state-chartered stock associations; (6) permission to savings and loan associations to sell subordinated debenture bonds and count them as part of their required reserves; (7) improved deposit insurance; (8) increased equity investments in service corporations; (9) trust services; (10) freedom to promote variable rate and flexible payment mortgages; and (11) placement of Treasury deposits in savings and loan associations. The detailed responses of the United States League of Savings Associations (USLSA) and the National Savings and Loan League (NSLL) to the proposed legislation are summarized below.

Section 1. Payment of Interest on Deposit Accounts

USLSA (a) Strongly opposes elimination of deposit interest rate controls and the differential because of the basic threat to the survival of savings and loan associations and diversion of savings away from housing.

        (b) Supports continued prohibition against interest on demand deposits.

        (c) Does not object to uniform ceilings on NOW accounts.

        (d) Recommends studying the regulatory consultation process.

        (e) Supports truth-in-saving but recommends restrictions on reporting burdens.

NSLL   (a) Supports rate controls and the differential to help housing.

        (b) and (c) Supports.

        (d) Supports consultations, but excluding Treasury.

        (e) Favors voluntary disclosure upon request.

Section 2. Expanded Deposit Liability Powers and Reserves

USLSA (a) Has not requested checking accounts and doubts that this power would be advantageous (would want authority if rate controls are eliminated); prefers third-party payment power to handle withdrawals from savings using "nontransferable nonnegotiable orders or drafts."

        (b) Opposes corporate savings and NOW accounts for national banks.

        (c) and (e) Does not oppose uniform rate ceilings for NOW accounts after consultation with FHLBB.

        (d) Opposes voluntary membership in FHLBB for insured state-chartered associations.

        (f) Does not support any specific range for reserves.

NSLL   (a) Supports third-party payment powers but objects to NOW accounts.

        (b) Takes no position.

        (c) Objects on the grounds that only FHLBB should set reserve requirements for members of the Federal Home Loan Bank system.

        (d) Supports requiring insured associations to belong to FHLBB.

        (e) Objects to NOW accounts and Federal Reserve System regulation.

        (f) Objects to changes in reserves for time and savings deposits.

Section 3. Expanded Lending and Investing Powers

USLSA (a) Favors consumer loan powers but doubts that associations will increase such loans substantially, so portfolio percentage limits are unnecessary.

(b) and (c) Strongly favors liberalization of real estate lending and authority to make construction loans.

(d) Favors community welfare and development investments and loans.

(e) Favors authority to buy high quality corporate commercial paper and debt securities but would add corporate equities.

(f) Portfolio percentage restrictions are not necessary.
Believes (g) and (h) are not necessary.

(i) Takes no position.

(j) Supports modernization of rules.

NSLL Essentially supports (a) through (j), but takes no position on corporate commercial paper and debt investments and suggests that 10 percent limit be applied to community welfare and development investments and loans.

Section 4. Charters for Thrift Institutions

USLSA (a) Supports concept of federal charters but opposes widespread conversion from mutual to stock charters and favors continued moratorium on conversions.

(b) through (e) Supports federal charters with related powers.

NSLL Supports (a) through (e) in granting federal charters provisions, provided federal savings and loan associations are granted powers equal to those of mutual savings banks.

Section 5. Credit Unions

USLSA Takes no position on recommendations (a), (c) through (e), (g), (h), and (j) on detailed changes in credit union powers.

(b) and (f) Points out that increased flexibility to make secured and unsecured loans with longer maturities would move them closer to making mortgage loans and that savings and loan associations would be at a competitive disadvantage because of the tax-exempt status of credit unions.

(i) Suggests that Congress should review the actual performance of credit unions and enforce the "consumer bond" membership rules if the tax-free status is continued.

NSLL Has no objection to the credit union modifications but believes that (1) credit unions should also be subject to the rate ceilings applied to thrift institutions, (2) the "common bond" rule should be enforced, and (3) the tax-exempt status should depend on the historic consumer loan function.

Section 6. FHA and VA Interest Ceilings

USLSA, NSLL Both support the removal of administrative mortgage interest rate ceilings. USLSA also encourages congressional support for variable rate mortgages.

Section 7. Taxes

USLSA (a) Strongly opposes the elimination of the procedure now used by mortgage-oriented institutions for calculating reserves for bad debts which was established as a special incentive to encourage mortgage loans; since commercial banks receive other special tax advantages and presently pay taxes at a lower effective rate than is paid by savings and loan associations, the equalization of bad debt procedures would widen that gap further; strongly opposes further erosion of the tax advantage already reduced by the Tax Reform Act of 1969.

(b) and (c) Remains undecided about the mortgage investment tax credit because of the diverse characteristics of USLSA members; suggests further analysis. Recommends that a sliding scale be used if the tax credit is adopted and that a tax exemption or credit for interest earned by small savers be considered as a preferred alternative.

NSLL (a) Strongly opposes the suggested equalization of bad debt reserve procedures which would reduce mortgage credit and erode the competitive position of savings and loan associations.

(b) Opposes use of a mortgage investment tax credit on grounds that it would not represent an adequate incentive to provide a stable flow of funds into housing and would create a windfall benefit for commercial banks even though they would not be a major supplier of mortgage credit or a stable source.

(c) Recommends use of a sliding scale if a tax credit is approved.

The detailed suggestions of both the U.S. League of Savings Associations and the National Savings and Loan League indicate their great interest in removing certain rules considered to be restrictive to real estate financing, but no desire to move away from their historical specialization functions. The suggested diversification of asset and liability powers recommended in the proposed act was largely ignored as being irrelevant to this specialization or inadequate to efforts in that direction. Only the liberalization of real estate lending rules for savings and loan associations, proposed in section 3(b) and (c), was of major interest, and both trade associations clearly preferred to pursue these legislative goals in Congress without getting involved in the trade-offs required by the administration's package of reforms.

They were also adamant about preserving the regulation Q rate controls and restoring the differential to at least one-half of 1 percent above the commercial bank rate paid on deposits. These measures are considered to be the cornerstones of their competitive position, and spokesmen from both groups were highly critical of the theoretical arguments used by academic and administration witnesses, which they claimed failed to recognize the realities of the marketplace. They found particularly irritating the July 1973 experience with 4-year certificates issued without rate ceilings, which Strunk had referred to as an "unfortunate experiment" with "free market rates." It was, they said, responsible for a rate war lasting three chaotic months and corrected only when Congress restored the "integrity of the rate control system." Without such a system, they argued, market forces would "threaten the very existence of the savings and loan business, and severely damage the housing industry by diverting funds that could be used for mortgage loans."[13]

The responses of savings and loan association officials are a natural reaction to the risks they feared from changes, after their many years of remarkably successful operations in financing much of the postwar housing boom. Their position was that this success could be sustained simply by improving their specialization functions. They justly criticized the errors in fiscal and monetary policy which had created the swings in economic activity and inflation and led inevitably to the disruptive waves of disintermediation. Their key objective was to avoid risking competition with commercial banks without the protective shield of regulation Q controls and the savings rate differential advantage. In that framework the threat of continued economic fluctuations, inflation, and disintermediation could be overcome by unilateral appeals to Congress to protect the housing industry.

Credit Unions

The fourth major financial intermediary presenting testimony on the proposed legislation viewed the administration's package of reforms negatively. Since most independent analysts felt that credit unions were favorably treated by the recommendations, their sharp rejection of the legislation was surprising, but their statements to congressional committees provide several insights into the legislative process and explain why they were so critical. Because of their relative size and their concentration on consumer credit services to members, credit unions have not usually been grouped with commercial banks, savings and loan associations, and mutual savings banks. The extremely rapid growth of credit unions has now changed their public image, but the period of legislative analysis straddled the transition and some of the issues were therefore confused.

13. Senate, Committee on Banking, Housing, and Urban Affairs, *Financial Institutions Act of 1973*, p. 1043. Letter from Norman Strunk to Senator McIntyre.

The views of credit unions were presented to the Senate subcommittee by the Credit Union National Association (CUNA) and the National Association of Federal Credit Unions (NAFCU). Both trade associations were critical of the general purposes and detailed recommendations put forward in the proposal. Spokesmen for both groups appeared to be somewhat defensive about the status of credit unions and repeatedly criticized the other financial institutions for attempting to limit the growth and diversification of the credit unions. They also vowed to work directly with Congress in promoting detailed reform of the credit union industry to provide broader powers. The credit union movement is still relatively small in terms of financial assets, despite its very rapid growth, but it has considerable political influence because of its grass roots organizations in every state and its vigorous lobbying efforts.

In expressing their negative reaction to the act, because of its numerous sins of commission and omission, credit union authorities pointedly emphasized that they would be much happier with passage of other legislation already pending before Congress (identical bills sponsored by credit unions had been introduced by Representative Wright Patman, chairman of the House Banking, Currency, and Housing Committee, and by Senator John Sparkman, chairman of the Senate Banking, Housing, and Urban Affairs Committee). Their original objections turned out to be significant. Comprehensive reform of financial institutions failed to gain congressional approval, but detailed legislation affecting credit unions was easily passed at the very beginning of the ninety-fifth Congress that convened in January 1977. Regulation Q authority was extended at the same time. Meanwhile, however, no comprehensive legislation such as the Financial Institutions Act of 1975, passed by the Senate, or the Financial Reform Act of 1976, considered by the House, has yet been submitted to Congress, and Treasury officials have indicated that their new initiatives will be limited to actions on NOW accounts and the payment of interest on demand deposits.

The somewhat defensive tone of the credit union statements is clear in the comments of Thomas E. Roby representing the Credit Union National Association:

> We are mystified as to why drafters of the bill, who reportedly drew upon the Hunt Commission, deliberately isolated credit unions outside normal thrift institutions. This marked discrimination and our lack of representation on the Hunt Commission give rise to grave concern as to the inten-

tions of the drafters of the bill or their lack of understanding of credit unions and their role in the savings and credit marketplace.[14]

The official statement by the Credit Union National Association expressed even more explicitly the disappointment of its members in being excluded from the Hunt Commission and in not being "significantly involved in the development of the legislative package."[15] Following a series of two-day seminars in seven cities, 1,300 credit union leaders decided that "because of the serious concerns the credit union movement has expressed, the Credit Union National Association cannot endorse the Financial Institutions Act. Rather, CUNA will seek to amend it in an effort to make it a more acceptable vehicle for financial reform."[16] The detailed reactions of the two major credit union trade associations are shown in the following summary.

Section 1. Payment of Interest on Deposit Accounts

CUNA (a) Opposes removal of deposit interest rate controls unless more equitable competitive balance between financial institutions is established.

(b) Supports payment of interest on demand deposits as fair and consistent with NOW rules.

(c) Takes no position.

(d) Opposes transfer of rate-setting authority for federal credit unions from the administrator to FRS or FHLBS.

(e) Supports truth-in-savings provisions, but believes cooperative nature of credit unions requires special disclosure rules.

NAFCU (a) Favors continuation of deposit interest rate authority and suggests that any change be experimental so controls can be restored if disintermediation returns.

Supports (b) through (e) except that National Credit Union Administration should be added to regulatory consultations.

Section 2. Expanded Deposit Liability Powers and Reserves

CUNA (a) and (b) Strongly opposes recommendations that checking accounts, third-party payment powers, NOW accounts, and credit card depository authority not be granted to credit unions.

(c) through (f) Supports recommendations on setting reserve requirements for demand deposits and NOW accounts; repeats claim that credit unions are being treated unfairly.

NAFCU (a) and (b) Opposes exclusion of credit unions from expanded powers; objects to general FIA 1973 exclusion of credit unions from definition of thrift institutions.

14. Senate, Committee on Banking, Housing, and Urban Affairs, *Financial Institutions Act of 1973*, p. 698. Statement of Thomas E. Roby.

15. Ibid., p. 762.

16. Ibid.

Section 3. Expanded Lending and Investing Powers

CUNA   (a) through (j) Objects comprehensively for failure to provide credit unions with the "full array" of secured and unsecured loan and investment powers recommended by the Hunt Commission; claims that failure to broaden lending and investment powers will seriously erode the competitive position of credit unions, particularly with regard to their income and liquidity needs.

NAFCU   Criticizes (a) through (j) on grounds that expansion of powers for other institutions would further erode competitive equality; supports the general expansion of powers but argues for competitive equality through legislation.

Section 4. Charters for Thrift Institutions

CUNA   (a) and (c) Supports interest of mutual savings banks in having access to federal charters but objects to the creation of federal stock thrift institutions.

(b), (d), and (e) Takes no position.

NAFCU (a) through (e) Does not object to chartering proposals but strongly opposes (1) premise that credit unions must convert to another form of financial institution before being allowed to offer expanded financial services and (2) theory that the tax-exempt status of credit unions should be based on types of services offered.

Section 5. Credit Unions

CUNA   (a) Supports creation of a central banking facility but opposes FIA 1973 recommendation because it would (1) exclude state-chartered insured credit unions, (2) provide only temporary emergency liquidity assistance, and (3) be controlled by a single government official.

(b) Criticizes "minor liberalization" of unsecured and secured lending powers.

(c) through (h) Supports, but requests Congress to further liberalize the provisions.

(i) and (j) Vigorously supports continued tax exemption and rejects (1) argument that tax status depends upon the types of services offered and (2) recommendation that credit unions should convert to other forms of organization to acquire other powers.

NAFCU (a) and (b) Strongly supports liquidity facility for credit unions and extension of maximum loan maturities with limits set by National Credit Union Administration.

Supports (c) through (h) with further liberalization.

Objects to (i) and (j) involving possible taxation of credit unions and the forced conversion to obtain additional powers.

Section 6. FHA and VA Interest Ceilings

CUNA   Supports abolition of FHA and VA interest rate ceilings.

NAFCU   Does not object to a phaseout of rate ceilings, but recommends continuation of regulatory authority rather than complete elimination.

Section 7. Taxes

CUNA,   Neither commented, perhaps because the issue seemed prima-
NAFCU   rily to involve an argument between commercial banks and
           thrift institutions.

The objections of the credit union organizations can be grouped under four general headings. First, spokesmen claimed that the section dealing with the expansion of credit union powers did not go far enough and represented only "minor liberalization" of credit union laws, as the original Treasury Department publication described the legislation. The major point of contention appeared to be that Treasury officials had failed to include the detailed recommendations which the credit union associations had suggested during the two preparatory sessions preceding submission of the legislative recommendations to Congress. Since these detailed proposals were included in the specific legislation introduced by Representative Patman and Senator Sparkman, the credit unions naturally felt that they were being ignored.

Defending their set of recommendations, Treasury officials reminded their critics that the comprehensive Financial Institutions Act of 1973 could not cover all of the detailed objectives of each group of financial institutions, since it was intended to focus on the broader structural issues. While their response was perhaps a logical rebuttal, and entirely consistent with other Treasury goals of improving the efficiency of all types of financial intermediaries and giving them more equitable treatment, it did little to mollify the credit union leaders.

Second, both trade associations resented the explicit exclusion of credit unions from sections 2 and 3, which outlined the expanded asset and liability powers to be granted to other financial intermediaries. The intensity of their disappointment was apparent in the testimony presented by the Credit Union National Association.

> As proposed in the bill, those credit unions that aggressively seek the powers needed to serve the modern financial needs of their members would be required to convert to an organizational status decidedly different from what they now have and thereby cease to be a credit union. Those which did not opt for the modern powers would be allowed to continue to operate as they have in the past with only minor modifications in their powers. Thus, they would be left behind to wither away while other financial institutions would be empowered to take away their members by providing the financial services demanded by the contemporary consumer borrower and saver.[17]

17. Ibid., p. 721.

Third, every credit union spokesman vigorously objected to any suggestion that their tax-exempt status should be questioned or that the granting of additional asset or liability powers should be made contingent on converting into some other type of financial intermediary and giving up the tax-exempt privilege. Credit union leaders adamantly opposed any change and vigorously argued that their tax treatment is properly based on the uniqueness of the credit unions— the common-bond feature of their membership, and their cooperative, nonprofit form of organization—and has nothing to do with the size or scope of financial services provided. They were particularly upset by the Treasury Department's appearing to argue that if credit unions wanted to add services they would have to convert to another form of institution, a tax-paying thrift institution.

> We vehemently disagree with this type of reasoning which in effect could lead to the demise of credit unions as we know them today. Credit unions would be faced with the choice of either not offering competitive services or else converting into a different type of financial institution. We reject this entire approach and urge that the Committee do so too.[18]

Fourth, credit union leaders decided to oppose the elimination of existing controls on deposit interest rates and of the differentials, even though their organizations are not directly affected. It is interesting that one official recommended continuation of controls by suggesting that "this proposal should be deferred and studied carefully."[19] The questionable logic of calling for a new comprehensive study of an issue that had already been analyzed to death for over a decade is evidently just as popular in the private sector as it is in Congress and the Executive Office.

In summary, credit unions strongly denounced the proposed recommendations in the Financial Institutions Act of 1973 as inadequate for meeting their goals and as explicitly discriminating against their competitive interests. The political impact of their strong rejection cannot be measured quantitatively, but many analysts believe that credit unions played a major role in the ultimate failure of Congress to act favorably on the comprehensive reforms of financial institutions proposed in the Financial Institutions Acts of 1973 and 1975.

18. Ibid., p. 750.
19. Ibid., p. 1067. Letter from Credit Union National Association to Senate Subcommittee.

7

OTHER FORCES OPERATING AGAINST THE
REFORM PROPOSALS

Even if the proposed legislation could have prevailed against the arguments detailed in the foregoing chapters, there were other groups making their views heard by Congress. Economic conditions also played a part in defeating the proposed reform. Finally, the fact that introduction of the Financial Institutions Act of 1973 coincided with one of the most critical events in the nation's political history was probably a major factor explaining its legislative failure.

Consumer Interests

Anticipating the submission of the Financial Institutions Act of 1973 to Congress, Treasury officials held a large orientation meeting with representatives of various consumer groups to solicit their active support for the comprehensive package of reforms.[1] At that meeting a variety of administration officials, including the President's Special Assistant for Consumer Affairs, attempted to convince the consumer organizations that the new legislation was specifically designed to meet their needs in saving and borrowing. Consumer groups did give strong support to specific reform proposals, particularly the payment of interest on demand deposits and the expansion of NOW accounts, but they did not play a significant role in the Senate hearings. From the viewpoint of the administration, their limited involvement was unfortunate because their support was needed to persuade Congress to act favorably on the reform proposals. Consumer groups did send

---

1. For a complete summary of that meeting see U.S., Congress, Senate, Committee on Banking, Housing, and Urban Affairs, *Financial Structure and Regulation*, pp. 41–93.

letters to Senator McIntyre's subcommittee, however, expressing their views on some of the specific sections, and they presented formal statements at the hearings held in September 1974. Their responses to the various sections can be briefly summarized.

Section 1. The Consumers Union supported the removal of regulation Q controls and the differential and argued strongly for granting new powers to pay interest on demand deposits.

Section 2. The Consumers Union supported the granting of checking and NOW account authority to savings and loan associations, mutual savings banks, and credit unions. The Consumer Federation of America also expressed strong support for expanding NOW accounts as a means of stimulating competition for consumer deposits.

Section 3. The Consumers Union approved the broadening of thrift institutions' investing and lending activities.

Section 4. The Consumer Federation of America backed the granting of federal charters to mutual savings banks.

Section 6. Consumer representatives supported the elimination of administrative interest rate ceilings on FHA and VA mortgages because they had not really benefited consumers.

Organized Labor Interests

The views of organized labor were expressed in the statement of Nathaniel Goldfinger, director of research of the American Federation of Labor–Congress of Industrial Organizations (AFL-CIO). Commenting on the stated goals of the proposal, to increase the efficiency and flexibility of the financial system as a means of promoting sound economic growth, the AFL-CIO expressed its skepticism that the comprehensive package would help housing, consumers, state and local governments, and small businesses, or that it would fulfill other social needs.

> The AFL-CIO supports the goal of sound objective growth, including the provision of adequate funds for housing. However, we do not believe that S.2591 can achieve that goal. Indeed, it is our view that this bill, if enacted, would aggravate the difficulties that already exist and would add to present obstacles in reaching the stated goal.[2]

Given the prominent role of the construction trade unions of skilled workers in the AFL-CIO and their long involvement in various social issues, particularly housing priorities, the emphasis

2. U.S., Congress, Senate, Committee on Banking, Housing, and Urban Affairs, *Reform of Financial Institutions: 1973*, p. 609.

shown in the Goldfinger statement to avoid any actions that might restrict residential construction was to be expected. As Lane Kirkland, secretary-treasurer of the AFL-CIO, explained in his statement rejecting the Hunt Commission's report, the mandatory allocation of capital to residential construction is a responsibility of all financial institutions because the operation of the markets will not provide adequate funds for social needs unless the government intervenes.[3] The statement of Goldfinger elaborated on this theme by claiming that the legislation would add to this discrimination in the marketplace and lead to "very sharp declines in housing, and in these other vulnerable sectors of the economy. But," he continued, "high interest rates also are redistributing income from the less affluent to the more affluent."[4]

In expressing his strong support for lower interest rates and mandatory allocation of credit based on social priorities to be identified by Congress, Goldfinger stated:

> And what is urgently needed, in our judgment, is a specific method of mandatory allocation, which would allocate available credit into areas of high social priority, such as housing, public facilities, public utility expansion and regular operations of business; while at the same time to reduce and curb the flow of credit for such purposes as land speculation, commodity market speculation, the considerable degree of hoarding that has been going on in the past year and a half, and foreign borrowers.[5]

As secondary options the AFL-CIO statement also advocated direct lending through existing government programs or through a new National Development Bank that would lend directly to state and local governments, corporations, and individuals to achieve social benefits. However, direct credit rationing was clearly the preferred solution. One possible way in which such a program might be structured was suggested by Goldfinger in responding to a question from Senator Proxmire.

> *Senator Proxmire:* One final question, Mr. Goldfinger. Some have argued that financial institutions should be mandated by law to invest a certain proportion of their funds in homebuilding—5, 6, 7, 8, 10 percent, whatever—as one way of seeing that homebuilding gets its fair share.
> Do you think that that is a practical approach?
> Do you think it would work?
> Do you think it is fair?

3. Ibid., pp. 616–17; see Chapter 4, pp. 67–68 for a summary of the Kirkland statement.
4. Ibid., p. 595.
5. Ibid.

Mr. Goldfinger: Yes. I think it would work. I think it is practical, and I frankly think it is a good way to do it. That would be along the lines that we in the AFL-CIO advocate.[6]

In considering the individual sections of the Financial Institutions Act of 1973, the AFL-CIO particularly criticized the removal of regulation Q controls because of the possibility that pushing up interest rates would discourage residential construction. They were equally critical of the expanded investment powers and urged that the proposals be rejected because of the possible diversion of funds away from the housing sector. The argument that diversified lending and investment portfolios would strengthen thrift institutions and improve their earnings, making them a better source of stable mortgage credit, was not accepted by the AFL-CIO spokesmen. They continued to argue that thrift institutions would never be able to compete on a broad scale with commercial banks and that it was better to continue their narrow specialization, given the overriding importance of mortgage lending. With minor reservations the AFL-CIO generally supported the expansion of deposit powers for thrift institutions and the recommendations regarding credit unions but vigorously opposed the elimination of administrative interest rate ceilings on FHA and VA mortgage loans. Finally, the AFL-CIO spokesmen were highly critical of the proposed changes in the tax law. They felt that the adjustments would not attract additional funds into mortgage markets but would simply create another tax loophole for commercial banks. In short, the proposed legislation was considered to be a poor trade-off for thrift institutions and to portend serious disadvantages for home buyers, the housing industry, and construction workers.

Housing Industry Interests

The housing industry is a basic part of the economic, social, and political structure of America. It affects almost every person, and the quantity and quality of available housing is often used as a measure of social welfare and economic progress. The housing industry also provides employment for a large share of the labor force, both di-

---

6. Ibid., p. 608. In hearings on the Financial Reform Act of 1976 Congressman St Germain asked an AFL-CIO official about the extent of real estate investments made by union pension funds. Of the six national unions that responded for the record, two had zero percent of their assets invested in real estate loans, three had portfolio commitments ranging from 6 to 14 percent, and one had 46 percent of its total portfolio so invested; see, U.S., Congress, House, Committee on Banking, Currency, and Housing, *Financial Reform Act of 1976*, p. 382.

rectly in construction and real estate selling and financing, and indirectly in many other industries that supply materials and services for construction, household furnishings, and maintenance services. The political system has always recognized the fundamental importance of mortgage and construction financing, and much of the structural and regulatory framework of the financial markets reflects the evolution of housing finance in this country. The impressive size of the housing finance sector at the end of 1973, when the Financial Institutions Act was first proposed, is summarized in Table 9.

Serious concern about the volatile cyclical pattern of residential construction and mortgage financing was the original motive for the reform proposals. Administration representatives claimed that the housing sector would actually benefit from the recommended legislation, but critics responded that the uncertainties created by the structural changes might irreparably harm the housing industry and thrift institutions. Since the administration could not present any stronger evidence that future mortgage markets would behave as they hoped than a handful of theoretical econometric studies based on traditional assumptions, the critics could successfully argue that comprehensive change was too risky because of the possible effects on competition and the unique social and economic importance of housing. This unresolved controversy ultimately dominated the course of decision making.

No official statement from housing interests was presented until December 11, 1974, when Nathaniel H. Rogg, representing the National Association of Home Builders and its 77,000 members, appeared before Senator McIntyre's subcommittee just as consideration of the 1973 Financial Institutions Act came to a close. After correctly noting that changing the financial system simply because it does not work well during times of crisis would unfairly ignore its many positive accomplishments during normal periods, Rogg went on to explain that his association was "extremely concerned" about the recommendations in the proposed act.

On balance, as we now perceive S. 2591, it appears to us that the bill, if enacted into law in its current form and taken as a package, would be counterproductive to our national goal of providing a decent home for every American family. We, therefore, urge that further consideration be given to the bill's impact on the availability of funds for financing housing, not just its impact on the competitive position of thrift institutions in relation to commercial banks, before further action is taken.[7]

7. U.S., Congress, Senate, Committee on Banking, Housing, and Urban Affairs, *Housing and Financial Reform*, p. 5.

Table 9

HOLDINGS OF RESIDENTIAL MORTGAGE LOANS AND OF SECURITIES OF HOUSING-RELATED FEDERAL AND FEDERALLY SPONSORED AGENCIES BY MAJOR DEPOSITORY INSTITUTIONS, DECEMBER 31, 1973
(In Millions of Dollars)

	Commercial Banks	Savings Institutions		
		Total	Savings Banks	Savings and Loans
1. Residential mortgage loans	$ 74,188	$271,725	$60,641	$211,084
2. Securities of federal and federally sponsored agencies	10,568	4,491	1,724	2,767
FHA debentures	35	49	33	16
GNMA participation certificates	411	241	177	64
Federal Home Loan Bank securities	4,185	1,672	536	1,136
FNMA securities	5,937	2,529	978	1,551
3. Total (1 plus 2)	84,756	276,216	62,365	213,851
4. Household time and savings deposits	287,800	323,750	96,496	227,251
Percent of Household Time and Savings Deposits				
1. Residential mortgage loans	25.8	83.9	62.8	92.9
2. Securities of federal and federally sponsored agencies	3.7	1.4	1.8	1.2
3. Total (1 plus 2)	29.5	85.3	64.6	94.1
4. Household time and savings deposits	100.0	100.0	100.0	100.0

Source: National Association of Mutual Savings Banks; Federal Reserve System, Board of Governors; Federal Home Loan Bank Board; U.S. Department of the Treasury.

Note: Data for the securities of federal and federally sponsored agencies shown in the Table are taken from the Treasury Survey of Ownership of Federal Securities published monthly in the *Treasury Bulletin.* These data seriously understate the amount of such securities held by savings and loan associations, since the associations covered in the survey account for only about 50 percent of all such securities held by savings and loan associations. By contrast, the Treasury survey coverage includes virtually all mutual savings banks, while the commercial banks included in the survey account for about 90 percent of all such securities held by commercial banks. The table does not show GNMA mortgage-backed securities, since it was not possible to obtain an ownership breakdown. At the end of 1973, mutual savings banks held $1.9 billion of these securities.

The association's statement vigorously questioned the benefits for housing that proponents claimed would result from the "major overhaul" of the system and indicated that serious injury to the housing industry was more likely. Spokesmen were particularly concerned about the planned elimination of regulation Q controls, which they considered necessary to give "thrift institutions a fighting chance to attract savings in competition with commercial banks" and to assure that the long-term mortgage borrower has a chance to compete with short-term borrowers during periods of escalating inflation. They joined with the thrift institutions in arguing for the restoration of the "traditional" one-half of 1 percent differential on savings deposits.

The new mortgage investment tax credit was similarly criticized because the cutoff point of 70 percent would be well below the existing portfolio shares already committed to mortgage loans, and thrift institutions might therefore divert funds away from housing. The results of the econometric model, indicating increased housing credit after adoption of the proposed tax credit, were rejected because of the usual problems about the correctness of the assumptions used in developing the quantitative simulations.

Finally, the Rogg statement expressed strong opposition to the timing and procedures used in evaluating the proposed law and claimed that the subcommittee had made no detailed assessment of the impact of the recommendations on housing. Some resentment was apparent in the association's statement about the legislative process followed by the subcommittee: "Yet, the proposal is proceeding to the brink of full committee consideration without, as far as we are aware, the kind of analysis and attention afforded to housing that has been given to financial institutions."[8] That irritation could hardly have been caused by the pace of decision making, since the structural recommendations affecting the four financial intermediaries had begun with the announcement of a presidential commission in January 1970 and the subcommittee's report was submitted in December 1974, after fourteen months of Senate subcommittee hearings. The sharp reaction must have been the result of the subcommittee's not following the rules of the game expected by the association; that is, they had been dealing with controversial legislation when a session of Congress was about to end.

In general, the opponents of the proposed law concentrated their criticism on the possibly disruptive impact the changes might have on the housing industry and made this the basis for rejecting the

8. Ibid., p. 2.

recommendations. Their arguments can be summarized under four general classifications:[9] first, that the supply of mortgage credit determines the number of new homes built; second, that private financial markets are unwilling or unable to provide an adequate supply of mortgage credit; third, that government intervention in the financial markets successfully reallocates credit to the mortgage markets; and fourth, that controls on interest rates, like regulation Q, protect the thrift institutions and increase the supply of mortgage credit.

Advocates of the proposed legislation attempted to refute these claims by arguing that the pace of housing construction is also directly influenced by demand factors related to demographic variables, current interest rates, the stability of the flow of funds into housing, and general economic conditions; that the private markets have historically supplied adequate mortgage financing; that government intervention may simply shift the sources of mortgage credit from private institutions to public agencies without increasing the total amount available, since the sale of government securities to fund the public programs may simply be draining from the private markets money that might otherwise be committed to mortgage financing directly by private financial intermediaries; and that regulation Q controls actually distort the mortgage markets by preventing competitive responses to changing interest rates. Both sides presented a series of actual examples to support their rival positions, but more heat than light was created by the long series of claims and counterarguments.

Unfortunately, empirical evidence on such issues is very difficult to develop. Controlled econometric studies to simulate market conditions can be used to arrive at crude estimates of the results of alternative policies; but such studies are always suspect because they generally rely on past information and traditional assumptions that may be questionable, and the results are subject to a wide margin of error. In short, the extrapolation of past experience into the future, no matter how sophisticated the mathematical techniques are, is always vulnerable to criticisms that conditions have changed. The uncertainty of economic forecasts makes it impossible to rely on them for firm evidence in attempting to resolve disputes on such public policy issues as the impact that reform of financial institutions might have on the housing sector.

The econometric studies prepared to simulate the effect that the

9. Senate, Committee on Banking, Housing, and Urban Affairs, *Reform of Financial Institutions: 1973*, p. 4.

reforms recommended by the Hunt Commission and embodied in the Financial Institutions Act of 1973 would have on housing construction and mortgage credit flows indicated that a positive benefit would occur. The first major study was conducted by Professors Roy C. Fair and Dwight M. Jaffee of Princeton University using a large-scale model (the Federal Reserve–MIT–University of Pennsylvania econometric model of the U.S. economy) to simulate the results of adopting the Hunt Commission's recommendations. According to their findings, mortgages held by thrift institutions might decline slightly, but housing credit from other sources would increase, so that the "net effect of extended investment powers was found to be small, either positive or negative depending on the assumptions used."[10] In a subsequent publication, following additional econometric simulations, Professor Jaffee concluded:

> These results are quite clear in indicating that the Hunt Commission proposals will aid, rather than hurt, the housing and mortgage markets, once all the ramifications of the proposals are taken into account. . . . The broad implication of the results discussed in this section is clearly that the mortgage and housing markets will on net gain under the Hunt Commission proposals.[11]

In his testimony before the Senate subcommittee, Professor Jaffee argued that any reduction in mortgage holdings by savings and loan associations as a result of diversifying their portfolio assets would be offset by the increase in funds available to mortgage borrowers because of the improved earnings and increased deposits made possible by the new powers.[12]

In a second econometric study, prepared by the Federal Home Loan Bank Board and covering the five-year period from 1967 through 1971, it was estimated that new housing starts and investments in residential structures would have been increased by allowing savings and loan associations to offer checking accounts and consumer loans. The conclusion of this study stated:

> Reference was made earlier to a similar simulation study by Fair and Jaffee. The results presented here are consistent with those presented in the earlier analysis. However, as explained in the technical appendix to

10. Senate, Committee on Banking, Housing, and Urban Affairs, *Financial Structure and Regulation*, p. 96.
11. Dwight M. Jaffee, "The Extended Lending, Borrowing, and Service Function Proposals of the Hunt Commission Report," pp. 990–1000.
12. Senate, Committee on Banking, Housing, and Urban Affairs, *Financial Structure and Regulation*, p. 31.

this study, the results of the two studies are not directly comparable because different models, time periods, and assumptions were employed. Nevertheless, when expanded S&L powers were simulated, the results of both sets of simulations showed a positive impact on residential construction.

Econometric simulations are only as accurate as the assumptions used to generate them, and the results of such simulations should be taken as suggestive rather than specific. Given this caveat, the results presented in this chapter show that the probable impact on housing of a restructured S&L industry is positive. This is due to the fact that restructured S&L's will be in a much better position to compete for the consumer savings dollar, and as a result will have a larger and more stable supply of funds to invest in the residential mortgage market.[13]

How a broadening of consumer services and investment powers for thrift institutions might affect the long-term flow of housing credit has also been analyzed in at least four other major studies. Summaries of these reports, prepared by three widely respected academic experts and the Commissioner of the New York State Banking Department, all indicate a positive result from diversifying the asset and liability powers. In the New York State study it was noted:

> The offering of checking accounts and personal loans by MSBs will not have a significant effect on the supply of funds to mortgage markets. The establishment of MSBs [mutual savings banks] as full service household banks will increase their ability vis-a-vis CBs [commercial banks] and other investment alternatives to attract savings, partly because of the greater convenience of their full service offerings and partly because of the improvement in the level and stability of their earnings. These increased total flows will add to the mortgage flows.[14]

The Wharton School's comprehensive study of the savings and loan industry, directed by Professor Irwin Friend, concluded:

> . . . a judicious combination of changes both in the lending (assets) and borrowing (liabilities) power of the industry could effect a significant improvement in the industry's overall economic performance without risking a severe adverse impact on the housing market. These changes include additional flexibility in the areas of consumer credit, mortgages on

13. *A Financial Institution For the Future Savings, Housing Finance & Consumer Services, An Examination of the Restructuring of the Savings and Loan Industry*, prepared by the Office of Economic Research of the Federal Home Loan Bank Board, Washington, D.C., in Senate, Committee on Banking, Housing, and Urban Affairs, *Housing and Financial Reform*, p. 48.

14. Leonard Lapidus et al., *Public Policy Toward Mutual Savings Banks in New York State: Proposals for Change* (New York: Federal Reserve Bank of New York and New York State Banking Department, 1974), chapter 1.

multifamily residences (including limited use of equity participations), longer term savings accounts, capital notes or debentures, and checking accounts.[15]

Professor Leo Grebler's benchmark study of thrift institutions made the following recommendation:

> On the whole, then, it seems highly improbable that authority for thrift institutions to invest a moderate proportion of assets in consumer loans would divert any significant amount of funds from the housing sector. On the other hand, failure to grant the institutions this kind of lending flexibility may inhibit their growth sufficiently to diminish their vital role in the mortgage and housing markets.[16]

Professor George J. Benston arrived at a similar position in his study of mutual savings banks.

> . . .assuming that it is in the public interest to assure a stable flow of funds at relatively low cost to the housing industry, there is reason to believe that MSBs making consumer installment loans will benefit rather than harm the mortgage market.[17]

These academic studies, using sophisticated econometric methods to simulate the behavior of the financial markets under different policy assumptions, were hailed by the advocates of the proposed law as additional evidence of the positive benefits to be expected from financial institution reform. But critics summarily rejected the conclusions as being too theoretical and not an appropriate basis for changing policies in the real world. In other words, academic studies are accepted or rejected depending on whether or not they match predetermined preferences. In this case Congress was left with the difficult problem of evaluating such technical studies in attempting to decide the complex policy issues.

Summary of Progress for the Financial Institutions Act of 1973

The broad package of financial institution reforms submitted to Congress represented the most comprehensive approach to structural change since the proliferation of banking legislation during the 1930s. The legislative plan began during a period of improving economic conditions and escalating dissatisfaction with existing statutes

15. Irwin Friend, "Summary and Recommendations," p. 54.
16. Leo Grebler, *The Future of Thrift Institutions: A Study of Diversification Versus Specialization*, p. 72.
17. George J. Benston, "Savings Banking and the Public Interest," p. 182.

and regulations, and it attempted to sustain the momentum created by the President's Commission on Financial Structure and Regulation. In the beginning, hopes were high that the recommendations would contribute to a stronger and more flexible financial system, giving management greater control in deciding how best to respond to changing economic conditions, and thus providing more services to consumers, a more stable flow of funds to residential housing markets, and equitable returns to all savings deposits. The basic strategy was to provide enough incentives to forge a workable compromise despite the acknowledged loss of special competitive advantages for each group.

Role of the Treasury

Treasury officials continued to provide leadership for the administration's legislative effort throughout the Senate hearings. Their arguments focused on the need "to create an efficient financial system" by emphasizing competition, flexibility, and managerial choice in determining policies regarding asset portfolios and consumer services. While real estate finance was not the dominant variable in their legislative planning they were obviously sensitive to the unusual social and economic importance of housing and its use in political maneuvering. They did make a special effort to argue that the proposed act would improve the amount and stability of mortgage credit. Their recommendations, however, assumed adjustments to housing needs by the marketplace, rather than continued emphasis on more government involvement. Given the basic orientation of Congress, this is a difficult position to argue—as subsequent legislative events demonstrated. Finally, the Treasury representatives recognized the controversial nature and complexity of financial institution reform when they called for a supportive consensus among financial intermediaries, consumers, and housing interests to gain congressional approval.

Instead of the broad consensus hoped for by Treasury officials, the proposed reforms encountered strong criticism from the Independent Bankers Association of America and the major trade organizations representing savings and loan associations, credit unions, and housing interests. The American Bankers Association did give a qualified endorsement, and consumer groups and mutual savings bank representatives strongly supported specific sections; but the general reaction of interest groups was more negative than positive, and this attitude effectively eliminated the pressures and incentives for Congress to respond quickly or affirmatively. Because all of the pending legislation would be automatically terminated at the end of the ninety-third Congress in December 1974, each interest group realized that it could simply wait out the congressional calendar and that they need not agree to compromise during the first set of hearings. In fact, the National Association of Home Builders did not even submit a formal statement to the Senate subcommittee hearings on the proposed bill until December 11, 1974; and organized labor groups were not aggressively active because it was widely recognized that the Senate would not have time to act and that the House of Representatives had not even started formal hearings.

Despite the inconclusive fate of the Financial Institutions Act of 1973, the Senate subcommittee hearings were definitely not the "exercise in wasted motion" that Senator McIntyre had warned against. They did provide a forum to collect and analyze the various views of the administration, of regulatory agencies, and of the private interest groups that would be affected. Although the polarity of much of the material presented and the unalterable positions taken by each interest group give the impression that the hearings were often only a "dialogue among the deaf," this review procedure is evidently a necessary phase in which issues and background information must be set forth before congressional committees are willing to consider legislative decisions. Fortunately the various interest groups prepared their public statements carefully, and the vast amount of material they collected was a valuable resource when the Treasury and Congress prepared for the next legislative step.

Economic and political events

During the planning stage leading up to the formal submission of the Financial Institutions Act of 1973 the U.S. economy experienced rapid real growth; inflation moderated, housing construction boomed, and interest rates declined to the lowest levels reported in several years. Unfortunately the economic situation had changed dramatically by the time actual recommendations were sent to Congress in October 1973, and it continued to deteriorate throughout the next eighteen months until economic recovery started in March 1975.

The pace of real output gains reached a peak level in early 1973 when the gross national product (GNP), expressed in constant dollars to remove the distorting effects of inflation, increased at a seasonally adjusted annual rate of 9.5 percent during the first quarter. By mid-1973 the economy was already slowing down. Then came the OPEC embargo on shipments of oil to the United States begin-

Table 10

NEW HOUSING UNITS STARTED, 1963–76
(In Thousands of Units)

1963	1,603	1970	1,434
1964	1,529	1971	2,052
1965	1,473	1972	2,356
1966	1,165	1973	2,045
1967	1,292	1974	1,338
1968	1,508	1975	1,160
1969	1,467	1976	1,538

Source: Council of Economic Advisers, *Economic Report of the President* (Washington, D.C.: Government Printing Office, Jan. 1978), Table B-44, p. 308.

ning in October. This move had severe psychological effects as well as the more immediate one of causing the real GNP to decline at an adjusted annual rate of 3.9 percent during the last three months of the year. The national economy was temporarily stabilized during the first half of 1974, but economic disaster occurred in the late summer when consumer spending, business investment, and residential construction all faltered, causing the real GNP to decline at a seasonally adjusted annual rate of 4.0 percent during the last six months of 1974.

As the U.S. economy slumped after its overheating early in 1973, ushering in the worst recession of the postwar era, the enthusiasm of financial institutions for financial reform also slackened. The residential construction industry was one of the earliest casualties of the severe recession, and the extreme decline in housing starts so discouraged those involved in this basic industry that they opposed any change in the financial system which might further reduce mortgage credit. The pace of new housing starts is usually volatile, but the sharp decline during this period was particularly disruptive to the housing industry and mortgage-oriented financial institutions.

A dominant factor in the disappointing economic developments was the surge of inflation beginning in late 1972. After slowly declining from the 1969 peak of 6.1 percent to 3.4 percent in 1972, inflation, as measured by the consumer price index (CPI), seemed to explode, rising to double-digit rates by 1974 before receding to a 5 percent level in 1976 (from December 1975 through December 1976 the CPI increased 4.8 percent).

As inflation accelerated and monetary policies reacted to moderate the distorting effects of strong private demand and increasing gov-

Table 11

ANNUAL RATE OF INCREASE OF CONSUMER PRICE INDEX,
DECEMBER 1963–DECEMBER 1976 (In Percentages)

1963	1.6	1971	3.4
1964	1.2	1972	3.4
1965	1.9	1973	8.8
1966	3.4	1974	12.2
1967	3.0	1975	7.0
1968	4.7	1976	4.8
1969	6.1	1977	6.8
1970	5.5		

Source: Council of Economic Advisers, *Economic Report of the President* (Washington, D.C.: Government Printing Office, Jan. 1979), Table B-54, p. 244.

ernment spending, short-term interest rates rose rapidly, and a third round of financial market disintermediation occurred, topped off by the massive shift in the flow of funds from thrift institutions to commercial banks associated with the "wild card" certificates introduced in the summer of 1973.

The combination of severe economic recession, double-digit inflation, a decline in residential construction, rising interest rates, and

Table 12

SELECTED BOND YIELDS AND INTEREST RATES, 1969–76
(In Percentages per Annum)

	3-month Treasury Bills	Prime Commercial Paper	Federal Funds Rate	Corporate Bonds Moody's BAA	New Home Mortgage Yields FHLBB
1969	6.677	7.83	8.21	7.81	7.81
1970	6.458	7.72	7.17	9.11	8.45
1971	4.348	5.11	4.67	8.56	7.74
1972	4.071	4.69	4.44	8.16	7.60
1973	7.041	8.15	8.74	8.24	7.95
1974	7.886	9.87	10.51	9.50	8.92
1975	5.838	6.33	5.82	10.61	9.01
1976	4.989	5.35	5.05	9.75	8.99

Source: Council of Economic Advisers, *Economic Report of the President* (Washington, D.C.: Government Printing Office, Jan. 1977), Table B-63, p. 260.

financial market disintermediation created severe economic problems and caused a sharp drop in business confidence.

It would be impossible to describe a more disadvantageous economic environment for proposing reforms affecting financial institutions. The loss of enthusiasm for legislative change during such a chaotic period is readily understandable, even though the recommendations included in the new act were intended to alleviate the very problems being experienced. The combination of opposition by special interest groups and the severe economic recession and inflation meant that the Financial Institutions Act of 1973 started the legislative process with two strikes against it.

The third strike quickly became apparent as the political scandal known as Watergate brought Congress even closer to impeachment proceedings against the incumbent President, Richard Nixon, at exactly the same time that the Senate subcommittee was holding its hearings. Historians will find it difficult to describe the excruciating pressures on government officials and the internal confusion prevailing in that tragic period when Congress and the Executive Office were going through the unprecedented experience of watching the President of the United States struggle for survival and eventually resign his office on August 8, 1974.

Although the proposed legislation would probably not have been able to beat the congressional deadline even with the full support of a powerful President, the collapse of presidential leadership during that period clearly diverted attention and political support away from the administration's recommendations. Just when daily lobbying in Congress was most needed to push the bill along, the congressional liaison staff in the White House was busy tracking the progress of hearings that might lead to the President's impeachment. Similarly, the recommendations of the President's Commission on Financial Structure and Regulation lost much of their force when President Nixon's resignation left the administration's sponsors of the new legislation without the leverage of strong presidential leadership needed to push through such initiatives.

Vocal opposition from key interest groups, severe economic recession and related inflation, rising interest rates, plummeting housing starts, and increasing financial market disintermediation, combined with the unprecedented resignation of an incumbent President of the United States and the nationwide shock waves caused by that event made it impossible to gain affirmative action on the proposed Financial Institutions Act. In fact, the House Banking, Currency, and Housing Committee did not even initiate formal hearings, although Chairman Patman did continue to work on his special proposals, particularly his ideas for reforming the Federal Reserve System; and the committee's staff prepared an extensive background study of financial reform options.

In the Senate, the twelve days of formal hearings that had begun with submission of the administration's recommendations in October 1973 culminated in the action of Senator McIntyre's subcommittee to approve and report out the bill to the full Senate Banking, Housing, and Urban Affairs Committee on December 3, 1974. Eight days later the full committee considered the bill and decided not to submit it to the entire Senate for a formal vote. Thus the Financial Institutions Act of 1973 died at the conclusion of the ninety-third Congress without ever having been put to a vote in the Senate or the House of Representatives.

The record of this proposal is an interesting example of how legislative initiatives are born and how they fail. Despite the failure of the Senate and the House of Representatives to act affirmatively on the proposals the overall effort succeeded at least partially in collecting the information and the views of interest groups that Congress needed for consideration. When the effort ended the new President of the United States, Gerald R. Ford, was in office and beginning to develop his own legislative priorities, which included extensive regulatory reform. The national economy was about to begin a relatively strong recovery phase; inflation pressures were moderating, and Treasury officials were once more moving ahead with other Executive Office representatives to develop a revised financial institution reform proposal. This was soon to be submitted to Congress as the Financial Institutions Act of 1975.

8

THE FINANCIAL INSTITUTIONS ACT OF 1975

On March 19, 1975, President Gerald R. Ford submitted the revised Financial Institutions Act of 1975, a bill "to expand competition, provide improved consumer services, strengthen the ability of financial institutions to adjust to changing economic conditions, and to improve the flows of funds for mortgage credit."[1] In his message to Congress accompanying the administration's revised legislative recommendations, the President emphasized that the reform of financial institutions was a "key element" in his program to review all government regulations and to eliminate those that entailed greater costs to the American consumer than benefits.[2] His message went on to emphasize that at the peak of the financial crisis in the summer of 1974 home mortgages were virtually unavailable in many parts of the country, the returns paid to small savers continued to be restricted by arbitrary government rules, widespread disintermediation occurred in the financial markets, and new residential construction declined to a cyclically depressed level. The President also reviewed the appointment in 1970 of a presidential commission to study the recurring problems of financial institutions and referred to his previous endorsement of the Financial Institutions Act of 1973, which included a personal appeal to Congress to give it high priority. In summary, the President outlined the administration's position as follows:

> This bill contains certain notable changes from the legislation put before you in 1973. But the overall objectives remain the same—providing new opportunities for *savers* to earn a competitive return on their investment, and providing *homebuyers* with greater assurance that the flow of

1. U.S., Department of the Treasury, *Financial Institutions Act of 1975*, p. 1.
2. Ibid., p. 2.

funds for home mortgages will not be dramatically disrupted during periods of high interest rates. To achieve those objectives, the bill permits
institutions engaged in serving small depositors more flexibility both in
obtaining and investing funds. It will permit the payment of higher interest rates to small savers, and it will also offer a new tax incentive to most
financial institutions to make residential mortgage loans.[3]

The Senate subcommittee chaired by Senator McIntyre reconvened
in May to begin the final round of hearings required to evaluate the
administration's legislative proposals. Continuing his pattern of blunt
commentary intended to hasten the analysis in preparation for a Senate vote on the pending legislation and to make it more objective,
Senator McIntyre's opening remarks included an unusually stern
warning to his congressional colleagues and everyone else involved
in the prolonged legislative proceedings.

> This morning the Subcommittee on Financial Institutions is beginning
> what I expect will be the final, formal legislative inquiry into the Financial
> Institutions Act. We either get it going here now or we're going to forget
> it.
> The batting practice of the 93d Congress is over. The time has now
> come for the actual contest to begin.
> I reread last night with interest a number of points which I made in my
> opening statement back on November 6, 1973, when the subcommittee
> first began its deliberations on the original Financial Institutions Act. At
> the time, I made it clear that the hearings on the FIA would not be an
> exercise in wasted motion, that structural change and reform at the legis-
> lative level was necessary and would take place. That point bears empha-
> sis today.[4]

Senator McIntyre then briefly summarized four basic points that
he hoped would direct the subcommittee to a positive conclusion.[5]
Although these guidelines proved no more effective than earlier
attempts to forge a necessary consensus of opinion, they are well
worth reviewing as an example of the frustrations felt by at least one
responsible senator over the organization, jurisdiction, pace, and
decisiveness of congressional hearings.

First, he reminded the participants that the focus of his subcommittee was financial institutions rather than housing, which generally receives adequate congressional support elsewhere. Moreover,
he said, "the proper course for good government in the housing

---

3. Ibid.
4. U.S., Congress, Senate, Committee on Banking, Housing, and Urban Affairs,
   Financial Institutions Act of 1975, May 14–16 and June 11, 1975, p. 1.
5. Ibid., p. 2.

area demands that housing problems be treated directly and not through the ad hoc, special-interest, piecemealing approach of legislation pertaining to financial institutions."

Second, as to legislation affecting financial institutions, he noted that Congress has demonstrated a "never-ending inclination to ad hoc, piecemealing approaches, when the only way we can do it is through a comprehensive approach" to the various problems that disrupt the financial markets.

Third, he repeated his criticism of regulation Q rate controls as being not only "anticompetitive" but "an artificial crutch to the thrift institutions," which no longer provide real support because of the increasing sophistication of consumers and the continual innovations in the capital markets.

Fourth, he expressed his firm conviction that the legislation to be considered represented "an essential first step in the educational process to bring our financial institutions into the twentieth century of electronic fund transfers."

Considering the powerful special interest groups involved, these forthright opening comments by Senator McIntyre were courageous, but they did not significantly alter the attitudes of the administration or the various financial institutions. In fact the basic goals of credit unions were included in S. 1475 (a bill to amend the Federal Credit Union Act), and the savings and loan associations were mainly interested in S. 1540 (a bill to provide for family financial centers as proposed by the National Savings and Loan League). Both of these specialized legislative proposals were assigned to Senator McIntyre's subcommittee to be considered during the hearings for S. 1267 (the Financial Institutions Act of 1975).

The decisions of the politically powerful savings and loan associations and credit unions that they would work unilaterally through their trade organizations for passage of their own legislative initiatives, as described in Chapter 7, clearly demonstrate their preference for working directly with Congress to avoid the compromises required by comprehensive reform proposals. Their efforts to gain specific liberalization of existing regulatory guidelines and additional powers for their own members in the matter of lending, investment, and deposit accounts may also have reflected a fundamental skepticism about the prospects for the Financial Institutions Act of 1975, particularly in the House of Representatives. Additional political pressures were created by the vigorous opposition of small commercial banks and the intense criticism from the National Association of Home Builders and from the AFL-CIO, representing organized labor unions.

Against this impressive group of opposing organizations the administration could count on strong support only from mutual savings banks and the tentative endorsement of the American Bankers Association. Many academic experts also favored the recommendations in the Financial Institutions Act of 1975, on the basis of their participation in the Commission on Money and Credit and the President's Commission on Financial Structure and Regulation, but professors usually concentrate on their academic interests and have little political power. Finally, some consumer groups continued to support individual sections of the revised legislation, but their somewhat fragmented backing could not begin to match the cohesive pressures emanating from the housing interests and organized labor. In short, the resumption of Senate hearings on the Financial Institutions Act of 1975 began in an improved economic and political environment, but the overwhelming consensus among key special interest groups indicated resistance to the administration's comprehensive plan and a clear preference for directly working out their own legislative goals.

Administration Arguments Favoring
the Financial Institutions Act of 1975

The proposed legislation was submitted by the administration, but there was considerable variation among different agencies concerning specific recommendations.

Views of the Treasury

Despite the expiration of the Financial Institutions Act of 1973 at the end of the ninety-third Congress, Treasury officials expressed optimism that a revised bill could be made acceptable to the hitherto critical financial institutions and that the objections of housing interests could be moderated.[6] While readily admitting that the existing reform proposal was not the ultimate solution, they argued that "it is a clear first step in the right direction and should receive continued strong Administration support."[7] At the same time they recognized that the legislation remained controversial and arranged meetings with many special interest groups to seek broadened support. Attention was also given to other public relations efforts, by

6. Treasury Department staff memorandum, Dec. 18, 1974.
7. Treasury Department staff memorandum, Jan. 18, 1975.

emphasizing the goals of "improved consumer services" and the "flows of funds for mortgage credit." Once again the Treasury staff prepared a special report on the potential impact of administration recommendations on housing and added a separate section to the public brochure published by the Treasury Department to describe the five major benefits provided to consumers by the new legislation: (1) expanded and more convenient services at lower costs to consumers; (2) new nationwide access to NOW accounts; (3) more equitable treatment for small savers by eventually eliminating regulation Q controls; (4) more dependable sources of mortgage credit with less financial market disintermediation; and (5) elimination of the confusing "points" charged by lenders on FHA and VA mortgage loans to adjust the controlled interest rates as market conditions change.[8]

The opening statement for the administration was presented by Stephen S. Gardner, the new Deputy Secretary of the Treasury.[9] His basic theme was:

> Nothing has happened since the original drafting of similar legislation in 1973 that invalidates the concept and purpose of the legislation. On the contrary, the need for granting expanded powers has been demonstrated by our problems with inflation and disintermediation.[10]

In fact, Treasury officials had decided to follow the legislative strategy of reintroducing the same recommendations with only minor modifications to clarify the language of the lending and investment guidelines, along with specific adjustments in section 1 (deposit interest rate controls) and section 5 (credit unions) to neutralize earlier objections to the Financial Institutions Act of 1973. Major changes in the new bill were these:[11]

> *Section 1:* The proposal continued to recommend elimination of deposit interest rate controls within five and one-half years of final enactment of the bill; but six months before the termination date the Secretary of the Treasury, after consulting with the coordinating committee of regulatory agencies, would be required to submit a comprehensive report to Congress on the economic and financial consequences of such action. During the interim period the coordinating committee would continue to determine deposit interest rate ceilings and differentials. No reference was

8. U.S., Department of the Treasury, *Financial Institutions Act of 1975,* pp. 9–10.

9. Ibid., pp. 3–32. A special report on financial reform and housing was attached to the Treasury statement.

10. Ibid., p. 3.

11. For a detailed description of the FIA 1973 recommendations see Chapter 5.

made to phasing out the existing differential during the transition, but it was noted that the need for government intervention should decline as financial institutions gained the additional powers granted by the other sections.

Section 5: The 1975 legislation provided for a substantial expansion of credit union powers, including: (1) extension of first-lien home mortgage loans to members, with maturities up to 30 years; (2) 15-year loans for mobile homes and home improvements; (3) increased limits on amounts and maturities of secured and unsecured personal loans; (4) limited checking account powers for members; (5) more flexible interest rates on loans to members as permitted by the National Credit Union Administration; (6) use of share certificates with varying dividend rates and maturities; and (7) creation of a central discount fund to provide emergency liquidity assistance.

Section 7: The proposed legislation preserved the mortgage interest tax credit for all individual and corporate investors having at least 10 percent of their assets in residential mortgages, the amount of relief to be determined by a sliding scale according to the total percentage of mortgages held. For savings and loan associations and mutual savings banks, the new tax credit would replace their special treatment in calculating the bad debt reserve. However, thrift institutions were to be given the option of using either the new tax credit or their existing bad debt reserve procedure until 1979, when the tax credit would become mandatory.

Views of other government agencies

Major testimony supporting the Financial Institutions Act of 1975 was also presented by Thomas R. Bomar, chairman of the Federal Home Loan Bank Board.[12] As part of his statement, Chairman Bomar reviewed the results of the Board's extensive study of the future of savings and loan associations: the findings strongly supported the recommendations contained in the proposed legislation, particularly the emphasis on additional powers to make consumer loans and to provide third-party transfer payments to customers. According to Chairman Bomar, the study indicated that extending the asset and liability powers would actually help satisfy the need for mortgage credit by strengthening the thrift institutions in the competitive markets. Support for the passage of the Financial Institutions Act of 1975 was also submitted during the hearings in a letter written for the record by Chairman Arthur F. Burns of the Federal Reserve Board of Governors:

As indicated in that testimony, the Board believes that changes in our financial system should be designed to increase competition and improve

12. U.S., Congress, Senate, Committee on Banking, Housing, and Urban Affairs, *Financial Institutions Act of 1975,* pp. 43–108.

the flexibility of financial institutions to respond to changing needs of individuals and businesses while maintaining a base for effective monetary policy and preserving a sound and resilient financial system. The Board believes that enactment of S. 1267 would further these objectives, and urges favorable consideration of the bill by Congress.[13]

Similar letters were received from Chairman Frank Wille of the Federal Deposit Insurance Corporation, who said, "We continue to support congressional enactment of the substance of the Administration's Financial Institutions Act,"[14] and from the Comptroller of the Currency James E. Smith: "I endorsed the original F[inancial] I[nstitutions] A[ct], which was carefully conceived and meticulously constructed, and I urge with equal conviction the passage of the revised bill."[15]

In summary, the administration continued to emphasize its original arguments about the value of more efficient and competitive financial markets, but placed additional stress upon the expected benefits to consumers, including mortgage borrowers. The various regulatory agencies responsible for monitoring the operations of financial intermediaries similarly endorsed the substance of the proposed bill, offering suggestions about the details and timing of certain sections. The only major changes proposed by these agencies were the concession to prepare a comprehensive report on the potential economic and financial impact of removing regulation Q controls six months before the end of the transition period, the extensive broadening of provisions affecting credit unions, and the decision to make the mortgage investment tax credit optional for thrift institutions until 1979. Treasury officials hoped that this modified package would be passed by the Senate, and that a favorable vote might then encourage the House of Representatives to give formal consideration to financial institution reform.

Responses of Financial Institutions and Other Interest Groups

The extensive presentations of special interest groups at the Senate subcommittee hearings on the 1973 proposals were summarized in Chapter 6. Most of these groups merely repeated their previous arguments in evaluating the Financial Institutions Act of 1975. The following sections will note the position of each group as the Senate approached its decision on the 1975 legislation.

13. Ibid., p. 452.
14. Ibid., p. 450.
15. Ibid., p. 452.

Commercial banks

The American Bankers Association renewed its support for comprehensive financial reform as the "most promising means of managing the changes we inevitably face in our financial operations," despite serious reservations about the proliferation of NOW accounts and any premature removal of regulation Q controls. The association pledged to work with Congress to provide broadened powers to banks and nonbank thrift institutions, coupled with uniformity in imposing deposit interest rate ceilings, taxes, reserve requirements, and supervisory patterns.[16] The association also argued that the overall recommendations, particularly the new mortgage interest tax credit, would increase mortgage credit and extend needed services.

The Independent Bankers Association of America reaffirmed their members' "basic objections to the Financial Institutions Act of 1973 and its successor" in a letter to Senator McIntyre.[17] This letter also emphasized that they were shifting their support away from the Senate bill proposed by the administration and favoring instead a study advanced by the House Banking, Currency, and Housing Committee. This legislative strategy ultimately proved effective in bottling up comprehensive financial reform in the ninety-fourth Congress. An even stronger rejection was submitted by the Bankers Committee for Tax Equality, representing 3,000 commercial banks in small cities and rural areas. In an unusually candid statement which possibly revealed the real complaints and fears of members more clearly than the relatively guarded comments of other interest groups, they strongly criticized the encroachment of thrift institutions into traditional commercial banking activities and the disruptive impact of government economic and housing finance policies.

> We hold that any maladjustments in our financial system and failure to fulfill its obligations are not occasioned by an outmoded banking and thrift system but by uncontrollable inflation and an invasion of the financing field by government and governmental credit agencies such as the Federal Home Loan Mortgage Corporation, the Federal National Mortgage Association, the various agencies of the Farm Credit Administration, the Government National Mortgage Association and other government agencies [that were] created to assist our financial institutions but in so doing compete for the savings dollar. It is quite apparent that banks and

16. Ibid., p. 265. Statement of American Bankers Association, presented by Rex J. Morthland.

17. Ibid., p. 804. Letter from the Independent Bankers Association of America, written by Kenneth J. Benda.

thrift institutions have become more and more dependent on these institutions that have billions of dollars of debt.

Our banker friends have been aware for a number of years of the various proposals of thrift institutions to secure more and more functions that have been reserved for banks. They have been alarmed at some of these, such as checking account privileges, wider loan and investment powers, right to convert to banks, etc., and have opposed them from the start. They feel that we have a sufficient number of commercial banks to satisfy commercial needs and that the thrift institutions can do a better job concentrating on home financing and other specific consumer credit. To permit them to take on banking functions would severely handicap the housing industry and possibly call for more government assistance and financing in this area.

Since the late 1940's the federal government has followed international and domestic policies that have led to a series of large deficits which inevitably bring inflation. As a result of these undisciplined monetary and fiscal policies, the government and government agencies have had to pay ever increasing rates of interest to attract funds. This brought about the disintermediation which has disrupted the flow of funds into our financial establishments and thus into housing and commercial businesses.

The solution lies not in restructuring our financial institutions but in removing the conditions that led the government and its agencies to compete for national savings. Inflation must be stopped and some discipline instituted in our fiscal and monetary policies. Deficits must be eliminated and a sound monetary policy instituted.[18]

Mutual savings banks

The National Association of Mutual Savings Banks reaffirmed its support for comprehensive reform, with relatively minor amendments to the Financial Institutions Act of 1975, as the best way to "accomplish a long overdue modernization of the nation's thrift institutions and thereby provide significant benefits to consumer savers and home mortgage borrowers."[19] Sections 2, 3, and 4 were favorably cited as creating opportunities for mutual savings banks to develop into full service family finance centers. The association again denounced the recommendation that controls on deposit interest rates should eventually be removed, however, and strongly urged the restoration of "meaningful differentials" for mortgage-oriented thrift institutions to pre-July 1973 levels (at least one half of 1 percent). Opposition to allowing mutual thrift institutions to convert into stock organizations was once again emphasized, and the asso-

18. Ibid., pp. 774–75. Statement of Arthur T. Roth for the Bankers Committee for Tax Equality.
19. Ibid., p. 553. Statement of Morris D. Crawford, Jr., for the National Association of Mutual Savings Banks.

ciation recommended that thrift institutions be granted permanent authority to use either the proposed mortgage interest tax credit or the existing deduction of reserves for bad debts.

Finally, on the controversial subject of the potential impact of comprehensive reform on the housing industry, the National Association of Mutual Savings Banks presented an extensive argument, supported by a complete bibliography of published studies, that such diversification of asset and liability powers would actually benefit the housing industry by increasing mortgage credit and creating more stability. Their statement also included a tough indictment of the federal government's economic policies, citing them as the principal cause of distortions in the financial market and the housing sector.

> The major culprits for this situation are easy to identify: inflation, and excessive reliance on monetary policy and skyrocketing interest rates to fight inflation in the absence of adequate federal fiscal restraint. It is clear that feast and famine conditions in the mortgage market will continue so long as economic and financial conditions remain highly unstable, inflation remains a recurrent long-run problem, and major reliance is placed on "stop and go" monetary policies.
>
> The single most important means of ending the roller coaster pattern of deposit flows at savings institutions, and accompanying feast and famine conditions in mortgage and housing markets, therefore, will be the implementation of better-balanced federal policies to control inflation and restore more stable economic and financial conditions. Increased fiscal discipline at the federal level after the economy has recovered from the present recession—through spending hold-downs and tax increases, when necessary—will be essential if inflation is to be brought under control and wide swings in open-market interest rates are to be avoided in future years.[20]

Savings and loan associations

The same objections that the two major savings and loan associations raised against the 1973 proposal were repeated during the hearings on the Financial Institutions Act of 1975. Continuing their opposition to several sections of the administration's proposal, the U.S. League of Savings Associations submitted a revision of section 5(c) of the Home Owner's Loan Act dealing with investment and lending powers; and the National Savings and Loan League prepared alternative legislation, known as S. 1540, the Family Financial Centers Act of 1975.

The U.S. League continued to emphasize as its first priority the

20. Ibid., p. 557–58.

extension of rate control authority beyond December 31, 1975, and statutory restoration of meaningful differentials favoring thrift institutions. How strongly they opposed the administration's recommendation to eliminate controls is evident in their statement:

> Thus, you can see the overriding importance of Title I of S. 1267 to our institutions. Rate control is not perfect, but for the most part it has spared the country the added disruption of savings rate wars between financial institutions. The exception, of course, was the "wild card" period in the summer of 1973, when commercial banks siphoned away $6 billion in consumer deposits from thrift institutions (Exhibit D)—thus triggering the housing market collapse which still plagues our economy today. Rate control does disadvantage our institutions in times of high short term rate competition; but the temporary disintermediation from Government securities, money market funds, and Citicorp-type schemes cannot compare with the potential disruption and concentration of financial resources in the hands of the large commercial banks which would occur if savings rate ceilings were lifted.[21]

The U.S. League intensified the debate by calling on Congress to extend the rate controls to institutions not covered by federal deposit insurance and to credit unions. The growing practice of automatically switching funds by telephone from savings deposits receiving interest income to demand deposits was also criticized as a clever evasion of the prohibition against paying interest on demand deposits.

In reviewing the other sections of the Financial Institutions Act of 1975, the U.S. League continued to urge the elimination of provisions under which commercial banks may offer savings accounts to corporations, existing thrift institutions may convert into stock organizations, and credit unions may enter long-term mortgage lending markets and expand deposit account services. This group also opposed the granting of additional tax relief to commercial bankers through the proposed mortgage interest tax credit. At the same time, their suggested revision of existing laws would have significantly increased the asset and liability powers of savings and loan associations.

Their continuing battle with commercial banks and their growing concern about the encroachment of credit unions were apparent throughout the policy statement they submitted to the Senate hearings. For example, the U.S. League opened up a particularly sensitive issue when they objected "strongly" to the expanded powers

---

21. Ibid., p. 168. Statement by Tom Scott, Jr., for the U.S. League of Savings Associations.

proposed for credit unions in the new legislation. In turn, the statements submitted by the credit unions to Senator McIntyre represented a thinly disguised rebuttal of this sweeping criticism. Since the credit union legislation was passed in April 1977, credit unions appeared to win the debate, at least temporarily. The struggle to win competitive advantages through legislation and regulatory rulings is a never ending battle, however, and competition among private financial intermediaries remains unusually intense.

> Another problem is the proposed diminution of the "common bond" principle which, since passage of the Credit Union Act after the Great Depression, has distinguished credit unions from other lenders. For example, the alterations proposed by the new legislation would make it possible to form a credit union for almost any group and on almost any basis. If the "little man's bank" is to undergo a virtual metamorphosis so as to compete directly with other lending institutions, then the metamorphosis should be altogether complete and credit unions should be required to pay Federal taxes on the same basis as those institutions with which they are to compete as well as be made to observe similar statutory and regulatory constraints.[22]

The National Savings and Loan League also presented a very strong statement advocating a continuance of the mortgage-oriented specialization functions of savings and loan associations by requiring that they must go on committing 70 percent of their assets to housing or related investments. Under the provisions recommended in its Family Financial Centers Act, the league supported expanded consumer services and diversified lending powers, but strongly criticized the Hunt Commission and Treasury officials for allegedly threatening their unique housing finance specialization. In taking the offensive against the Financial Institutions Act of 1975, the league sharply criticized the administration's recommendations and demanded that two basic points be recognized. First, savings and loan associations do not receive special tax advantages, and allegations of such advantages should not enter into considerations of the competitive powers to be legislated for each financial intermediary. To support its position the league cited a study of taxes paid by commercial banks and savings associations.[23] The author, Professor Kenneth R. Biederman of Georgetown University, concluded:

22. Ibid., p. 183. Statement of the U.S. League of Savings Associations.
23. Kenneth R. Biederman, *Federal Income Taxation of the Savings and Loan and Commercial Banking Industries*, prepared for the National League of Insured Savings Associations, May 1973. Published in full in U.S., Congress, Senate, Committee on Banking, Housing, and Urban Affairs, *Financial Institutions Act, 1973*, pp. 454–606.

. . .savings and loan associations pay substantially a higher effective tax rate than do commercial banks.

The study shows that on average the savings and loan industry is paying an effective tax rate of approximately 22 to 24 percent as compared with an effective tax rate of 15 to 16 percent for the commercial banking industry.

Further, the study indicates that because of the built-in increase in the effective tax rate that was in the 1969 tax reform bill, by 1979 the savings and loan industry will likely be paying an effective tax rate nearly double that paid by the commercial banking industry.

Our point is a simple one. If it was a valid argument to prohibit the savings and loan industry from having greater authority, greater power to serve the consumer because of the tax inequality, then that battle, it would seem to us, has been fought and there should be no argument over whether the industry should have the broader powers which are provided for in the Family Financial Centers Act and which the administration is proposing in the FIA.[24]

The second point urged by the National Savings and Loan League was that regulation Q controls should be extended indefinitely, with a restoration of a one-half of 1 percent differential. Congressional failure to so act would be a signal "that housing no longer is a priority for the nation" and would indicate "to prospective homeowners that they will have to pay whatever the traffic will bear in interest on their homes."[25]

The unusually aggressive attacks from both of the savings and loan trade associations on sections 1 (rate controls), 5 (credit union powers), and 7 (taxes) hint at a decision that the best defense is a good offense. Following the rather general debate on the 1973 recommendations, which were never really intended to be voted on by Congress, the sharpness of the testimonies by all of the participants in the second round of hearings in 1975 is a fascinating example of the intense competition among financial intermediaries and the extreme emotions aroused by many of these issues. The reason why they have occasioned such acrimonious debate over the years is clear. Although claims and rebuttals are usually expressed in the abstract language of economics, the daily competition in the marketplace for the flows of savings and investments is a very real issue because it ultimately determines the success or failure of each institution.

24. U.S., Congress, Senate, Committee on Banking, Housing, and Urban Affairs, *Financial Institutions Act of 1975*, p. 187. Statement of Edwin G. Alexander, President, National Savings and Loan League.

25. Ibid., p. 197.

Credit unions

Credit unions received unusual attention during the second round of Senate hearings. One of the four days of testimony was devoted exclusively to statements from the Administrator of the National Credit Union Administration and representatives of the Credit Union National Association and National Association of Federal Credit Unions.[26] Despite their critical evaluation of the 1973 proposals, largely because credit unions were excluded from the broadened asset and liability powers granted to other financial intermediaries, credit union spokesmen were generally satisfied with the expanded scope of section 5 in the Financial Institutions Act of 1975, but they vigorously objected to granting even broader powers to competing institutions and to the continued absence of many of the detailed provisions advocated by their two trade associations.

With regard to expanding the powers of other financial institutions, credit union authorities claimed that their group would be uniquely at a disadvantage, in a competitive sense: thrift institutions would be encouraged to expand into the consumer credit markets, but credit unions would be left without checking accounts, NOW accounts, full credit card powers, and equal access to electronic systems for transferring funds. Their representatives repeatedly emphasized that they were not trying to prevent the expansion of asset and liability powers for other institutions. They were simply trying to hold their own against the intense competitive pressures developing in the marketplace.

Credit unions were not happy with the Financial Institutions Act of 1975 as a total package, or with the greater competition they foresaw from the legislation sponsored by the savings and loan associations, that is S. 1540, the Family Financial Centers Act of 1975. They welcomed the positive provisions included in the expanded section 5 of the 1975 proposals, but claimed they would be worse off competitively with respect to consumer finance if the administration bill were approved without major changes. The irony of this attitude was that other financial institutions believed that credit unions were already ahead competitively—because of rapid growth and aggressive promotion efforts—and that any further expansion of their powers would only add to their existing advantages.

Their deep dissatisfaction with the current competitive environment, and what they considered to be the narrow scope of section 5 in the 1975 bill, caused the credit union industry to submit separate

26. Ibid., pp. 582–724.

legislation known as S.1475, a bill to amend the Federal Credit Union Act, in the hope of improving their competitive status and obtaining congressional approval of several specific reforms. In addition to the provisions in the expanded section 5 of the Financial Institutions Act of 1975, the special credit union bill called for new authority enabling them to: (1) provide demand deposits comparable to commercial bank checking accounts; (2) gain full participation in future electronic funds transfer systems; (3) have increased flexibility in purchasing government securities and making unrestricted "leeway" investments up to 5 percent of total assets; (4) make major changes in their operating and managerial structures; (5) offer a variety of deposit accounts; (6) reorganize the National Credit Union Administration to improve its status and regulatory powers; and (7) create a National Credit Union Central Liquidity Facility to provide continuing assistance for unusual emergencies.

In return for these increased powers, credit union industry spokesmen claimed that their member firms would continue to function as member-owned, nonprofit, cooperative financial institutions serving the personal financial needs of small savers and borrowers. Their legislative strategy of seeking a separate legislative package at the same time that Congress was considering the Financial Institutions Act of 1975 is summarized in the following statement by the National Association of Federal Credit Unions:

> Because the credit union industry felt that the provisions of Title V— when contrasted with the expansionist provisions devoted to savings and loan association and mutual savings bank powers—were insufficient, it drafted as a substitute for Title V the Credit Union Financial Institutions Act Amendments [CUFIAA] of 1975. These amendments were sweeping in scope, and designed to maintain parity between credit unions and competing financial institutions in the event the Financial Institutions Act [FIA] of 1975 was passed into law largely intact.
>
> From the beginning, there was discussion over what was properly part of the CUFIAA/FIA package. Those elements of FIA either repeated in CUFIAA or expanded in CUFIAA—such as the mortgage lending power, the variable rate share concept, and the creation of a Central Liquidity Fund more powerful than FIA's Central Discount Fund—have been generally accepted as being a proper part of the FIA concept of overall financial institution change.[27]

Housing interests

In attempting to neutralize the strong opposition of various housing interests, Treasury officials argued that the amount and stability

27. Ibid., pp. 686–87. Statement by B. David Goble for the National Association of Credit Unions.

of mortgage credit would be improved by the Financial Institutions Act, even though competition for deposits might intensify and other lending and investment opportunities for thrift institutions would be increased. They claimed that the competitive position of thrift institutions would be strengthened and their deposits stabilized; new tax incentives would encourage more participation in the mortgage markets; disintermediation pressures would moderate; and a better match between the maturities of loans and investments and deposit liabilities would improve the liquidity of mortgage-oriented financial institutions.

In the Senate hearings on the proposed legislation, two of the four sessions were devoted to clarifying these housing issues. The first day included the supportive testimony of Carla A. Hills, Secretary of Housing and Urban Development, and criticism presented by major housing interests.[28] During the second session, statements were made by representatives of the Consumers Union, the Consumer Federation of America, and the Public Interest Research Group (an organization affiliated with Ralph Nader in various consumer causes), as well as by Professors Almarin Phillips, Dean of the School of Public and Urban Policy at the University of Pennsylvania, and Donald P. Jacobs, Dean of the Graduate School of Management, Northwestern University.[29]

As the former co-directors of the Hunt Commission research staff, Professors Phillips and Jacobs strongly supported the substance of the Financial Institutions Act of 1975, particularly the elimination of regulation Q controls and diversification of powers. They also emphasized that accelerating technological changes in the marketplace made institutional reforms necessary. The three consumer representatives also supported many aspects of the 1975 recommendations, although they also expressed specific objections.

The Consumer Union spokesman supported the removal of regulation Q controls, the inclusion of truth-in-savings provisions and broadened deposit and asset powers, federal chartering of thrift institutions, expanded credit union powers, and elimination of administrative interest rate ceilings on FHA and VA mortgages. He was very critical, however, of the continued prohibition against paying interest on demand deposits and did not take any position on the tax proposals. The representative of the Public Interest Research Group limited his comments to supporting the removal of

28. Ibid., pp. 475–550.
29. Ibid., pp. 725–66.

regulation Q controls and the direct use of subsidies "to allocate credit into the housing sector should Congress continue to believe that preferential treatment for housing is still desirable as a national policy."[30] Finally, the Consumers Federation of America supported the removal of rate controls and the diversification of deposit and asset powers but was critical of the tax credit and truth-in-savings suggestions. This group also argued strongly for direct credit allocation programs, similar to the major AFL-CIO recommendations, to ensure that housing and other social activities would receive adequate financing.

The powerful National Association of Home Builders and AFL-CIO labor leaders continued to argue the other side of the housing issue and repeated their criticism of Treasury claims that housing and consumer interests would actually benefit. The major objection of this group was that if rate controls were removed, if the deposit differential favoring thrift institutions were eroded, and if authority to diversify loans and investments, including construction loans, were granted, the result might be a massive shift of funds away from residential mortgage financing. They rejected the Treasury's position that stronger thrift institutions would provide a larger absolute amount of mortgage credit even though diversification of their portfolios might reduce the relative percentage of housing loans. Their general views are summarized in the following excerpt from their Senate subcommittee testimony.

> We urge the subcommittee, as it proceeds to consider this far-reaching legislation, to examine carefully what its impact will be on meeting our Nation's housing needs and whether a neater system of financial institutions is worth the further disruption to the housing financing system which we see flowing from many of these proposals.[31]

Similar concern about the legislation's potential impact on the housing sector was expressed by the National Association of Realtors, an unusually large trade association representing 1,600 local boards and 500,000 realtors.[32] Their testimony requested a new and comprehensive analysis of housing issues and recommended that congressional action be delayed until the House Banking, Currency, and Housing Committee could complete its pending study of financial

---

30. Ibid., p. 735. Statement of Jonathan Brown, Public Interest Research Group.
31. Ibid., p. 499. Statement of J. S. Norman, Jr., President of National Association of Home Builders.
32. Ibid., pp. 518–32. Statement of Harlan E. Crowell for the National Association of Realtors.

institutions in the nation's economy. With regard to the Financial
Institutions Act of 1975, the realtors' association favored continued
controls on deposit interest rates and restoration of the differential,
along with authority to offer checking accounts; but they opposed the
diversification of lending and investment powers. Finally, the National Lumber and Building Material Dealers Association wrote to the
Senate subcommittee that thrift institutions should remain specialized mortgage-oriented institutions protected by rate controls and a
meaningful interest rate differential.[33]

During the Senate hearings on the Financial Institutions Acts of
both 1973 and 1975, many witnesses claimed that thrift institutions
should not be allowed to diversify their asset portfolios because commercial banks cannot be depended upon to provide a stable source of
significant amounts of mortgage credit. This accusation caused a serious concern among commercial banks about their public image because of the importance of housing as a social and political issue.

To improve its legislative position at least, the American Bankers
Association prepared a special report, "The Banking Industry's Relative Contribution to Housing Finance," which was included in their
presentation at the hearings on the 1975 legislation.[34] The study acknowledged that residential mortgage loans do not account for a large
share of the asset portfolio of most commercial banks. It emphasized,
however, that other loans and investments by commercial banks are
vitally important to the overall development of the housing sector.
The group's representative also challenged the claim that commercial
banks are undependable, fair weather friends, who quickly curtail
mortgage loans whenever more attractive alternatives become available. Their rebuttal stressed the growth of commercial banks' residential mortgage debt outstanding: from $46 billion at the end of 1970 to
$81 billion by the end of 1974. Four examples of the important role of
commercial banks were cited in their report:

1. *Distribution of residential mortgage loans.* Commercial banks are
the second largest source of mortgage loans; most of their credit is
allocated to family residences.

2. *Mobile home loans.* Commercial banks provide two-thirds of the
credit used to purchase mobile homes, which have become a dominant factor in the low-cost housing markets. By the end of 1974

33. Ibid., p. 814. Letter from National Lumber and Building Material Dealers Association.

34. Ibid., pp. 283–85. Included in statement of Rex J. Morthland for the American
Bankers Association.

Table 13

MORTGAGE LOANS OUTSTANDING, BY TYPE OF LENDER, FOURTH QUARTER 1974
(In Billions of Dollars)

	One- to Four-Family	Multifamily	Total
Savings and loan associations	$201.9	$23.8	$225.7
Commercial banks	74.0	7.4	81.4
Mutual savings banks	44.8	17.3	62.1
Life insurance companies	22.4	20.0	42.4
All others	71.1	23.4	94.5
Total	$414.2	$91.9	$506.1

Source: U.S., Congress, Senate, Committee on Banking, Housing, and Urban Affairs, *Financial Institutions Act of 1975;* American Bankers Association.

commercial bank loans outstanding for mobile homes totaled $7.6 billion.

3. *Construction loans.* Commercial banks are the major supplier of residential construction loans. They had provided $10 billion of credit for this important part of the housing industry at the end of 1974.

4. *Loans for the infrastructure of housing.* A wide variety of financial requirements are filled by loans from commercial banks, including in 1974: (1) investments totaling $14 billion in government securities issued by federal agencies; (2) investment holdings of $75 billion in municipal securities, used to finance roads, sewers, and other utilities; (3) home improvements totaling $5.2 billion; and (4) a total of $17 billion supplied to other financial institutions involved in housing finance such as savings and loan associations, mortgage bankers, life insurance companies, and real estate investment trusts.

The combined total of $212.2 billion of housing-oriented assets held by the commercial banks at the end of 1974 placed them second to savings and loan associations in providing assistance to the housing sector. Nevertheless, the thousands of pages of congressional testimony and hundreds of journal articles on financial institution reform rarely mentioned this crucial point, and the hearings appeared to be dominated by a concern with housing, to the neglect of broader issues of economic policy.

As so often happens when public policies are debated, the empirical information needed to make informed decisions was not available. The technical data used in the hearings were usually supplied by one of the financial intermediaries, a fact that naturally raises questions about the objectivity of the analysis. In general, even when professional studies are available, such as the several econometric studies and institutional monographs prepared by professors and private analysts in this instance, the representatives of special interest groups often reject them for being too theoretical, or out-of-date. The congressional evaluation of the two Financial Institutions Acts provides a striking example of how the lack of theoretical and empirical analysis can limit the effectiveness of debates on public policy.

Senate Action

Following the second round of public hearings the full Senate Banking, Housing, and Urban Affairs Committee met in executive session on September 30 and October 1–2, 1975, to consider the Financial Institutions Act of 1975. After careful consideration and the addition of several key amendments, the committee unanimously ordered the bill reported to the Senate with the recommendation that it be passed. The committee report stated:

> Its purpose is to eliminate unnecessary and outdated regulation that prevents depository institutions from competing effectively and operating efficiently; it would allow depository institutions to offer new services to the public and permit depositors to earn a rate of return that more clearly reflects prevailing market conditions; it would provide a more stable flow of funds to the sectors of the economy that rely on depository institutions to meet their credit needs, particularly housing; and it would provide direct incentives for all institutions to support the residential housing markets.[35]

The committee report was particularly critical of the controls on deposit interest rates, which had restricted the ability of depository institutions to compete for funds during periods of financial market disintermediation and thus created an unstable flow of mortgage credit. The Senate Banking Committee went on to support the eventual elimination of regulation Q controls with four specific stipulations: (1) thrift institutions must first receive expanded asset and

---

35. U.S., Congress, Senate, Committee on Banking, Housing, and Urban Affairs, *Financial Institutions Act of 1975*, Nov. 20, 1975, pp. 2–3.

liability powers enabling them to compete for deposits and improve their earnings; (2) to preserve competition, all depository institutions must have access to the evolving systems for electronic funds transfers; (3) a system of uniform taxes and reserves against transactional accounts (demand deposits and NOW accounts) is required; and (4) continued financial support for the housing markets is necessary to achieve national social goals. Given these four legislative requirements, and the amendments described below, the committee report strongly supported the bill as "a comprehensive, integrated package for financial reform and the provisions in the Act have been considered as an interrelated package."[36]

In supporting the seven principal sections of the proposed bill the committee agreed that under "reasonable assumptions" the termination of regulation Q controls, combined with expansion of asset and liability powers and implementation of the mortgage investment tax credit for all institutions, would have a "positive effect" on housing.[37] Nevertheless the committee added a number of important amendments that would improve the bill and reflect the Senate's fundamental interest in housing.[38]

Section 1. Payment of interest on deposit accounts. The proposed amendments included: (1) a directive to regulatory agencies to enforce regulation Q controls during the transition period, so as to avoid disintermediation and to assure a fair return to savers by setting the rate ceilings closer to market rates;[39] (2) repeal of the prohibition against payment of interest on demand deposits, the effective date being for January 1, 1977; (3) expansion of the Coordinating Committee of Regulatory Agencies, which is charged with setting deposit interest rate rules and is composed of representatives of the Board of Governors of the Federal Reserve System, Federal Home Loan Bank Board, and Federal Deposit Insurance Corporation, to include the Secretary of the Treasury, the National Credit Union Administrator, and the Secretary of Housing and Urban Development; and (4) deletion of the truth-in-savings provisions.

Section 2. Expanded deposit liability powers and reserves. The committee strongly supported this section, including the granting of check-

---

36. Ibid., p. 18.
37. Ibid., p. 22.
38. Ibid., pp. 18–38.
39. The regulatory agencies were also directed to maintain "appropriate" interest rate differentials on deposits to enable thrift institutions to compete against the full line of financial services offered by commercial banks.

ing account authority to thrift institutions, unrestricted expansion of NOW accounts on a nationwide scale, and corporate savings accounts at commercial banks. It added one major amendment making it unlawful for anyone who is providing clearing or settlement services for checking and NOW accounts to refuse to serve, on a nondiscriminatory basis, any depository institution.

Section 3. Lending and investment powers. After the introduction of the Financial Insitutions Act of 1975, the committee decided to accept a comprehensive revision of section 5(c) of the Home Owner's Loan Act of 1933 concerning the lending and investment powers of federal savings and loan associations, and the administration supported this change along with the committee's amendment to grant federal associations personal trustee and fiduciary powers. The revised section, prepared by the Federal Home Loan Bank Board, eliminated many of the detailed percentage requirements for portfolio assets and simplified the rules by creating a maximum 30 percent ceiling on commitments to education loans, consumer loans, development and construction loans for residences, commercial real estate loans, community development loans, service corporations, commercial paper and other debt securities, and bank deposits and acceptances, leaving a minimum requirement of 70 percent to be allocated to traditional residential mortgage loans.

Section 4. Charters for thrift institutions. The liberalization of chartering rules, including the granting of federal charters for mutual savings banks, was approved; but the prohibition against the conversion of mutual thrift institutions into stock organizations was continued.

Section 5. Credit unions. The extensive expansion of asset and liability powers was accepted by the committee, and further liberalization of the rules was accomplished by adding many of the amendments proposed by credit union representatives in the Credit Union Financial Institution Act of 1975.

Section 6. Government-insured and guaranteed mortgage loans. The abolition of rate ceilings on such loans was approved, with standby authority granted to the Secretary of Housing and Urban Development and the Administrator of the Veterans Administration.

Section 7. Taxes. The committee report supported this section, which was designed to provide a uniform tax rate for all financial institutions involved in the same investment activity and to establish a mortgage investment tax credit to encourage mortgage lending. The maximum percentage ceiling was raised to 80 percent from the 70 percent figure suggested in the proposed bill. The committee report also carefully specified that the effective date of the mortgage investment tax credit would not occur until enactment of the entire Financial Institutions Act of 1975. This requirement was particularly significant because of the complexity of completing tax law changes, which must be approved by the House Ways and Means Committee and the Senate Finance Committee. The early prospect of any actual financial reform was therefore complicated by the comprehensive nature of the legislation.

It was also significant that the committee report was unanimously reported out with only two supplementary statements. The eight Democrats making up the majority of the committee added an extensive comment on the importance of protecting the housing industry and what might happen to mortgage credit, and they directed the regulatory agencies to monitor marketplace developments carefully to preserve meaningful interest rate differentials and avoid disruptions such as the "wild card" experiment in July 1973. Senator Tower of Texas, the ranking Republican on the committee, also added a comment calling for further study of the amendment to permit interest payments on demand deposits.

On December 11, 1975, the Senate passed S.1267 as amended, the Financial Institutions Act of 1975, by a vote of 79 to 14. After so many years of internal planning and legislative liaison efforts, Treasury officials were naturally pleased by the positive results and the overwhelming majority of votes in favor of the reform measure. They also recognized, however, that the Senate vote was only the first step in a protracted series of congressional actions that they hoped would lead to final approval of a conference report combining the Senate and House versions of legislation for financial institution reform. Treasury officials were particularly aware of at least four favorable circumstances in the Senate proceedings which could not be expected to occur during the House hearings: (1) the partial defusing of opposition from the housing interests by segregating the mortgage investment tax credit so that it could not take effect until the entire legislative package was passed, which meant that housing interests could block the reform efforts at a later date if they were still unhappy with the bill; (2) the compromises made by the administration in agreeing to the major amendments and to the revision of section 3, dealing with lending and investment powers; (3) the leadership of Senator McIntyre in moving the bill to a Senate vote so quickly; and (4) the growing support of credit unions following the inclusion of many of their specific suggestions in the committee's report.[40]

40. Treasury Department staff memorandum, March 23, 1976.

Following the Senate vote, the impetus toward financial institution reform shifted to the House of Representatives, where Congressman Henry S. Reuss of Wisconsin had initiated a massive study of the entire financial market system in April 1975 as preparation for committee hearings scheduled to begin just as the Senate completed its vote. At the same time, Senator Proxmire, chairman of the full Senate Banking, Housing, and Urban Affairs Committee, continued to thrust ahead with other financial reform legislation that would extend far beyond the Financial Institutions Act of 1975 and that he wanted to have ready to match with pieces of the comprehensive initiatives being considered by the House of Representatives. The results of the effort in the House of Representatives and of Senator Proxmire's pushing separate pieces of legislation to consolidate the various regulatory agencies into one organization, reform the bank holding company act, and create new guidelines for foreign banking in the United States are the subject of the next chapter.

9

THE FINANCIAL REFORM ACT OF 1976 AND THE FINE STUDY

Government credit programs and tax policies are generally recognized to be crucial in the allocation of resources, which is the core subject of economics. Using its legislative and oversight powers, Congress attempts to direct these policies toward achievement of its national goals. Throughout the six-year effort to restructure the financial system the key issues involved the complex problems of meshing housing requirements with marketplace efficiency and the intense competitive struggle between thrift institutions and commercial banks.

The final phase in this example of the government's decision-making process was completed in the House Banking, Currency, and Housing Committee. The House began its evaluation of the comprehensive legislation needed to match the Senate's efforts by initiating another massive study of the entire financial system, using the extensive resources of its own staff and many outside consultants. The major project, known as the Financial Institutions and the Nation's Economy (FINE) Study, later served as a foundation for the Financial Reform Act of 1976 considered by the House of Representatives. The ultimate fate of that legislative initiative and its relation to the Financial Institutions Act of 1975 passed by the Senate are the subjects of this last descriptive chapter.

The House Banking, Currency, and Housing Committee has a long and impressive history of detailed legislative and oversight interest in financial institution reform. In 1967 its proposed Federal Savings Institutions Act was almost reported out for a House vote, and in 1973 a comprehensive report by a committee staff was published.[1] Under the leadership of Congressman Wright Patman of

---

1. U.S., Congress, House, Committee on Banking and Currency, *Financial Institutions: Reform and the Public Interest.*

Texas, a constant stream of reform proposals on detailed financial issues had been developed. Many of these reports and legislative initiatives were particularly critical of the organization and operations of the Federal Reserve System and also of commercial banks.

The change of committee chairmen in February 1975, at the beginning of the ninety-fourth Congress, resulted in even more interest in financial issues in Congress. Following the reorganization, the Senate Committee on Banking, Housing, and Urban Affairs, chaired by William Proxmire of Wisconsin, included eight Democrats and five Republicans; the House Committee on Banking, Currency, and Housing, chaired by Henry S. Reuss of Wisconsin, was composed of twenty-nine Democrats and fourteen Republicans. Both Proxmire and Reuss are considered to be unusually hardworking, bright, ambitious, and articulate, and they have shown themselves to be philosophically committed to housing and to a widespread reform of the financial system. At the time of the changeover in committee leadership it was widely anticipated that legislative and oversight activities would accelerate and become more comprehensive under their leadership, although some financial executives were apprehensive about their views on regulatory reform, particularly about Congressman Reuss's interest in establishing government guidelines for the allocation of credit and his pressure to make the Board of Governors of the Federal Reserve System more responsive to Congress.

The House Committee approached financial institution reform on an extremely comprehensive basis that initially included many more issues than those dealt with in the Financial Institutions Act. On April 24, 1975, almost five years after the creation of the President's Commission on Financial Structure and Regulation, Congressmen Reuss and St Germain of Rhode Island, the chairman of the House Subcommittee on Financial Institutions Supervision, Regulation, and Insurance, jointly announced the FINE Study to review the nation's financial institutions and their regulation by the federal government. Congressman Reuss summarized the scope of the study as follows:

> If we can deal with the commanding problems of the institutions themselves, the Federal Reserve System, the regulatory agencies, and foreign banking here and U.S. banking abroad—particularly where they interrelate, so that we do not legislate in one field and then find that we are in conflict with another—we will have done a pretty good job.[2]

2. "Mr. Proxmire and Mr. Reuss Talk About Banking," pp. 41–42.

The almost overwhelming breadth and complexity of the FINE Study caused serious doubts among critics about the feasibility of the project and its compatibility with the Financial Institutions Act, which was nearing final approval in the Senate. Some cynics even claimed that the FINE Study was deliberately designed to overload the system for making legislative decisions so that it would collapse of its own weight, thereby frustrating all attempts at financial institution reform in 1976, including passage of the Financial Institutions Act by the Senate. Congressman Reuss strongly denied these accusations and boldly established an ambitious schedule calling for these steps: completion of the FINE Study in time to pass a House bill by March 1976; issuance of a joint conference report with the Senate by May 1976; and submission of the entire package for the signature of the President by July 1976. He also adamantly defended the remarkable breadth of the House approach.

> The only way you can rise above the jungle of pressure groups is by taking an overall view. Then when you know what's in the public interest, you can wrest the individual congressman from the lobby taking hold of them.[3]

The FINE study group was able to prepare a challenging set of general principles, which they called "Discussion Principles." These were published as a committee print in November 1975. Following a series of exploratory hearings on those issues during the next two months, the comprehensive outline of the Financial Reform Act of 1976 (FRA 1976) was released as a committee print in February 1976. In early March, when the extensive hearings began before the House subcommittee, chaired by Congressman St Germain, the proposed legislation had grown to 275 pages covering seven topics: the depository institution and housing issues analyzed in the Financial Institutions Act; additional sections on the reorganization of the federal government's regulatory functions; bank holding companies; changes in the Federal Reserve System; activities of foreign banks in the United States; and the regulation of U.S. banks operating abroad.

The unusual breadth and complexity of the bill apparently created severe problems in management and strategy, which eventually forced Congressman St Germain to split the omnibus package into three parts, including one bill comparable to the Financial Institutions Act of 1975, passed by the Senate in December 1975.

3. "Drive for Sweeping Financial Reform," p. 86.

Further efforts to arrange compromises that would move the specific bills along were unsuccessful, however, and the political pressures caused by the approaching 1976 national elections made it difficult to muster widespread support in the face of intense opposition of several special interest groups. The entire project for comprehensive financial reform was therefore abandoned during the summer of 1976. Specific reform measures have continued since then, but no effort has been made to revive the total package which generated so much controversy among the special interest groups.

Despite the acknowledged sense of urgency created by three successive waves of financial market disintermediation—in 1966, 1969–70, and 1973–74—the federal government was unable to develop an acceptable reform package even with the combined efforts of the executive branch and the two important congressional committees. There were three principal reasons for this failure.

1. The special interest groups adamantly refused to compromise on the basic issues to arrive at a consensus. During the initial consideration of the Financial Institutions Act, beginning in 1973, the American Bankers Association and National Association of Mutual Savings Banks supported the administration's proposals, with certain reservations, while the Independent Bankers Association of America, as well as both of the savings and loan association groups, the credit unions, organized labor, and the housing interests opposed the reforms. The contingent support of the American Bankers Association was later reversed when the Senate markup session added amendments to permit payment of interest on demand accounts and to allow nationwide NOW accounts.

By 1976 the various positions had become even more polarized as each group refused to compromise on the basic issues. The thrift institutions and credit unions did support the Financial Reform Act of 1976; but the AFL-CIO and the housing interests rejected the proposals, and the American Bankers Association mounted a major lobbying effort against the bill. Treasury officials continued to argue for legislation comparable to the Financial Institutions Act, but delay on the other provisions added by the House caused the other representatives of the Executive Office and the regulatory agencies to raise criticial comments on specific parts of the comprehensive bill. After almost six years of detailed analysis and extensive congressional hearings the various interest groups were even more intransigent, and their conflicting positions made agreement impossible.

2. The basic approach of increasing competition in the financial markets by expanding asset and liability powers to stabilize the availability of mortgage credit and attract additional lenders was never accepted by the AFL-CIO and the housing interests; and their skepticism on this point eroded their crucial support for comprehensive reform. Perhaps the most ironic aspect of the congressional hearings was the evolution in the attitudes of special interest groups on the critical issue of expanding asset and liability powers for thrift institutions and credit unions. The American Bankers Association first supported the Financial Institutions Act as a means of aiding the housing sector, but the same group subsequently opposed the Financial Reform Act of 1976 on the grounds that expanded powers would hurt housing construction. Thrift institutions and credit unions originally criticized the Financial Institutions Act as a threat to housing but later embraced the Financial Reform Act of 1976 as a means of creating "family financial centers." The arguments remained essentially the same, but the final conclusions were reversed.

3. The unusual scope and complexity of the proposals made it extremely difficult to develop a legislative strategy that could produce positive results within the arbitrary two-year schedule of congressional sessions. At the conclusion of each two-year session of Congress all pending legislation expires automatically. Similar bills can, of course, be introduced in the next session, but it is sometimes difficult to restore the previous momentum if the proposals are controversial.

In addition to the usual rules of the game for public policy decisions, Congress often requires that its legislative proposals be based on studies conducted by its own staff with the assistance of carefully selected consultants. The FINE Study, completed in April 1975, and the publication of "Discussion Principles" in November 1975 created a basis for holding public hearings leading to consideration of legislation. Together they enabled the members and staff of the House Banking, Currency, and Housing Committee to present a distinct set of recommendations covering the usual financial reform issues, plus some fundamental suggestions for reorganizing the development of monetary policy by the Federal Reserve System. The trade-off for following such an independent approach, however, is added complexity and controversy, which often prevent effective action on many issues that would otherwise be readily resolved.

The FINE Study included a series of position papers drafted by the staff and outside consultants and the summary of recommendations published under the title "Discussion Principles."[4] The apparent goal of Congressmen Reuss and St Germain and of Dr. James L. Pierce, who directed the study, was to emphasize public interests as distinguished from the interests represented by financial institutions. As Congressman Reuss stated:

> What is needed at this point is a Congressional review starting from the viewpoint of what the public needs from its financial institutions. Congress must define what the basic issues are, where the public interest lies, and should constitute a solid financial system for a nation approaching the 21st century.[5]

The end result was a broad set of measures that attempted to foster efficiency and competition in the financial markets by adopting the basic recommendations advocated in the Financial Institutions Act, with special emphasis on housing interests. In exchange, the regulations applying to financial institutions, including bank and savings and loan holding companies and commercial banks involved in international activities, would be considerably stronger and more concentrated.

Provisions of the Financial Reform Act of 1976

The proposed Financial Reform Act of 1976 was carefully considered in March 1976 by the House Subcommittee on Financial Institutions Supervision, Regulation, and Insurance, chaired by Congressman Fernand J. St Germain, in extensive hearings lasting seven days. Sponsors of the legislation argued that the entire 275-page bill should be taken up only as a comprehensive package, just as the administration had earlier tried to avoid a piecemeal approach when the Financial Institutions Act was analyzed by the Senate. This procedure greatly extended the scope and number of witnesses invited to testify; but the hearings moved rapidly, and an amazing amount of information was collected concerning each of the seven main sections summarized below.[6]

Section 1: Regulatory Agencies. (a) A new Federal Banking Commission with five members, appointed by the President and confirmed by the

4. U.S., Congress, House, Committee on Banking, Currency, and Housing, *FINE: Financial Institutions and the Nation's Economy.*

5. Harry Guenther and Philip Meyer, "Banking Control: New Hands at the Helm," p. 1075.

6. U.S., Congress, House, Committee on Banking, Currency, and Housing, *The Financial Reform Act of 1976.*

Senate, would be created and given expanded enforcement powers to absorb all of the chartering, branching, examination, supervision, and regulation of national banks and holding companies from the Comptroller of the Currency (office would be terminated) and the Federal Reserve Board; (b) the Federal Deposit Insurance Corporation would remain as an insuring agency and would examine state-chartered insured banks until state bank regulatory agencies could assume responsibility; (c) the Federal Home Loan Bank Board, expanded to five members, would regulate federal savings and loan associations and the National Credit Union Administration, expanded to three members, would supervise federal credit unions.

The FINE Study had recommended an even more comprehensive reorganization by calling for one superagency, the Federal Depository Institutions Commission, to absorb the regulatory and supervision functions of all existing agencies and to be responsible for state-chartered institutions until state authorities could demonstrate adequate proficiency at conducting examinations. This arrangement would limit the Federal Reserve Board to functions related to monetary policy and would eliminate entirely the Comptroller of the Currency and the National Credit Union Administration. The aim of this sweeping reform was to reduce the confusing and conflicting jurisdictions and improve the scope and quality of regulation. Such major reforms were evidently unacceptable in a financial system dominated by allegiance to the separation of federal and state powers, however, and critics were able to argue effectively that a regulatory superagency would disrupt the existing patterns of supervision during a long transition, that a single agency would stifle innovation and flexibility by exercising excessive power, and that the quality of regulation would deteriorate. Arguments about equity and efficiency are often used to mask the real reasons for policy decisions, which in this case involved the untouchable status of the dual system and the power of the established regulatory agencies.

Given the comprehensive nature of the FINE Study, it is puzzling that some of its key recommendations did not even survive long enough to be included in the proposals for the Financial Reform Act of 1976. One may see in this fact an analogy to the administration's decision that it would completely ignore regulatory issues in the Financial Institutions Act, even though the President's Commission on Financial Structure and Regulation had recommended extensive reorganization and concentration of existing functions.[7] Public com-

---

7. Senator Proxmire subsequently introduced S. 2298, the Federal Bank Commission Act, which recommended the consolidation of the regulatory functions of the

missions and external consultants are evidently listened to only when their recommendations confirm the views of the executive branch and Congress, particularly if the dual system of financial institutions is threatened. Another example of the same problem was the significant deletion of the FINE Study's recommendation to permit interstate branching, or at least branching within a metropolitan area, if existing laws prohibit crossing state boundaries. These topics are admittedly political dynamite, but why bother to conduct analytical studies if they evade controversial issues?

Section 2: Depository Institutions. (a) Regulation Q interest rate ceilings on time and savings deposits would be removed within five and one-half years; an evaluation to determine the economic and public interest repercussions of this action was to be prepared six months prior to the final expiration; (b) a differential interest payment of one-fourth of 1 percent would be permitted on time and savings accounts placed in depository institutions, including qualifying commercial banks, holding a substantial portion of their assets in residential mortgages; (c) a formal Coordinating Committee (composed of officials from the new Federal Banking Commission discussed in section 1, the Federal Reserve Board, the Federal Home Loan Bank Board, and Federal Deposit Insurance Corporation) would have authority to administer the rates during the transition period to provide reasonable returns for small savers and to prevent future financial disintermediation; (d) the existing statutory prohibition against the payment of interest on third-party payment accounts (principally checking accounts) would be removed by 1978 under direction of the Coordinating Committee; (e) the new Federal Banking Commission was directed to develop disclosure requirements for banks and bank holding companies; (f) the acquisition of checking accounts by federal credit unions, savings and loan associations, and mutual savings banks would require that they meet legal reserve requirements against such deposits, the amounts to be established by the Federal Reserve Board, which was also directed to prepare a report on the possibility of paying interest on such reserves; (g) mutual savings banks would be granted authority to obtain federal charters and would receive additional asset and liability powers; (h) savings and loan associations would also be granted greater asset and liability powers; and (i) credit unions would be given the extended powers requested, and a central discount fund would be created to provide liquidity assistance.

The second section dealing with deposit interest rate controls and extended asset and liability powers for thrift institutions and credit

---

Federal Reserve Board and the entire Federal Deposit Insurance Corporation and Comptroller of the Currency into a single agency roughly equivalent to the reorganization proposed in Section 1 of the FRA 1976. The Federal Reserve Board would continue its monetary policy functions in the S. 2298 reorganization.

unions closely paralleled the Senate's Financial Institutions Act of 1975, except for minor differences in regulatory responsibilities and the treatment of legal reserves. There was also very little change from the FINE Study's recommendations, except for one important difference in strategy. The FINE "Discussion Principles" called for an absolute termination of deposit interest rate controls at the end of the five-year transition period, rather than a delay in preparing a final evaluation until six months before the expected expiration. By this change, financial institutions would be forced to begin the necessary policy adjustments, instead of deferring them in the hope of postponements of the deadline.

The close similarity between the recommendations for deposit interest rate controls and expanded asset and liability powers in the House's 1976 Financial Reform Act and those in the Senate's Financial Institutions Act of 1975 suggests that this section of the comprehensive proposal could have been approved independently, even if the entire package of reforms could not be accepted. This simple solution was never a viable option, however, because of the polarized positions of the powerful special interest groups and the complex political maneuvers between the majority Democrats and minority Republicans as well as between the House and Senate committees. The intense controversy surrounding the recommendations to eliminate deposit interest rate controls eventually, to continue the differential payment advantage for thrift institutions, to remove the ban against paying interest on demand deposits, and to approve extensive liberalization of asset and liability powers for savings and loan associations, mutual savings banks, and credit unions made even this scaled-down version of financial institution reform impossible in an election year.

Section 3: Housing. (a) The advantageous one-fourth of 1 percent interest rate differential on time and savings deposits would be limited to financial institutions committed to financing residential housing (thrift institutions would be required to hold 80 percent of their assets in residential mortgages, housing related investments, and liquidity investments; and commercial banks could become eligible to pay the higher return by committing 35 percent of future additions to assets to mortgages and housing-related investments); (b) the Federal Home Loan Bank Board would be authorized to increase its program of extending "advances" (loans for five years) to member institutions for up to thirty years, with the requirement that the funds provided be loaned for purchases of "nonluxury" housing at interest rates that would reflect their lower costs of obtaining capital directly in the financial markets or from the Treasury through its Federal Financing Bank.

Housing goals are clearly affected by financial institution reform because thrift institutions are the main source of mortgage funds. Congressional committees and their staffs have always been responsive to these issues and their political implications. The past failures of deposit interest rate controls to stabilize the mortgage markets, and pragmatic skepticism about the results of various econometric simulations indicating that the housing sector would actually benefit from the comprehensive financial institution reforms, left the Congress in a difficult position regarding the positive incentives for residential construction that the proposed reform might provide. The Senate bill finally recommended a mortgage interest tax credit designed to increase as a larger share of the total asset portfolio was committed to housing investments. The FINE "Discussion Principles" suggested three possible approaches: (1) a tax credit linked to mortgage investments; (2) direct loans to financial institutions active in making mortgage loans; and (3) credits against the legal reserves required for deposits at financial institutions, so that funds would be released for mortgage loans. All of the incentives mentioned in the FINE report were limited to financial institutions extending loans to construct housing for low- and moderate-income families.

In drafting its 1976 financial reform proposals the House committee rejected the Senate recommendations for a new tax credit and elimination of the FHA and VA mortgage interest rate ceilings. The FINE Study's suggestion for allowing credits against legal reserves was also passed over in favor of using the existing authority with respect to the deposit interest rate differential to encourage continued emphasis on mortgage loans and a new program of long-term "advances" from the Federal Home Loan Bank Board to bolster the supply of housing credit during periods of tight money and financial disintermediation. In defending its choice of the incentives proposed in the Financial Reform Act of 1976, the House subcommittee argued that these incentives would be a technically more efficient and less costly means of accomplishing the housing goals than the tax credit in the Senate bill, entailing an estimated annual loss of $800 million of tax revenues.

Section 4: Bank Holding Companies. (a) Responsibility for the regulation of bank holding companies would be transferred from the Federal Reserve Board to the new Federal Banking Commission described in section 1; (b) a list of permissible activities for bank holding companies would be prepared and any additional powers granted by the Federal Banking Commission would be subject to veto by either house of Congress within ninety days; (c) bank holding companies would be prohibited from acquiring control of a savings and loan association.

Bank holding companies have remained a controversial issue despite the benchmark legislation passed in 1970, which assigned regulatory authority to the Federal Reserve Board. The Senate bill did not include any coverage of this subject, but Senator Proxmire introduced legislation to prohibit acquisitions or mergers by which a bank or a bank holding company would control more than 20 percent of the total banking assets in any state. The recommendations of the FINE Study were incorporated in the proposed Financial Reform Act of 1976.

Section 5: The Federal Reserve System. A number of changes would be made in the organizational structure and functions of the Federal Reserve System which the committee print claimed would help focus its actions on monetary policy: (a) the four-year term of the Chairman of the Board would be changed to coincide with that of the President, with a six-month lag; (b) district Federal Reserve bank presidents would be appointed by the President and confirmed by the Senate; (c) the Boards of Directors of the district Federal Reserve banks would be enlarged, and six of the twelve members would have to be representatives of business, farming, labor, education, and consumers; (d) the Federal Reserve Board would be required to pursue the policy objectives of the Employment Act of 1946; and (e) the House Concurrent Resolution 113 of March 1975, which requires the Federal Reserve Board to consult with the Congressional Banking Committee each quarter to explain its monetary policies for the next twelve months, would be made permanent.

Although these recommendations seem relatively innocuous when they are buried in a massive piece of legislation, few, if any, matters have greater bearing on the formulation and conduct of economic policy than the organization and procedures of the Federal Reserve System. At the present time the Fed operates as an autonomous public agency responsible for directing domestic monetary affairs and performing many international monetary functions. The professional and personal qualifications of its Board of Governors and staff should be of the highest order to preserve the objectivity and independence of their policy decisions on issues whch profoundly concern the condition of the national and world economies. Most of their decisions deal with complex and controversial problems. Those who created the Federal Reserve System clearly meant it to be carefully insulated from the intense political pressures that are generated when Congress and the executive branch fear the effect of economic conditions on elections and other public affairs. At the present time the seven members of the Board of Governors are appointed to staggered fourteen-year terms; and during their tenure great emphasis is placed on preserving the independent judgment of each member, as it should be. Perhaps the closest analogy in public affairs to being named to the Board of Governors is appointment to the Supreme Court.

Defenders of the existing organization and procedures argue that the independence of the Federal Reserve System is absolutely necessary to avoid political manipulation of established economic policy in favor of short-term benefits, without adequate regard for the longer-term consequences. In general, the Federal Reserve System has earned an unmatched reputation for professional service and careful judgment, and its chairman from 1970 until 1978, Dr. Arthur F. Burns, is respected around the world as much for his personal integrity and sound advice as he is for his extraordinary qualities as a professional economist and senior government official serving for an unusually long period.

Critics of the present system argue that the independence of the Federal Reserve System frustrates the election process by preventing the President and Congress from exercising full power over both fiscal and monetary policies. This argument was summarized in the House committee print of FINE "Discussion Principles" as follows:

> Congressional and public involvement in monetary decisions which affect all Americans has been peripheral, and easily ignored. In contast with fiscal policy, which is hammered out on the forge of public debate and in give and take between the executive and legislative branches, monetary policy is shaped largely in secret.
>
> In its virtually complete control over monetary policy the Fed can largely offset the effects of fiscal policies determined by democratic process. The Fed can—by either intent or by error—precipitate inflation or recession. The experiences of 1966, 1969, 1973, and 1974 bear witness to this power.
>
> The removal of monetary policy from public pressure is both a virtue and a vice. It allows monetary policy to be flexible in a way that is virtually impossible for spending and taxation policy. It exempts monetary policy from narrow political considerations. But the balance between independence and public accountability is tipped too far in one direction. The Federal Reserve has become almost a fourth branch of government, exempt from the system of checks and balances written into the Constitution for other areas of public policy.[8]

This debate will undoubtedly continue to arouse strong reactions from both sides, suggesting not only a fundamental difference of opinion about how political and economic power should be exercised but considerable concern about how the issue will be resolved.

8. U.S., Congress, House, Committee on Banking, Currency, and Housing, *Financial Institutions and the Nation's Economy (FINE) Discussion Principles*, p. 15.

The efforts of the Congress and executive branch to gain increased control over monetary policy involve more than simple organizational matters or abstract economic principles. On the contrary, they are central to the allocation of power. When the time comes to make a fundamental decision about the future role of the Federal Reserve System the American people deserve to be part of the debate, and the argument should be stated in the clearest possible terms rather than confused by the jargon of economics and politics. The issue requires the most careful analysis if the public interest is to be well served.

Section 6. Foreign Banks in the United States. (a) It would be required that all banking branches and agencies of foreign banks be chartered by the new Federal Banking Commission proposed in section 1; (b) foreign banks would be permitted to establish Edge Act corporations comparable to such corporations formed by U.S. banks; (c) foreign banks would not be required to join the Federal Reserve System, but they would have to maintain a surety deposit with the Federal Deposit Insurance Corporation; and (d) all current activities of foreign banks not permitted for domestic banks would have to be phased out within five years. (This would have a significant impact on their underwriting of securities and multistate branching activities).

Both the Federal Reserve Board and the congressional committees had long been concerned about the disparities between foreign and domestic banks in the United States. Section 6 essentially attempted to give foreign banks domestic treatment. That is, they would be granted the same privileges but would be subject to similar supervision and regulation. The most controversial aspect of the 1976 reform proposal and the comparable legislation considered in the Senate, which is discussed later in this chapter, was requiring a phaseout of current activities within five years, rather than permitting them to continue under "grandfather" clauses. Some witnesses felt that this requirement would be punitive and might result in foreign retaliation against U.S. banks operating abroad.

Section 7: U.S. Banks Abroad. (a) U.S. banks with foreign operations would be subject to the supervision and regulation of the new Federal Banking Commission proposed in section 1, particularly regarding the adequacy of capital and antitrust concerns; and (b) U.S. banks would be permitted to perform international functions comparable to foreign branch activities by operating separate departments in their domestic offices.

This section did not receive much attention during the public hearings, although there was some discussion of the need to improve the supervision and regulation of U.S. banks' foreign operations.

Responses of Financial Institutions and Other Groups

The seven full days of hearings on the Financial Reform Act of 1976, held in March 1976, produced another extensive set of background materials to be drawn on by the government's decision makers. After the long series of detailed statements presented to the President's Commission on Financial Structure and Regulation, the Senate hearings on the Financial Institutions Acts, and the earlier hearings on the FINE Study, which took place in December 1975, the viewpoints expressed by each group were easily predictable. The specific arguments were analyzed in Chapters 4 through 8 and need not be repeated, except to note the narrower focus of much of the testimony on the 1976 proposals, which reflects the breakdown of previous compromises. The sharp polarization of viewpoints together with the pressure of political events created a deadlock on the comprehensive legislation considered by the House Subcommittee on Financial Institutions Supervision, Regulation, and Insurance.

Responses of government agencies

The Administration's principal statement, presented by Deputy Secretary George H. Dixon, argued that the Financial Institutions Act of 1975, which included a provision for a mortgage interest tax credit, had offered a better approach to necessary reform. The Treasury statement strongly opposed the two key housing incentives proposed in the 1976 legislation: (1) continuation of deposit interest rate controls, with a one-fourth of 1 percent differential payment advantage authorized for all financial institutions that were willing to emphasize mortgage loans as measured by minimum shares of total asset commitments; and (2) long-term loans from the Federal Home Loan Bank Board to mortgage-lending institutions, these loans to be financed by direct claims against the Treasury or its Federal Financing Bank, as well as by the sale of government agency securities in the private capital markets.

The Treasury also criticized the 1976 proposals recommending consolidation of the various regulatory functions under a single agency. In arguing that "now is not the time to reorganize or consolidate our regulatory agencies," the Treasury repeated the familiar assertion that diverse agencies provide flexibility and competitive innovation.[9] The Treasury's claim that the regulatory reforms re-

9. House, Committee on Banking, Currency, and Housing, *The Financial Reform Act of 1976*, p. 335.

quired more "careful study and deliberation in an atmosphere free of the heat and emotion of the moment" was particularly irritating to many congressmen, since these reforms had been a major part not only of the final recommendations of the President's Commission on Financial Structure and Regulation but of the FINE Study as well.

Administration officials had often complained with reason about the tediously slow progress of financial institution reform and the intransigence of special interest groups in opposing changes. But now the same officials seemed to adopt the same strategies and stonewalling arguments in their reactions to the recommendations for regulatory legislation. While it may be true that "a foolish consistency is the hobgoblin of little minds, adored by little statesmen and philosophers and divines,"[10] the exasperation of Congress was understandable when the Treasury argued for haste and at the same time urged delay in making reform decisions. The resulting deadlock is typical of the governmental process.

The Department of Housing and Urban Development joined the Treasury in criticizing the interest rate differential and direct loans to financial institutions from the Federal Home Loan Bank Board, considering these provisions a poor substitute for the mortgage interest tax credit proposed by the administration. The Assistant Attorney General also submitted an impressive statement extolling the virtues of increased competition and decrying the deposit interest rate controls and numerous regulatory barriers to more efficient markets.[11] The Justice Department was particularly critical of the recommendation in the 1976 proposals that checking accounts and other third-party payment systems be restricted to thrift institutions, according to individual state laws. The powerful logic and analytical evidence presented in the Justice Department statement was unfortunately ignored during the subsequent congressional deliberations.

The Federal Reserve Board, the Comptroller of the Currency, and the Federal Deposit Insurance Corporation all objected to the proposal to consolidate their regulatory functions into a new Federal Banking Commission. The Federal Reserve Board did support the specific recommendations for requiring uniform legal reserve re-

---

10. Ralph Waldo Emerson, *Essays and Journals,* ed. Lewis Mumford (Garden City, N.Y.: International Collectors Library, Nelson Doubleday, 1968), p. 95.

11. House, Committee on Banking, Currency, and Housing, *The Financial Reform Act of 1976,* pp. 597–633. Statement of Thomas E. Kauper, Assistant Attorney General, Antitrust Division, Department of Justice.

quirements and strengthening the regulation of foreign and domestic banks operating in the United States, but it was emphatic about the necessity of maintaining its existing regulatory functions in order to avoid the erosion of its control over monetary policy.

> Second, the proposal to lop off the Board's bank regulatory role, would, whether by intent or inadvertence, drastically diminish the ability of the Federal Reserve to perform its monetary policy mission. Monetary policy and bank regulation are organically intertwined. Over the years, Congress has consistently rejected attempts to diminish the effectiveness of the Federal Reserve. If there is to be any move now to emasculate the Federal Reserve, the public interest requires that this be argued explicitly rather than in the name of "reform" of the bank regulatory structure.
> Third, not only have the proponents of "reform" failed to make a factual case for restructuring the agencies, but the proposal before the subcommittee will not cure the defects with which the present system is charged.[12]

One of the most interesting statements was presented by the Federal Home Loan Bank Board. The board had operated without a chairman for eight months prior to the hearings on the Financial Reform Act of 1976, and in the absence of the other two members of the board the research director presented the official statement.[13] As anticipated, the board strongly agreed with the sections that would promote the development of thrift institutions as "family financial centers." What was not expected was their overwhelming support of deposit interest rate controls and the severe criticism of commercial bank competition. In previous testimonies on the financial institutions acts, the board had argued for a transition period in phasing out the controls but had concentrated chiefly on the positive aspects of diversifying the asset and liability powers of thrift institutions without modifying their traditional emphasis on housing finance. This agreement with the administration apparently changed during their preparation of testimony: the Federal Home Loan Bank Board became an advocate of continuing the controls for an extended period, particularly the one-fourth of 1 percent differential. Their statement also noted that the 1976 proposals for reform would favor thrift institutions; but it went on to say they would "hardly view this as an inequity" because commercial banks were already alleged to have powerful competitive advantages and to enjoy numerous tax shelters. Hence it was unnecessary to give them the added differen-

12. Ibid., pp. 888–89. Statement of Arthur F. Burns, Chairman of the Federal Reserve Board of Governors.
13. Ibid., pp. 232–323. Statement of Donald M. Kaplan, Chief Economist and Director of the Office of Economic Research, Federal Home Loan Bank Board.

tial for shifting into housing loans, because the extra incentives would increase competition in mortgage markets and create an unwanted windfall for commercial banks. The board's testimony did indicate that a mortgage interest tax credit might be a useful incentive to increase commercial bank mortgage loans. These views differed sharply from the recommendations of the administration's task force, which had worked on position papers since 1970. With regard to the "rate control issue," the board's statement included the following summary comment:

> As we have said many times, we believe that an adequate rate differential for savings and loan associations will continue to be necessary for some time, certainly until thrift institutions are able to take full advantage of their new powers and have these reflected in their asset and liability structure, their market shares and their earnings. We have noted that it will take a long time before this comes about, if at all.[14]

On the basic point of contention between the special interest groups, involving the balance of competition, the Federal Home Loan Bank Board presented the following unusually clear summary of the real issues, which also explains why no comprehensive financial institution reform occurred in the 1970–77 period.

> Events of recent years have, if anything, put S&Ls in a less competitive position. The administration of Regulation Q by banking regulatory authorities has made it possible, since the mid-1960's, for commercial banks to compete much more aggressively for savings and time account business and expand into an area that had previously been dominated by thrifts. Commercial banks have clearly been competing much more strenuously in areas that had formerly been left largely to thrifts. The rate differential possessed by thrift institutions has been narrowed since 1966. Studies have shown that the traditional savings and loan association needs an average rate differential more on the order of one half to three quarters of one percent in order to be competitive with commercial banks. Yet, FRA only mandates a minimum of a one quarter of one percent differential, although it will take a long time for new powers to reduce or eliminate the needed rate differential. We hardly see how anyone can object to such a modest rate differential, let alone claim that it would destroy competitive parity between S&L's and banks. For S&L's to lose their rate differential at this point of time would be catastrophic for the solvency of the S&L's and the flow of funds into housing credit.[15]

Responses of private interest groups

The tentative compromises developed by the President's Commission on Financial Structure and Regulation and in the Financial Insti-

14. Ibid., p. 257.
15. Ibid., pp. 242–43.

tutions Act of 1975, passed by the Senate, did not survive the tough debate on the Financial Reform Act of 1976 in the House of Representatives. The earlier accommodation may have been simply an illusion that disappeared as soon as the House began the final phase of its decision making. Whatever the reason for the changed environment, the various special interest groups were clearly unwilling to develop a consensus on the proposed legislation.

Savings and loan asociations. The United States League of Savings Associations expressed "substantial support of your committee print," particularly the recommendation to continue the crucial deposit interest rate differential and expand the investment and deposit powers needed to compete against commercial banks.[16] The National Savings and Loan League similarly supported the proposals as a means of providing "the necessary viability for thrifts to survive the economic ups and downs created by imbalances in our monetary and fiscal policies and which at the same time would create a climate whereby the thrifts would maintain their preeminence as housing finance specialists of this Nation."[17] The National Savings and Loan League further advocated the mortgage interest tax credit and agreed that continuing the interest rate controls and differential, along with the Federal Home Loan Bank Board's new program of long-term advances, would effectively direct money into housing finance. Both groups criticized some specific suggestions, such as the rule that would require all financial institutions to maintain legal reserves for demand deposit accounts, to be held by the Federal Reserve System; and some amendments were proposed to improve the competitive position of savings and loan firms in relation to commercial banks, but there was general support for the recommendations.

Mutual savings banks. The savings bank industry also enthusiastically testified "to support the basic thrust of the Financial Reform Act of 1976," particularly the provision of a federal charter alternative for savings banks and the broadened powers with respect to investment and consumer services.[18] The statement of this group repeated the

16. Ibid., p. 3. Statement of Tom B. Scott, Jr., representing the United States League of Savings Associations.
17. Ibid., pp. 8–9. Statement of Harold W. Greenwood, Jr., representing the National Savings and Loan League.
18. Ibid., p. 30. Statement of Morris D. Crawford, Jr., representing the National Association of Mutual Savings Banks.

fundamental arguments for maintaining the interest rate controls and differential, as well as for granting federally chartered thrift institutions the authority to provide third-party payment accounts regardless of restrictive state laws. The savings bank industry endorsed most of the other provisions in the 1976 proposals.

Credit unions. The Administrator of the National Credit Union Administration and both trade associations advocated the Financial Reform Act of 1976. In it were amendments to existing legislation which they had developed and which had also been incorporated into the Financial Institutions Act of 1975. The Credit Union National Association expressed strong support for the House recommendations, with two exceptions: the rule limiting third-party payment deposits to federally chartered institutions operating in states with permissive legislation; and the suggestion that required reserves be held by the Federal Reserve System.

> It is a pleasure for me to appear before this Committee on behalf of the credit unions in the United States. It is a pleasure because we in the credit union system hopefully see the successful completion of more than five years of effort at the federal level to obtain the powers that credit unions need to serve the financial needs of their members. It is a pleasure also because I can offer an almost unqualified endorsement of the Financial Reform Act of 1976. And it is a pleasure because it gives me an opportunity to thank the members of this Committee for the courteous consideration of our amendments many of which are included in FRA '76.[19]

The association's statement went on to summarize their goals for "survival," or expansion into broader markets, and then joined with the thrift institutions in attacking the commercial banks.

> Our first observation is that it is the savings and loan associations, credit unions, and mutual savings banks, that are seeking and getting broader powers. With certain exceptions, commercial banks would gain less than these other institutions. We think this is significant since it is a recognition of the practical realities of the competitive imbalance in the marketplace.
> Commercial banks have been pushing forcefully into the consumer credit and savings market with a range of powers that have had the effect of placing the other financial institutions at a distinct disadvantage. And they have been the beneficiaries of a diverse base of asset and liability powers that enabled them to adjust more readily to recent economic dislocations. So there has been a natural reaction by competing institutions to seek additional powers.[20]

19. Ibid., p. 106. Statement of Mandy R. Hellie, representing the Credit Union National Association, Inc.
20. Ibid., pp. 109–10.

The statement submitted by the National Association of Federal Credit Unions was almost identical except for their continued support for the existing common bond rules. After criticizing the restriction of third-party payment powers to federally chartered institutions located in states that already have permissive legislation, and the requirement that legal reserves be held by the Federal Reserve, this group warmly endorsed the Financial Reform Act of 1976 as a "far-reaching and a farsighted proposal," which would "offer credit unions their rightful place in the financial marketplace by allowing them to provide modern financial services to their consumer members." It "modernizes," they said, "the overall balance among financial institutions and financial institution regulatory agencies."[21] This association of credit unions also joined the attack on commercial banks with the following statement.

> As pointed out in our written statement, market advantages enjoyed by credit unions in the past are today being eroded. Some are being eroded because other lenders, especially commercial banks, have realized that the consumer market is an important one. So banks have moved into serving customers. Credit unions, however, have been barred by law and regulation from offering members other services to compensate for this banking assault on traditional credit union lending and saving activities.[22]

American Bankers Association. In some ways the appearance of the American Bankers Association at the hearings was analogous to the entry of the villain during a melodrama. Prior to these hearings the president of the American Bankers Association had delivered a speech in Texas in which the printed text described the Financial Reform Act of 1976 as "totally abhorrent." That strong accusation was omitted from the actual speech, but its presence in the printed version released to the public created a storm of protest, which erupted during the hearings when Congressman St Germain responded to the American Bankers Association's testimony during the question period.

> Today continues the American Bankers Association's 60 year record of opposing responsible financial reform legislation. In 1913, your predecessors opposed the proposal through which the Federal Reserve Board was created, calling it socialism, because it might impair, in your view, bank profits. In 1933, during the Depression, the ABA opposed Federal Deposit Insurance, stating, and I quote:
> "Taxing properly managed banks to make up losses of failed banks is

---

21. Ibid., p. 162. Statement of B. David Goble, representing the National Association of Federal Credit Unions.

22. Ibid., p. 161.

not only unfair and unreasonable but it weakens the whole banking structure. We are, therefore, opposed to the passage of any law carrying a guarantee of bank deposits."

And you kept right on with that line in 1966 when we raised deposit insurance to $15,000, in 1969, when we raised it to $25,000 and in 1974 when we raised it to $40,000. Today, the American Bankers Association pronounces itself in total, all-out opposition to our 1976 financial reform proposal which you call totally abhorrent. The ABA, as far as I can see, just wants to be protected by law against having to pay the small saver a fair market interest rate on his deposit. The ABA, as far as I can see, just wants to be protected by law against any competition from other lenders which might help to bring interest rates down. In short, in my view, the ABA is a selfish and petulant dinosaur and it's about time you entered the 20th century.[23]

Since many witnesses approach congressional hearings with the expectation of experiencing a public flogging, the tone of the questions that followed and the uniform criticism from other interest groups was probably no surprise to the banking officials. The spokesman for the American Bankers Association even began his statement defensively by reviewing the group's record of general support for the President's Commission on Financial Structure and Regulation, the original version of the Financial Institutions Act of 1975, and selected parts of the FINE Study. Their support for the 1975 proposals, however, quickly disappeared when the Senate Banking Committee added an amendment permitting the payment of interest on demand deposits. This was done during the markup session after the public hearings. The American Bankers Association had already experienced great difficulty in developing support for the 1975 reforms because of the overwhelming opposition of small commercial banks to the phasing out of regulation Q controls. The Senate's amendment shattered even that fragile consensus. By early 1976 the association had become opposed to any financial reform legislation during the ninety-fourth Congress.

During testimony on the Financial Reform Act of 1976, the American Bankers Association put forward a number of objections: (1) the bill would divert funds away from housing into consumer, corporate, and government debt; (2) thrift institutions would withhold funds from the mortgage markets in anticipation of legislative changes; (3) payment of interest on third-party payment accounts would increase costs for small borrowers and seriously erode the earnings of small financial institutions; (4) commercial banks would be discriminated against in the proposed bill; (5) an excessive banking structure would result from expanding the powers of thrift institutions; (6) "tax-free" credit unions would receive unfair advantages; (7) the proposed Federal Banking Commission would confuse and delay needed regulatory improvement; (8) uniform treatment of depository institutions with respect to taxation, reserve requirements, regulation and supervision, and deposit interest rates would not be provided; (9) the reorganization of the Federal Reserve System would impair its independent status, making it vulnerable to political pressures; (10) the mortgage interest tax credit would be deleted; (11) the Federal Home Loan Bank Board's program of long-term advances would disrupt the capital markets without providing much assistance to the housing sector; (12) mutual savings banks should not be granted federal charters to expand into new states; and (13) the existing activities of foreign banks operating in the United States should be permitted to continue under grandfather clauses in any future legislation.

The overwhelmingly critical response of the American Bankers Association concluded with the following total rejection:

> After careful consideration, the American Bankers Association has come to the conclusion that the Financial Reform Act is not amendable. For 4½ years—since the Presidential Commission on Financial Structure and Regulation—the Hunt Commission—issued its report—the banking industry has supported comprehensive financial reform, reform that is fair to all consumers and competitors and is in the public interest. But this bill is not in the tradition of the proposals emanating from the Hunt Commission. Its erratic yet massive approach to change would increase competitive inequities among depository institutions and, therefore, work to the detriment of the consuming public.[24]

Independent Bankers Association of America. The trade association dominated by small banks, the Independent Bankers Association of America, also rejected the Financial Reform Act of 1976 because "it is so incredibly complex and would result in so drastic a modification of the entire body of Federal legislation regulating the Nation's depository institutions that it is well nigh impossible to assess its precise effects with any degree of certainty."[25] This group repeated the arguments used in its previous appearances: the expansion of asset and liability powers would hurt housing; thrift institutions should concentrate on mortgage loans rather than becoming family

24. Ibid., p. 737. Statement of J. Rex Duwe, representing the American Bankers Association.

25. Ibid., p. 779. Statement of Charles O. Maddox, Jr., representing the Independent Bankers Association of America.

financial centers; and changes in regulation Q controls and the payment of interest on demand deposits would seriously hurt smaller financial institutions. In short, they pressed for a fine-tuning rather than comprehensive reform.

American Federation of Labor–Congress of Industrial Organizations. The AFL-CIO disappointed the sponsors of the Financial Reform Act of 1976 by refusing to support this proposed legislation "because it attempts a mechanical restructuring of the Nation's financial system while failing to come to grips with the needs that these institutions are supposed to serve."[26] Their major criticism focused on the increased asset and liability flexibility proposed for thrift institutions. This provision, they argued, would serve "to greatly reduce the proportion of their new funds going into residential mortgages in coming years."[27] They repeated their familiar arguments that government guidelines should be established to provide selective credit allocation, and that they should include requirements that financial institutions place a minimum percentage of their assets in home mortgage loans.[28]

National Association of Home Builders. The powerful National Association of Home Builders also refused to endorse the Financial Reform Act of 1976 despite its significant improvement over the FINE "Discussion Principles," because "it does not address itself to the root causes of the residential mortgage money problem and in fact, if enacted, could well worsen that problem."[29] The home builders strongly endorsed the continuation of regulation Q controls and the one-fourth of 1 percent differential but criticized the liberalization of thrift institutions' asset and liability powers and the Federal Home Loan Bank Board's new long-term advances program. They also joined with the AFL-CIO in requesting legislation which would in-

26. Ibid., p. 371. Statement of Henry B. Schechter, representing the American Federation of Labor–Congress of Industrial Organizations.

27. Ibid., p. 374.

28. Ibid., p. 382. In an interesting exchange of comments between Chairman St Germain and Dr. Schechter the amount of union pension funds committed to home mortgage loans was reviewed. Of six major union pension funds willing to report their investment portfolios to the House Banking Committee, two did not have any real estate loans and mortgages, one had 6 percent, one had 11 percent, one had 14 percent, and the International Brotherhood of Electrical Workers had 46 percent of their total assets committed to mortgage loans.

29. Ibid., p. 976. Statement of John Hart, representing the National Association of Home Builders.

crease real estate lending by pension funds and insurance companies. At the same time, they criticized the 1976 legislation for proposing incentives to attract commercial banks into the mortgage markets, a seeming contradiction of their assertion that larger and more stable sources of funds are needed to help the housing sector.

National Association of Realtors. The National Association of Realtors joined with the AFL-CIO and the National Association of Home Builders in rejecting the Financial Reform Act of 1976, because it did not provide enough incentives to increase mortgage financing. In commenting that "the bill in its present form is not acceptable to our association," the realtors' group sharply criticized the deletion of the mortgage interest tax credit included in the 1975 proposals. They also opposed the Federal Home Loan Bank Board's new program of advances, arguing that it would create additional distortions in the private financial markets.[30] Proposals to liberalize the powers of thrift institutions were also opposed by this group because of the risk that support for the mortgage markets might be reduced if consumer loans became a popular asset for savings and loan associations and mutual savings banks.

Consumer organizations. Two major consumer groups presented statements warmly endorsing an extensive set of amendments proposed by Chairman St Germain and designed to increase the disclosure requirements of financial institutions. The representative of the National Consumer Congress complimented the House subcommittee for attempting to "balance the interests of the banking industry against the desires and needs of the savings and loan associations" but criticized the entire package for failing to "address matters of concern to consumers" other than the amendments proposed by Chairman St Germain.[31] He expressed support for the expansion of powers for thrift institutions including the authority to offer checking accounts, liberalized branching rules for commercial banks, removal of regulation Q controls, and consolidation of the bank regulatory functions into a new agency, including the transfer from the Federal Reserve Board of functions established under the new Consumer Credit Protection Act. The statement from the Consumer Federation of America was more positive in its support, although its

---

30. Ibid., p. 991. Statement of Philip C. Smaby, representing the National Association of Realtors.

31. Ibid., p. 847. Statement of Michael C. Harper of the Center for Law and Social Policy, representing the National Consumer Congress and Americans for Democratic Action.

representative admitted that the 1976 proposals should be significantly improved and could only be graded "a very unenthusiastic
plus."

> CFA supports the principles of the Financial Reform Act of 1976 and if
> adequately modified to accommodate our concerns, we can endorse the
> bill when it is introduced. It represents a much-needed and appropriate
> step in the right direction toward more vigorous competition among and
> regulatory coordination of financial institutions of this country. Only a
> combined approach can afford consumers reasonable assurance that, one,
> there will not be a continued discrimination against small savers; two, the
> housing needs of this country will not continue to suffer from a cyclical
> pattern of boom and bust; three, that regulation will be more comprehen-
> sive and subject to greater accountability; and four, customers of all finan-
> cial institutions will be provided with the expanded benefits and services
> they deserve.[32]

The Consumer Federation also jumped on the bandwagon to criticize commercial banks with a statement which probably caused
more concern among depository institutions trying to meet the aggressive entry of banks into consumer lending and savings markets
than it did among officials of the American Bankers Association,
who are used to such attacks:

> Bankers resist with haughty disdain efforts to expand consumer bene-
> fits and services, and even insist on maintaining a 3 P.M. closing time as
> the norm, so as to further maximize their already quite comfortable prof-
> its. They veil themselves in a self-righteous secrecy, and adamantly op-
> pose even reasonable disclosure requirements. They decry the payment of
> interest on checking accounts, and exhibit little if any commitment to the
> housing needs of this country.
> Incredibly, bankers now enter the debate on financial reform with a
> preannounced policy which states, there will be no good faith discussion
> on the merits, no compromise, no accommodation, and an all out war
> against this proposed legislation. Their insensitivity and their sheer arro-
> gance lead consumers to wonder if the time is not long overdue for
> consumers to squeeze this Scrooge.[33]

During the extensive hearing on the Financial Reform Act of 1976
each group became more unwilling to compromise, and their lobbying efforts seemed to intensify. Special interest groups, as noted

---

32. Ibid., p. 865. Statement of Kathleen F. O'Reilly, representing the Consumer Fed-
    eration of America which includes the Consumers Union, seventeen cooperatives
    and credit union leagues, forty-five state and local consumer organizations, sixty-
    six rural electric cooperatives, twenty-seven national and regional organizations,
    and sixteen national labor unions.

33. Ibid., p. 864.

throughout this study, usually concentrate on preserving their existing powers and competitive advantages before seeking additional responsibilities. The proposed comprehensive reforms evoked little interest, and there were very few references to the future structure of the financial system, other than serious concern about the potential impact of the electronic transfer of funds systems. The conflicting arguments usually emphasized qualitative factors and historical experiences rather than theoretical and analytical evidence.

Also prevalent was a tendency to attack commercial banks as the common enemy. Even the smaller banks joined in the general criticism of larger banking institutions. This adversary relationship ultimately prevented the trade-offs necessary for structural reform, because each group believed that competing organizations should be required to pay an admissions price before receiving additional powers. Thrift institutions and credit unions argued that because the full-service commercial banks already have such a dominating competitive advantage their own powers should be expanded to enable them to survive. Commercial banks responded that if other depository institutions are authorized to provide new services historically reserved for banks they should be made to conform to the same regulatory, tax, and reserve requirements as banks. The resulting stalemate prevented comprehensive structural and regulatory reforms.

Legislative Results

At the conclusion of the congressional hearings on the Financial Reform Act of 1976 each group had to devise a new strategy for responding to the legislative stalemate, since it was clear that the comprehensive package proposed in the House could not be passed. After six years of intense debate the critics of broad reform were even more reluctant to compromise, and each special interest group preferred to work independently for its own goals while delaying any action on the pending legislation. For example, credit unions lobbied throughout this period to gain favorable congressional consideration of their detailed proposals without waiting for final action on either the Financial Institutions Act of 1975 or the Financial Reform Act of 1976. By delaying legislative reform beyond 1976 the special interest groups evidently hoped to avoid the uncertainties of change and the risks of increased competition, but at the same time to preserve and expand their present advantages.

The administration's position

Within the administration a diversity of views had evolved by the spring of 1976. The Federal Reserve Board proposed several changes in their powers to supervise and enforce regulations, and Senator Proxmire was preparing to hold hearings on these proposals. The Board continued to be concerned about the pressures to reorganize the functions and independent status of the Federal Reserve System. The Department of Housing and Urban Development was principally alert to the housing aspects of the reform legislation, which somewhat limited its interest to the mortgage interest tax credit that had been included in the 1975 proposals and recommended in the FINE Study but deleted from the Financial Reform Act of 1976. The Federal Home Loan Bank Board concentrated on moving the thrift institutions toward their goal of creating family financial centers with expanded asset and liability powers and continued mortgage market protection. This left the Treasury Department to develop a general strategy for the administration to follow in reacting to the legislative status of the 1975 and 1976 legislative proposals. On February 17 a task force comprising officials from the Treasury Department, the Council of Economic Advisers, and the Office of Management and Budget was formed to prepare the administration's response to the Financial Reform Act of 1976.

The crucial issue involved how much the administration would be willing to compromise for the sake of salvaging its preferred depository institution reforms and the eventual elimination of deposit interest rate controls. The administration had four options: (1) to do nothing until the markup of the proposed 1976 legislation was completed; (2) to oppose vigorously the House proposals for the Financial Reform Act of 1976; (3) to attempt to salvage some type of reform legislation by matching the Senate bill with pieces of the 1976 act, while continuing to avoid any major overhaul of the existing regulatory organization and allocation of functions; and (4) to continue developing new housing incentives to make the Financial Institutions Act of 1975 more attractive to special interest groups who refused to support either bill because of the alleged risks for mortgage markets.

The final decision, submitted to the Economic Policy Board on March 5 and summarized on March 11 in the Treasury testimony at the House hearings on the Financial Reform Act of 1976, was the third of these options. This position was reaffirmed in a letter from Deputy Secretary Dixon of the Treasury Department, written March

18 to Congressmen Reuss and St Germain, which limited Treasury support to proposals in the Financial Institutions Act of 1975.[34] Finally, on March 25, Deputy Secretary Dixon wrote to Congressman Rousselot of California, the ranking Republican on the House Subcommittee on Financial Institutions Supervision, Regulation, and Insurance, asking that he again support the 1975 proposals because they were the most likely to gain the necessary bipartisan support: "We propose to stand behind that bill, but would not oppose amendments which minority members might desire so long as they did not change its basic thrust."[35]

The Treasury first listed the bare-bones minimum of these measures: expanded asset and liability powers for thrift firms and credit unions; federal charters for mutual savings banks and elimination of the one-fourth of 1 percent interest differential; and the return of deposit interest rate control decisions to the regulatory agencies, with instructions to change the rules as necessary to respond to financial disintermediation. Beyond these the Treasury presented a variety of possible amendments to the 1975 proposal that might help defuse the intense controversy: (1) eliminate or defer provisions permitting interest on demand deposits, but provide authority for preauthorized transfers between savings and checking accounts; (2) eliminate either demand deposits for thrift institutions or NOW accounts for all institutions; (3) eliminate trust powers for savings and loan associations and mutual savings banks; (4) eliminate the provision for conversion from mutual to stock ownership of thrift institutions; (5) eliminate references to ceilings on FHA and VA mortgage interest rates; and (6) eliminate the mortgage interest tax credits for thrift institutions, permitting them to retain their existing tax treatment of special reserves for debt losses.

Deputy Secretary Dixon reported to Secretary Simon on April 10 that the House Republicans were not going to support the Treasury strategy for pushing the 1975 proposals as a substitute for the 1976 package because the adverse political climate would probably prevent the passage of any legislation.[36] During the next few months

---

34. Letter from Deputy Secretary of the Treasury George H. Dixon to Congressmen Henry S. Reuss and Fernand J. St Germain, dated March 18, 1976.

35. Letter from Deputy Secretary of the Treasury George H. Dixon to Congressman John H. Rousselot, dated March 25, 1976.

36. Treasury Department memorandum from Deputy Secretary George H. Dixon to Secretary William E. Simon, dated April 10, 1976.

Treasury officials continued to lobby for the 1975 proposals. At the same time they opposed the entire Financial Reform Act of 1976, which included the consolidation of bank regulatory agencies into a single superagency and thus eliminated the office of Comptroller of the Currency, which is part of the Treasury Department. On April 20 the administration's internal task force on mortgage credit was disbanded, and a Treasury staff memorandum expressed the view that acceptable legislation would not be forthcoming from the House. The memorandum further stated that no simple housing incentive was available as an alternative to the mortgage interest tax credit.[37]

From this time the Treasury staff concentrated on responding to the specific bills created by splintering the 1976 package into three parts and to the parallel proposals made in the Senate Banking, Housing, and Urban Affairs Committee. On June 9 Deputy Secretary Dixon informed Secretary Simon that Chairman Reuss had already announced the impossibility of legislative action in 1976. Meetings had been held between Treasury officials and Congressman St Germain, he said, and these sessions confirmed the Treasury's judgment that no financial reform would occur in 1976.[38]

The Treasury and Congressman St Germain had also come to an agreement that piecemeal actions during the remaining months of 1976 would be avoided and that the administration would cooperate with Congress in developing a new package of reforms. These could be introduced upon the convening of the ninety-fifth Congress and final action could be expected by March 1977. One last review session took place on July 1 between the Treasury staff and representatives of the House Subcommittee on Financial Institutions Supervision, Regulation, and Insurance. After that the administration ended its effort to accomplish a comprehensive reform of financial institutions.[39]

During the transition from President Ford's administration to that of President Carter, the new Treasury officials appointed by the President were thoroughly briefed on the seven-year history of the reform effort and the fundamental dilemma of choosing between comprehensive or specific legislative strategies. As described below,

---

37. Treasury Department staff memorandum, dated April 20, 1976.
38. Treasury Department memorandum from Deputy Secretary George H. Dixon to Secretary William E. Simon, dated June 9, 1976.
39. Treasury Department memorandum from Thomas J. McDowell to Deputy Secretary George H. Dixon, dated July 1, 1976.

legislation extending deposit interest rate controls and granting the detailed expansion of asset and liability powers requested by credit unions quickly passed the House and Senate in early 1977, soon after Congress reconvened; but no effort has been made to revive the entire package of comprehensive reforms. In fact, the new Secretary of the Treasury, W. Michael Blumenthal, informed the Senate Subcommittee on Financial Institutions on June 20, 1977, that the Carter administration would limit its new initiatives to two specific proposals dealing with the payment of interest on demand deposits and NOW accounts and the payment of interest on legal reserves required by the Federal Reserve System. This reversal of strategy by the Treasury Department is discussed in the next chapter.

House committee's position

By late March 1976 the House Banking, Currency, and Housing Committee faced a difficult decision. The extended hearings on the Financial Reform Act of 1976 had clearly demonstrated that the comprehensive package could not be reported out favorably for a House vote. In addition to criticism from several powerful special interest groups and the opposition of the administration, which continued to push for its own 1975 proposal already passed by the Senate, the unusual scope and controversial nature of the seven sections comprising the 1976 proposal had confused and alienated many of the House committee members at a time when political pressures related to the approaching national elections were rapidly accelerating.

Legislative History after the 1976 Proposal

It had become increasingly obvious during the hearings that the comprehensive legislative proposals could not be passed. Congressman St Germain responded by splitting the broad bill into three parts to make it more manageable. The legislative history of these bills and parallel efforts in the Senate Banking, Housing, and Urban Affairs Committee, chaired by Senator Proxmire, are briefly outlined in the following chronology of hearings and committee reports on individual subjects covered by the 1976 Financial Reform Act.

Section 1. Regulatory Agencies

House of Representatives	Senate
FINE Study, *April–Nov. 1975.*	Hearings on the Federal Bank Commission Act, S. 2298, to consolidate federal bank supervisory and reg-
Hearings on the FINE Study, *Dec. 1975.*	

Hearings on the Financial Reform Act of 1976, H.R. 10183, *March 1976.*

ulatory functions into a single agency, *Oct. 31, Dec. 1, 8, 1975; Feb. 3, March 1, 19, 1976.*

Hearings on Financial Institutions Supervisory Powers, S. 2304, to strengthen the supervisory authority of federal banking agencies, *March 26, 1976.*

Committee report recommending passage of the Financial Institutions Supervisory Act Amendments of 1975, S. 2304, to strengthen the enforcement powers of bank regulatory agencies, *May 13, 1976*

Committee report recommending passage of the Financial Institutions Supervisory Act Amendments of 1977, S. 71, to strengthen the enforcement powers of bank regulatory agencies. The bill follows the recommendations proposed by the regulatory agencies themselves, *June 20, 1977* (similar to S. 2304).

Hearing on Federal Branching Policy concerning state regulations for bank branching, *Dec. 6–8, 13, 1976.*

Section 2. Depository Institutions (including deposit interest rate controls)

House of Representatives

FINE Study, *April–Nov. 1975.*

Hearings on the FINE Study, *Dec. 1975.*

Hearings on the Financial Reform Act of 1976, H.R. 10183, *March 1976.*

Markup of Financial Reform Act of 1976, H.R. 13077, covering the subjects of depository institutions and strengthened enforcement powers for banking regulatory authorities parallel to the Financial Institutions Act of 1975 and section 1 of the Financial Reform Act of 1976. This bill was the first part of the splintered 1976 FRA, *March 1976.*

Senate

Hearings on Financial Institutions Act of 1973, S. 2591, to improve the efficiency and flexibility of the financial system and to provide adequate funds for housing, *Nov. 1973; May and Dec. 1974.*

Hearings on the Financial Institutions Act of 1975, S. 1267, to expand competition, improve consumer services, strengthen financial institutions, and improve the flows of funds for mortgage credit, *May 1975.* Favorable committee report, *Nov. 20, 1975.* Favorable Senate vote, *Dec. 11, 1975.*

Hearings on H.R. 1901, a bill to extend regulation Q, expand the asset and liability powers of federal credit unions, permit federally chartered New York savings and loan associations to establish demand deposit accounts, and extend the authority of Federal Reserve banks to purchase U.S. government obligations directly, *Feb. 7, 1977.*

Committee report recommending passage of the Depository Institutions Amendments of 1977, H.R. 3365 (replaces H.R. 1901 above), *Feb. 22, 1977.*

H.R. 3365 considered and passed by the House, *March 1, 1977.*

House agreed to conference report, *April 5, 1977.*

Public Law 95–22 effective, *April 19, 1977.*

House approval of one-year extension of existing controls, including the one fourth of 1 percent differential, from Dec. 15, 1977, through Dec. 15, 1978, *Nov. 2, 1977.*

Committee report recommends passage of Extension of Interest Rate Control Act, S. 756, to extend deposit interest rate ceilings, *March 1, 1977.*

Amended H.R. 3365 considered and passed by the Senate in lieu of S. 756, *March 1, 1977.*

Senate agreed to conference report, *April 4, 1977.*

Public Law 95-22 effective, *April 19, 1977.*

Senate passed H.R. 1910 as described under the House column, *Nov. 2, 1977.*

Section 3. Housing

House of Representatives

FINE Study and the Financial Reform Act of 1976 included housing incentives; House Banking, Currency, and Housing Committee continued to hold legislative and oversight hearings each session.

Senate

The Financial Institutions Acts of 1973 and 1975 included housing incentives; Senate Banking, Housing, and Urban Affairs Committee continued to hold legislative and oversight hearings each session.

Section 4. Bank Holding Companies

House of Representatives

FINE Study, *April–Nov. 1975.*

Hearings on the FINE Study, *Dec. 1975.*

Hearings on the Financial Reform Act of 1976, H.R. 10183, *March 1976.*

House approved the Federal Reserve Reform Act of 1977, H.R. 9710, including amendments to the Bank Holding Company Act of 1956, *Nov. 2, 1977.*

Senate

Hearings on Competition in Banking Act of 1976, S. 2721, to amend the Bank Holding Company Act to restrict nonbanking activities, control bank acquisitions by holding companies, and promote competition, *March 4, 5, 1976.*

Section 5. The Federal Reserve System

House of Representatives

FINE Study, *April–Nov. 1975.*

Hearings on the FINE Study, *Dec. 1975.*

Hearings on the Financial Reform Act of 1976, H.R. 10183, *March 1976.*

Hearings on the Federal Reserve Reform Act of 1976, H.R. 12934, extracted from the Financial Reform Act of 1976 to amend the procedures for appointing regional Reserve bank presidents and to require quarterly congressional oversight hearings for the Federal Reserve Board, *April 9, 1976.*

Committee report recommending passage of H.R. 12934, the Federal Reserve Reform Act, *April 30, 1976.* This bill was the second part of the splintered 1976 act.

Committe report recommending passage of H.R. 8094, a new Federal Reserve Reform act comparable to H.R. 12934, which expired at the end of the 94th Congress, *Aug. 2, 1977.*

House approval of the Federal Reserve Reform Act of 1977, H.R. 9710, with the following provisions: monetary and credit aggregates to expand at the rate required to achieve national economic goals; the Board of Governors to consult with the House and Senate committees semiannually to explain objectives and plans for monetary and credit aggregates, with specific authority to change these objectives and plans if conditions change; boards of directors of Federal Reserve Banks to be selected without discrimination and with regard to the interests of agriculture, commerce, industry, services, labor, and consumers; beginning Jan. 1, 1979, the persons designated to

Senate

Hearings on the Federal Reserve Act Amendments of 1975, S. 2298, to require Senate confirmation of nominations for chairman of the Federal Reserve Board and presidents of district banks, to limit Federal Reserve System expenditures to approved congressional appropriations, add labor and consumer representatives to the board, and to authorize the Government Auditing Agency to audit the Federal Reserve System regularly (the GAO audit was separately recommended in S. 2509), *Oct. 20, 21, and Nov. 17, 1975.*

Committee report recommending passage of an amended Federal Reserve Reform Act as proposed in H.R. 12934 by the House to change the structure and functioning of the Federal Reserve System and make it more responsive to the Congress, *Aug. 20, 1976.*

Passed H.R. 1910 as described under the House column, *Nov. 2, 1977.*

serve as chairman and vice chairman of the Board of Governors would be subject to confirmation by the Senate. Cleared and sent to the President, *Nov, 2, 1977.*

Section 6. Foreign Banks in the United States

House of Representatives

FINE Study, *April–Nov. 1975.*

Hearings on the FINE Study, *Dec. 1975.*

Hearings on the Financial Reform Act of 1976, H.R. 10183, *March 1976.*

Committee report recommending passage of the International Banking Act of 1976, H.R. 13876, which would authorize the Federal Reserve Board to regulate foreign banks operating in the United States, *May 26 1976.* This bill was the third part of the splintered 1976 act.

Subcommittee approval of a modified bill that would apply domestic regulations to foreign banks in the United States, except that they would be permitted to continue branching in more than one state and would retain existing activities except for the underwriting of securities which must be phased out, *Oct. 12, 1977.*

Senate

Hearings on the Foreign Bank Act of 1975, S. 958, to amend various federal statutes to require domestic regulatory rules for foreign banks operating in the United States, *Jan. 28–30, 1976.*

Hearings on the International Banking Act of 1976, an analysis of H.R. 13876, which would authorize the Federal Reserve Board to regulate foreign banks operating in the U.S., *Aug. 31, 1976.*

Section 7. United States Banks Abroad

House of Representatives

FINE Study, *April–Nov. 1975.*

Hearings on the FINE Study, *Dec. 1975.*

Hearings on the Financial Report Act of 1976, H.R. 10183, *March 1976.*

Senate

On April 26 the House Banking, Currency, and Housing Committee (hereafter referred to as the House Banking Committee) commenced markup sessions on three separate pieces of legislation extracted from the Financial Reform Act of 1976. The first bill, H.R.

12934, known as the Federal Reserve Reform Act of 1976, was comparable to section 5 of the original 1976 proposal and was strongly supported by several members of the House Banking Committee and some private interest groups. This particular piece of legislation reflected a long-held conviction among many congressmen that the Federal Reserve System frustrates the goals of Congress by following its own independent monetary policies. At one point Congressman Reuss sponsored a bill, H.R. 3160, that would have required the Federal Reserve to expand monetary growth more rapidly and to allocate credit according to priorities that would lower interest rates for worthy projects and increase the interest rates for those considered unworthy.

Although that proposal was defeated in the House Banking Committee, the Federal Reserve Board was directed to make quarterly appearances before the House and Senate committees to explain monetary and credit policies; this was done under the terms of House Concurrent Resolution 133, which was passed in early 1975. (Such resolutions are not binding and are not signed by the President.) After the passage of that congressional resolution Chairman Arthur F. Burns appeared before the House and Senate banking committees to explain the target ranges for monetary growth, which are expressed in general terms.

The original 1976 reform proposals called for several changes in the organization and operation of the Federal Reserve System: making the terms of the chairman and vice chairman coterminous with that of the President; making the appointments subject to Senate confirmation: enlarging the boards of directors to include more public members; requiring that the presidents of the Federal Reserve district banks be appointed by the President and confirmed by the Senate; requiring explicit recognition of national goals for economic growth in the Board's conduct of monetary policies; and specifying that the quarterly testimony from the Federal Reserve Board on their targets for monetary growth was to be a permanent arrangement. When the Financial Reform Act of 1976 was splintered, the new bill, H.R. 12934, salvaged part of those proposals, although the House Banking Committee deleted some of the most controversial suggestions before reporting it out on April 30.

The Senate Banking Committee began in October 1975 to consider similar legislation, S. 2298, known as the Federal Reserve Act Amendments of 1975, and eventually reported out the House version of the bill on August 20, 1976. The essence of the congressional recommendation was that the formulation of monetary policies should be more open to participation by various private interest groups and much more responsive to the direction of Congress and the Executive Office.

Both the Treasury and the Federal Reserve Board opposed this legislation. They considered it not only unnecessary but potentially harmful. It would erode the professional quality of the entire Federal Reserve System, and it would take away some of the insulation protecting the Board from strong political pressures to use monetary policies to affect economic growth, particularly during election years. Despite the positive support of the leadership of both congressional banking committees, the Federal Reserve reform proposals were not accepted by either the House or the Senate in 1976.

Although H.R. 12934 and S. 2298 expired along with all of the other financial reform bills at the end of the ninety-fourth Congress, observers have been aware for some time that comparable legislation will be introduced in every session of Congress. Given the overwhelming importance of the basic issues, it is unfortunate that very few congressmen and members of the general public understand the complexity of the policy debate. The abstract nature of national economic policies and the confusing jargon used by the few officials and economists who are knowledgeable obscure the real significance of the issues. In fact, the public decisions being made on these matters will ultimately determine our success or failure in meeting our goals for national growth and stability.

Considering how eager several leading congressmen were to revise the organization and procedures of the Federal Reserve System, it is not surprising that many of the now familiar reform proposals were again submitted early in the ninety-fifth Congress. The Senate Banking Committee favorably reported to the full Senate a bill to improve banks' regulatory powers, S. 71, on June 30, 1977. This action came after a proposal to require Senate confirmation of future nominees to be chairman of the Federal Reserve Board had been narrowly defeated.

In the House Banking Committee two important bills were quickly prepared to replace the expired recommendations in the 1976 Financial Reform Act. The first bill, H.R. 8094, was directed at changing the appointment procedures for the chairman and vice chairman of the Federal Reserve Board to make their terms roughly coterminous (allowing a one-year lag) with the President's elected tenure and to require Senate confirmation for both positions. Under the existing procedures the President simply designated one of the Governors of the Federal Reserve Board to serve in each position, and Senate confirmation was required only at the time of their initial appointment to a fourteen-year term. Chairman Burns had originally given tentative approval to the procedural changes, but he shifted his position, thinking the new rules might create political pressure on the Federal Reserve Board during the final consideration of H.R. 8094.

Other important provisions of the legislation included: (1) quarterly testimony by the Federal Reserve Board; (2) expanded representation of more diverse interests on the boards of directors of the district banks; and (3) application of federal conflict-of-interest laws to the Federal Reserve System's activities. Several controversial proposals were eliminated, such as a requirement that the Federal Reserve Board include specific projections of interest rates, the velocity of the monetary aggregates, and the expected mix of Federal Reserve assets in their quarterly testimony before Congress. The House Banking Committee then approved the modified version of H.R. 8094 by a unanimous vote of forty members on August 2, 1977. The Senate Banking Committee, however, did not have comparable legislation to consider at that time.

The second bill considered by the House Banking Committee called for the General Accounting Office to carry out comprehensive audits of Federal Reserve Board activities, other than monetary policies and foreign transactions, and the operations of the Federal Deposit Insurance Corporation and the Comptroller of the Currency. The original pressure for the audits came from the House Government Operations Committee, and even some of the House Banking Committee members reacted against the potential encroachment in the matter of monetary policy. Chairman Burns was sharply critical of the audit proposals, calling them a threat to the continued independence of the Federal Reserve System. Governor Coldwell summarized the Board's opposition:

> We do not see what advantage there is to be gained either in requiring the General Accounting Office to duplicate the audit of the Federal Reserve Banks that has been carried on by the board for decades, or in substituting GAO for the board as the auditor of the banks.[40]

The strong opposition of the regulatory agencies has resulted in considerable modification of the proposals for audits by the General Accounting Office, but no House vote has been taken. The Senate

40. Mary Eisner Eccles, "House Democrats Renew Challenge to Federal Reserve," *Congressional Quarterly* (Sept. 3, 1977), p. 1879.

Banking Committee does not have comparable legislation at this time.

The most recent legislative initiative occurred November 2, 1977, when both the House and the Senate passed and sent to the President a bill to extend regulation Q controls for one more year, that is, through December 15, 1978. This legislation, H.R. 9710, also included some routine amendments to the Bank Holding Company Act of 1956. More significantly, it included amendments to the Federal Reserve Act which apparently represent current decisions on the various proposals to reform the Federal Reserve System. The pertinent amendments call for the Federal Reserve Board to carry out these directives: increase the monetary and credit aggregates at a rate commensurate with national economic goals; present semiannual testimony to the two congressional banking committees on its monetary objectives and plans for the next twelve months, recognizing that the plans must remain flexible to adjust to changing conditions; and assure that the directors of Federal Reserve district banks are selected without discrimination and represent various public interests. Future nominees to the chairmanship and vice chairmanship of the Federal Reserve Board were to be confirmed by the Senate after January 1, 1977.

The legislative actions finally approved by the House and Senate in early November 1977 are considerably watered down from the many proposals considered by the House Banking Committee in the 1976 and later legislation, but the deleted provisions may well be introduced in future sessions of Congress. As with any compromise, probably most participants in this decision-making process are dissatisfied with the actual results. The Federal Reserve Board remains uneasy about the continued threat to its independence, and many congressmen are still critical of the present arrangements because they do not make the Federal Reserve Board directly responsible to the directives of Congress. The final outcome, of course, will not be known for many years, and there is little point in speculating about it here. One general observation may be made, however. As so often happens, the process of making economic decisions in the Congress was confused by procedural details that prevented the public at large from recognizing the real significance of the issue. Considering how fundamental the conduct of monetary policy is to the development of national economic strategies, a much more open and comprehensive debate, involving not only the entire Congress but the public as well, should precede such basic decisions.

The second bill, H.R. 13077, known as the Financial Reform Act of 1976, included recommendations covering depository institutions and consolidation of bank regulatory activities. It was overwhelmingly opposed by numerous special interest groups and by the Treasury. This opposition limited the chances for its success, and it was not reported out of the House Banking Committee. At the same time, the Treasury did support the recommendations contained in S. 2304, under consideration in the Senate. This legislation had been suggested by the federal banking agencies themselves to strengthen their existing supervisory and regulatory powers without creating the consolidated agency proposed in section 1 of the Financial Reform Act of 1976.

One of the most interesting aspects of this sequence of events was the vigorous effort by the Treasury to prevent further "piecemealing," in which one special interest group might gain congressional approval for specific measures, even though the comprehensive proposals of 1975 and 1976 remained stalled. Treasury officials met frequently with representatives of the special interest groups and congressional leaders to argue against passage of specific legislation during the waning days of the ninety-fourth Congress. Both Senator McIntyre and Congressman St Germain agreed with the Treasury's view and cooperated in effectively preventing "piecemealing" legislation.

Nevertheless, credit unions continued to try to gain separate action on the package of detailed legislative changes which they had previously proposed to Congress and which had been largely incorporated in both the 1975 and 1976 acts. Although in this case the Treasury and both congressional banking committees supported the requests, they considered it unfair and potentially disruptive to respond to only one group among the financial institutions.

At one point it appeared that the credit unions might be successful in adding their entire package as a floor amendment to a bill, favorably reported to the Senate by its Banking Committee, that would replace the single Administrator of the National Credit Union Administration with a new board composed of three members. The political appeal of most credit union legislation might have made it relatively easy to gain a favorable Senate vote in an election year, and then to arrange for a conference report with the House by adding the proposals as an amendment to one of their bills. Senator McIntyre's strong commitment to comprehensive reform was enough to prevent such action in the Senate, however, and

Congressman St Germain for similar reasons delayed consideration of separate credit union legislation in the House. As he explained in his opening statement at subsequent hearings:

> Last year, when it became evident to all that there was not sufficient time to resolve many differences over the Financial Reform Act, H.R. 13077, which included the credit union amendments, many of my colleagues urged the separate consideration of the credit union amendments which had already passed the Senate as a part of the Financial Institutions Act of 1975.
>
> Despite the strong support for the credit union legislation, no further action was taken because of the basic belief that we should not legislate for one segment of the financial industry.[41]

The approach to financial institution reform changed dramatically when the new ninety-fifth Congress convened on January 4, 1977. With regulation Q scheduled to expire on March 1 and the credit unions still applying strong pressure to have their legislative package considered immediately, both the House and Senate were compelled to act quickly. On January 13 Congressmen St Germain and Reuss introduced new legislation, and on February 7 the House Banking Subcommittee held hearings on H.R. 1901, "a bill to extend the authority for the flexible regulation of interest rates on deposits and accounts in depository institutions, and for other purposes." The "other purposes" beyond the simple extension of the deposit interest rate controls referred to three additional sections, including the detailed credit union proposals so often introduced in Congress but delayed until this time because of the preference for a comprehensive approach to financial institution reform. H.R. 1901 contained four sections.

Title I would extend regulation Q controls until June 1, 1977. The final bill cleared by Congress extended the new deadline through December 15, 1977. The bill also maintained the one-fourth of 1 percent differential for thrift institutions.

Title II would extend the authority for federally chartered depository institutions in three more states, including New York, to offer NOW accounts. Considerable opposition to extending NOW accounts beyond the six New England states developed, however, and the House Banking Committee then dropped its proposed extension of authority to three additional states and recommended instead that federally chartered savings and loan associations in New York be

41. U.S., Congress, House, Committee on Banking, Finance, and Urban Affairs, *To Extend Regulation Q*, Hearing Before the Subcommittee on Financial Institutions Supervision, 95th Cong., 1st sess., Feb. 7, 1977, p. 12.

permitted to offer non-interest-paying checking services, as state thrift institutions were already allowed to do. The conference version agreed to by the House and Senate dropped this provision on April 15.

Title III would extend the authority of the Federal Reserve System to purchase U.S. government obligations directly. The final bill extended the authority through August 31, 1977.

Title IV would broaden the asset and liability powers of federal credit unions and make many detailed administrative changes, including: (1) an increase in the limits on the size and maturities of both secured and unsecured loans; (2) authority to grant residential mortgage loans with maturities of up to thirty years; (3) authority to grant mobile home loans with maturities up to fifteen years; (4) authority to offer revolving lines of credit; (5) provisions for loans to other credit unions and participation loans; (6) flexibility in rates of return and maturities of deposit accounts; (7) new leeway provisions to diversify assets; and (8) new liquidity assistance.

The decision to respond specifically to credit union interests along with the necessary extension of regulation Q, pending decisive action regarding its permanent status, was explained by Congressman St Germain:

> As we resume our deliberations on comprehensive financial institution reform proposals which will include further consideration of the recently introduced Credit Union Modernization Act, H.R. 1528, it must be recognized that, pending final determination, certain interim action is imperative to insure the continued viability of federally chartered institutions and to provide parity of treatment, not an unfair advantage.[42]

The one day of hearings produced statements from the new Administrator of the National Credit Union Administration, as well as from spokesmen for the National Association of Federal Credit Unions and the Credit Union National Association. As would be expected, all of the testimony endorsed the new legislation but took note that some of the detailed administrative changes requested by credit unions had not been included:

> We are pleased that, in the main, Title IV is drawn from H.R. 1528, the Credit Union Modernization Act, which is the culmination of six years of effort by credit unions to design and draft a legislative package which will permit us to meet the competitive challenges posed by other financial institutions. H.R. 1528 is much more comprehensive than the rather modest proposal we have before us today.[43]

42. Ibid.
43. Ibid., p. 49. Statement of Jim R. Williams, President of Credit Union National Association.

Additional written comments were received from these sources: the Federal Reserve Board, which supported Titles I and III, suggested delay on Title II, and deferred comment on Title IV; the Acting Comptroller of the Currency, who supported the bill but suggested that Title IV be made part of comprehensive reform; the Federal Home Loan Bank Board, which approved of Titles I and II but deferred comment on III and IV; and the Federal Deposit Insurance Corporation which did not object to the bill, despite many specific questions, but suggested deferring action on Title IV.

In the private sector, the American Banking Association agreed that regulation Q should be temporarily extended but argued that the expansion of credit union powers and NOW accounts should wait for general reform. The AFL-CIO endorsed the bill. The two major savings and loan associations strongly endorsed regulation Q controls but felt that the other expansion of powers should be delayed (the letter from the National Savings and Loan League did support the expansion of NOW accounts; the U.S. League of Savings Associations recommended further delay).

All of these viewpoints were predictable to anyone familiar with the many years of public statements. Perhaps the only surprise was the total absence of involvement by the Treasury Department after it had provided leadership during the preceding six years. The last paragraph in the letter written by the Acting Comptroller of the Currency referred to the Treasury's role as follows: "The Treasury Department is currently reviewing the question of financial reform and these comments do not necessarily reflect the views of the Department."[44]

Legislation to extend regulation Q was also quickly introduced in the Senate, but the proposal that was reported out by the Senate Banking Committee on March 1 was limited to controls on deposit interest rates rather than providing the broader coverage contained in H.R. 3365 (a replacement for the original H.R. 1901). Also on March 1, the latter bill, H.R. 3365, was approved by the House, and later in the day the full Senate decided to pass the amended version of this bill, the compromise making it possible to complete the conference report in early April. The important extension of regulation Q controls and the controversial expansion of specific asset and liability powers for credit unions became a public law taking effect April 19. Anticipating the expiration of the deposit interest rate controls scheduled for December 15, 1977, the House

44. Ibid., p. 87. Letter from Robert Bloom, Acting Comptroller of the Currency.

and Senate approved another extension for one year and sent the bill to the President for his signature on November 2. A presidential task force is now preparing a new study of the long-term future of regulation Q controls.

The third bill extracted from the Financial Reform Act of 1976 concerned the operation of foreign banks in the United States. The House Banking Committee reported out H.R. 13876, the International Banking Act of 1976, on May 26, 1976, and the Senate held hearings on the House bill on August 31, but it was not possible to pass the legislation in either house of Congress before the year ended.

The proposed legislation called for application of domestic banking rules to foreign banks and for foreign banks to be denied any activities not permitted to domestic banks. Other specific provisions involved the establishment of an option for the federal chartering of branches, a screening process requiring the approval of the Secretaries of the Treasury and State Departments, surety deposits with the Federal Deposit Insurance Corporation, and Federal Reserve supervision and regulation. The Treasury generally supported the legislation except for the screening requirements, which would affect newly appointed Secretaries of the Treasury and State Departments, and the absence of grandfather exemptions allowing foreign banks to continue existing activities. The widespread support for this bill led to expectations that new legislation could be proposed in the ninety-fifth Congress; but it was not until October 12, 1977, that the House Banking Subcommittee approved a modified version of the 1976 initiative. A final version, the International Banking Act of 1978, was finally completed by Congress in March of 1978.

The scoreboard of legislative activities at the end of 1976 indicates that both the Financial Institutions Act of 1975 and the Financial Reform Act of 1976 expired without favorable action; the three specific bills extracted from the comprehensive House Banking Committee's proposal also failed to reach the floor of either the House or the Senate, despite the seven years of legislative effort and an even longer period of academic analysis of the issues. The complicated legislative procedures made the comprehensive packages vulnerable to many forces: the strong opposition of powerful special interest groups; the internal struggles between the executive branch and Congress for political power; and similar conflicts within the Senate and House of Representatives.

Summary

When the ninety-fourth Congress adjourned at the close of 1976 the outlook for comprehensive financial institution reform was bleak at best, a disappointing end to the bright expectations that existed when the President's Commission on Financial Structure and Regulation was announced on February 2, 1970. Similar optimism had prevailed when the Treasury Department introduced the Financial Institutions Act of 1973 on August 3, 1973, and when Congressmen Reuss and St Germain initiated the FINE Study on April 24, 1975. The comprehensive approach to reform had produced hundreds of articles and books, many thousands of pages of congressional hearing records, and had required many years of continuous effort by an executive branch task force and two important congressional banking committees. To one looking back, the final outcome was startling. By the end of 1977, only one public law had been passed as a result of eight years of work, and that single piece of legislation called only for the simple temporary extension of deposit interest rate controls, which have existed since 1966 in their present form, and for approval of the detailed package of credit union reforms developed independently by their private trade associations. Even that modest accomplishment was sharply criticized by those who believe that regulation Q controls are the chief cause of many financial problems, rather than a sound solution to recurring competitive strains, and that the reform of depository institutions requires a comprehensive set of balanced actions to encourage competition and moderate distortions.

In the final analysis, the fate of the Financial Institutions Act of 1975 and of the Financial Reform Act of 1976 was determined by the uncompromising attitudes of three power blocs: private interest groups, executive branch departments and agencies, and Congress. By the end of the legislative process the various special interest groups were intent on preventing widespread changes and had clearly decided to work independently in seeking their own specific goals. Analysis of their congressional testimonies and lobbying efforts demonstrates unmistakably the polarization of the views held by these key special interests. For example, Congressman Willis D. Gradison, Jr., of Ohio expressed the following conviction during the hearings on the 1976 proposals:

> But more to the point of what we are talking about today, Mr. Chairman, my feeling is that the testimony so far today has, for the first time in this second round of hearings, indicated that this measure in its present form

is in trouble and that there are serious problems that are going to require major changes if this legislation is going to do the job of reform which it is supposed to do.

It seemed to me before today that we had a classic confrontation shaping up of the bankers on the one side against the measure, and maybe the savings and loans and trade union groups and builders, perhaps, on the other side. But it seems to me, if there ever was such a coalition, it seems to be crumbling.

Certainly, Mr. Schechter's testimony, which I have glanced over and which we will hear later today, suggests something less than wild enthusiasm for this measure on his part as a representative of the AFL-CIO, a group which carries great weight in this body. And the testimony given by Dr. Kaplan [Federal Home Loan Bank Board] suggests to me, as a representative of one of the strongest savings and loan areas in the United States, that once individual savings and loans start taking a look at the numbers in this bill and comparing it with their own internal operations, a lot of them are going to find that they are not going to get the differential that they have become so accustomed to and looked upon as essential to their operations.[45]

The strong position of the Treasury Department was succinctly summarized in a set of talking points distributed as the House Banking Committee started the markup sessions:

We are strongly opposed to the Financial Reform Act being considered in the House and to any proposals which would benefit only isolated industry groups to the detriment of others.[46]

Finally, Congressman St Germain expressed his frustration with the course of the hearings on the 1976 bill, in an exchange of views with Dr. Henry B. Schechter, representing the AFL-CIO.

Mr. St Germain: Now, on page 2, you state, "The opportunity will be lost for many years to come, because enactment of comprehensive financial reform legislation is very time-consuming and infrequent."

Are you in a sense saying that you intend to hold this bill hostage, despite the jurisdictional problems and limitations we have in this subcommittee and on the full committee?

Dr. Schechter: Mr. Chairman, may I ask—

Mr. St Germain: Until we deal with the housing-related problems?

Dr. Schechter: Well, what we are concerned with is not getting into a situation which will be worse than what we have had, and this is what we fear.

Mr. St Germain: Well, do you not fear more the possibility, and the very real possibility, of the adoption of FIA 1975?

Dr. Schechter: We would strongly oppose that.

45. House, Committee on Banking, Currency, and Housing, *The Financial Reform Act of 1976*, p. 356.

46. Treasury Department staff memorandum, dated April 27, 1976.

Mr. St Germain: Well, the facts of life are that the probabilities of that, if this does not receive support, improve every minute of the day, because some of the major trade associations want FIA 1975. And you heard the administration witnesses; they have been pushing this now since 1973. And since it has passed the Senate by a very dramatic vote—I think 14 votes in opposition—they have a very strong feeling that if they are able to defeat this committee print, that prior to the end of this Congress, they can have adopted FIA 1975. And I think that is a fact of life to be viewed very, very carefully.[47]

47. House, Committee on Banking, Currency, and Housing, *The Financial Reform Act of 1976*, p. 384.

10

LEGISLATIVE RESULTS AND OUTLOOK

In developing policies for making financial institutions more adaptable to changing conditions, the federal government failed to rationalize the various competing interests. When time ran out at the end of 1976, it had been eighteen years since the private Commission on Money and Credit began its broad review of the nation's entire financial system, six and one half years since the President's Commission on Financial Structure and Regulation was created to prepare recommendations for basic reform, and three years since comprehensive legislation, in the form of the Financial Institutions Act, was presented to Congress. This failure in the decision-making process had occurred despite the universal recognition that the financial system is rapidly changing and requires basic reform. As a result, the private financial markets and individual regulatory agencies were left to work out their own solutions to competitive problems in an environment of unnecessary confusion and obsolete legislative barriers to change.

Financial institution reform is only one example of the hundreds of difficult legislative issues that Congress must consider during each session. It should not be surprising or discouraging that many controversial issues cannot be readily resolved or that existing governmental institutions and procedures often impede, rather than aid, the efforts to make necessary decisions. In fact, given the extreme diversity and technical complexity of the problems that government must deal with, it is impressive that they accomplish as much as they do. Nevertheless, the example considered in this study does demonstrate three important facts about our modern political system.

First, the federal government increasingly intervenes in our personal and economic lives by making decisions affecting private markets and individual behavior. In a complex society many controversial issues can only be resolved at the highest levels of government, and the familiar adage, "The buck stops here," clearly applies to the Executive Office, Congress, and the Supreme Court. The apparent trend toward collective approaches to problems further increases the role of a strong central government.

There are serious risks that personal freedoms and individual creativity may be eroded by government dominance. But there are also potential benefits in having a central authority that identifies and ranks national priorities and then marshals public support for the proposed solutions, as long as the democratic process for identifying the preferences of the majority and protecting the rights of minorities is preserved. For example, the federal budget can be used as a rigorous means of ranking national priorities and a basis for debating alternatives in allocating resources and assigning responsibilities to the private and public sectors. Unfortunately the budget can also be used as a simplistic device for courting political favor without regard for the economic distortions thus created. How effectively the government actually functions will depend on the quality of the people in leadership roles and the involvement of the electorate, but the federal government can provide broad perspectives and discipline in efforts to make the system work better.

Second, the structure of government too often leads to delay—or outright prevention—of responsible and workable decisions that could avoid unnecessary frustrations and inequities. The fate of each legislative initiative depends upon actions by the relatively few powerful officials in the Executive Office and Congress who use the complicated committee processes to control events. In the case considered here the key issues and the conflicting arguments of the special interest groups and expert witnesses had long been well known and could be easily summarized as a background for a relatively quick legislative response. The issues involved were clearly controversial but they were at least understandable.

The details given in the preceding chapters explain why the decisions required for financial institution reform were not made: in a political sense there was little prospective advantage but considerable risk in forcing the powerful special interest groups to accept the compromises required by the proposed comprehensive legislation. This same dilemma exists in considering legislation dealing with the environment, energy, welfare, transportation, education, health, agriculture, and every other controversial issue confronting Congress. The preferred solution is too often simply a continuation of the status quo to avoid rocking the boat.

Third, the present fragmented approach to making decisions within the government dilutes the quality of analysis and confuses the assignment of authority and responsibility. We should seriously ask how much detail Congress should consider in debating legislative rulings which assign specific programs to the executive branch and regulatory agencies. So much time is spent arguing about details that the philosophical and organizational issues are often ignored. No matter how conscientious the individual members of Congress are, the flood of legislative proposals in every session makes it impossible for them to understand the details of most bills.

This problem leads many to argue in favor of delegating authority to specialized committees to consider complex legislation, but such an approach can also cause delay or prevent decisions. The history of financial institution reform is a clear example. An alternative would be to have Congress consider fewer issues and function in an oversight role, leaving the operating details to administrative officials. Congress could then be expected to arrive at judgments more quickly and to involve more of its members in the final decisions. Congress does need to give broad directions to prevent the bureaucracies from becoming too independent.

The general political, social, and economic shocks experienced over the last fifteen years have demonstrated the complexity of legislative issues and caused increased concern about the organization and procedures for making important national decisions. Unfortunately, examples such as the financial institution reform effort have added to the general disillusionment about the quality, efficiency, and objectivity of actions by the executive branch and Congress. Disagreements over specific government acts will, of course, always exist, but the current degree of cynicism among the general public and experts outside the government is unnecessary. It exists because the institutions and procedures of government have too frequently been allowed to frustrate the decision-making process.

Financial Institution Reform Goals and Results

The chief goal of any financial system is to provide an efficient means of collecting and allocating capital resources in a way that best serves national economic and social goals. Analysts have been concerned for many years about the severe cyclical swings in interest rates and related financial disintermediation, the volatile earnings of financial institutions, major shifts in historical patterns of competition, disrupted housing markets, and the increasing intervention in the private economy that governments at all levels have used to achieve various social goals. Rapid changes in consumers' financial needs and in the operating characteristics of financial institutions and the national economy have led many to doubt the appropriateness of preserving a framework of government legislation and regulation that was designed forty years ago, largely as a reaction to the traumatic experiences of the Great Depression. Originally those rules were intended to foster fair competition and restore public confidence in the financial system. But adapting to changing conditions is also an important goal.

During the 1960s and 1970s the personal income and ways of life among most consumers changed dramatically. These changes in turn caused major adjustments in the competitive environment and made the statutory specialization of financial institutions a pressing issue.

> Statutory specialization committing the thrift institutions to mortgage lending developed at a time when passbook accounts were the only significant source of funds, when the institutions were investing mainly in local mortgage markets, when management was often relatively unsophisticated, when deposit insurance was not available, and when safety for the public's savings was necessarily the main concern.
>
> The case for statutory specialization may have been clearer when government first began to regulate the thrift institutions. It was plausible for legislators and regulators to assume that when financial intermediaries specialize in one class of assets, it would simplify management tasks, enhance the institution's safety, and provide financial services to the public at lower cost.[1]

As the assumptions underlying the regulatory framework have evolved, two major changes in the financial markets have occurred: (1) competition based on managerial innovations and new technology has become more intense; and (2) severe distortions have resulted from the periodic economic booms and recessions and chronic inflation pressures. In this difficult environment the preferred functional specialization of earlier years made competition difficult for many depository institutions because of the mismatch between the short-term stability of their liabilities, largely passbook savings accounts, and the long-term maturities of mortgage loans that comprised the bulk of their assets. As the postwar economy continued to evolve, risks were created by "borrowing at the margin" (the rate of return paid on the vast majority of savings accounts) and "lending at the

---

1. U.S., Congress, Senate, Committee on Banking, Housing, and Urban Affairs, *Reform of Financial Institutions: 1973*, p. 188.

average" (the cumulative earnings on mortgage loans acquired over many years in which the average return lags behind rising current interest rates). During the same period the secular trend of interest rates turned sharply upward as inflation pressures escalated. This unfortunate combination of events trapped many financial institutions, putting them at a disadvantage competitively. Nevertheless, functional specialization continued, since statutory rules restricted managerial discretion in changing institutional asset and liability policies. By the late 1960s, as we have seen, the accumulation of economic distortions and the accelerating pace of technological change in the financial markets provided clear signals that widespread reform was necessary.

The creation of the private Commission on Money and Credit in 1958 marked the beginning of a comprehensive restructuring of financial depository institutions. That monumental study was followed by similar initiatives to pass new legislation involving a cabinet-level White House task force in 1963 and the Federal Savings Institutions Act that was favorably reported by the House Banking and Currency Committee in December 1967. A fourth attempt started in 1970, when the President's Commission on Financial Structure and Regulation was formed. The key recommendations from that study were subsequently included in a broad package developed by an Executive Office task force and submitted to Congress in October 1973 as the Financial Institutions Act and again in a slightly revised form in March 1975. Finally, the House Committee on Banking, Currency, and Housing prepared a massive staff report and attempted to draft an unusually comprehensive piece of legislation, known as the Financial Reform Act of 1976, which was later broken into three parts.

The fundamental recommendations of all of these studies concerned the need to strengthen the relative competitive positions of financial intermediaries and improvement in the efficiency and range of asset and liability services provided for their customers. Although the specific details of each set of recommendations offered for reform are different, the goals showed a similar pattern.

    1. The overall financial system, including depository institutions, should be flexible enough to adapt to changing competitive conditions. However, expanded asset and liability powers should be permissive rather than mandatory, allowing each financial institution to select its own approach to specific markets and the degree of specialization it prefers.

    2. Financial institutions should become a more stable source of credit and a reliable depository for savings. The repetitious swings in savings

flows and in the availability of credit associated with financial disintermediation are extremely damaging. At the same time, long-term shifts in
savings flows and sources of credit in response to changes in the competitive roles of different types of financial intermediaries should not be artificially restricted by arbitrary government controls.

3. Efficient and convenient savings and lending services for a variety of
customers should be available in the financial markets, even though specific firms may restrict the range of their own activities. All savers should
receive a rate of return on their deposits more commensurate with overall
market yields and the specific costs and risks associated with each type of
account. Small savings accounts should not be discriminated against.

4. Financial intermediaries should be concerned for savers as well as
borrowers and should have adequate powers to offer safety, convenience,
and a range of financial services, including different savings instruments
and types of loans. These powers should be discretionary, to allow each
firm to determine its special interests.

5. Basic social goals should continue to be emphasized. Housing requirements that affect financial intermediaries should receive particular
attention, but the diversity of worthy credit needs should also be recognized. In those situations where special assistance is considered necessary, such as support for low- and moderate-income housing, direct subsidies clearly identifiable in the government budgets should be used,
rather than complicated credit allocation programs which disrupt the normal flows of credit to all borrowers and make such preferential assistance
inefficient and more costly.

6. All financial institutions competing in the same markets should have
an equal competitive opportunity undistorted by significant differences in
taxation, reserves, or regulatory requirements.

7. The entire financial system should remain flexible enough to respond
to changing technology, so that consumers receive maximum services at
the lowest possible cost; and all firms should have access to such technology to avoid unfair competitive disadvantages.

These suggestions for comprehensive reform have never been successfully combined in a legislative package with enough popular
appeal to win congressional action because of the opposition of most
special interest groups. Although numerous bills dealing with specific issues that affect financial institutions are passed by Congress
during each session, the broad proposals have failed, beginning
with the bill recommended by the House Banking and Currency
Committee in 1967, which was not put to a floor vote. The Financial
Institutions Act analyzed in Chapter 5 was finally approved by the
Senate in December 1975, by an overwhelming vote of 79 to 14, but
that action was generally recognized as only the first step in a difficult sequence. Ultimately the House of Representatives would have
to pass comparable legislation. Then necessary compromises would
have to be agreed on in the preparation of a conference report for
final approval by both houses of Congress.

The House of Representatives did not even begin its efforts until April 1975, when Congressmen Reuss and St Germain jointly announced that another massive study of the financial system was needed before hearings could begin. By the time the House subcommittee responsible for financial institutions finally received the FINE Study and initiated hearings in late 1975 and early 1976, it was obvious that internal jurisdictional disputes and the approaching national political elections would preclude any timely consideration of the extremely broad Financial Reform Act of 1976 discussed in Chapter 9.

Even when that bill was splintered into three parts to make it somewhat compatible with the Financial Institutions Act passed by the Senate and with other specific legislative initiatives being considered by the Senate Banking, Housing, and Urban Affairs Committee, there was never any real hope that a meaningful compromise on such a controversial bill could be developed in the partisan political environment preceding the national elections scheduled for November 2, 1976.

The most striking contrast between the way Congress reacts to comprehensive legislation affecting financial institutions and the way it has dealt with the more specific initiatives sponsored by special interest groups, or the projects personally advanced by powerful members of Congress, was evident in 1977. The new session of Congress began the year with a pro forma approval of legislation extending the authority of regulatory agencies to continue controls over the payment of interest on savings, including a continuation of the yield differential advantage for thrift institutions; the legislative package previously proposed by the credit unions during the Senate hearings on the Financial Institutions Act of 1975 was also rapidly passed.

An even more striking example was the hearings that both the Senate and House committees responsible for issues related to financial institutions quickly arranged on the specific problems of commercial bank correspondent loans, overdrafts, and other questions of bank management during the fall. These actions resulted from continuing widespread publicity about earlier actions by Bert Lance, head of the Office of Management and Budget, when he was president of a Georgia bank. Both committees had been concerned for some time about the specific bank management issues that were involved, and the hearings probably served a constructive role in helping Congress to fulfill its responsibilities for overseeing such matters. But one would have to be unusually naive to believe that the stories on the front page of every newspaper and on most radio and television news broadcasts for several weeks were not what made these topics a matter of priority, especially since Congress had not been able to respond to the comprehensive list of eighty-nine general and twenty-seven specific recommendations made by the Hunt Commission in 1971, or to the numerous suggestions contained in the Financial Institutions Act and the Financial Reform Act which were submitted for consideration beginning in 1973.

While Congress reacted quickly to the need to extend government controls and to investigate bank management practices in this widely publicized case involving a prominent public official, the comprehensive legislation described in this study was quietly buried on June 20, 1977, following testimony by Secretary W. Michael Blumenthal of the Treasury Department to the Subcommittee on Financial Institutions of the Senate Committee on Banking, Housing, and Urban Affairs. Secretary Blumenthal emphasized in his support of S. 1664 that it would be the "principal reform legislation that the Administration expects to propose this year."[2] He then explained the Treasury Department's strategy as follows:

> The approach the Administration is recommending through the proposals contained in S. 1664 is to concentrate on two related areas that clearly need to be addressed and to resist the temptation of addressing all real or perceived inequities and thereby invite continuing stalemate.[3]

The two recommended changes were: (1) granting authority to the Federal Reserve System to pay interest on the legal reserves that are required of banks belonging to the system, in order to halt the attrition of members; and (2) removal of the existing prohibition against the payment of interest on demand deposits and clarification of the rules governing NOW accounts. The interesting recommendation to allow interest payments on demand deposits is similar to the amendment added by the Senate before it passed the Financial Institutions Act of 1975. According to the suggestion about NOW accounts, authority to set interest rate ceilings on such accounts would be given to the coordinating committee of financial institution regulatory agencies, and the Federal Reserve Board of Governors would be enabled to set uniform reserve requirements for NOW and share-draft accounts at all depository institutions. Avoidance of the contro-

---

2. Statement of the Honorable W. Michael Blumenthal, Secretary of the Treasury, before the Subcommittee on Financial Institutions of the Senate Committee on Banking, Housing, and Urban Affairs, 95th Cong. 1st sess., June 20, 1977, p. 1.
3. Ibid., p. 2.

versial issue of regulation Q controls was once again finessed by asking for extension of the existing powers from December 15, 1977, until December 1979 and by establishing a task force of all concerned agencies to "study the impact of these deposit rate ceilings on financial intermediaries, the individual saver, and the mortgage market."[4] The new task force would at least have abundant resource materials in the form of previous studies.

These two proposals are important and consistent with the recommendations made in earlier studies and legislative initiatives. They represent only a minute share of all the past recommendations, however, and they do not consider any of the controversial questions that still cause resentment and frustrations. The current strategy of the Treasury Department may represent a realistic assessment of the decision-making process in the government, but Secretary Blumenthal's statement makes a better funeral eulogy for comprehensive reform than a justification for backing away from the long tradition of previous recommendations.

> Despite substantial past efforts by Congress and previous Administrations, Federal laws dealing with depository institutions have been largely unresponsive to pressures for change. Elaborate attempts to enact comprehensive packages of financial reform to deal with a wide range of difficult issues have failed . . . because they linked a number of proposals on which there is obvious need to measures on which the need for prompt action is less pressing.[5]

The Rejection of Comprehensive Reform

The Financial Institution Act and the Financial Reform Act failed because of procedural difficulties and the outside opposition of most special interest groups. Within the administration the task force charged with converting the recommendations of the Hunt Commission into legislation took almost two years to prepare its first proposal, and revisions continued during the next three years of public hearings. The constant adjustment of legislative strategies resulted in compromises that occasionally eroded the support of agencies represented by task force members. Senior government officials are not philosopher-kings interested only in the general public welfare. They must also defend and promote the jurisdictional interests of the agencies they represent. In a pragmatic sense the legislative

4. Ibid., p. 5.
5. Ibid., p. 1.

initiatives prepared by the executive branch are usually a broad compromise representing the historical preferences of different departments. This generalization has been particularly true of legislation for financial institution reform.

The regulatory agencies cautiously supported comprehensive reform, but they were particularly sensitive to their institutional constituencies and their specialized responsibilities. Similarly, the Department of Housing and Urban Development was principally interested in the potential impact of legislative changes on the housing markets and concentrated most of its attention on supporting the proposed mortgage interest tax credit. The Treasury Department served as the administration's major representative in contacts with Congress and private special interest groups. Several other executive branch agencies also had important roles, although their participation varied as internal pressures for compromise increased and as outside groups became more strongly opposed to the comprehensive proposals.

Once the legislation reached Congress the measure immediately became subject to the complicated committee procedures, which require a progressive series of hearings and reports at different levels of authority before a final vote occurs. At each level, powerful members of the subcommittees and committees, particularly the leaders, can delay or destroy the initiatives by various parliamentarian tactics. These can be simply "stonewalling" the proposal, to delay hearings or a formal vote long enough to allow the congressional calendar to expire, or the familiar practice of adding enough objectionable amendments to make the bill unacceptable. There are many other possibilities in between. Even when broad legislative support continues throughout the committee phase of analysis, the progress of major bills is usually slow and complicated. Political compromises are ordinarily required at each stage of analysis, as special interest groups press their claims directly during the public hearings and indirectly through personal lobbying among individual members of Congress. Since only a few congressmen have the specialized knowledge or interest in a particular bill that would lead them to become personally involved with its passage, particularly if the proposals are controversial or difficult for most of their constituents to understand, the fate of most legislative initiatives depends upon the views of a few key congressmen whose judgment the majority must rely on. This, of course, opens up the possibilities for trading votes.

An effective chairman of a committee or subcommittee can usually either expedite or delay indefinitely most pieces of legislation by adroitly managing the work schedule, which usually includes frequent congressional recesses and occasional national political elections. The processing of legislation becomes a unique art form in which power to control the course of events is determined by structured patterns of seniority and protocol. In consequence, the submission of controversial legislation by a President representing the Republican Party to a Congress dominated by representatives of the Democratic Party is hardly a promising situation. For financial institution reform, the complexity of the broad changes recommended and an unprecedented combination of adverse external pressures proved to be overwhelming added disadvantages.

Perhaps the most important external event significantly reducing the prospects for acceptance of the reform was the shift in the national economy from booming expansion to a severe recession. Large increases in unemployment occurred along with a precipitous drop in housing constructions. Meanwhile inflation surged upward to double-digit levels. These serious distortions made many critics even more skeptical about the free-market recommendations advocated in the financial institutions reform acts. Their suspicions were aggravated by the return of strong financial disintermediation in 1973 and again in 1974. Further doubts arose from the large loss of savings deposits among thrift institutions following the regulatory rulings early in June 1973, which temporarily permitted the distribution of 4-year savings certificates without any interest rate ceilings. By November 1973 the strong objections of thrift institutions had moved Congress to restore the interest controls. From this time onward, opponents of the comprehensive reform legislation repeatedly claimed that the experience with "wild card" savings certificates provided irrefutable evidence that free-market solutions based on more flexible asset and liability powers would not work.

During the same 1973-74 period the collapse of a large bank in New York City and a smaller bank in San Diego, following the widely publicized failure of a bank in West Germany, created a wave of concern about the stability of the entire financial system. At times the pessimism became almost hysterical, despite the underlying strength of most U.S. financial institutions and the rapid corrective actions of the Federal Reserve System. Later analysis indicated that these specific failures were caused by unauthorized speculation in foreign currencies and other improper—in some cases illegal—management practices, but the popular impression was that the entire financial system was threatened. In that pessimistic atmosphere, recommendations to grant more managerial flexibility and to reduce governmental controls were obviously out of step with the current mood of Congress. Since many members of Congress and the general public believe that government controls are more effective than competitive market incentives in achieving national economic goals, the general themes expressed in the Financial Institutions Acts and the Financial Reform Act were also suspect.

Finally, the unprecedented political scandal of Watergate, and the extensive congressional hearings leading to the forced resignation of the same President who had originally appointed the Commission on Financial Structure and Regulation, severely eroded the prestige and power of the executive branch. These developments occurred at a crucial time, when total support from the administration was absolutely necessary if the proposed legislation was to have any real chance for success. Even after the resignation of President Nixon on August 8, 1974, the disruption of the general political environment took its toll. Economic conditions deteriorated, and President Ford was forced to concentrate on the problems of restoring leadership in government and rebuilding the confidence of the general public.

In the time covered by the congressional hearings on financial reform legislation there was also great anxiety over inflation and unemployment, rising interest rates, depressed housing construction, renewed financial disintermediation, the rapid increase in federal spending from \$247 billion in fiscal 1973 to \$366 billion in fiscal 1976 (a jump of 48 percent in three years), and the cumulative budget deficits of \$116 billion. During the hearings several thoughtful witnesses had emphasized the disruptive effects of the federal government's fiscal and monetary policies from the mid-1960s and their impact on many of the issues considered in the reform proposals. Then as now, however, no immediate solutions to the fundamental problems of economic instability, inflation, unemployment, and the rapid growth of federal spending and related budget deficits were likely as long as political interests dominated economic decisions.

In the adverse environment described here the only means of creating enough pressure to force a positive reaction from Congress would have been a solid, united front of special interest groups representing the financial institutions, consumer interests, and the housing industry. Ironically enough, the reactions of most of the key interest groups were generally negative. They appeared to prefer the familiar advantages and disadvantages of the status quo to the uncertainties created by change, despite the prospects of increased efficiency and stability once the competitive adjustments were over.

Most of the witnesses participating in the congressional hearings argued that regulation Q controls are still absolutely necessary for the survival of thrift institutions and small banks. Secretary William E. Simon, representing the Treasury Department, identified this controversy as the key issue in the entire package in his early public statements about the Financial Institutions Act. Senator McIntyre also referred to the recommendations on interest rate controls as the "pivotal issue" in questioning Mr. Morris D. Crawford, Jr., the prominent Chairman of the Bowery Savings Bank and a member of the Hunt Commission:

> During the hearings this week, Mr. Crawford, each witness representing thrift institutions has testified that they are not opposed to expanding their permissible authorities, but that they are opposed to the elimination of regulation Q.
> There is no doubt in my mind that this is the most pivotal issue in the Federal Institutions Act. The purpose of these hearings and the stated purpose of S. 2591 is to provide greater equality to the various types of institutions in our financial system.
> How are we in the Congress, how can we enhance competition if we simply grant those parts of the bill expanding permissible powers, but yet continue to maintain Federal controls on interest rates?[6]

By refusing to accept the administration's proposed compromise of eliminating both interest rate controls and the advantageous differential granted to thrift institutions in exchange for expanded asset and liability powers, the special interest groups effectively rejected the entire package. Critics of the Financial Institutions Act argued that even with the expanded powers proposed for thrift institutions and credit unions they would still not be able to compete with large commercial banks offering a full line of commercial services. Their view was that the new powers would not particularly strengthen their position but that the loss of regulation Q controls on interest and of the differential would disastrously affect their competitive position. Even the mutual savings banks refused to support the entire package, although it included their principal aim of gaining access to federal charters.

Representatives of the financial institutions expressed their opposition to the total package of recommendations not only because they had specific grievances but because they were generally concerned about the uncertain impact of the proposals on the housing industry. Stressing the latter reason was an effective strategy, since

6. U.S., Congress, Senate, Committee on Banking, Housing, and Urban Affairs, *Financial Institutions Act of 1973*, p. 832.

it recognized economic and social importance of the housing sector and its powerful political position.

The status of housing construction and the related consumer durable goods industries is always a key variable in the overall performance of the U.S. economy, and the quantity and quality of housing is considered one of the most important measures of social progress and equity. The short-term problem of volatile mortgage credit flows has induced the federal government to protect the housing sector by measures such as regulation Q controls on interest rates, direct advances from the Federal Home Loan Bank Board to strengthen the liquidity positions of member institutions, favorable tax treatment, and various direct government subsidies for housing construction.

Critics have challenged the equity and efficiency of this favored status of the housing interests as a basic contradiction of the historical emphasis on competitive markets and private enterprise. Others have argued that special treatment to the housing sector should only be in the form of direct subsidies to low- and moderate-income owners and renters rather than indirect incentives to builders and financial institutions. Nevertheless it is unlikely that Congress will reduce its support of the housing interests. In fact, the political power of this sector of the economy is likely to lead to even more assistance in the future.

As a consequence congressional support for comprehensive financial reform will be exceedingly difficult to gain as long as there is uncertainty about the potential impact of such changes on the housing industry. The most effective argument against the recommendations offered in the various studies and legislative proposals has been the claim that housing interests might suffer. The feast-and-famine experience of this essential industry over the years certainly indicates that the statutory requirements of the past have not prevented serious distortions. Nevertheless, the housing interests refused to support the financial institution reform, and their opposition was effective in blocking favorable congressional action.

Looking Ahead

The central point of this review of financial reform legislation has been that significant changes in the structure and regulation of depository institutions are needed. Merely expanding the patchwork of existing controls will not achieve the desired goals. As Professor Eli Shapiro stated in his testimony:

The problem at the moment is to accept the reality that our thrift system and mortgage market must change in the ways that have been suggested for at least the past fifteen years and move to deal with the very difficult problem of bringing about those changes.[7]

At issue are the competitive problems created for financial institutions by the mismatch of assets and liabilities, and the consequent necessity for new regulations to stabilize deposits and provide more flexibility in the asset portfolios. While the need for reform is obvious, there is apparently no sound solution that can pass the necessary political tests. Most special interest groups strongly rejected the comprehensive reform which the Commission on Money and Credit and the President's Commission on Financial Structure and Regulation recommended and which was used in preparing the Financial Institution Acts. That refusal of support and the political risks of backing a controversial piece of legislation, in which the issues were so little understood by the public, ultimately caused Congress to back away. The testimony of Secretary of the Treasury Blumenthal in June 1977 completed the cycle by withdrawing the support of the current administration for comprehensive reform and focusing its efforts on only two specific regulatory changes.

Despite this disappointing sequence of events, widespread structural and regulatory changes have occurred and will undoubtedly continue. The pace and type of adjustments, however, are likely to resemble the "salami approach" to policy decisions—repeated small slices of reform, just enough to avoid major disruptions that could once again cause insoluble controversy.

On the legislative side special interest groups will continue to push for congressional action on their specific reform goals. This strategy has worked in the past, most recently when credit unions had their extensive legislative package approved in April 1977. Marketplace adjustments to consumer needs and changing technology will be even more extensive in the future. The combined results of specific legislation, new administrative rulings by the regulatory agencies, and competitive pressures in the private financial markets will ultimately lead to the general reforms proposed for more flexible asset and liability powers. But the actual transition will be unnecessarily slow and costly because of the breakdown in the decision-making process that has been described here.

The efforts of the Commission on Money and Credit, the Presi-

---

7. Senate, Committee on Banking, Housing, and Urban Affairs, *Reform of Financial Institutions*, p. 35. Statement of Eli Shapiro.

dent's Commission on Financial Structure and Regulation, the Executive Office task force directed by Treasury officials, the special studies prepared by regulatory agencies and academic consultants, the lengthy Senate and House hearings, including the FINE Study, and the detailed presentations by the many representatives of special interest groups were definitely not wasted. The years of study and debate provide a solid foundation of increased knowledge about the structure and regulation of financial depository institutions:

1. Key competitive issues and goals were more clearly identified, and written views from various special interest groups and government agencies were collected.

2. A vast amount of descriptive and statistical material concerning the financial system was prepared and is now available for developing future reform proposals.

3. Many specific legislative and administrative changes have already been made on the basis of the special studies and extensive congressional hearings.

4. A clear distinction was developed between policies which favor private markets and competition and those which advocate an increasing role for the federal government in the private economy, including allocation of capital according to predetermined government guidelines.

5. State governments have responded to the reform recommendations by approving specific changes rather than waiting for a comprehensive agreement at the national level.

6. The fundamental link between social issues, particularly housing, and economic policies was carefully reaffirmed.

7. Each special interest group affected by the reform proposals was given an opportunity to participate in the decision-making process—a tangible example of how the democratic system operates.

Nevertheless, the effort to achieve financial institution reform was obviously not a success in every respect. The basic issues identified twenty years ago are still unresolved, and decisions needed to improve the financial system have not been made. Given the fundamental strength of the U.S. economic system and the adaptability of the depository institutions within the existing set of rules, these failures have not been fatal, but the related inefficiency and periodic financial crises are unnecessary. Decisions involving controversial issues are not easy to make, but making them is a primary function of senior government officials.

Beyond this, we can learn a number of lessons from the negative side of the experience with financial institution reform:

1. The decision-making process in the federal government is fragmented and extremely slow. Senior officials and their staffs must therefore commit considerable time and effort to preparing and arguing each legislative proposal, no matter how detailed and technical it may be.

2. A large share of the time spent on evaluating proposals is devoted to debates about the validity of basic statistics and information on institutional characteristics. Data should be collected and refined long before the final decision is made. In many situations even the most rudimentary information needed to make an intelligent judgment is not available, or erroneous information is used to avoid the task of collecting valid material.

3. Government officials often use the complicated decision-making procedures to bury controversial issues, even though the delays make the problems even more difficult. The continuing risks associated with financial market disintermediation are a classic example of the results of such procrastination.

4. Concentration on specific issues often conceals the underlying causes of problems. For example, the greatest challenge confronting financial depository institutions has been the disruptive impact of the periodic booms and recessions that began in the mid-1960s. The major role of federal fiscal, monetary, and regulatory policies in creating these cyclical swings was occasionally mentioned during the congressional hearings, but nothing meaningful was done to relate the reform proposals to the fundamental issue of stabilizing the national economy.

5. Government decisions affecting long-term goals are extremely sensitive to short-term developments. The experience with "wild card" certificates during the summer of 1973 was a major factor in shaping the general reaction of Congress to the financial institution reform proposals.

6. Many special interest groups apparently prefer the security of government controls which curtail competition to the risks associated with free markets. Businessmen usually claim that they generally favor competition and free enterprise, but they justify government intervention in their own activities because of what they call unique conditions. Advocating competition for others and special protection for their own interests apparently does not seem inconsistent to most businessmen. The prevalence of this attitude explains why public officials seeking political advantages respond so frequently to appeals for special consideration.

7. Special interest groups that understand how the federal government decisions are really made and that develop close contacts with the relatively few key officials in the Executive Office and Congress have a major advantage in promoting their specific legislative goals and frustrating the efforts of other groups.

Some analysts claim that the unequal advantage possessed by special interest groups is the natural result of our political system with its separation of powers and delegation of authority to specialized committees. This pragmatic viewpoint may be realistic, but it does not allay the frustration that develops when a single group delays consideration of legislation for several years, even though in a given case most analysts might believe the general public would benefit. These tactics, allowing form to dominate over substance, may be considered clever politics by some; to many of those concerned about the general public interest, however, first-hand observation of lobbying, as it influences the Executive Office and Congress, is a disillusioning experience.

Perhaps the most disheartening aspect of this problem is that most government officials recognize the unfortunate results of the existing arrangements and sincerely support efforts to improve the system, but actual progress in correcting the faults rarely occurs. As a result, the attitude of the average citizen vacillates between angry resentment and ugly cynicism, while conscientious public officials become more frustrated by their inability to surmount the flood of detailed legislative proposals. Meanwhile, comprehensive recommendations to improve the decision-making process have no more chance of being accepted than the comprehensive financial institution reform proposals had when they were first presented to Congress in 1973.

These observations about the federal government's decision-making procedures do not offer any new or startling conclusions. Other analysts have noted and criticized the same characteristics. The purpose here has been to describe a specific example showing the institutions and procedures in action. In this instance senior officials of the Executive Office, members of Congress, representatives of special interest groups, and expert academic witnesses converged in the analytical process. Despite their extensive efforts, no important decision was put forward. Even with such controversial issues a yes or no response could have been given much earlier for the entire package and for each of the specific recommendations. This experience is a sobering commentary on the effectiveness of the system.

11

THE ROLE OF PRESIDENTIAL COMMISSIONS AND CONSULTANTS

The next four chapters shift the focus of the discussion from the analysis of the case presented here to an interpretation of the role of key institutions involved in the legislative experience. This chapter examines the functions and limitations of commissions and consultants, after which we will consider the role of congressional hearings, the structure and operations of Executive Branch task forces, and the marketplace adjustments of financial institutions as they attempt to adapt to changing conditions. The earlier historical analysis and these chapters of interpretation combine to provide an overview of how economic policy develops in such matters as financial institution reforms.

Advantages of Commissions and Consultants

Commissions and outside consultants provide expert advice that broadens the perspectives and capabilities of policy-making officials and gives substance to their recommendations. Such collaboration ideally creates a blend of technical expertise and reasoned judgment when complex issues of national significance are being considered. The diversity of interests involved in most policy questions, it is reasoned, can best be recognized by combining the independent views of eminent generalists, specialists, and representatives of the groups most affected by the issues being considered.

The actual performance of hundreds of public commissions and thousands of consultants results at one extreme in failures traceable to irrelevancy and obsolescence; at the other are the occasional successes which do influence public policies. On balance, most of their reports have value in documenting expert views and accumulating empirical information. But very few outside advisers have a significant impact on the final decisions of the executive branch or Congress because the ultimate effectiveness of most public commissions and consultants is limited by four fundamental factors: (1) outside advisers usually emphasize the technical aspects of issues and the feasibility of familiar government solutions rather than the pressing political needs of the President or Congress; (2) the compromises required to gain a consensus ordinarily undermine the necessary support of the idealists, who prefer logic and efficiency, and of the pragmatists, who demand immediate action, and the thrust of most reports is consequently dissipated before the government makes its decision; (3) government leaders normally listen only to the advice they want to hear, avoiding the need to respond to criticisms and recommendations that might alienate the electorate; and (4) the resources and internal cooperation that are made available to commissions and consultants rarely match the grandiose nature of their assignments.

As long as these constraints are recognized, the use of outside advisers can contribute to better decisions. Their semiofficial status and the recognized quality of most commissioners and professional staff members are valuable assets in increasing public understanding and forcing the government to act. The credibility of many commissions and consultants gives them unique access to senior government officials, the news media, and special interest groups involved in developing recommendations.

Their temporary standing is another major advantage which eliminates the crisis atmosphere, both real and imagined, that pervades most government offices. Commissions and consultants are not forced to defend mistaken policies of the past or the existing bureaucratic arrangements, and hence they can be more objective and creative in preparing proposals. Even the necessary compromises can be constructive if they result in more comprehensive and realistic reports. Finally, the internal processes of many commissions often create a more balanced analysis that recognizes the diversity of goals and constraints.

The President's Commission on Financial Structure and Regulation was a good example of these benefits. The commission's report provided a comprehensive view of a serious policy issue having national significance; the diversity of problems and the necessary trade-offs were clearly noted; and each special interest group was given an opportunity to express its views. The Hunt Commission was also able to develop a broad set of recommendations that provided a framework for subsequent legislative and administrative proposals. Although the total package was not adopted, many of its detailed suggestions have already been implemented. Even when specific recommendations were ignored, or explicitly rejected, by government officials, the commission's report was a convenient lever to force them to justify their actions and develop alternative solutions.

From the viewpoint of the executive branch the Hunt Commission was also useful as a damage control device which enabled the administration to show its interest in an important problem without committing itself too quickly on specific reform proposals. In fact, the long delay between the submission of the commission's final report in December 1971 and the consideration of actual legislation, beginning in November 1973, suggests that the administration effectively controlled the pace of events. By allowing sufficient time it was able to respond to the rules of the game by demonstrating the qualities of presidential leadership—foresight, concern, fairness, and objectivity—to obtain rigorous analysis of a problem, broad participation in its discussion, and comprehensive proposals for solving it. The commission's recommendations were consistent with the philosophical preferences of senior officials in the executive branch, who were able to use this "authoritative source" in hammering out the legislative proposals subsequently submitted to Congress.

The Hunt Commission study also served as a primary source for the extensive congressional hearings and reports. The thousands of pages of congressional testimony clearly indicate the weight given to the Commission's report, particularly to such themes as the need for increased asset and liability powers and the advantages of competitive markets. Although most special interest groups eventually rejected the total package of comprehensive reforms because of the disagreeable trade-offs required to reach a compromise, the legislative and administrative actions since then have reflected the influence of the Hunt Commission's efforts. The disappointing fate of the Financial Institutions Acts and the Financial Reform Act do not detract from the commission's success in forcing a more comprehensive and rigorous analysis of the issues.

The popular image of public commissions and consultants is that they are used to put off making decisions and that their reports are generally ignored. The positive achievements of the Hunt Commission tend to refute this critical generalization and confirm the findings of Professor Thomas R. Wolanin in his study of ninety-nine public commissions created between 1945 and 1969.

The evidence indicates, quite to the contrary, that commissions are created to be instruments of action, reform, and change, not of obfuscation and standpatism. The primary presidential purpose for the largest number of commissions is to formulate innovative domestic policies and to facilitate their adoption.[1]

Professor Wolanin also applied to the ninety-nine commissions a qualitative rating measuring the level of official response according to the following scale: 0, no authoritative response; level 1, minimal administrative action or legislation passed; level 2, substantial action; and level 3, major response, including modification of administrative policies or comprehensive legislation passed by Congress.

Public commissions and consultants have often contributed to public policy decisions by providing the substance and validating authority for important presidential messages to Congress and the general public, for the introduction of new legislation, and for affirmative actions within the executive branch. This positive evaluation was particularly true for the Hunt Commission. Nevertheless, it would be an exaggeration to claim that public commissions and consultants have played a major role in determining public policies. Most issues are considered without calling on such outside advisory groups. Even when external studies are requested, the executive branch and Congress usually extensively revise the original recommendations, and they obviously add their own ideas before they arrive at final decisions. Commissions and consultants can occasionally be helpful, but they are not a panacea for the problems that afflict the federal government's decision-making process.

The Drive for Consensus

Most commissions' and consultants' studies strive to develop a consensus. In some cases such agreement may simply result from general recognition that the recommendations are obviously the best. Participants who begin with divergent, even contradictory, views may also come to agree on a common answer as part of the educational process that occurs in group studies. But in most cases of consensus the reports mask earlier disagreements and compromises made to present a united front. The compromises may represent reasonable adjustments, but there has usually been a tough give-and-take, and the final recommendations represent the "least worst" solution that could hold the group together. The formation

---

1. Thomas R. Wolanin, *Presidential Advisory Commissions*, p. 11.

Table 14

GOVERNMENT ACTION IN RESPONSE TO COMMISSION
RECOMMENDATIONS

Level of Government Action	Number of Commissions	Percentage of All Commissions
0	35	35
1	6	6
2	8	8
3	50	51
Total	99	100

Source: Thomas R. Wolanin, *Presidential Advisory Commissions* (Madison, Wis.: The University of Wisconsin Press, 1975), p. 138.

of such a consensus in itself helps to identify the boundaries of feasible actions: the very process of developing an acceptable compromise usually eliminates the extreme suggestions that might cause legislative controversies. Furthermore, if prominent citizens, experts, and representatives of special interest groups can agree, the problem seems manageable. The entire political process is often described as the art of the possible, and most commissions and consulting groups are good examples of this realistic approach to making decisions.

The results of a group consensus based on compromises may be advantageous, but there are numerous obstacles to achieving a significant agreement. The process of compromise begins as soon as the commission members or consultants are appointed. The usual approach is to create a balanced group—a Noah's Ark of representatives from each political party, as well as from groups with special interests. Commissions have included men and women representing labor and business as well as racial and ethnic groups; a few generalists, usually university professors or former government officials, are also found on most commissions. This cross-section of characteristic national groupings is sometimes supplemented by adding members of Congress and Cabinet officials. Over the years the nominating procedures have become so stylized and predictable that the same people are constantly being asked to serve, particularly if they can symbolically represent two or more of the political, racial, ethnic, religious, age, sex, geographical, or special interest groups that White House officials attempt to have appointed to every general public commission.

Once this complicated and time-consuming job is completed, the same process is repeated in selecting the executive director and staff. The next step is usually to meet with senior government officials—sometimes with the President responsible for creating the commission—to build up enthusiasm for the project and provide some guidance about what is expected. After the formal sessions begin, the drive for consensus quickly dampens the more grandiose expectations of most members, and the major effort is directed at finishing a report. Since most members join commissions expecting to achieve their own predetermined goals without giving away too much to competing interests, the first few sessions are usually very general. Then the bargaining begins, and each participant discovers the difference between major and minor issues and what compromises can be arranged.

The culmination of this process occurs at the plenary session, where the final report is considered in great detail. In most instances the commission staff prepares a draft of the final report, working under the direction of the chairman and a few key members. That draft is then submitted to the entire membership for their individual approval by means of an excruciating collective review of the text one line at a time.

The experience of spending hours quibbling over the specific wording and nuances of a general report is like taking part in a long forced march. If the group is fortunate the personal idiosyncrasies of each member can be accommodated, but the congenial mood that accepts changes in wording can also break down. Then there are tedious delays until the most persistent member prevails or the majority bands together and applies arbitrary pressure to move on. Major disagreements during this final review are unusual. Philosophical disputes have usually been resolved or discarded in earlier sessions, although precise details are often a matter of contention.

In the rush to finish the editing in the plenary session, many controversial points are simply deleted. The wording is modified again and again, not only to make it more general and thus susceptible to individual interpretations but also to obtain the necessary compromises. The final result is often a bland report that avoids offending anyone. Like every other average, this consensus supposedly represents the middle position but not the specific views of individual members. The ultimate irony is that this diluting process, designed to eliminate controversy, often adds to the chance of disagreement. Everyone dislikes the final version of the report because his individual views and objections are not included.

The drive for collective agreement is a paradoxical aspect of public commissions. Individual members are selected on the basis of their recognized professional expertise and their personal reputation for judgment and integrity. But they then seem to be expected to submerge their views in the collective statement. The loss of individual opinions that might well produce effective results is a heavy price to pay for conformity. Dissenting views on specific points may of course be added as footnotes, or statements disagreeing with the total report may be submitted separately, but such exceptions receive little attention compared to the general consensus.

The high quality of most commissions makes it puzzling that some alternatives, calling for something less than full agreement, have not been tried. One would be to prepare a summary section covering the topics that have won universal agreement. This could be followed by a series of individual statements from each commissioner, which would, of course, combine to form a comprehensive overview of all the relevant arguments.

A second alternative would be to have the commission identify and rank a series of different recommendations. Their analysis should go beyond the mere listing of options. It should concentrate on ranking the alternative solutions and explaining the relative advantages and weaknesses of each. Since Congress and the executive branch have to perform this function eventually, the independent judgment of a commission or consultant about the ranking of several different approaches might be more productive than only one general view. The main difference would be in presenting the individual recommendations of each expert member and consultant rather than emphasizing conformity. It may well be that these individual views are more valuable than the conclusions agreed upon by the entire group.

Irreconcilable Disputes

In some cases the personal beliefs of commissioners or political pressures from outside create irreconcilable differences which prevent a consensus. Although members participate and sign the final report as individuals, they usually represent a certain constituency. In order to preserve their standing with their constituencies—sometimes their professional status or their jobs—commissioners must occasionally take an intransigent position against the majority. Commissioners who find themselves in this difficulty usually refuse to sign the final report and may add a dissenting statement to the published material.

An excellent example of an irreconcilable dispute occurred in the deliberations of the Hunt Commission, when Lane Kirkland, the respected secretary-treasurer of the AFL-CIO, refused to sign the report and strongly criticized the overall recommendations as being "designed to promote the interests of private financial institutions without genuine regard for the most urgent problems and needs of the nation."[2] As the second-ranking official in the leadership of organized labor, Kirkland had to reject the overall recommendations, which were contrary to his personal views and the basic position of the AFL-CIO. Both he and the group he represented believed that public guidelines should be established to control the allocation of credit in the financial markets so that more funds would be available for housing and other specified social needs.

His strong dissent and detailed arguments actually did more to create a meaningful debate on a controversial issue than could have been achieved by any perfunctory signing of the report merely to preserve an artificial consensus. His position, representing the political power of labor unions and other housing interests, clearly signaled that no financial institution reform could be legislated that might curtail the availability of credit for housing. Advocates of comprehensive reform argued that the flows of mortgage funds would in reality be larger and more stable, particularly if the mortgage investment tax credit was adopted, and that the financial system would be more efficient and consistent with the concepts of competitive markets. Housing interests, however, remained unconvinced that the proposed changes would improve mortgage credit conditions, and their continued opposition was the major factor preventing favorable congressional action.

Emphasis on New Research

Commissioners and consultants are usually selected for their sound judgment and their expert knowledge about the issue being considered. Nevertheless, there is a common tendency to go back to square one and invent the wheel once again, when they should rather turn directly to debating the basic issues and rely on the combined abilities of the commission members. During the early sessions a well-intentioned decision is usually made to initiate a broad research program, called by Professor Charles E. Lindblom

2. U.S., *Report of the President's Commission on Financial Structure and Regulation*, pp. 129–33.

the "rational-comprehensive model" of decision making. Few decisions can or should be based on this theoretical model, but most commissions and consultants take this approach to honor the rules of the game.[3]

As the collected material begins to swamp the analysis of issues which are usually obvious to begin with, the group eventually reverts to the knowledge and judgment of the members, but by that time the delays threaten to disrupt the schedule. If the focus is not shifted back to the relatively limited number of fundamental issues the report remains mired in details. As a consequence the recommendations will call only for tinkering with established institutions and procedures rather than comprehensive change. This playing-it-safe approach makes consensus easier and minimizes the risks of criticism from special interest groups, but the purpose of a special study to attack a national problem is frustrated.

In most situations it would be more productive to leapfrog over the research phase and quickly begin analyzing and debating issues that are already familiar to most commissioners and consultants, since they were selected at least partly for that reason. Decisions about fundamental issues are normally judgmental; and rather than seeking consensus above all, commissioners and consultants should concentrate on analyzing and ranking the alternative solutions, which are usually apparent but always controversial. When background statistical and descriptive information is needed, the staff should carefully monitor its quality and quantity so that the analysis is not diverted into examining the trees rather than surveying the forest.

Government Use of a Selective Screen

The most serious limitation of public commissions and consultants is that those with authority and responsibility for developing and directing public policies—the executive branch and Congress—as a rule respond only to recommendations they want to hear. Suggestions that contradict established policies are simply ignored, particularly if they threaten to dilute the power of incumbents or to hurt their image with the electorate. In some cases the established power centers may even counterattack. They attempt to refute the authority and credibility of a critical report by issuing a press release or internal government study supporting the existing views of Con-

3. Charles E. Lindblom, "The Science of 'Muddling Through,' " pp. 79–81.

gress and the President. A more subtle approach is to restrict the publicity given to external reports, or to upstage them by convening public hearings, commissioning a new study, or engaging in similar defensive actions.

The selective screening of the recommendations of public commissions and consultants that government officials resort to obviously frustrates the purpose of such efforts to develop original and independent ideas for improving public policies. In many situations government officials are too involved in the specific activity to be aware of their bias against outside views. At other times they consciously ignore unpleasant advice from advisory groups because it is embarrassing or inconvenient. Over the years government officials have become increasingly insulated from the realities of the world beyond the Potomac River; Washington, D.C., has become an unusually introverted community, which is unfortunate because of the increasing concentration of power in the central government located there. No matter how effective commissions and consultants are, their usefulness is usually restricted by the unwillingness of government officials to respond objectively to unpopular recommendations.

This strong aversion to outside advice is partly the result of the "bunker mentality" that many senior government officials develop once they are in office. Presidents and senior congressional leaders typically rely on a trusted inner circle, people who are looked to for advice on the entire spectrum of issues. To become part of this elite team of insiders requires much more than mere appointment to a position of responsibility in the government. Even Cabinet members are frequently frozen out of top-level decisions, and only a few members of Congress exercise real power in the complicated committee operations.

The extreme exclusiveness of this inner circle of advisers, and its tendency to usurp the leadership of the executive branch and Congress, prevent public commissions and consultants, no matter how well regarded or productive they are, from having direct access to those with real decision-making powers. The chief limitation on outside commissions and consultants is imposed by the inner circle of advisers close to the President and to powerful leaders of congressional committees, who filter out unwanted advice leaving only the suggestions that support their favored policies.

This critical failing is widely recognized, but there seems to be no feasible alternative. Few commissions and consultants have enough public backing to coerce a reluctant government into adopting their recommendations. Paul W. McCracken, the only person to serve twice on the Council of Economic Advisers and a consultant to national and international groups and governmental institutions for over thirty years, once summarized part of the problem: "Practical men of affairs have always found it difficult to suppress their inclination to make light of long-hair advice."[4]

Aside from their skepticism toward advice from outsiders, government officials with authority and responsibility to shape public policies may ignore such advice because they want to control the entire decision-making process. The eventual effects may not be as disadvantageous as one might think, because elections can change the distribution of power. Still the existing procedures restrict the effectiveness of public commissions and consultants, particularly if senior government officials have already decided what to do.

Inside and Outside Perspectives

Beyond the inherent skepticism of senior government officials toward everyone who does not belong to the inner circle is the gap between the perspectives of inside and outside advisers. The President has unmatched responsibility for all public policy issues and constituencies. To an increasing degree in today's collectivist society the President is credited or blamed for every success or failure of public policy.

This concentration of power and responsibility does not mean that every issue and constituency has the same importance, or even that specific problems and interest groups will receive any attention at all. Each President explicitly ranks priorities in accordance with his particular sensitivity to different pressures, particularly if he is striving for reelection. But the breadth and complexity of the issues and interest groups that must be considered at all times are unique. The very nature of the President's responsibilities necessarily creates insights and constraints that cannot be imagined by anyone who has not served in that awesome role or been a close adviser. The functions and constraints of key members of Congress are similar, although they normally relate to more specialized areas, because those in Congress are dealing with specific issues affecting their committees and the interests of the people in their home states.

In contrast, outside advisers do not have the same perspectives as

---

4. Paul W. McCracken, "Reflections on Economic Advising" (Los Angeles: University of California, Dept. of Economics, International Institute for Economic Research, March 1976), p. 4. Original Paper no. 1.

government leaders when they analyze a particular issue. It is only to be expected, therefore, that the way the President and Congress perceive possible solutions to a problem may be entirely different from the recommendations of public commissions and private consultants. There are many reasons for this difference.

First, the President and Congress cannot consider a single issue in isolation; public commissions and consultants are specifically directed to do so. A problem like restructuring the social welfare programs seems extremely urgent to many, but it is only one in the total range of domestic and international issues that a President must simultaneously consider. Before the President and Congress can support or reject any policy recommendation, they must take into account a set of interrelated budget and legislative priorities.

For example, a request by the Russians to buy grain from private dealers in the United States in 1975 triggered a series of top-level meetings of the Economic Policy Board. The issue was finally taken directly to the President, and each affected Cabinet member presented conflicting arguments. The Secretary of the Treasury analyzed the inflationary impact of the proposed sale on the U.S. economy and the effects on our international trade policies and balance of payments. The Secretary of Agriculture argued in favor of maximizing agricultural exports to create future markets and current income benefits for American farmers. The Secretary of State presented a strong case that the final decision should be made within the context of détente between the two superpowers and should take careful account of the international political and military factors. The chairman of the Council of Economic Advisers, director of the Office of Management and Budget, chairman of the Board of Governors of the Federal Reserve System, and other Cabinet officials who were present also discussed related domestic and international issues.

The result was a compromise to permit limited grain sales to Russia in 1975 up to a maximum target level. In exchange the United States received guarantees of more open trading arrangements. An agreement was also reached setting a predetermined minimum and maximum figure for grain exports to Russia during the next five years. As the next step, these arrangements had to be coordinated with the key congressional committees having oversight responsibilities. During these complex discussions the interrelation of public issues involved in policy decisions was very clear.

Second, public commissions and consultants have only an advisory role; they are not responsible for implementing their recommendations or responding to changing events. The Executive Office and Congress are left the difficult tasks of working out the details and monitoring the actual results of policy decisions. Advisory groups have a tendency to focus on the broad goals, and to have less regard for the complexities of specific programs and the operating problems that constitute the daily challenges of government officials. For example, government officials who have been involved in counterproductive programs like wage and price controls often respond to advisory recommendations with the sarcastic comment: "Anyone who advocates wage and price controls should be condemned to manage them."

Third, the rapid pace of change in modern society often makes the recommendations of public commissions and consultants obsolete by the time they are finally presented to the President and Congress. Most commissions take one to two years to complete their analysis and prepare written reports, and many major issues can change dramatically during that time. Partly to blame for the delay in presenting reports is the usual schedule of meeting one or two days each month, or even less frequently, to give the staff time to prepare the research studies and background material.

Fourth, the final reports of public commissions and consultants are often highly critical of existing policies and organizations. The most frequent recommendation is to call for new procedures and institutions requiring more government spending. While such critiques may provide "fresh and independent insights," they may also be embarrassing and threatening to the executive branch and Congress, who created and operate the programs being criticized. For example, the Hunt Commission's criticism of regulation Q controls over interest rates paid on deposits had eventually to be considered by the congressional committees that legislated the controls and the regulatory agencies responsible for enforcing them.

Setting up a commission or a study by consultants is often forced upon the President or Congress by a sudden crisis, especially when no other alternatives which might demonstrate leadership are at hand. Government officials do not enjoy having their efforts criticized, and they quite naturally feel defensive when their work is challenged by outsiders who have not had the same responsibilities. Government officials also tend to discount reports of outside advisory committees that depict a situation as "serious but not hopeless if new and imaginative government action programs are adopted." This tendency in most reports sometimes causes officials to believe, on the contrary, that the particular situation may be "hopeless but not serious."

Fifth, outside groups do not share the same political goals as the President and Congress. In fact, most commissioners and consultants are cautioned to avoid considering the political feasibility of their recommendations so that they may preserve their independence and the technical quality of their analysis. This guideline is also based on realistic appraisals of most political judgments made by commissions and consultants, which are usually amateurish at best.

Most Cabinet-level officials in the executive branch would also be more effective if they would concentrate more on the technical aspects of their responsibilities and leave the political judgments to specialists. This fact is seldom accepted either by most officials or by outside advisors, who quickly become fascinated with the political aspects of public service and try to anticipate political reactions. Not only does this effort too often dilute the professional quality of their analysis; it is also completely unnecessary, since every report must eventually be adapted to the political realities affecting the President and the Congress, and such adjustments should be made by them.

Executive Branch Opposition to Outside Reports

The attitude of the bureaucracy within the executive branch is a key factor in the ultimate acceptance or rejection of the recommendations made by public commissions and consultants. These permanent government employees apply the same types of qualitative screens as the President, his inner group of advisers, and Congress. The position of the bureaucracy is difficult, however, since they are responsible for directing the thousands of programs under which the government actually functions. In many instances the recommendations by outsiders concern programs which these career officials not only administer but which they have designed and whose legislative and regulatory framework they have personally arranged. The tensions when public commissions and consultants criticize the failure of existing programs and institutions obviously provoke defensive reactions from the government officials who feel threatened by the critics.

Even when the studies by outsiders support existing governmental activities, usually with the caveat that public spending should be increased, they are sometimes resented by insiders. Such commissions have been used, it is felt, to bypass the established bureaucracy on the grounds that they will provide objectivity, independent views, fresh insights, and necessary credibility. The creation of outside studies seems to cast doubt on the career officials. No one likes to be told that others can do a better job of analyzing complex issues that he has personally struggled with over the years. To career government officials, the implication that they are biased, controlled by political appointees, lacking in credibility, and bogged down in the details of existing programs and daily crises is insulting. They feel this particularly if the commission's or consultants' reports are superficial and fail to justify the need for changes. There are many good reasons for appointing commissions and consultants other than to gain support for ideas the bureaucracy may favor, but the resentment and skepticism such appointments arouse are in many instances understandable.

Experienced career officials recognize the rules of the game much better than the average presidential appointee, who has an average tenure of less than two years. Such officials usually stay on through many different administrations and are adept at responding to policy changes and reorganizations when a different political party takes over. The bureaucracy copes with these sporadic flurries of political activity much as ancient China absorbed invading armies, with little change in actual functions and goals. They expect each new President and Cabinet member to reorganize and reevaluate priorities before settling into the routine of government activities. And they realize that the promised revolutions soon return to the familiar evolution that existed before the new administration.

Nevertheless, it is still a serious problem to accommodate sensitive egos and departmental jurisdictions when outside studies are commissioned. The federal government is not a monolithic bloc of faceless bureaucrats that can be mechanically manipulated by clever leaders, although each newly elected President and his advisers try at first to make it function that way. Each of the government programs is directed by people with individual characteristics and needs. Most career officials are dedicated to public service and approach their assignments with a commitment to efficiency that makes their performance match or exceed that of most private executives. But it is naive to assume that they will support the recommendations of outside advisers if their personal security and administrative power are threatened.

The intricate web of personal relationships and decision-making procedures that make up the real base of power within the federal government cannot be changed unless the established bureaucracy supports the recommendations. In the example of the President's Commission on Financial Structure and Regulation, the departments and agencies of the executive branch generally supported the comprehensive reform proposals, but each group—and the congressional committees as well—carefully guarded its jurisdictional turf until the legislative effort died a natural death at the end of 1976.

The internal response to most public commissions was apparently found to be even more negative by Professor Wolanin:

> The Federal Executive Branch is also likely to regard the recommendations of commissions with suspicion. Commissions are one means used by the President to bypass the federal bureaucracy. They are a technique for generating policy analysis and options outside of the normal channels. When commissions fail to receive the support of the President, the bureaucracy is more likely to applaud the vanquishing of the usurpers than to rally in their defense. The unsympathetic treatment that commission reports often receive when reviewed by Executive Branch agencies (described below) supports the interpretation that there is a basic conflict of institutional interests between commissions and line agencies.[5]

Career government employees have many opportunities to influence commissions' and consultants' studies by volunteering or withholding help during the analysis. Once the final report is submitted they may express their specific reactions directly to the President. Or they may choose the normal procedure of circulating the report to all affected departments and agencies for formal comments. Task forces headed by the key department agencies—the Treasury in the case of the President's Commission on Financial Structure and Regulation—or under the direction of the Office of Management and Budget are often formed to conduct this review.

After the internal analysis is completed the President may issue a separate message to Congress. Many times a discussion of the issue is included along with other important views on policy in the State of the Union message, the *Economic Report of the President*, and the *Budget of the United States Government*, which are prepared by senior government officials in the executive branch.

The next steps have already been traced in our example: the drafting of legislation for submission to Congress; the creation of formal task forces to prepare the legislative package; and the assembling by the Office of Management and Budget of written responses from all interested departments and agencies. During the congressional hearings the different organizations continue to participate by preparing and presenting testimonies representing their official views. At each step in the process, from evaluating the final report through the congressional hearings, the views of career government employees are

---

5. Wolanin, *Presidential Advisory Commissions*, p. 168.

influential, even though they may not outweigh the official position of the administration, in developing the messages and legislative proposals. Later, when the process comes back to the starting point and new legislative and administrative decisions are transmitted to the Executive Office to be implemented, the established bureaucracy has a powerful role at each point in this involved sequence of events because of its responsibility for carrying out programs and its extensive contracts with the Congress and special interest groups.

Congressional Reactions to Commissions and Consultants

If the recommendations submitted by outside advisory groups survive the internal review conducted by the executive branch, the next step is to make the necessary administrative and legislative changes. In some instances operating departments and agencies can unilaterally take the appropriate actions under existing authority. To formalize this process, task forces may be organized to prepare internal procedural directives, administrative rulings may be filed in the *Federal Register*, the President may issue an Executive Order, and the responsible regulatory agencies may issue official rulings. The key factor in successful internal adjustments is to develop a coordinated package which has the strong backing of the President. It is also crucial that the congressional committees be aware of what is happening because of their increasing responsibilities for oversight.

The final step is to submit to Congress, for their consideration and final vote, whatever legislative initiatives are required to achieve the desired reforms. The executive branch often begins this phase by sending a message from the President to Congress announcing the goals and suggested actions. At the same time an extensive public education program may begin, including press conferences, speeches, briefings to special interest groups by senior government officials at the White House, and a carefully programed strategy of legislative liaison.

Since Congress has the final authority to accept or reject the legislative proposals and also has specific responsibilities for monitoring administrative changes, there is a tenuous link between its specialized committees and the executive branch officials responsible for shepherding the legislative proposals. Cooperative efforts between the two branches of government are always difficult to conduct because the normal problems with personalities and communication are exacerbated by special jurisdictional disputes involving the separation of powers.

Congress tends to be suspicious of proposals from the White House and jealously guards its legislative prerogatives. Even the simplest proposals from the executive branch are more often substantially changed by committee staffs and in formal hearings before one can hope that Congress will finally approve specific legislation and thus demonstrate its absolute authority.

Sometimes this jurisdictional suspicion becomes particularly abrasive, and the decision-making process is disrupted or breaks down completely. Such occasions often occur as a consequence of open disputes between the administration and Congress, when rival political parties refuse to cooperate: for example, when one political party dominates Congress and the administration represents the other party; when liberal versus conservative disputes cut across the normal party loyalties; when disagreements arise between the Senate and the House of Representatives; when unusual crises involving leadership create a serious erosion of presidential power; or when irreconcilable disagreements within the Congress produce sustained filibusters. Because these disagreements frequently delay, or even prevent, necessary government actions, one of the most serious issues confronting our society is how to avoid them without damage to the democratic ideal. The case of financial institution reform reviewed earlier is an example of how seriously they can disrupt the decision-making process.

Changes in the Governmental Environment

One of the most difficult aspects of preparing effective reports by commissions and consultants is the constantly changing environment affecting public policies. Executive branch officials and congressional committees and staffs can adjust rather rapidly, once the course of events is properly identified, but the long lead times required for preparing and publishing the commissions' and consultants' reports makes them very vulnerable to being made obsolete, or even harmful to the cause, by unexpected events. Perhaps the most obvious change in the environment for public policies stems from the pattern of elections, which can at one stroke remove the President from office, along with other senior officials in the executive branch, and alter the membership of Congress and of its standing committees.

The degree of interest and active support the President gives to a public commission is usually the key to the environment in which it makes its impact on the legislative and administrative processes, as well as on the general public. A positive response from the President and his close advisers means that public messages will be issued and legislative initiatives are likely. A negative response means the end of the commission's efforts unless the Congress or general public aggressively supports further consideration. Accordingly, a lame-duck commission reporting to a new President rarely attracts much attention.

The President's Commission on Financial Structure and Regulation, appointed by Richard Nixon in 1970, had already submitted its report to him before the Watergate scandal sapped his power of leadership and forced him to resign on August 8, 1974. But the political turmoil of the times nevertheless severely damaged its prospects for favorable consideration.

Changes in the composition of congressional committees can strongly influence subsequent legislative actions. There were also changes in the leadership of both the Senate Committee on Banking, Housing, and Urban Affairs and the House Committee on Banking, Currency, and Housing during the period when Congress considered the legislative proposals that were based on the commission's study.

The fact that national elections were scheduled for November and the Democratic party candidate Jimmy Carter held a large lead in the public opinion polls was the final political factor influencing the legislative initiatives throughout the summer of 1976, when concluding discussions of comprehensive financial institution reform were taking place. While the exact effects of these political developments can never be determined, they dominated the legislative strategies that the administration, congressional leaders, and various special interest groups adopted in connection with the Financial Institutional Act and Financial Reform Act that followed the Hunt Commission study.

Even more fundamental changes are constantly occurring in the economic, social, international, and technological environment, and all of these influence the efforts and results of commissions and consultants: shifts in the business cycle take us from booms to recessions, and the related surges of inflation and unemployment not only force major adjustments in the analytical approach to national issues but affect the general nature and flexibility of recommendations. Longer-term issues involve the balance of investment and consumption, the pace of economic growth, the distribution of resources, and the incidence of taxation. All of these also change in the course of time. In a social context, the age and composition of the population, urban and rural conditions, and the attitudes and aspirations of people must be considered. The approach of a commission studying the structure of welfare programs in the mid-1970s would be much different from that of a group assigned to a comparable project in the mid-1960s or the mid-1980s.

The increasing integration of different nations in the world economy, particularly the income flows to oil-exporting countries and the acceleration of economic growth in others, has dramatically changed the international environment influencing public policy issues in the United States, which had been relatively insulated from external pressures until the 1960s. Finally, an array of technological developments in energy, transportation, communication, health care, and education have affected not only the world economy but the total environment, including the environment for making governmental decisions.

It is clearly too much to ask commissions and consultants that they correctly anticipate all of these environmental changes, particularly the political developments. Nevertheless, they do need to give careful attention to these externalities in structuring their projects and preparing recommendations. In extreme cases environmental factors will make reports by advisory groups outdated by the time they are submitted, while in other situations the pace of progress in economic, social, international, and technological affairs may make their well-intentioned suggestions premature or impossible.

Criticism from Dissatisfied Special Interest Groups

Special interest groups that remain dissatisfied with the final reports of public commissions and consultants may try to discredit their work and in this way prevent, or at least restrict, the recommended legislative and administrative changes. Such groups make their criticisms to both the executive branch and Congress through public statements and vigorous private lobbying programs, directing most of their objections to the recommendations that threaten their protected status.

For example, representatives from several associations of financial institutions argued that the Hunt Commission's package of reforms would seriously disrupt the competitive balance of the financial markets and prevent the achievement of social goals, particularly for housing construction.

Critics sometimes also attack the structure and procedures of commissions and consulting groups, trying to detract from the credibility of their substantive recommendations. By claiming that the groups did not observe proper procedures, critics attempt to discredit them for failing to observe the rules of the game. For instance they are charged with failing to represent the diverse interest groups that are affected; with being too narrow or too broad in their consideration of the issues; with having conflicts of interest and showing bias; with failing in expertise; with setting up an inadequate staff or dominating the staff; with being too conservative or too radical; premature or out of date; too fast or too slow; too attentive to expediency or too naively idealistic; too politicized or too isolated from the real world; and so eager to finish the final report that they do not thoroughly consider the issues. Some of these accusations may be true of many commissions and consultants. But they appear to miss the very reason why such studies are created: to provide a set of recommendations that will be independent of these pressures from special interest groups.

Summary

A study of the President's Commission on Financial Structure and Regulation and general observation of other public commissions and consultants indicate that they have made a contribution to the analysis of several important issues. A few outside studies have even affected public policy decisions and led to administrative and legislative changes. Most advisory groups, however, have provided only the necessary background for the executive branch and congressional efforts that must follow.

Proposed studies by advisory groups are taken, as we have said, as a symbol of the President's concern and his intent to study the issues thoroughly and objectively before making a final decision. The analysis submitted by commissions and consultants usually constitutes a useful trial balloon by which the President can measure the reactions of his executive branch bureaucracy, of Congress, and of the general public.

Even more important, such studies bring to the fore the controversial issues and policy positions of the relevant special interest groups. The strong drive for consensus in most reports eliminates the most revolutionary suggestions, and the President usually receives a package of recommendations representing the "least worst" set of ideas that can survive the pressures for consensus and the final editing process. Even when the President and his advisers assume the leadership role in advocating part, or all, of the recommendations, the original report serves as a benchmark, providing background authority and independent credibility. Public commissions and consultants can thus mark a beginning step in decision making, if they are given reasonable assignments and are so structured that they are respected by the general public and at least tolerated by powerful special interest groups.

The weaknesses of public commissions and consultants have been reviewed in this chapter: the delayed timing of reports, the universal drive for consensus, the irreconcilable disputes among members, the emphasis on new research rather than evaluation of obvious issues, the selective screens used by government officials to ignore unpopular recommendations, the differences in perspectives, the problems with congressional liaison, the opposition from the executive branch bureaucracy, the influence of external events and conditions, and the continued criticism and lobbying by dissatisfied special interest groups. These clearly limit the effectiveness of commissions and consultants in influencing public policies. But even if these drawbacks were not present, the contributions of advisers from outside the government would still not correct the problems inherent in making public decisions. At best, outside analysts can provide background information and recommendations. They cannot substitute for the elected and appointed government officials who must ultimately face up to the most difficult of all human actions—the final decision on a controversial issue. The rationale of appointing public commissions and consultants is basically valid, but they cannot be expected to develop definitive solutions leading directly to administrative and legislative changes. To do so would represent an abrogation of the responsibilities of government officials that would be both illegal and certain to fail.

12

THE ROLE OF CONGRESSIONAL HEARINGS

When both the executive branch and Congress agree that fundamental administrative and legislative changes are needed, why is the government's response so fragmented and delayed? The disappointing example of comprehensive financial institution reform provides insights into the organizational and procedural problems that prevented a final decision—thus leaving individual interest groups to pursue their unilateral legislative goals, and the marketplace to work out competitive adjustments within the existing framework of administrative and statutory rulings. Details of that failure have been covered in earlier chapters. Here we will take a broader look at the role played by Congress and its committees in governmental decisions.

Congress is involved in the decision-making process at both the beginning and completion of the sequence.[1] Congressional committees are charged with oversight responsibilities to review the administrative actions of the executive branch and conduct hearings relating to the allocation of the federal budget to competing programs. Members of Congress are also expected to respond to developments in the private sector, particularly to unexpected events which are unusually serious or are likely to attract widespread publicity and have political consequences. Recently Congress has been rapidly expanding its oversight activities in public and private affairs. A second major responsibility of Congress involves the consideration of legislative proposals resulting from oversight activities and from

---

1. This brief summary does not discuss Congress as an institution or its broad functions. It is limited to specific congressional responsibilities in dealing with the executive branch and outside groups in the decision process. For an unusually perceptive and thorough analysis of this subject see Charles E. Lindblom, *The Policy-Making Process* (Englewood Cliffs, N.J.: Prentice-Hall, 1968).

251

the initiatives of the executive branch and a multitude of special interest groups.

Of the many thousands of legislative proposals submitted during each session only a small fraction are eventually considered by congressional committees, and even fewer survive to be sent forward for formal votes. Nevertheless, the responsibility for comprehensive oversight and legislation represents an overwhelming workload for conscientious members of Congress. In addition, they must respond to individual requests from constituents, satisfy a continuous need for political campaigning, attend and address endless meetings with individuals and groups, plan leadership and strategy, travel many miles, and meet with private lobbyists and representatives of the executive branch—all this without neglecting personal and family affairs. Since it is obviously impossible for any individual to carry out all of these responsibilities adequately, Congress has created an intricate system of specialized committees and staffs who can share some of the responsibilities and burdens. Final authority, however, cannot be delegated, and responsible congressmen prefer to remain involved in the details of oversight and legislation because they have undertaken personally to represent the general public and various special interests. The result is too often a chaotic system of confusing parliamentary procedures, putting heavy pressures on individual members as they strive to carry out their extensive duties.

In too many situations the congressional system becomes so overloaded that it does not function. When this happens the oversight reponsibilities are ignored, important legislation stagnates, and the executive branch and regulatory agencies are left to function independently or to delay necessary actions until Congress finally responds. As would be expected, these breakdowns typically involve the increasing number of issues that are both complex and controversial. When this happens, crucial needs, such as the great need for a national energy policy, may be ignored for years. Festering problems lead to crises, and important legislative matters, such as comprehensive financial institution reform, are allowed to expire quietly at the end of the congressional calendar.

A major paradox is thus evident: Congress has greatly expanded its oversight and legislative efforts that affect the private sector, but is too often unable to make the necessary policy decisions because of the cross-currents of political pressures and its cumbersome operating procedures. The rules of the game designed for the slower pace and simpler issues of a previous era are not adequate for coping with the flood of new legislation and increasing oversight requirements.

Political activity is an intriguing subject and the manipulation of government processes through the use of power has been the fascinating topic of thousands of books and articles. But the welfare of over two hundred million individual Americans and our role in international affairs should not be pawns in a game where points are awarded for political expertise. More rigorous and objective analysis of issues, uninhibited by partisan political pressures, is needed in preparing for congressional oversight and legislative decisions. And a more dynamic schedule of decisive work is required if the current disillusionment with the processes of government is to be replaced by public respect and support.

The average citizen feels very vulnerable to external forces and believes that the powers of governments are used against rather than for his personal interests. Many people develop apathy and cynicism, and the existing problems are made more difficult by their lack of interest in public affairs. This is all the more true because they leave a vacuum to be exploited by aggressive special interest groups.

The goal of our political system should be to find ways to improve procedures and organizational arrangements so that Congress plays a more effective role in decision making. History and current international developments clearly indicate that when the representative body of government fails to fulfill its responsibilities for arriving at crucial decisions, an unfortunate shift to some kind of authoritarian leadership occurs.

The Structure of Congressional Analysis

Given the extremely busy schedule of most congressmen, the selection of issues to be considered and specific committee assignments are key decisions. Routine oversight by committees turns up many problems requiring analysis, and individual congressmen and leaders often submit proposals. A second major source of initiatives is the executive branch, and proposals are also submitted by independent regulatory agencies and special interest groups. Congress also reacts to various events presented as crises, such as serious economic developments, natural disasters, major scandals, or such unexpected developments as the oil embargo against the United States by certain oil-producing nations in 1973. Once the topics are identified, the majority leaders and committee chairmen in Congress negotiate specific assignments and tentative schedules so that the staffs may prepare background studies.

The first step is usually to convene public hearings under the auspices of an entire committee or subcommittee. Hearings may take up only one day or require several sessions lasting many months, as was the case with financial institution reform. As a rule opening comments are made by the chairman and others from the committee who desire to speak. Next to be heard are other members of Congress and invited representatives from the executive branch, regulatory agencies, major interest groups, and academic institutions. Witnesses typically present long written statements and brief oral summaries as a basis for an extended question-and-answer exchange. Speakers also commonly submit additional written material that expands the original statements and responds to written questions from the committee. Individuals and groups not invited to the hearings may also submit written statements.

The chief purpose of congressional hearings is to provide a forum for the exchange of views that will serve as a background for evaluating proposed legislation. At best, this process can be a classic example of effective governmental leadership, when serious and well-briefed committee members direct probing questions on substantive issues to other government officials and outside experts. Responsibly conducted congressional hearings create meaningful dialogue that provides necessary guidance for the committee and the general public. The exchange of strongly held views is often abrasive, but unwarranted personal attacks and empty rhetoric are generally avoided. In the best hearings the substance of discussions justifies the long preparation of witnesses and the time and effort of the full committee members and staff. When reality matches this ideal, a sound foundation is created for subsequent analysis and decisions.

At worst, congressional hearings represent a mere show of interest or deteriorate to the level of a carnival. Disappointing sessions often begin with a predictable harangue by the chairman of the committee or subcommittee, who is usually the only congressman present unless the minority party sends a representative to be a watchdog. The chairman's bombastic opening comments are designed to appeal to political motives and impress his constituencies. He is followed by a series of witnesses carefully selected to express views that reinforce his own. These witnesses usually read long statements to take up time and then answer a few perfunctory questions supplied by the committee staff. Other committee members may wander in and out during these presentations but do little except read or talk to their colleagues, unless it is their turn to ask partisan questions aimed at solidifying their own views or embarrassing the witness. Such hearings are worse than a waste of time for the witnesses and committee staffs who work hard to prepare for the sessions, but the sessions receive little public notice because the news media have learned to ignore them.

The results of most congressional hearings fall somewhere between the extremes of substantive dialogues and partisan political displays. The concept behind the hearings is sound, and results are positive if the committee members are willing to listen and ask pertinent questions. As a minimum contribution, hearings comply with the ubiquitous rules of the game that shape the form of government. At best they result in a comprehensive discussion, objective views from experts, challenging questions from committee members, a written record, a chance for the public to view the entire process, and, allegedly, a consideration of all views before the committee makes its decision.

More realistically, most hearings are limited to identifying the issues, hearing the opinions of various interest groups, and accumulating valuable information and arguments for the committee members who are interested. They also provide publicity for the issue being considered and open up communication with the interest groups that want to be heard. The formal statements presented by the interest groups usually represent only the tip of the iceberg, compared to their private lobbying among individual congressmen and administration officials, but the question-and-answer periods are sometimes useful in showing the scope and intensity of their views.

Once the sessions are completed, the group conducting the hearings submits its summary to the full committee, which must then decide whether to recommend new legislation or a congressional resolution based on their analysis and the results of the hearings. In most cases the public hearings provide a useful background if the committee decides that action is necessary, but the hearings seldom produce the major motive for a new legislative initiative.

The real power over the fate of most legislative proposals is centered in the various committees that conduct the bulk of the work of Congress. For example, in 1976 the Senate had 31 committees and 174 subcommittees and the House of Representatives had a parallel organization. These groups have the ultimate authority, working closely with the congressional leaders, to determine what bills are sent forward for final votes and when the decisions will be made. They form a small elite of changing power blocs responsible for piecing together specific legislation. This is where the trade-off decisions are made which ultimately result in compromises.

It is also the place in the entire decision-making process where all of the specific forces converge. Individual congressmen add their special amendments. Executive branch officials conduct the give-and-take negotiations necessary to move legislation out of the committees. Private lobbyists push their particular interests with key committees and staffs. And at the center of this political maze the committee chairman controls the schedule and sequence of discussions among the members and staff aides that leads to the final outcome representing the interactions of the entire group.

Political party affiliations are usually the key in marshaling support or defeating minority viewpoints, but fluctuating coalitions are constantly being created—and just as rapidly abandoned—to represent the specific interests of the committee members and the diverse constituencies they represent. This committee process is the very essence of the political decision, bringing into play all of the rules of the game, or what Professor Charles E. Lindblom calls the "play of power."[2] The public hearings that precede the committee's sessions are an interesting and sometimes useful prelude, and the subsequent vote in the Senate and House of Representatives is the formal symbol of representative government, but the real action in hammering out congressional decisions actually occurs in the committee sessions.

The dominant power in this extremely complicated and highly politicized process is the committee chairman, who applies persuasive and arbitrary techniques to direct the members toward compromise agreements. The chairman has the formal power to call committee meetings and hearings, to appoint the members to various subcommittees, and to allocate assignments. Even more important, the chairman can delay or expedite all bills and resolutions considered by the committee. One political analyst has aptly described the atmosphere of committee deliberations:

> In time, every senator comes to understand this. The more successful, and the occasional great ones, learn how to move that collection of conflicting interests and egos onto a common path. People sneered, for instance, at Lyndon Johnson's Dale Carnegie approach to human relations as applied to the Senate. But, in truth, human relations were decisive in his unexcelled ability to lead that body.
>
> Johnson knew, better than anyone in our lifetime, that he could not order a senator to vote this way or that; he could not decree legislative compromises. He understood that his only real power was the power of persuasion, and that power rested on his relationship to his peers. "There

2. Lindblom, *The Policy-Making Process*, p. 18.

are different viewpoints and different emphases on nearly every matter," he once said of the Senate. "There are 50 different states with different backgrounds, different environments, different geographical and economic interests . . . all of them sent by sovereign states to speak for their states. Now, these men don't always see everything alike."

The art was in achieving a compromise—or "consensus," in that much maligned term—among those strong disparate views and also in understanding that each senator bore special personal and political pressures that only he could entirely fathom.[3]

The actual preparation of legislation begins with a staff markup of a proposed bill, which is then modified by the committee members. Once the committee markup is completed, the final compromises are negotiated and the chairman arranges a stategy for reporting out the bill to the full Senate or House of Representatives. The staff also prepares a committee report that explains the legislative background to other congressmen, who probably will not have the time or interest to review the record of public hearings and the details of the legislation.

Throughout this entire process unusual power is delegated to the committees, particularly the leaders, to determine what oversight and legislative initiatives will be made. Legislation rarely comes to the floor of the House or Senate without first being evaluated by a committee, and amendments suggested during the formal floor vote are usually rejected and returned to the responsible committee for further consideration. Once the bill is reported out favorably by a committee, the final vote usually follows the committee's recommendations because of the delegation of responsibilities and specialization of functions used by Congress to accomplish its diverse assignments.

Accordingly, committee chairmen can often prevent formal votes on issues simply by bottling up the proposed legislation in their committees. On the other hand, new legislation and resolutions can be rapidly moved along by a supportive committee chairman if he can forge a consensus within his group.

Much of the effectiveness or inefficiency of the government's decision-making process is thus centered in the organization and procedures of congressional committees. Numerous proposals for reform have been made in the hope of breaking the committees' hold on the functions of Congress, but the system continues to function almost unchanged except for some recent minor alterations by the House of

3. Haynes Johnson, "Cracks in the Senate Floor," *Washington Post* (Oct. 9, 1977), p. A3.

Representatives. The existing system has many advantages, and such specialization of assignments is probably the only feasible way of handling the overwhelming number and diversity of legislative proposals, but there is also a great risk that the interests of the general public may be frustrated.

After the intensive analysis of issues by committees, the formal vote on the floor of the Senate or House is often an anticlimax. Most new bills and resolutions are passed quickly with little discussion and minimal changes. Major issues, such as the massive energy act debated throughout all of 1977 and much of 1978, require extended parliamentary discussion, and competing interests continue to propose amendments right up until the final vote. At this point another important factor is the possibility of a veto by the President. Formal votes in the Senate and House are sometimes a test to determine if a threatened veto can be overridden. Votes on key amendments are similarly used to gauge the probable reaction to the entire bill.

There are also instances in which relatively minor issues stir up extreme controversy and completely disrupt the entire congressional schedule until leaders figure out a way to force a vote or simply delete the bill from the agenda. The legislative history of the common situs picketing bill, involving the powers of single labor unions to picket entire construction projects, is interesting in this connection. It was a classic example of a somewhat obscure bill, which few people really understood but which caused strong controversy lasting several months until it was surprisingly rejected in early 1977. When such delays occur, the congressional leaders and committee chairmen must work out an acceptable scheduling compromise which respects the complicated procedural rules and historical protocol.

When the formal vote occurs, the issues tend to be decided along political party lines, although some create temporary coalitions where the divisions are conservative versus liberal, urban versus rural, old versus young, or even one geographical region versus another. While most votes are predictable, there is always an element of uncertainty, particularly on emotional issues, and the actual results are sometimes surprising even to congressional leaders. The classic analysis by Stephen K. Bailey of the famous Employment Act of 1946, a benchmark in legislation that identified national economic goals, emphasizes this point:

> The fate of any piece of legislation cannot be understood without an appreciation of the fact that Congressmen are people, with all that that banality implies. Like the rest of us they become bored by tedious de-

bates, angered by personal affronts, inspired by the words of leaders they respect, irritated by the weather, confused by technical problems, upset by domestic misunderstandings or the illness of loved ones. Like any cross-section of the American public, they have been molded in their thinking by scores of influences: parents, teachers, friends, enemies, social status, occupation or profession, personal success and failures, adult associates, regional interests, local opinions, party loyalties, and the general social, economic, moral, and intellectual milieu of their generation and culture.[4]

The last step by Congress requires a reconciliation of any differences that might exist in the final bills passed separately by the Senate and the House. Committee chairmen are responsible for appointing representatives to meet to develop a unifying compromise whenever disparities exist. The resulting conference report provides one last opportunity to develop a consensus. If a compromise can be worked out, the conference report is then returned to each House for final approval and is then sent to the President for his signature, completing the process.

If the President signs the bill it becomes effective immediately, but if he vetoes the proposed legislation both the Senate and the House must vote to override the veto before the statute can become binding. Even at this late stage various interest groups continue to exert intense pressure on the President and his senior advisers to approve or veto bills passed by Congress.

These complicated procedures have been carefully designed to preserve the representative forms of government. But, as we have said, effective leadership is often delayed or even prevented by the involved process.

Organizational and Procedural Problems

Along with the complexity of the entire decision-making process, several specific procedural problems hinder efficient operations. Although these restrictions have existed for many years and are by now firmly established in the system, they are often frustrating to congressmen and outside groups involved in legislative activities. Typical examples of such procedural limitations are these:

1. *Specialized committees and subcommittees.* The oversight and legislative responsibilities of Congress are normally handled by a large number of autonomous committees and subcommittees. The official leadership and political party allegiances provide some cohesion,

4. Stephen K. Bailey, *Congress Makes a Law,* p. 189.

but each committee and some important subcommittees represent separate power blocs. Comprehensive issues rarely fit into such neat compartments, so there is often a fragmented approach to major problems which makes scheduling and coordination difficult. Many congressional hearings and studies are also redundant because each committee and subcommittee jealously guards its jurisdictional prerogatives. It is not unusual for senior officials from the executive branch to present similar testimony to several different committees in both the House and Senate, and this has also been true of private witnesses. The natural tendency to seek additional power by broadening the scope of committee and subcommittee activities makes the degree of overlapping greater each year and causes leadership disputes and confusion as well.

2. *Parliamentarian procedures and protocol.* The prerogatives of individual congressmen and the committee structure have created a set of customs and guidelines that usually determines procedures and important protocol requirements. These traditional practices make Congress a more pleasant and predictable place to work, but they restrict the pace of activity and often lead to inefficiency. The complex rules also make it a relatively easy matter to stonewall the progress of new legislation and resolutions, particularly by the leaders and the committee chairmen who control the schedules and assignments.

3. *Information flows.* Individual congressmen are deluged by reports, hearings, speeches, letters, telephone calls, meetings, and petitions for special attention. They cannot possibly absorb even a small fraction of this information and are forced to rely extensively on their personal and committee staffs. It is sometimes claimed that staff aides dominate congressional activities because of their specialized knowledge of technical matters. But such charges exaggerate the role of most staff officials, who usually concentrate on serving the interests of their personal congressmen or committee leaders.

4. *Mutual reciprocity in voting.* Congressmen use the same sort of selective screens to filter information whether they are preparing to vote or conducting hearings, but because their oversight and legislative interests are usually relatively narrow they must rely on respected colleagues to help them decide how to vote on many technical issues. This mutual dependence creates reciprocal arrangements by which members exchange support within the general framework of party loyalties and the specific interests of constituencies. The exchange of support is usually limited to simple persuasion by the sponsors of new bills and congressional leaders, but more outright

pressures are resorted to if the running counts of votes for or against controversial measures turn out to be close.

5. *Emphasis on details.* The growing emphasis on oversight responsibilities and the crush of new legislation result in an excessive concentration on details. This, in turn, limits the perspectives of congressmen and prevents them from spending enough time on the broad questions that need to be considered in establishing national priorities. Both the House and the Senate should devote more of their attention to resolving these controversial issues and give less time to the details of committee oversight and legislative activities.

6. *Crisis orientation.* A problem related to deciding what activities should take precedence arises from the common tendency of Congress to shift its attention to external events that are sometimes real crises but sometimes only imaginary ones. The difficulty, of course, is to distinguish between the two. There are many situations to which Congress must respond decisively, but most cases that come before Congress do not require an immediate response. Interruptions of the regular business to deal with emergencies exemplify an unfortunate aspect of the schedules and committee arrangements used by Congress.

7. *Commitments of time and resources.* Congressional hearings require an extensive commitment of time and institutional resources on the part of congressmen, their staffs, and the participating witnesses. Representatives of special interest groups usually welcome an opportunity to express their views to congressmen and the general public. The reaction of witnesses from the executive branch is usually less enthusiastic unless the hearings are established to give them a public forum. Most of the exchange of views and responses to congressional questioners could be more efficiently accomplished by written statements. In fact, very few congressmen attend the hearings, and they could easily have their staff aides summarize the major points. The drama and media coverage associated with major hearings would be lost, but the long hours and large financial costs that would be saved would justify a reduction in the number and length of many hearings.

8. *Advantages of hearing from selected special interest groups.* Congressmen are constantly expected to respond to pressures from various special interest groups. In doing so they must decide whether they are a public trustee, concerned about comprehensive national issues, or a constituent delegate, representing the specific interests of the people who elected them. The political reality, of course, is that each congressman must serve in both capacities. On issues that affect

their constituencies they must be delegates if they want to be re-elected, but on other questions they can adopt a broader perspective. There is nothing insidious about being responsive to outside interests as long as the pressures are limited to persuasion and the exchange of views.

There is, however, the fundamental problem that different interest groups vary widely in their access to political blocs of power. Political scientists believe that such inequality is a natural consequence of the decision-making process in a representative government. This seems too ready an acceptance of an unfairness in the political system that frustrates the average citizen and leads to cynicism and a general lack of interest in political elections among approximately one half of the eligible voters. Congressional hearings are one way to open up the public decision-making process, although the real decisions will still be made in the committees where only certain pressure groups have the advantage of access to the members and staffs.

Comprehensive or Specific Legislative Strategies

The dilemma for congressmen in choosing between the roles of public trustee and constituent delegate also leads to another difficult decision: the proper strategy to use in submitting new legislation. In 1973 the administration argued that financial institution reform should be comprehensive, and congressional leaders supported that approach. By mid-1977 the Treasury Department, under a new Secretary, decided that sweeping changes were not feasible and that only two specific proposals would be submitted to Congress. This experience demonstrates the difficult choice between comprehensive and specific legislative strategies.

Most questions of public policy are related to other problems, and few specific changes can be made without affecting the overall balance. Economic issues, such as federal spending and taxation, inflation, unemployment, capital investment, energy, the environment, transportation, welfare programs, foreign trade, and so on, are obviously interrelated and require a broad perspective. In the real world, however, it is difficult to develop comprehensive recommendations, and most legislative proposals call for only marginal changes in existing policies. The government's fragmented organizational structure along with political pressures to preserve the existing competitive balance are partly to blame for such an ad hoc approach, but there are many other factors that limit the timing and scope of rec-

ommendations for change. Sponsors of new administrative and legislative proposals must therefore carefully compare the theoretical
advantages of comprehensive plans against the pragmatic benefits of
specific adjustments that may gradually achieve the same goals.
They must also adjust their strategy as conditions change and be
willing to accept compromises combining both comprehensive and
specific approaches.

Arguments favoring the comprehensive approach

The major advantage of comprehensive administrative and legislative reforms is that such a plan recognizes the integrated nature of
important issues. Piecemeal changes are often uneven and create
unexpected distortions because some problems are strongly emphasized while others are neglected. It is frequently argued that specific
interests can be helped without injuring other groups, but this ignores the truism that when a chosen few receive special advantages
everyone else suffers relative disadvantages. The government has
authority to provide compensatory programs through spending,
taxation, and the use of regulatory incentives or penalties to achieve
certain goals; but the real costs and pervasive effects of such activities should be fully explained to the electorate. The vending-
machine approach—providing specific palliatives in response to
pressures from each of the many special interest groups—effectively
neutralizes the advantages that a strong central government has
from its broader perspective and longer time frame for ranking national priorities and allocating resources.

The comprehensive approach also helps maintain a more equitable
balance among various groups because it requires trade-offs. For
example, the administration's strategy for financial institution reform assumed that thrift institutions and housing interests would
accept a phasing out of interest rate controls and the advantageous
yield differential in exchange for a broadening of their asset investment and liability powers, which would theoretically strengthen
their competitive position and lead to improved mortgage market
conditions. Similarly, although commercial banks would suffer competitive disadvantages if expanded operating powers were granted
to other depository institutions, it was hoped that they would accept
this proposal in exchange for the elimination of regulation Q controls, which would improve their overall position in the financial
markets. The underlying assumption was that a sweet-and-sour
compromise could be arranged in which each group would accept

increased competitive risks and give up some existing advantages to acquire expanded powers and flexibility.

A third advantage of comprehensive reform is that the base of political support may be enlarged by considering the needs of more interest groups. If this strategy succeeds, changes are more likely and the transition is usually simpler and less costly. These advantages sometimes cause officials representing the private groups to develop broad policy recommendations to serve as the political equivalent of a "preemptive strike," to seize the initiative and force Congress and the executive branch to react to the entire range of relevant issues. This approach is often associated with a crisis situation such as the energy legislation submitted in 1974 and 1977. The initial thrust often helps to focus public attention on important issues and to get the decision-making process started. Unfortunately, government procedures and political pressures have a way of neutralizing popular enthusiasm for reform.

A fourth reason why comprehensive recommendations are favored rests on the familiar bargaining technique of beginning with a demand for major concessions and gradually working back to a reasonable compromise. For example, some suggest that many of the approximately one hundred government regulatory agencies should be critically evaluated all at once in the hope that at least a few remedial changes might survive the review process in the executive branch and Congress. In other words, a simultaneous attack on many sacred cows might result in at least a few casualties. This argument may appeal to the cynical but it rarely works in the real world.

Finally, the comprehensive approach has the major advantages of being logical and efficient as well as enlarging the perspective of policy officials. Broad recommendations may also enlist greater public support and effective political pressure from citizens. It would be an exaggeration, however, to claim that this is the normative model for government decisions. The organization and operating procedures of the executive branch and Congress are not such that they lend themselves to comprehensive strategies, and extensive political opposition quickly develops whenever sweeping reforms are proposed.

Arguments favoring the specific approach

Despite the theoretical superiority of comprehensive policy proposals, the government approaches most problems through a continuous series of small decisions that eventually accumulate to form major actions. The principal reason for using this "incremental gradualism" is that such a procedure minimizes the political risks while providing tangible evidence that the government is actually doing something. Gradualism usually avoids the harsh reality of abrupt changes and provides government officials with more flexibility to react to the daily "mini" crises that characterize public service. Since each special interest group concentrates on its own goals rather than the system as a whole, this compartmented response is an effective way for government officials to prove that their reactions to problems of individual groups are compassionate, imaginative, analytical, and effective, even though the problems are minor in the national context.

The term *gradualism* may be misleading. Actually this approach necessitates frenetic activity to consider the thousands of new bills and resolutions intended to respond to these specific concerns. The idea is to relieve the responsible officials from working painfully through the entire problem and its repercussions on related issues. But the general result is an overwhelming maze of governmental programs, which often overlap and are occasionally contradictory.

For example, in 1975 there were fifteen different programs to improve the nutritional standards for children, but most analysts remained critical of the fragmented results. Many were particularly troubled by the disadvantages suffered by many children from low-income families, and the continued subsidies to provide school lunches for children in the wealthy suburbs of Washington, D.C., and other heavy concentrations of military and civil service employees.

Nor is it unusual to find different government programs promoting mutually exclusive goals: agricultural projects providing incentives to some farmers to increase their output, while others are given cash payments to restrict production; or the development of national programs to promote productivity, while individual regulatory agencies and federal tax policies consistently discourage capital investment. The resulting waste of human and material resources, along with the personal frustrations of the individuals directly affected, represents a serious problem even in a nation as affluent as the United States.

The incremental gradualism approach appeals to many government officials, however, because it enables them to concentrate on positive responses to each group while delaying the inevitable counterbalancing actions. This arrangement does not always work, because each interest group is affected whenever concessions are granted to rival constituencies, but the disjointed timing, massive size, and confusing complexity of government activities make it difficult for them to assign the blame for disappointing results.

In a positive sense, this approach does enable specific problems to be corrected as they develop without resorting to the time-consuming process of comprehensive reform. In many instances, in fact, these detailed issues must be cleared away before an overall evaluation of existing policies can begin. The specific approach is also more compatible with the specialized committee structure of Congress and the fragmented distribution of program responsibilities within the executive branch.

Nevertheless, marginal policy adjustments and continual responses to pressures from special interest groups do not solve fundamental problems. Most government officials accept this fact because in the normal course of events they anticipate another chance during the next session of Congress, in next year's budget, during the next administration, when another public commission's or consultant's report is issued or the next major reorganization of the executive branch takes place. Given the serial nature of most policy decisions, it is safer to tolerate minor problems than to commit a major mistake, particularly if the issues are politically sensitive.

A further advantage to the pragmatic approach of concentrating on specific policy adjustments is that it avoids difficult procedural problems. The all-or-nothing commitment of comprehensive proposals increases the risks of total rejection because the broad scope of suggested changes tends to splinter both popular and official support: the effort that government officials can devote to specific issues is necessarily limited, and interest groups concentrate on their own goals. The necessary compromises also consolidate the opposition, since there is usually something for everyone to hate, and most groups adopt defensive positions to protect their present advantages and avoid concessions. In this situation they play to avoid losing rather than to win. Once a comprehensive initiative fails it is difficult to get the program started again, and the usual practice is simply to salvage the uncontroversial parts of the package.

All of these problems affected the Financial Institution Acts and the Financial Reform Act. Each special interest group decided to reject the entire package rather than accept the required compromises. As a result, the Treasury Department shifted from a comprehensive to a specific strategy in 1977, at the same time that the administration was attempting to promote broad revisions relating to energy, tax, and welfare policy. Each of these efforts to achieve comprehensive reform has had considerable difficulty getting started in Congress, where various specialized committees have divided the jurisdictional responsibilities. The legislative history of financial institution reform and current debates about several other complex issues suggest that comprehensive efforts will continue, but the familiar pattern of gradual change is likely to dominate the decision-making process.

Summary

The oversight and legislative functions of Congress are the key factor in decision making. All of the public and private strategies, the power plays, and the pushing and shoving from political pressures converge at this point. The admirable record of the United States in domestic and international affairs indicates that representative government has served this nation well for two hundred years. The separation of powers and familiar checks and balances have generally prevented excessive centralization of authority. Because of the division of responsibilities, institutions have continued to function despite the growing number of complex and controversial issues. The operating procedures and protocol rules, while often frustrating and occasionally silly, generally prevent arbitrary or devious national decisions.

As a result, the necessary framework for making decisions and exercising follow-up control is firmly in place and very few Americans would favor any alternative form of government. Given the extreme complexity of issues that must be considered during each session and the extraordinary pressures on the time and abilities of congressmen, they deserve more compliments and less criticism for what is accomplished. The procedural problems and the incremental gradualism approaches to making decisions discussed in this chapter indicate that constructive improvement is needed, but the primary role of Congress is a major strength in the American system. In fact, a strong and independent Congress is our best hope for the future preservation of representative government in the face of a diversity of interests and a collectivist environment with increasing centralization of power in the executive branch, where only the President and Vice-President are elected by the people.

Despite this positive evaluation of Congress it is equally clear that serious problems prevent the decision-making system from functioning as well as it should. The piecemeal approach of Congress to administrative oversight and legislative proposals too often leads to delays, patchwork results, and excessive emphasis on details, while fundamental issues are conveniently ignored. Occasionally the entire process is halted because of indecisiveness, stonewalling tactics of filibusters, and clever manipulation of the parliamentarian procedures to prevent action. The disappointing fate of the Financial Institution Act and Financial Reform Act is only one example of important breakdowns in responding to crucial issues involving energy, taxes, welfare, defense, foreign affairs, and many other national priorities.

For example, for over a decade individual experts and some government officials pleaded for a national energy policy that would recognize not only the pressing need for extensive development of domestic resources and meaningful conservation but even more fundamental issues involving international monetary problems, trade and investment, and the long-term outlook for national economic growth, inflation, and employment. Those pleas were largely ignored until the traumatic oil embargo, beginning in October 1973, dramatically demonstrated the serious economic, political, and military risks in the current situation. The return to normal supplies of energy—with oil import prices quadrupled—by the spring of 1974 and the severe economic recession that soon followed quickly eroded public support for the broad recommendations on energy policy submitted to Congress by President Ford in late 1974.

By the time a new administration arrived in January 1977, over three years after the energy crisis of 1973, the United States had become significantly more dependent on foreign sources of oil; our balance of trade had swung from a sizable surplus of $9 billion in 1975 to a deficit of $34 billion for 1978; and little real progress had been made in promoting conservation or developing the available resources for domestic energy. In short, the United States was even more vulnerable to the devastating shocks of another energy crisis caused by natural or political developments.

Following an unusually severe winter, marked by serious shortages of natural gas, President Carter once again proposed a comprehensive energy policy which included many of the recommendations that had been ignored or rejected over the years. In launching his energy crusade in April 1977, President Carter repeatedly emphasized that the energy problem is "the single most important item before us, second only to our nation's security," and he promised to make his package of recommendations the central item in his entire

legislative program.[5] Six months later the scoreboard indicated that
the House of Representatives had passed a heavily modified comprehensive bill, but the Senate had rejected the major proposals. It was
still trying to act on five different bills, which would then have to be
submitted to a conference report, with conferees from the House, to
see what could be salvaged. In reporting on President Carter's intention to make a personal tour of the country to marshal public opinion,
the *Washington Post* described the situation as follows:

> President Carter yesterday accepted part of the blame for the demolition
> of his energy bill in the Senate and promised a new offensive to try to
> arouse public opinion to save it.
>
> "There is no need for me to beat the energy horse," the President was
> quoted as saying at his weekly breakfast with Democratic congressional
> leaders. "The situation is obvious to everyone."
>
> He referred to the fact that the Senate Finance Committee has killed his
> three proposed taxes—on crude oil, gas-guzzler cars and natural gas—
> which were the main parts of his energy conservation plan. The full
> Senate, meanwhile, has gutted his electric utility rate structure revision
> proposal, weakened his coal conversion plan and voted to lift price con-
> trols from natural gas, which he would continue to control, but at a
> higher price.
>
> According to members of Congress present, Carter said: "Part of the
> problem may be my own. When the situation was before the House I met
> two or three times a week with members of the House, but I did not do
> much of that with the Senate."[6]

The failure of financial institution reform, and continuing difficulties in developing broad policy revisions affecting energy, taxes,
welfare, capital investment, transportation, agriculture, foreign
trade, and other basic issues, cannot be blamed on the composition
of the political system or the actions of individual special interest
groups. The political system is merely the mechanism for making
decisions. It does not determine the quantity or quality of decisions.
Nor is it inherently biased for or against any specific policy or particularly responsive to external pressures. Congress functions as it
does—with all of the resulting benefits and disappointments—because it is representative. Every congressman understands that reelection depends upon responding to the diverse interests of his
personal constituents. The output of Congress reflects the input of
the electorate. To blame our decision-making problems on "the gov-

5. Richard L. Lyons and Edward Walsh, "Carter Vows New Offensive to Save
   Energy Bill in Senate," *Washington Post* (Oct. 13, 1977), p. A3.
6. Ibid.

ernment," as if some monolithic entity independently determines the laws and administrative rulings, is grossly simplistic and totally unreasonable.

Government officials do exactly what they think the voting electorate wants them to do. The United States has reported massive federal budget deficits in eighteen of the last nineteen fiscal years and will continue to do so for the foreseeable future, because the people want the programs and services provided by the public spending. If the electorate did not want those programs and services the extraordinary deficits would not have occurred. The United States has had inadequate capital investment for many years. This situation has led to excessive inflation, unemployment, slowdowns in productivity, production bottlenecks, and erosion of our competitive position in world markets, because Americans prefer current consumption over investment for future benefits.

Despite the frightening risks to our economic, political, and military capabilities, the United States has not developed an effective energy program because Americans are unwilling to sacrifice current consumption or make the investments needed for developing available resources. A modified energy bill did become law in late 1978, but the final compromise bore little resemblance to the original proposal. Legislation for comprehensive financial institution reform did not pass because few people were concerned about it, and those who did express their views to Congress were chiefly against it. If a villain is to be identified it must be the American people, not the government, because the actions of public officials are responsive to the interests that citizens express. To behave otherwise in a representative form of government would lead to political failure.

In summary, the decision-making process described here will continue to function as it has in the past because it represents the preferences of the majority. Whether this approach is right or wrong is not the relevant issue in a representative form of government. If Americans are to enjoy the blessings of this political system they must also recognize the disadvantages that limit the efficiency of our policy making. We should strive to improve the system by organizational and procedural reforms that will correct the problems discussed in this chapter. Some changes have already been proposed in Congress.[7] But we cannot expect any major adjustment in the process by which policy is made, or in the existing role of Congress in

---

7. Several internal reforms have been adopted by the House of Representatives in recent years. One immediate effect was the replacement of several senior commit-

oversight and legislative affairs. The system will not change unless the American people change first. This point is well expressed by Professor Lindblom:

> Policy making, however, is what it is because participants in the policy-making process behave as they do. Men make policy; it is not made for them. They also make the policy-making machinery. Much of what might be called the "irrationality" of the policy-making system is, therefore, the consequence of the irrationality of the participants in it. It may be serious—even disastrous. But it represents the quality of man's control over policy-making, not the absence of it.[8]

---

tee chairmen at the beginning of the ninety-fourth Congress in January 1975. The House also adopted an ethics package in early 1977 which limited outside earned income of members and required reports about expenditures made from official allowances. On October 12, 1977, an internal commission proposed an additional set of recommendations but the House defeated the proposal by vote of 262 to 160. That negative vote occurred one day after publication of the first report on how individual members had spent funds from their "district allowances." One of the recommendations in the reform package called for the establishment of a select committee to review and cut down the number of House committees and subcommittees.

8. Lindblom, *The Policy-Making Process*, p. 108.

13

THE ROLE OF EXECUTIVE OFFICE TASK FORCES

The familiar separation of functions required by the Constitution of the United States helps control the arbitrary abuse of power, but it also limits the scope of the authority exerted by the Executive Office. In addition to being the symbolic leader of the Nation, the President is responsible for balancing the national interests by coordinating the diverse programs of the executive branch and working with Congress to develop legislative plans and budget appropriations. In reality, the power of the President in these roles is more limited than is generally assumed, and he must use it with great discretion if his administration is to sustain its effectiveness.

Leadership requires the President to create a process for decision making that honors the rules of the game in dealing with political pressures. The process should be responsive to the internal authority of departments and agencies responsible for statutory and administrative programs. It should also insulate the White House from premature or otherwise mistaken involvement in controversial actions. The President should generally function as a point of final arbitration rather than as an original advocate of programs. An incumbent President typically emphasizes government programs that are compatible with his political goals, which means that White House officials must monitor the activities of departments and agencies. Finally, the decision making within the executive branch should provide effective liaison with Congress and various special interest groups. The usual approach to meeting these organizational needs is to create an interagency task force of representatives from the departments and agencies that will be affected by the particular decisions.

Cabinet Committees on Economic Policy

Major decisions on economic policy always involve several departments and agencies within the executive branch. Necessary coordination is often assigned to top-level interagency committees that include Cabinet officials. For example, in September 1950 President Truman established the Economic Stabilization Agency "to control inflation and maintain stabilization of the national economy."[1] That organization was terminated on April 30, 1953, and one month later President Eisenhower appointed an Advisory Board on Economic Growth and Stability to "keep the President closely informed about the state of the national economy and various measures necessary to aid in maintaining a stable prosperity."[2] In January 1959 President Eisenhower created the Cabinet Committee on Price Stability for Economic Growth "to study the problem of maintaining price stability as an essential basis for a high and sustainable rate of economic growth."[3] President Kennedy formally abolished these two organizations on March 12, 1961, and replaced them with the National Advisory Board on Economic Policy, which was subsequently replaced by the Cabinet Committee on Economic Growth in August 1962.[4]

When the administration of President Nixon began in January 1969, a new interagency committee known as the Cabinet Committee on Economic Policy was immediately appointed to "advise and assist the President in the development and coordination of national economic programs and policies and perform such other duties as the President may from time to time prescribe."[5] The membership and functional assignments of that Cabinet committee are indicated in the official Executive Order which follows. It is interesting to note the careful wording of the authorizing order designating the President as the chairman, and the chairman of the Council of Economic Advisers as an executive director. The emphasis on coordinating economic policy activities without usurping the functional responsibilities of existing departments and agencies was also a significant gesture.

1. U.S., *Government Manual 1975/76*, Appendix A, pp. 667–758. Executive Order 10161, dated Sept. 9, 1950.
2. Ibid. Letter from President to Congress dated June 1, 1953.
3. Ibid. Letter from President to Vice-President dated Jan. 28, 1959.
4. Ibid. Established by direction of the President.
5. Ibid. Executive Order 11453, dated Jan. 24, 1969.

Executive Order 11453[6]

ESTABLISHING THE CABINET COMMITTEE ON ECONOMIC POLICY

By virtue of the authority vested in me by the Constitution and statutes of the United States, and as President of the United States, it is ordered as follows:

Section 1. Establishment of the Committee. (a) There is hereby established the Cabinet Committee on Economic Policy (hereinafter referred to as "the Committee").

(b) The President shall preside over meetings of the Committee. The Vice President shall preside in the absence of the President.

(c) The Committee shall be composed of the following:

The Vice President
Secretary of the Treasury
Secretary of Agriculture
Secretary of Commerce
Secretary of Labor
Director of the Bureau of the Budget
Chairman of the Council of Economic Advisers
Counsellor to the President

and such other heads of departments and agencies as the President may from time to time designate.

Section 2. Functions of the Committee. The Committee shall advise and assist the President in the development and coordination of national economic programs and policies and shall perform such other duties as the President may from time to time prescribe. In addition to such duties, the Committee shall:

(1) Assist the President in the formulation of the basic goals and objectives of national economic policy;

(2) Develop recommendations for the basic strategy of national economic policy to serve as guides for decisions concerning specific economic programs and policies;

(3) Promote the coordination of Federal economic programs;

(4) Consult with individuals from academic, agricultural, business, consumer, labor, and other groups to assure the consideration of a wide range of views about national economic policy; and

(5) Recommend procedures for evaluating the effectiveness of Federal programs in contributing to our national economic objectives.

Section 3. Administrative Arrangements. (a) The Chairman of the Council of Economic Advisers will coordinate the work of the Committee.

(b) In compliance with provisions of applicable law, and as necessary to effectuate the purpose of this order, (1) the White House Office shall provide or arrange for supporting clerical administrative and other staff services for the Committee, and (2) each Federal department and agency which is represented on the Committee shall furnish the Committee such information and other assistance as may be available.

Section 4. Construction. Nothing in this order shall be construed as subjecting any department, establishment, or other instrumentality of the

6. *Code of Federal Regulations*, 1966–70 compilation (Title 3—The President), p. 774.

executive branch of the Federal Government or the head thereof, or any function vested by law in or assigned pursuant to law to any such agency or head, to the authority of any other such agency or head or as abrogating, modifying, or restricting any such function in any manner.

THE WHITE HOUSE,   RICHARD NIXON
January 24, 1969

The orientation of the group toward domestic policy made coordination difficult, and Cabinet officials from the Justice, State, and Transportation departments were subsequently added to expand the scope of issues considered. In February 1973 the Council on Economic Policy was appointed to replace the original Cabinet Committee on Economic Policy, as wage and price controls increasingly dominated domestic economic policy.[7] Finally, the forced resignation of President Nixon on August 8, 1974, resulted in the establishment of the Economic Policy Board.[8]

Despite the shifting nature of the problems they consider, all of these interagency committees have had approximately the same membership and operating procedures. They have essentially served as a general forum for discussing current economic problems, but a number of very important economic studies have been prepared by task forces operating under the direction of the Cabinet committees. For example, in 1969 the Cabinet Committee on Economic Policy prepared a benchmark review of future claims against the gross national product. This study, prepared under the direction of Herbert Stein, a member of the Council of Economic Advisers, directly influenced major policy decisions. Similar studies on specific domestic and international issues probably represent the principal accomplishment of these organizations. They do not solve the problems of coordinating actual operating activities, but at least they give senior officials an opportunity to discuss their views on important policy questions.

Functions of the Task Forces

The executive branch is not a monolithic institution. It is actually a loose alliance of hundreds of separate organizations with different program priorities, loyalties, constituencies, histories, and customs. Each one is characterized by the goals of its personnel, its particular problems, and its links with the congressional committees that con-

7. U.S., *Government Manual 1975/76*, Appendix A, pp. 667–758. Memorandum from the President, dated Feb. 2, 1973.

8. Ibid., p. 644. Executive Order 11808, dated Sept. 30, 1974.

trol its budget, specify its responsibilities, and conduct oversight hearings. Policy issues rarely match the neat jurisdictional boundaries described by government organization charts. Instead, most national problems involve a wide range of programs and departments, and this complex mixture of goals and responsibilities leads to a degree of competition for formal authority and real power that must be experienced to be believed. Although each department and agency in the executive branch is supposedly a member of the same team and striving for a common public goal, the characteristic shared by most government organizations is their relentless struggle to gain more power and defend existing functions.

For example, in the proposed sale of grain to Russia in 1975 the jurisdictional issues involved groups concerned with domestic agriculture, agricultural exports, the international balance of payments, foreign affairs, maritime policy, labor, defense, antitrust, inflation, employment, and farm income. Decisions with high national priority that affect energy, social welfare, transportation, tax policies, human and natural resources, military security, international relations, and foreign trade and investment are even more complex. The ultimate battleground for resolving these jurisdictional priorities is the annual federal budget, which forces the Executive Office, including the President, and Congress to make fundamental decisions about the allocation of money and the even more crucial issues of organizational responsibilities and personnel quotas.

The President and senior White House officials can directly participate in only a small fraction of the jurisdictional rivalries that characterize much of the political activity within the government. For this reason permanent or temporary interagency committees are created to provide some of the necessary coordination and discipline. Unfortunately, these committees are often swamped by the size, complexity, and controversial nature of the government programs they are expected to deal with. The design of the programs is to begin by developing expertise through specialized compartments and then to combine the findings into packages that provide comprehensive responses to national needs. The frequent failures of government institutions to satisfy these theoretical goals are disappointing. More impressive is the fact that the massive structure of thousands of overlapping programs and people functions as well as it does.

Task forces are used not only because most problems cut across formal organizational jurisdictions but for several other pragmatic reasons. First, interagency committees enable the President to refer critics to studies he has commissioned as an example of active leadership and rigorous analysis of problems. At the same time, internal control can be maintained over the schedule and format of committee activities and reports. The White House also retains flexibility in the choice of responses to the resulting recommendations: they can be favorably received if that is advantageous or disavowed if they turn out to be too controversial or inconsistent with the administration's overall goals.

Second, creation of an interagency committee often assembles the most competent technical experts within the government to exchange ideas and information. Most organizations designate their best people to serve on such bodies, and work with the group often provides excellent training. Committee sessions also inform each organization about the interests and capabilities of other departments and agencies.

Third, the interagency approach establishes a necessary foundation for final decisions by senior officials. Problems are analyzed and the available options identified. Controversial points and internal opposition can be isolated and resolved before senior officials commit themselves to specific policy recommendations. This analysis is then the basis for drafts of legislation and testimonies for congressional hearings and for the White House fact sheets that are distributed to the news services and the general public.

Fourth, task forces are used to control the internal bureaucracy by requiring them to participate in joint study projects. The final recommendations allegedly represent a consensus among the participants and are used as a benchmark in judging their commitment to the final decisions and the actual results. At times the participating organizations renege on the agreement in order to promote their own interests, but the hypocrisy of such actions is at least evident, and senior officials can enforce conformity if they are really concerned. Despite the fragmentation arising from organizational interests and the independence of each task force, positive coordination and communication within the group and among the internal agencies does result.

Fifth, task force projects are useful in maintaining contacts with congressional committees and private groups with special interests. These exchanges are sometimes made formal by holding public hearings and by distributing official working papers and preliminary reports to other groups for review. Opening up government activities to invite broader participation is a constructive step that improves the quality of the analysis and the credibility of internal decisions.

In other situations communication with outside groups is informal and simply reflects the close working relationships that make up the famous "iron triangle" links between program directors in the executive branch, congressional committee staffs, and special interest groups. It is standard operating procedure to keep powerful groups outside the administration fully informed even when the internal studies are supposed to be confidential. In fact, it is assumed that internal memos and summaries of committee discussions will be routinely distributed to outside groups, the news media, and congressional staffs. Giving the internal documents a security classification and pleading for confidentiality tend to increase the likelihood that the information will be leaked.

Committees continue to proliferate in public and private enterprises because of the complexity of problems and the manner in which human organizations develop collectivist decisions. Nevertheless, committees are constantly criticized for being too time consuming, powerless, and inconclusive. Some say they are too much oriented toward consensus and are resorted to as a device for either avoiding a decision or assuring that responsibility will at least be shared.

Analysts have even claimed at times that government committees are usually collections of officials who do not know what to do as individuals but who can collectively agree that the solution to most problems should be another spending program. One particularly experienced government official has accurately described the general attitude: "Interagency committees are the crabgrass in the garden of government institutions. Nobody wants them but everyone has them."[9]

Political candidates and government officials habitually ridicule the enormous number and scope of committees, promising to eliminate these symbols of waste and bureaucratic gamesmanship. And each new set of government leaders begins by mounting a sweeping reorganization drive to reduce the number and functions of existing committees, thus demonstrating their commitment to efficiency and vigorous leadership. Such efforts are inevitably brief and ineffective. After the smoke clears there are even more committees and the scope of their activities is increased.

Despite all of the criticism there is no effective substitute for committees and task forces, and their use is likely to grow because problems cut across formal organizational responsibilities and because the growing preference is for collective decisions. It is unrealistic to talk about eliminating the committee style of government

9. Harold Seidman, *Politics, Position and Power*, p. 171.

operations in the executive branch, just as it is naive to believe that the procedures and protocol of specialized congressional committees can be significantly changed. At the very most, it may be possible to improve task forces by identifying their limitations and establishing higher operating standards of performance.

The Limitations of Executive Office Task Forces

To the outsider, major policy decisions often appear to be improvised hurriedly by a small group, meeting in an atmosphere of crisis and acting under pressure from special interest groups. Some decisions match this stereotype, but most actions are the result of long and careful analysis. Task forces bring together technical experts and policy officials, and generally they work hard to represent the public interest. Although this study is critical of many of the procedures and organizational details of the government's decision-making process, particularly the disappointing results of financial institution reform, the broad efforts of the national government deserve credit for being representative. It is ironic, however, that as collectivist pressures increase the centralization of government power, the complexity of urgent issues and the controversy they occasion often neutralize the decision-making process. Some of the operating limitations of Executive Office task forces are summarized below.

Concentration on defending jurisdictional authority

Government programs often overlap, and the priorities set up by each agency and department create cumulative pressures, each group striving to protect its own interests and expand its sphere of influence. Committees are intended to develop agreement on recommendations and to monitor the results of previous policy decisions, but this theoretical objective is difficult to achieve because each group concentrates on its own goals, protecting its own turf.

The institutional identities that are developed over time lead to serious jurisdictional battles when new programs are assigned or reorganization proposals threaten to shift existing functions within the executive branch. The resulting bureaucratic warfare usually brings out the worst in each organization and effectively defeats the efforts of interagency committees as members become preoccupied with power struggles that may go on for years. Government organizations are like private special interest groups: they play to avoid losing, rather than to win. Instead of concentrating on larger goals, they place most importance on protecting their existing powers. Status within the Executive Office is based on each one's access to the President and on the number and importance of the programs for which each organization is assigned responsibility. Since direct access to the President is usually sealed off by the inner circle of advisers, the symbol of power for most government officials is the number of people their agency employs and their budget appropriations.

Each representative on an interagency committee serves as an instructed delegate explicitly responsible for defending the particular interests of his organization. Strategic and tactical gamesmanship assumes special importance in committee activities, and objectives are fragmented to make them compatible with existing procedural and organizational arrangements. At worst, task force members simply stonewall any committee actions which threaten the established pattern, irrespective of what the analysis has revealed and of their instructions from senior officials to agree to necessary compromises. At best, the resulting consensus is usually constrained by each member's institutional obligations. It is naive to believe that most task forces function as a cohesive team even though all of the participating agencies and departments belong to the executive branch. Each member actually serves a specific constituency comprising groups within the government as well as private interest groups. As a result, there is often more competition than cooperation when task forces consider complex issues that spread across jurisdictional lines of authority.

Presidential appointees committed to the central goals of an incumbent administration usually have difficulty in meeting the expectations of the organizations they represent. The pressure to serve the interests of the White House is intense, and equally strong forces within the permanent bureaucracies urge appointed advisers to be responsive to their goals. Presidential appointees are caught in the middle, like actors expected to play two conflicting roles. Special interest groups and career government employees withdraw their support if officials do not try to advance their programs. But these same officials must continuously demonstrate their loyalty to the White House if they wish to be included in policy decisions. The trade-off between being a program manager and an adviser to the President is difficult to manage.

The internal struggle to defend existing powers makes coordination difficult since policy decisions inevitably promote some interests at the expense of others. Formal task forces find it hard to provide this coordination, and informal arrangements must be made. As described by Harold Seidman in his perceptive study of government:

> Without informal or so-called "lateral" coordination, which takes place at almost every stage in the development and execution of national programs and at every level within the Federal structure, the Government probably would grind to a halt. Skilled bureaucrats develop their own informational networks. Managers who are motivated by a desire to get something done find ways and means of bridging the jurisdictional gaps. Informal coordination is greatly facilitated when people share the same goals, operate from a common set of legal authorities and informational assumptions, agree on standards, have compatible professional outlooks, and can help each other. Where these conditions exist, there is no need for the intervention of third parties to secure harmonious action.[10]

When effective formal and informal coordination becomes impossible, competing organizations within the executive branch ordinarily appeal to their supportive constituencies in Congress and among special interest groups. At this point the President must intervene to restore order despite the significant risks of alienating congressional committees, private interest groups, career government employees, and even his own appointees. The diversity of priorities within the executive branch and the emphasis on defending each one's turf also make it difficult to maintain agreement and effective coordination.

White House intervention in task force activities

A variation of the turf issue involves the chronic tendency of White House officials to make important policy decisions that usurp the authority of agencies and departments with resulting confusion and frustration. In theory, the President and the Cabinet form a team in both an operating and a political sense. Cabinet officials do compete vigorously for appropriations and functional powers; but they are selected on the basis of their commitment to the goals of the President, and a natural alliance would normally be expected. The difficulty results chiefly from the fragmented reponsibilities that each Cabinet official is assigned: (1) advising the President on policy issues; (2) acting as program manager and administrative director; (3) conducting legislative liaison with Congress; and (4) serving as a contact point for private special interest groups.

In contrast, White House officials are expected to concentrate on promoting the interests of the President. When presidential appoin-

10. Ibid., p. 170.

tees attempt to improve their working relationships not only with their own bureaucracies, but with special interest groups and Congress, the White House staff tends to question their loyalty to the inner circle of elite advisers (this is referred to as "going native"). Cabinet officials who aggressively push their own programs are also suspect, and barriers are created to seal off the President from such influence. In extreme cases Cabinet officials may circumvent the system with direct personal appeals or even mount a media campaign to express public dissent, but they do so at great risk of being permanently ostracized, or even forced to resign, even if they are temporarily victorious on specific issues.

Cabinet officers are usually people of considerable standing who are not without personal ambitions or even vanity. They naturally dislike comforming to controls exerted by staff members. This is especially true when they believe that they serve the President directly and that they should be allowed to work independently with their program directors, relevant special interest groups, and congressional committees to fulfill their assignments. Presidential appointees thus often resent interference by White House staff, even if it is labeled coordination, when they consider that it encroaches on their areas of authority and responsibility.

There are many things that the White House staff cannot do because they lack technical expertise and must work under frenetic schedules. Senior White House officials function in an atmosphere of constant crisis, both real and imagined. Each new problem attracts immediate attention, and current assignments are downgraded in importance. In this turbulent atmosphere, planning and oversight become especially difficult, and the resulting discontinuity, the lack of any meaningful follow-up of assignments, and the generally superficial approach to technical issues is infuriating to Cabinet officials and career government employees who must deal with the congressional committees and private special interest groups having a permanent interest in these matters.

In its worst form, the coordinating efforts of the White House staff completely seal off the President from communication with Cabinet officials, and the inner circle of advisers make their own policy recommendations. Presidential appointees, angered or discouraged by this barrier to personal involvement in the real policy decisions, either withdraw to concentrate on the activities of their agencies and departments or find different ways to promote their views.

The perennial struggle between the inner circle of White House advisers and Cabinet officials for control of policy decisions is so abrasive and disruptive that most new Presidents begin by pledging that past mistakes will not be repeated. They promise that the Cabinet will become an important policy-making body, with general responsibilities and direct access to the President. Careful distinctions are drawn up between line and staff responsibilities, and White House staff officers are instructed to avoid usurping policy and administrative functions from agencies and departments within the executive branch. White House staff officials themselves show an equal readiness to limit their efforts to coordinating the flow of information between the President and operating officials and thus expediting the whole decision-making process. For example, President Franklin D. Roosevelt issued the following directive:

> In no event shall the administrative assistants be interposed between the President and the head of any department or agency or between the President and any one of the divisions in the Executive Office of the President.[11]

During the exciting transition when a new administration is assuming office this ideal model of line and staff cooperation functions reasonably well. A barrage of press releases describes the smooth working relations and unique personal rapport between the President and individual Cabinet officials. Pictures of a smiling President earnestly conferring with Cabinet appointees appear daily, and White House staff aides carefully maintain a low profile and give proper deference to the formal organization charts. This idyllic arrangement soon deteriorates as the tough realities of public service replace the rhetoric of the campaign and transition ceremonies. Perpetuation of power—that is, reelection—becomes the dominant theme, and the White House staff has the assignment of making the executive branch move ahead on programs that will improve the prospects of the incumbent administration. When this happens the inner circle of advisers no longer allows appointees to carry on independent operations. It usually does not take very long before real channels of communication and authority replace the formal organizational arrangements.

Another familiar development is that the young professionals who work diligently in the political campaign and are accordingly rewarded with staff appointments somewhere in the Executive Office discover that they enjoy part of the power of the presidency. When they telephone an outsider their secretaries curtly announce, "The

11. Executive Order 8248, dated Sept. 8, 1939.

White House is calling." The stunning effect of that beginning statement is too often achieved by some junior official calling to demand an immediate report on a policy issue that has perplexed government officials for many years. The response is likely to be a bundle of old memos, but the staff aide's sense of power is gratified, and a fallacious belief is created that the key to the issues is at hand. As this process continues, operating policy decisions are increasingly pulled into the White House: staff aides prepare brief talking points for senior officials to use in explaining welfare reform, tax policies, deregulation goals, international trade and investment, and other equally complex issues. What starts out as a participating organization based on open access to the President usually evolves into a maze in which coordinating officials produce mounds of position and options papers which slowly move upward through the White House hierarchy until a few make it into the President's night-reading packet. The amazing aspect of this common pattern is that each group can justify its own actions by claiming to serve the public.

The operating agencies and departments feel that White House aides unwisely isolate the President and influence his decisions without considering the technical advice that others have provided. White House assistants retort that Cabinet officials are immersed in operating details and become captives of institutional goals rather than concentrating on the needs of the President. Political appointees are placed in a no win situation: the career employees responsible for their programs resent pressures they believe are politically motivated, and White House officers argue that the appointed officials should be better team players. On occasion heads of departments and agencies may rebel by refusing to prepare the endless reports, or they may even try to end-run the staff system and present their views directly to the President. Such behavior confirms the suspicions of the White House staff that many Cabinet officers cannot be trusted to render effective support for the administration's entire program. Mutual respect and cooperation are dissipated, while the White House increasingly creates its own group of instant specialists to prepare policy recommendations based on the grand illusion that a bright young lawyer or economist can draft a good options paper on any public issue.

The pyramid of policy coordinators has so many layers that screening of staff material is repeated several times before it actually reaches the President. It is ironic that the President, who is elected to represent and balance the interests of all the people, winds up being almost totally isolated from any meaningful contact with ideas from any source except a small group of capable and well-intentioned but limited advisers. Few Cabinet officials are able to penetrate the staff environment that insulates a President. Some of them persevere just long enough to justify the transition costs of entering government service. Others simply relax and allow the perquisites of their position and the continuous round of social engagements, committee meetings, and travel to fill in their time.

This unfortunate result does not occur because the White House staff consciously plans to dominate the Executive Office. On the contrary, the preferred approach is deliberately planned to establish a skeleton organization that will assist the flow of information and decisions. The centralization of power which actually occurs is nevertheless easy to understand. Selecting the senior staff at the White House is the one set of decisions the President can make without the hassle of obtaining Senate confirmation or answering complaints from special interest groups. The appointments that recognize the contributions of various groups during political campaigns are usually concentrated in the agencies and departments; the President can appoint personal advisers who have already proved their loyalty in more particular ways. These assistants naturally believe that their role is mainly to look after the President's interests by creating a comprehensive program that will contribute to his reelection.

To achieve this paramount goal the inner circle of advisers gradually centralizes the making of decisions to avoid embarrassing mistakes. But meanwhile the entire system becomes less responsive, and the valuable program capabilities of the rest of the executive branch are partially ignored. The final and most unfortunate step in this sequence is to draw a veil of secrecy around important policy decisions so that only the inner circle of advisers and a few trusted officials who "think like the White House" are included. The views of everyone else are largely written off as outmoded and unimaginative, or, worst of all, obstructionist and oriented toward special constituencies.

If this narrowing process continues, the initial optimism and elitism of the White House staff eventually deteriorate into a surly bunker mentality: "these few against the world," consisting of an unresponsive and undisciplined bureaucracy, an irresponsible Congress, and ungrateful special interest groups who know only how to ask for more. In this unfortunate situation personal loyalty keeps the White House staff members working at their extraordinary pace, while the President rewards their commitment by increasing their responsibilities.

Throughout this experience the White House staff continues to believe that inordinately heavy work schedules and the individual brilliance of young generalists can resolve public policy questions that have long defied solution. All that is needed, they believe, is for the recalcitrant bureaucracy and Congress to cooperate and the general public to be educated to support the administration's position. Unfortunately, the decision-making system inevitably breaks down in such situations, wasting the vast resources that might otherwise be available. The final irony when this happens is that it is always the presidential appointees in the departments and agencies who are sent to appear before congressional oversight hearings and to meet with special interest groups. The President may occasionally present radio and television addresses, but the White House assistants never have to justify their decisions to Congress or the general public.

Structure of task force committees

Interagency committees function best in evaluating specific problems as a basis for advising the senior officials who are responsible for policy decisions. For each group, success depends upon the unique mix of personalities and institutional characteristics. The precise way in which this internal chemistry works cannot be predicted, but many patterns are similar. For example, most committees do not have the necessary authority to make final decisions, so they show a familiar tendency to push controversial issues to higher levels to avoid assuming risks. This centralization of decision making also results from a failure of senior officials to delegate the necessary authority and to give clear instructions about the goals and restraints that are involved. Tight administrative controls over committee actions come about not only because of the natural interests of senior officials but also because of their aversion to White House criticism when mistakes occur. Such personal involvement by highly placed officials strengthens the authority of committees, but it also slows down their activities because the time that officials can spare for preparation and meetings is limited, and convenient schedules are difficult to arrange. Even more serious is the effect of the increasing emphasis on technical subjects like energy, taxes, international trade and investment, welfare reform, structural unemployment, and so on. The complexity of such issues and the constant turnover of presidential appointees make it harder to sustain continuity and ensure competent analysis. Understanding public policies that involve technical and controversial matters presents a difficult challenge for the generalists who serve on interagency committees.

Government committees almost always recommend an aggressive response to perceived problems. Public officials naturally support the programs they direct, and there is strong pressure from the White House and Congress to promote new spending to demonstrate concern and positive leadership. Nevertheless, committees usually avoid suggesting drastic changes in existing policies. This conservatism is a legacy of past decisions which restrict current operating flexibility as well as a response to the combined influence of special interest groups. Important economic policies are always debated within a general political framework, and the range of feasible actions is usually only marginally greater than that of existing programs. The extended effort to achieve financial institution reform, described in this study, demonstrates how little flexibility of policy is possible on controversial issues and how great the influence of political variables is when powerful special interest groups become aggressively involved in legislative and regulatory affairs. An even more important example was the unsuccessful attempt to create a comprehensive national energy program throughout 1977.

The intensity of the internal conflicts and the external pressures that committees are subject to make it normal to work toward a compromise that will satisfy the necessary majority, including the inner circle of advisers to the President and congressional leaders, even though the anticipated results may not match the optimum goals. This general willingness to settle for less, rather than struggle for the most, is typical of most public and private organizations. It largely explains why many government committees simply recommend an expansion or reorganization of existing programs, calling for more spending, higher program priorities, greater commitment, improved coordination, and a higher degree of creativity and leadership.

The assumption appears to be that merely improving the scope and efficiency of government activities will solve public policy problems. There is also increasing pressure for simplistic solutions in the hope of immediate results, despite the complexity and controversial nature of most public issues. Faced with intimidating administrative pressures from within and the concern of special interest groups and Congress, interagency committees often try to survive by reverting to piecemeal recommendations that cautiously emphasize existing programs in the hope of producing satisfactory results. Such marginal adjustments rarely match the committee assignments, which ordinarily present the problem under consideration as a crisis. Wolanin's analysis of public commissions calls this tendency a "Perils of

Pauline" syndrome. It is also apparent in the activities of most interagency committees:

> The nation, or whoever or whatever the commission is examining, rests on the brink; it is the eleventh hour, and the situation is critical. The situation has not yet plunged over the edge, however, and the possibility of rescue and salvation remains open. So the grimness of the findings is always combined with a ray of hope and a touch of optimism about the future.[12]

Another reason why most interagency committees recommend only marginal changes in existing policies is that their members consider the decision-making process to be a continuous series of small actions leading gradually toward tentatively identified goals. They do not think of it as a search for a comprehensive, permanent solution. By limiting the size and scope of individual policy initiatives, government officials believe they can respond to specific issues quickly and avoid major blunders. In fact, minor mistakes and partial solutions are often tolerated because committee members assume that these imperfections will be corrected in the next series of committee deliberations, the next package of legislative and administrative proposals, or the next budget appropriations.

The case histories of tax reform, deregulation of natural gas prices, environmental standards, welfare reform, and continuous fiscal and monetary decisions for fine tuning the national economy are classic examples of this tactical approach, which is designed to avoid large errors in judgment by constantly making small legislative and regulatory adjustments in policy. Presidential appointees operating under politically imposed time schedules and personal standards of performance often press for larger and more immediate policy actions to demonstrate affirmative leadership, but these pressures are usually absorbed by Congress and the permanent bureaucracy, and the system changes very little.

Some political appointees with temporary government assignments go so far as to claim that the problems being considered must be solved immediately or the opportunity for constructive action will be permanently lost. Experienced government officials are rarely moved by such now-or-never arguments because they know that public policy issues repeat themselves. Opportunities to consider "comprehensive" reform of policies dealing with taxes, welfare, regulation of economic activities, the environment, short-term fiscal and monetary stabilization, and so on will continue to be available

---

12. Thomas R. Wolanin, *Presidential Advisory Commissions*, p. 126.

each year. This serial nature of public policy decisions is frustrating to outside advisers and temporary government officials, but it is an acknowledged way of life for career members of the bureaucracy who are largely responsible for making the system work despite the coming and going of political appointees.

Occasionally senior officials and dissatisfied members of inter-agency committees attempt to end-run the process of methodically arriving at a consensus by appealing directly to the President for preferential treatment. There is really no way to stop this procedure, even when everyone pledges to play the game by the committee rules, and it is probably a useful safety valve as long as everyone understands what is happening. In most committees it is automatically assumed that dissatisfied members will try to override the joint decision by appealing directly to higher authorities all the way up to the President. A strong President can usually handle the situation by listening to the appeals and then going ahead and making his own decisions with the assistance of the inner circle of White House advisers and those Cabinet members who actually participate in policy decisions. Trying to placate the interests of unhappy organizations takes up the President's time, but it is the only way to sustain the morale of disappointed officials who want to believe that they effectively represent their organizations. The major risk is that a weak President may base his decision on the last argument he hears rather than on the combined views of the entire committee and his personal advisers.

Finally, some important public policy problems cannot be solved despite the best efforts of the interagency committees appointed to prepare recommendations for the exercise of government leadership. Such a failure is especially difficult for committees to accept because their members, senior political and career government employees, are oriented toward action, and they are usually confident that government programs will work if only enough public funds are appropriated, if the participating departments and agencies are well coordinated, and if an effective public relations program can be launched to educate the general public and win support for the effort.

There is a limit, however, to what can be accomplished by these means. Recognizing the point of diminishing returns is always difficult, but it is particularly so for government officials because their assignment is to render public service. Senior officials in the Executive Office and on congressional committees with oversight responsibilities are expected to guard against the proliferation of government programs which are ineffective or worse. But the system is partially self-defeating, because many of these same officials have a direct interest in expanding the size and scope of the programs they are evaluating. Another ironic twist is that when government programs fail to solve the problems that they are addressing the normal reaction is to increase their budgets and responsibilities. Greater oversight efforts within the executive branch and Congress are needed to reverse this pattern. Improving the efficiency of governmental operations should particularly interest those who believe in limiting the concentration of power in a central government, since failures seem only to invite further encroachment.

Internal barriers to effective communication

Committees usually prepare extensive reports and statistical materials for discussion, but real communication among participating members and with senior officials is often restricted by the procedures used and the complexity of assignments. Such a limitation is unfortunate because an important function of committees should be to identify the issues objectively, summarize and evaluate the available information, and rank the feasible options. This threefold task is particularly vital in developing national economic policies, because the issues are nearly always complex and controversial and analyses by others are frequently based on erroneous assumptions. The quality of policy decisions ultimately depends on the way committees deal with preparatory staff work and how well this information is communicated to the participants.

At least six important barriers block effective communication among committee members and senior officials. First, the ideological preferences of committee members often cause them to reject some sources of information arbitrarily and to disregard policy options which are inconsistent with their beliefs. This narrow approach, sometimes a reflection of insecurity, destroys the objectivity and creativity of the committee before it has a reasonable opportunity to develop its recommendations. The philosophical commitments of senior officials will obviously influence the final decisions, which must always be made within a framework of political pressures, but it is a serious error to begin the decision-making process by automatically eliminating unpopular options. Senior officials should make certain that their subordinates consider the entire range of policy actions before they use a selective screen to arrive at the final decision.

Second, efforts by those involved in the decisions to inform themselves on the issues are frequently limited by unrealistic schedules and the personal priorities of committee members, who naturally prefer to concentrate on their regular assignments. A backlog of completed studies on the topic is seldom available, so most new committees must collect and compile information from the participating organizations. The constant turnover of political appointees further disrupts the continuity necessary to sustain rigorous analysis.

The typical crash schedule followed by these groups prevents the advance distribution of materials, and little is accomplished in the actual meetings, since participants are unfamiliar with the views of other agencies and know only that they must defend their own organization's interests. Experienced government officials have the necessary backgrounds for following the committee discussions, but unless other members are specialists they have difficulty understanding technical issues. Even when there is adequate time to distribute materials prior to the formal sessions, most of the memorandums are paste-and-scissors reports, which have not been updated or coordinated with other members of the committee.

These problems are not insoluble and many committees do function efficiently, providing agendas and substantive materials which are circulated in advance, so that the participants can communicate effectively. Still the usual pattern is somewhat disorganized, unless senior officials actively participate and demand a high standard of preparation and serious discussion.

Third, the descriptive and statistical material available for making important policy decisions is often surprisingly inadequate and occasionally even misleading. The earlier example of the large exports of grain in 1975 clearly demonstrated this difficulty when accurate information about domestic and international supply and demand could not be obtained quickly enough to influence an important decision. Most national issues present similar problems. In some situations the relevant materials are just not available. In other cases officials may have quantitative analyses at hand but choose to ignore them and depend entirely on their own views. Those with experience in both public affairs and private business say that many public policy decisions are made without the same amount of analysis that comparable private economic decisions receive.

In contrast, at times committee members are confronted with so many memorandums and statistics that they are overwhelmed with details and too confused to focus on the crucial issues. Too often the indiscriminate collection of materials results in what some describe as tons of information but only ounces of analysis. Developing the proper proportions of background information is the responsibility of the designated committee leaders, who must also depend on the cooperative spirit of participating organizations. Information gaps as well as a deluge of technical details can restrict communication among committee members; but even when the proper balance is achieved skeptical government officials, particularly political appointees, most often rely on their own analysis and ideological preferences.

Fifth, it is natural for interagency groups to become committed to their own set of recommendations. At the same time there is a tendency to avoid giving advice that the President and his inner circle of senior advisers do not want to hear. It is also unusual for a committee to report back that no feasible solution exists, or that the policies of the incumbent administration have so far been ineffective or mistaken. A selective screen has clearly been used, which makes the objectivity of the analysis suspect and suggests that internal communication is limited to good news and popular decisions that conform to the expectations of senior officials.

Sixth, in some interagency committees internal communication is purposely restricted to preserve the confidentiality of the analysis and recommendations. Such efforts are rarely successful, and planned leaks to others within the Executive Office, as well as to congressional committees and the news media are common. Anything that is said or written is likely to appear almost immediately in the news or on television, regardless of the confidentiality of the discussion and the mutual expressions of trust within the group. There is a very positive aspect to such a flow of information. Opening up the decision-making processes is actually desirable, and the quality and quantity of most committee activities would be improved by increased public awareness. Some discussions, however, should remain confidential until the recommendations are made final, to avoid giving false signals to outsiders.

The meaningful distinction between open communication and the occasional need for real confidentiality is not adequately recognized. In fact, the planted news story and off-the-record disclosure are essential to the organizational defense of turf and the strategies for personal aggrandizement that dominate top-level governmental activities. It is widely recognized that the government leaks from the top, and that officials attempt to use the news media to promote their own interests and restrict the progress of rival organizations.

Experienced officials recognize the risks involved in communication and respond by limiting the openness of their comments in memorandums and committee discussions, although the effectiveness of internal communication obviously suffers.

Distrust of the career bureaucracy

One of the most disheartening aspects of government service is the lack of real trust and cooperation between political appointees and the career officials who are responsible for the continuing functions of government. Both sides are guilty, but the appointees are usually the most suspicious and critical. Most career employees are committed to the concept of public service, and only a small minority have such serious ideological biases and personal weaknesses that they cannot function honestly and effectively if they are properly encouraged and directed. Presidential appointees too often develop a skeptical attitude which assumes that the career bureaucracy is purposely trying to sabotage their efforts by withholding support. The bureaucracy develops a similar belief that the appointees are too cavalier and do not understand the real problems. There are, of course, many examples of cooperation, but the unfortunate schism between the two groups sometimes leads to cynicism, backbiting, insubordination, inefficiency, and heavy opportunity costs. When power struggles do develop, the bureaucracy has the edge. Its members can usually play a waiting game, while appointees come and go in a rotation cycle that averages about two years.

Some presidential appointees believe that their career employees are being unnecessarily stubborn when they argue that instant solutions of chronic problems cannot be provided at low costs. What these temporary appointees take to be a limitation of the bureaucratic mind may actually be a great asset to the government. Stability, skepticism, long-term perspectives, detailed familiarity with technical and administrative problems, and familiarity with previous attempts to change policies can contribute much to policy making. Wise presidential appointees recognize these potential strengths and rely on their contacts with career employees to help run existing programs and design new initiatives.

They also respect the network of alliances existing among and between the bureaucracy, congressional staffs, and private interest groups, because these relations shape most public policies. When the technical and professional interests of career employees are meshed with the broader responsibilities and political contacts of presidential appointees, the Executive Office functions effectively. But this arrangement requires a mutual trust and spirit of cooperation, qualities that must be carefully developed rather than arbitrarily demanded.

Human failings

There is a common tendency to think of the executive branch as a monolithic entity, independent of the general public. People expect "the government" in distant Washington, D.C., to identify, solve, and pay for all of the problems of society. It is useful to remind ourselves that only individuals pay taxes directly and as part of the price of goods and services, and that the government is simply a collection of individual employees striving to accomplish the goals mandated by legislation and regulatory rulings. Individual presidential appointees and career employees have all of the human characteristics that make personal relationships so challenging when interagency committees are formed: all differ in their personal and institutional loyalties, biases and idiosyncrasies, professional commitments, physical stamina, ambition, pride, jealousy, insecurity, aversion to risk and embarrassment, education, training, experience, leadership qualities, decision-making abilities, and so on. Blending all of these individual traits into an efficient team creates the committee chemistry referred to earlier in this chapter. Perhaps the most surprising discovery during my eight years of public service was that it is the strengths and weaknesses of many ordinary individuals that largely determine the results of government activities, despite the overwhelming size and complexity of government institutions.

Given the fundamental importance of the individual, the quality of elected, appointed, and career government officials is the crucial variable in the entire decision-making process. It is hardly a unique discovery to observe that good people make good decisions, and vice versa, but selection of personnel in government is too often dominated by political considerations rather than technical competence and commitment to public service. Inexperienced individuals with little more than personal loyalty and a record of participating in political campaigns are quite frequently appointed to important staff positions. Appointments are also sometimes based on political affiliations and pressures from special interest groups. Most presidential appointees do not fall into these categories, but the grounds for such selections raise questions about the public appointee's commitment to service compared to his wish to advance his personal career. "Resumé grooming" is the popular term for the anxious effort to achieve titles and status.

A famous study of the Executive Office prepared in 1938 recommended that close advisers to the President should have "great competence, great physical ability and a passion for anonymity."[13] Most senior officials do have unusual ability and physical endurance but very few strive for anonymity. The drive to satisfy an image of themselves is more typical, and much of what is wrong with relations among government officials results from the unusual emphasis on personal power and publicty. While self-interests dominate the actions of officials in every type of organization, the effects of personal power struggles and petty bickering are more harmful in important government activities because these have a pervasive and powerful impact on the whole nation.

Government assignments create an exaggerated sense of personal power and an illusion of being indispensable, despite the government's having survived even the wrenching experience of seeing an incumbent President forced to resign. Changes in assignments to most government positions are barely noticed by the public and rarely disrupt the underlying course of events. Nevertheless, senior government officials often confuse the real importance of their position with their own personal popularity. (It is always interesting to observe how few groups want to hear the views of a former government official.) The constant stream of invitations to speak or give interviews, or to accept committee assignments, is not based upon the individual but reflects the importance of the official position.

The internal struggle for real power and the intense conflicts of personality at senior levels is surprising, given the importance of the decision-making process. A spirit of real trust and team unity, however, are too often missing in interagency committees. This serious failing will continue to limit the effectiveness of committees, and governments in general, until public service is more widely recognized as a responsibility to serve others rather than as a means of accelerating the advancement of a personal career and satisfying an individual ego.

---

13. President's Committee on Administrative Management, *Administrative Management in the Government of the United States* (Washington, D.C.: Government Printing Office, 1937), p. 2. The chairman of the committee was Louis Brownlow and the report is often referred to as the Brownlow Report.

External variables

The activities of important interagency committees must be carefully coordinated with those of many other organizations, including other executive branch committees and permanent agencies and departments, congressional committees, state and local governments, powerful special interest groups, and even international institutions and representatives. Committees must also be sensitive to major political, social, and economic developments if their analyses and recommendations are to be relevant to the real issues. This is a difficult assignment because government officials are often insulated from outside contacts by the pressures of their own jobs. Formal procedures, such as meetings of outside advisory boards, public hearings, and field trips, are used, along with public opinion polls and selected interviews, to reduce this isolation, but government officials have difficulty reaching the people who are actually affected by proposed measures and to ascertain their views. Congress has a better understanding of the specific interests of their constituencies but determining national priorities remains a demanding task. Although government agencies continue to conduct public education programs to disseminate their views, two-way dialogues are unusual.

Political constraints

Since interagency committees are customarily appointed by Cabinet officials who have both functional and political interests, their analyses and recommendations must always consider the political environment. Only a few decisions can be based solely on technical factors. The normal political variables influencing decisions create conflicts within committees which can only be resolved by strong leadership. For example, political appointees and congressional committees operate according to rigid schedules timed with regard to elections; career employees have different perspectives and professional interests.

It is only realistic to assume that political considerations will continue to dominate the government's decision-making process. This arrangement is natural to the representative form of government which has served America so well. The risk in this approach is that political factors will determine policy decisions before a careful professional analysis is completed. The American people can judge the political consequences of government decisions, but usually they cannot recognize and analyze the technical variables that need to be considered. Interagency committees therefore have an explicit responsibility not only to base their public policy recommendations on objective professional judgments, but to submit them prior to the political decisions of the Executive Office and Congress. Sustaining the widespread interest and support of the general public in national policy issues will ultimately depend on the quality of the professional analysis that is available before political considerations intervene.

Conclusion

The primary responsibility of the executive branch is to manage the specific legislative and regulatory programs needed to achieve national goals. It is expected to balance the various pressures on Congress and regulatory agencies so that the general public is served rather than specific constituencies. While each government organization has detailed responsibilities for programs, the Executive Office is supposed to provide overall planning and coordination. When the extensive experience and professional abilities of career government employees are properly combined with the general responsibilities and political authority of presidential appointees, this balancing works well and the official separation of powers leads to broader public perspectives and more efficient programs.

In reality, this positive union is difficult to achieve and even harder to sustain. Despite the seriousness of policy problems and their tendency to overlap, which creates a special need for cooperation, there is too often a disruptive power struggle between organizations that are supposed to be working together. Although the representative form of government has served our nation well and is clearly superior to totalitarianism, it is not functioning as effectively as it should, and this failure wastes human and material resources. The purpose of this chapter was not to condemn the efforts of interagency committees but to identify those procedural barriers to making decisions that can and should be corrected. Rhetoric and continuous reorganizations will accomplish very little until a unity of purpose is achieved and the process works more decisively. The example of comprehensive financial institution reform clearly demonstrates the need for broad improvement.

The remarkable complexity and scope of most national issues requires the use of interagency committees. Many of these groups have made signal contributions by analyzing policy issues and preparing recommendations, and this organizational approach is likely to be even more advisable because of the types of problems that must be considered and the growing emphasis on collective decisions. Committees are always criticized, but there is apparently no feasible substitute, given the existing procedures.

Most of the complaints are directed at the restrictive aspects of committee functions: (1) the tendency to defend organizational interests rather than emphasize broad public goals; (2) continuous White House intervention in the operating activities of departments and agencies; (3) frustrating structural limitations which limit the authority of individual departments and agencies, and the fear of risks, which permits only marginal changes in existing policies; (4) barriers to communication within committees and to meaningful contacts with Congress and the general public; (5) the breakdown of cooperation between political appointees and the career bureaucracy; (6) human failings that detract from general competence, and a lack of experience in dealing with public policy issues; (7) changing external circumstances, which force committees to adjust to new environments and different goals; and (8) pervasive political factors which too often shape the final decisions before completion of the professional analysis and the committees' recommendations.

The structural problems summarized here all affect the performance of interagency committees functioning under intense pressure. The logical conclusion is that the commitment of government officials to public service and their authority to exercise objective judgment before political pressures become overwhelming will continue to determine in large measure the success or failure of the decision-making process. In most cases the results are positive. But there are enough disappointments to justify efforts to improve the existing procedures. Public policy issues are too important to be influenced by ineffective or misdirected efforts by committees.

14

THE MARKETPLACE AS A SUBSTITUTE
FOR THE LEGISLATIVE PROCESS

As government decisions have become more influential in shaping the economic and social environment, concern about the quality, efficiency, and objectivity of the democratic decision-making process has increased. The challenge of public leadership is to do those difficult things today that will provide the necessary foundation for progress five or ten years from now. Since such foresight is rare, we continue to move from crisis to crisis, relying on our reservoir of human and material resources to overwhelm problems.

The disappointing failure of proposals for financial institution reform clearly demonstrates the great difficulty of making controversial decisions and the fundamental importance of continuous marketplace adjustments to changing conditions. National priority issues are so technically complex and politically sensitive that only a powerful central government can provide the broad perspectives and discipline necessary to make the economic system function properly. The success of the democratic approach will ultimately depend upon the personal competence and dedication of public officials and the efficiency with which government institutions sustain the creativity and productivity of the private sector.

Existing procedures too often delay or prevent decisions that could and should be made to avoid unnecessary frustrations and inequities. Aversion to change is a natural characteristic of most individuals and institutions, but the basic responsibility of government officials is to represent the general public interests by facing up to difficult policy issues. This chapter brings together the major conclusions of the study with particular emphasis on the continuous changes in the marketplace and in regulatory matters that have independently achieved many of the goals recommended in the Financial Institutions Act of 1975 and Financial Reform Act of 1976.

Major Conclusions

Comprehensive or specific legislative strategies

The beginning point of any effort at legislative reform is a decision about the type and scope of proposals to be considered by Congress. A comprehensive approach is logical because of the interdependence of most problems, particularly in the crisis atmosphere that usually dominates public affairs. Most officials recognize that reacting to specific problems only when they become too serious to ignore any longer is not an effective way to solve the broad issues. Moreover it may actually create distortions by disrupting the balance of the entire system.

In the case of financial institution reform the President's Commission on Financial Structure and Regulation proposed a package of 106 suggestions as a basis for widespread changes. The administration subsequently prepared the Financial Institutions Act, which advocated broad reform proposals in the structure of financial depository institutions. The House Banking, Currency, and Housing Committee finally considered an unusually comprehensive bill that would have profoundly changed the financial system. All of these comprehensive legislative initiatives were eventually rejected because the general public had little awareness of the broad reform proposals, and the special interest groups that the changes would affect preferred to continue the current competitive arrangements rather than risk the unknown results of comprehensive change. Similar difficulties have been experienced in considering broad legislation for energy, taxes, welfare, social security, education, transportation, international trade, and many other complex national issues.

The strategy of proposing comprehensive legislation has the important theoretical advantages of explicitly recognizing the complexity and integrated nature of most issues, preserving balance and equity among different interest groups, providing a framework for necessary compromises, and allowing for broad appeals to public opinion for political support. In reality, however, the pragmatic advantages of piecemeal legislative changes have greater weight in the decision-making process because incremental gradualism avoids the political risks of comprehensive change: it permits a separate response to the specific interests of each group. This approach is admittedly fragmented and confusing, but it is easier to manage than comprehensive reform because the private special interest groups can be satisfied by narrow changes, and because a number of such groups do not combine to defeat the recommendations through continuous lobbying that eventually erodes any support for pending legislation. Although the piecemeal approach ignores the plea of Congressman Reuss that comprehensive analysis be used to recognize the general public interest, attacking specific points is more realistically suited to the structure of the government's decision making. This conclusion is certainly not a new discovery, but its significance is heightened by tracing the experience with financial institution reform, which provides an example of how the system functions and why most legislation will continue to use the piecemeal strategy.

The drive for consensus recommendations

Perhaps the most common characteristic of the government's decision making is the overwhelming emphasis on compromises to make the recommendations politically feasible. Compromises are obviously necessary in a diverse and complex nation, and there is nothing strategically or morally wrong with seeking approval by broadening the acceptance of new legislation and administrative actions. In fact, compromises may often strengthen proposals by making them more realistic and responsive to the interests of many groups. Very few suggestions for legislative or administrative changes can be accepted without considerable modification, a safeguard that has been carefully built into our democratic system of government.

There are, however, risks associated with a governmental system that places so much emphasis on compromise solutions. The most obvious disadvantage is that the final recommendation may be so diluted that the major goals are no longer identifiable. The committee approach to making decisions often forces a consensus to avoid choosing between competing proposals. Forcing a consensus where no agreement actually exists might destroy potential support for necessary change because the participants were alienated. The potential strength of a policy recommendation may also be destroyed by compromises that create so many escape clauses or contradictory requirements that the resulting package becomes ineffectual or meaningless. The Christmas tree approach to legislation, in which the particular interest of each competing group is added to the basic proposal like an ornament, is a familiar government procedure, which dilutes much of the credibility and effectiveness of the process.

There are very few control devices in our system by which those outside the government can monitor and evaluate the legislative and administrative activities of the Executive Office and Congress. The making of decisions will therefore continue to be dominated by compromise rather than objective analysis of what actions will best serve the public interest. The bottom line of this issue is the simple fact that trade-offs are necessary in any decision, and such compromises involve the political risk that specific groups will be alienated. Our system apparently does not face up effectively to the problem of explaining that the general public interest transcends particular special interests.

Compromises are the natural recourse of those wishing to avoid the risks of comprehensive legislative and administrative actions. They clearly involve attitudes toward equality versus efficiency, change versus the status quo, minority rights in a democracy, the proper degree of tolerance accorded to dissenting views, and other key aspects of representative government. Compromises will continue to dominate the process in our present form of government, but increased consideration should be given to arriving more quickly at decisions and to requiring more explicit policy recommendations, thus forcing the governing officials and the general public to identify the single best solution, even though it results in changes that entail risks and disappoint special interests.

The dominating political factors

The dominating pressures of political factors in the decision-making process flow logically from the first two conclusions regarding the choice between comprehensive and piecemeal policy strategies and the great emphasis on compromises. Political sensitivities are natural in the representative form of government that has served America so well. Elected officials should be responsible to their various constituencies, and lobbying efforts by special interest groups are the channel through which people who will be directly affected by government actions can make known their goals. Structuring government policies to appeal to the majority of the people is entirely consistent with basic concepts of democracy and the preservation of cherished personal freedoms. Most government officials recognize that political motives are fundamental to the system and learn to adapt to political pressures without betraying their public obligation to serve the general interests. As a result most government officials do serve the general public, and the structure of the decision-making system as well as the fact that at least part of the process is public prevent repeated political abuses.

More insidious, however, is the overwhelming politicization of decisions, which permeates the top levels of the government. Because the dominant goal is most often reelection, the focus of decisions is on the near term. The form of leadership too often becomes more important than the substance, and disturbing amounts of time, money, and public resources are committed to the symbols of office and to self-serving public relations. Simplistic rhetoric is used to mislead the public about the risks and complexity of government actions. Despite the similarity of their behavior in office, political parties greatly exaggerate their disputes and differences. Meanwhile a relatively small group of administration and congressional officials make most of the important policy decisions, concealing or distorting bad news and exaggerating and making political capital of good news. Every decision is directed toward reelecting the incumbent official. In short, the political leaders begin to see policy issues through a selective screen that removes unwanted and unpleasant advice, and the bunker mentality mentioned earlier increasingly motivates the actions of the inner circle of powerful advisers. In some situations even the professional experts who serve in staff positions are drawn into the political drive for reelection, either voluntarily or because of overt pressure from political appointees.

There are, of course, protections against this politicizing: an active electorate, alert news organizations, dedicated career employees in government, and special interest groups that will undertake constant monitoring. Helped by the basic separation of powers required by the Constitution of the United States, these groups can identify and force the correction of the more blatant abuses of power for narrow political purposes.

But they can do little to shift the orientation of many senior government officials away from the expansion of personal political power. Government officials joke about the chronic spread of "Potomac fever" among newcomers to government service, but the excessive determination that some officials show to maintain the power associated with high political office and use it for personal ends is a matter of great concern, for these are the decision makers who directly affect the lives of every American and the course of international events. Today the collective powers of government officials evoke both fear and cynicism among the average citizen, who feels vulnerable but helpless to change the situation. Unfortunately, as we have said, the general apathy creates a vacuum which is then exploited by aggressive special interest groups anxious to expand their power within the political system.

Most of the serious problems confronting government officials have existed for many years, and solutions will continue to be delayed until they can pass the mandatory political tests. In Chapter 12 it was suggested that more rigorous and objective analysis of issues, uninhibited by partisan political pressures, is needed before starting the formal decision-making process, which will probably continue to be dominated by political considerations. A more decisive work schedule was also suggested. These improvements would help to emphasize in advance the substance of the policy debate, leaving until later the negotiations and compromises that make up the political side of the process. Important policy decisions will still be largely determined by political factors, but at least the background information and identification of options would be improved. Adoption of this idealistic reform will not result from actions by senior government officials. The real pressures for change will have to come from outside: from concerned citizens exercising their electoral power, from objective research on public policies by universities and study centers, and from the efforts of career employees dedicated to public service.

The existing decision-making system is merely the mechanism for processing problems. It does not determine the quality or quantity of decisions. Senior officials in the Executive Office and Congress function as they do because they believe they are responding to the interests of the people who will determine their prospects for reelection. If the American people want different decision-making procedures they will have to apply strong pressure on the existing system and continue it permanently. There is serious doubt that the American electorate will be willing to make such a commitment.

The need for presidential leadership

In the American political system the constitutional separation of powers leaves the President with the authority and responsibility to balance national priorities against the more specific goals of Congress and diverse special interest groups. In this lofty role the President receives credit for national progress and blame for failures, even though his actual power to control the government is fragmented and limited. The President does appoint senior officials in the Executive Office and regulatory agencies, with the approval of the Senate, and he can directly influence many governmental decisions, but Congress retains control of the legislative process, including the right to reject or approve federal budget decisions.

The requirement that the President consider each issue in the broader context of overall national and international goals automatically creates tensions and conflicts between the Executive Office and special interest groups or individual congressmen, who normally concentrate on more narrow problems. The President can veto legislation passed by Congress and even attempt to shape public opinion to support his position, but this adversary style of leadership is rarely a sound approach to developing public policies—as each administration learns after a few confrontations. The President must use the great powers of his office to persuade other government officials to support his broad program even though they may disagree on specific points. The abrasive political environment which has prevailed since the mid-1960s has made this conciliatory approach to leadership difficult, and the breakdown of presidential leadership on several occasions partly accounts for the delays in making necessary decisions affecting many national issues.

The pivotal role of the bureaucracy

Career employees in the executive branch and Congress are actually the backbone of the government, and their professional and administrative abilities determine the success or failure of government programs. They generally recognize the rules of the game and manage to adapt to changing organizations and personalities that come and go as the fortunes of each political party fluctuate. In my own personal experience most career officials are competent and dedicated to public service and professional service, qualities that greatly strengthen the effort to provide good service and guard against political abuses.

But the professional orientation and ambitions of most government employees also create problems because their perspective is often limited to their specific assignments rather than extended more broadly to include the many national issues that senior officials must consider. The inability or unwillingness of political appointees to work closely with career employees is a further obstacle to communication and credibility. In its worst form the barrier between the bureaucracy and political appointees may cause a breakdown of mutual trust and efficiency. At best, only a fraction of the talent and commitment of career employees is effectively utilized. The constant turmoil of organizational changes within the Executive Office and

Congress makes it very difficult to create an efficient team with long-term perspectives and broad goals.

A related problem is the dilemma that senior officials face in their dual roles of advisers to the President and managers of departmental and agency functions. The White House staff naturally expects officials appointed by the President to serve his interests by carrying out the operating details of his program and by supporting his political position. Presidential appointees are also expected to defend and promote the jurisdictional interests of the departments and agencies they represent. This is particularly true for those with line responsibilities for specific programs, as distinguished from staff roles.

If the bureaucracy feels threatened or ignored by the actions of presidential appointees in the Executive Office or Congress, obviously they will withhold their support and the functions of government will suffer. The bureaucracy also acts to protect itself by forming a powerful triangular relationship with special interest groups and the permanent staffs of congressional committees. Senior Cabinet officials and congressmen receive most of the publicity, including personal praise and criticism for events which are often uncontrollable or accidental, but the three groups comprising the triangle actually control most of the decisions made by the government. Given the pivotal position of the bureaucracy in determining the success or failure of government activities, it is surprising that few political appointees ever develop effective working relations with the career employees who have so much to contribute. The constant turnover of presidential appointees is a key reason, but the greatest barrier to cooperation continues to be the innate skepticism of each group about the political loyalties of the other. The irony of this situation is that by far the largest number of problems lend themselves to a bipartisan agreement that could ignore differences in political commitments.

Pragmatic considerations in government decisions

Theoretical arguments about equity and efficiency are often used during policy debates, and the rhetoric of legislative drafts is a model of idealism and noble objectives, but pragmatic reasoning and calculated trade-offs usually dominate final decisions. In fact, surprisingly little weight is given to theoretical analysis and empirical information in most government decisions, considering the serious nature of the issues. Even when competent academic studies are available, senior government officials often reject them as being too unreliable or hypothetical to serve as a basis for real policy decisions. A good example of this attitude occurred during the public hearings on financial institution reform. Numerous econometric studies demonstrated that the housing industry would probably benefit from an increase in the flow of mortgage funds, but they were ignored because the positive results could not be guaranteed. The actual outcome of theoretical studies will always be uncertain until the recommendations are applied to real problems, but such analysis can play a valid role in predicting the probable results. The strong criticism leveled against the mortgage investment tax credit by several special interest groups, which led to its deletion from the Financial Reform Act of 1976 considered by the House of Representatives, is another example. The defeat occurred despite the professional support of the Office of Tax Policy in the Treasury Department and several academic witnesses.

The importance of Congress

The rapid expansion of legislative and oversight responsibilities has made Congress the key factor in the governmental decision-making process, even though functional responsibilities for programs are concentrated in the executive branch and the independent regulatory agencies. Congress is also the best hope for the future preservation of representative government as the system becomes more centralized. Ironically, however, as Congress assumes a larger role, its ability to make decisions is increasingly limited by the complexity of issues and frustrating operating procedures. Some way must be found to focus the attention of Congress on policy problems having national priority rather than on the confusing details of operating programs. Political pressures obviously require individual congressmen to concentrate on legislative details in responding to special interest groups, but basic philosophies are too often ignored in working out the elaborate compromises necessary to gain widespread political acceptance. The inherent risk in this approach is that controversial issues will be avoided to prevent political opposition, even though procrastinating only makes many problems more serious and their ultimate solution more costly.

Even when there is general agreement that action is required, Congress often reacts slowly because of the fragmented nature of its organization and operating procedures. Reliance on specialized committees and subcommittees with overlapping jurisdictions to handle the bulk of analytical work in Congress is probably a necessary approach, given the technical complexity of most national issues, but the piecemeal recommendations that result after long delays often leave a large part of the problem unsolved. In this setting the real power in Congress is concentrated in a few important committees and subcommittees, giving particular power to their chairmen. Special interest groups with easy access to these important congressmen and committee staffs have great advantages in promoting their goals. The actual processing of legislation becomes, as we have said, a unique art form in which the power to control the course of events is concentrated in a few congressional leaders who use their expertise, experience, and detailed knowledge of procedures and protocol to expedite or delay the progress of specific legislation.

When the system works well, representative government is an efficient and equitable approach to determining the public interest. But there are also great risks, as demonstrated by the disappointing case of financial institution reform. Legislation may be delayed or frustrated by such political tactics as stonewalling, that is, blocking serious consideration by initiating new studies, slowing work schedules until the congressional calendar expires, adding so many complex or controversial amendments that the entire bill becomes unacceptable, or holding the proposals hostage until opponents agree to compromise. These and many other tactics have always been resorted to in political processes, and it would be hopelessly naive to expect the operating procedures to change drastically, but many congressmen and outside critics have recognized the need for reform to improve the effectiveness of Congress in the future.

Requirements for stable economic growth

According to several comments during the congressional hearings, the major problem confronting financial institutions is the unstable economic environment, not the structural and regulatory issues considered in the comprehensive legislative proposals. In the mid-1960s the United States began an unfortunate series of economic booms and recessions: serious overheating of the national economy created severe price pressures; accelerating inflation led to recessions by restricting housing construction, personal spending, and business investment; the recessions created unwanted unemployment which wasted resources and caused personal suffering; the rising unemployment triggered well-intentioned but poorly planned, ill-timed, and too frequent changes in government fiscal and monetary policy, setting off another round of excessive stimulus leading once again to the same cycle: overheating, inflation, recession, unemployment, and even more government intervention.

Government policies attempted to correct this vicious circle throughout the 1960s and 1970s, but the fine-tuning efforts tended to exaggerate the patterns of booms and recessions. While the gross national product rose from $753 billion in 1966 to $1.7 trillion in 1976, a gain of 126 percent, the federal budget jumped from a level of $135 billion in fiscal 1966 to $366 billion in fiscal 1976, a gain of 171 percent. In fiscal 1978 the federal budget increased to $451 billion, an increase of 23 percent over fiscal 1976. During this period of accelerating federal spending a budget deficit has been recorded in every year except fiscal 1969, and the cumulative total for deficits during fiscal 1975 through 1978 was $218 billion (includes one transition quarter).

Monetary policy has also changed significantly since the mid-1960s. From 1956 to 1966 the money supply, narrowly defined as currency and demand deposits, increased at a compounded annual rate of change of 2.5 percent (consumer prices rose at an annual rate of 1.8 percent); from 1966 through 1976 the money supply increased at an annual rate of 5.7 percent (consumer prices rose at an annual pace of 5.8 percent). The sharp accleration of inflation pushed interest rates to historically high levels causing severe disintermediation in the financial markets. The unemployment created by unstable economic conditions disrupted the flow of savings into depository institutions and restricted the purchase of homes and consumer goods.

Changes in structural and regulatory policy may help to improve the competitive balance and efficiency of private financial institutions, but real stability will not be possible as long as national economic conditions remain volatile. Government officials, of course, try to foster stable economic growth, but their policy decisions have frequently created uncertainty and unwanted distortions. In this context, the broader implications of national economic priorities must be examined to identify the entire range of public and private claims against the potential economic output of goods and services. The total capacity of the system must be considered and each competing claim ranked in order to counter the simplistic arguments that government programs can be multiplied indefinitely merely by increasing total output above the normal level for extended periods, or by shifting resources from the private to the public sector. There will always be honest differences of opinion about the proper functions of government, but new public obligations cannot be added if the total productive capacity of the economy is exceeded. This simple guideline has frequently been violated, and the current momentum of government spending and chronic federal budget deficits is the inevitable result of previous policy decisions. Legislation for special purposes, like the proposals for financial institution reform, obviously cannot correct such fundamental distortions.

Direct or indirect policy recommendations

One basic policy decision is whether to choose direct or indirect approaches to specific problems. For example, national goals have been established for improving and increasing the available housing, particularly for low- and moderate-income families. In line with those broad goals Congress has specified various programmatic efforts to supplement the actions of the private sector. One approach is to help eligible individuals and families acquire housing by providing a direct subsidy that will partly offset rent payments or mortgage interest costs. Since eligibility for direct subsidies is usually based on financial status, the objective of assisting low- and moderate-income families is explicitly recognized. An alternative is to provide comparable subsidies to suppliers of low-cost housing. The advantages of direct subsidies are that the actual costs can be readily identified and included in the federal budget along with competing claims, eligibility requirements can be controlled, and benefits can be restricted to those who continue to conform to the established guidelines. It is also easier to prevent windfall benefits from going to those who do not need special help, and the future costs of the program can be limited to the appropriations authorized during the tough reviews of the budget.

The major disadvantage of direct subsidies is that those who do not receive special benefits may object to paying taxes to support the programs, particularly if the costs are rising rapidly. One way to avoid the political risk of creating a rebellious electorate is to provide the benefits indirectly through special tax relief, subsidized government credit programs, and arbitrary government regulations. (Chapters 2 through 10 describe a wide variety of such actions designed to increase the flow of mortgage credit into the housing sector as mandated by Congress.)

Preferential credit arrangements, private loan guarantees, tax relief, capital grants, and various government services have been used to influence the allocation of national resources. Advocates of these indirect approaches often claim that they entail only minimal costs because no government funds are spent. This view ignores the opportunity costs of shifting resources away from other worthwhile purposes. Furthermore, when some borrowers are given special advantages all other borrowers are penalized, and when tax relief is granted on a selective basis other taxpayers are forced to carry a heavier burden.

In the case reviewed in this study the regulation of private financial markets to benefit the housing sector creates opportunity costs for personal borrowers interested in other goods and services, for business borrowers seeking credit needed to finance operations and investments that create job opportunities, and for government borrowers at all levels who are responsible for various social and investment projects. In fact, many doubt that these indirect methods actually benefit the low- and moderate-income families who really need help. Providing direct subsidies to needy persons would enable the regulatory agencies to concentrate on improving the efficiency and competitiveness of private financial institutions and still give attention to urgent social goals established by Congress. Economic arguments about efficiency and competition have little political appeal, but it is clear that tax incentives, subsidized government credit programs, and arbitrary portfolio loan and investment guidelines are popular both in Congress and among most special interest groups responsible for developing legislative proposals.

Presidential commissions and consultants

The frequent appointment of public commissions and consultants is a familiar technique whereby the government attempts to abide by the rules of the game as they relate to the scope and quality of public policy analysis. Commissions and consultants often serve as a clearinghouse for ideas and information and as a source of authoritative support for policy recommendations. As semiofficial organizations they have access to information and support from the administration but retain the autonomy necessary to preserve an independent image. In a tactical sense they usually have more credibility than internal advisers, who are always suspected of being primarily interested in the reelection prospects of the incumbent leaders, and they are insulated from the crisis atmosphere that pervades government offices as a consequence of the rapid pace of events, even though these events tend to repeat themselves. From the viewpoint of senior officials, outside commissions and consultants serve as useful damage control devices, permitting a show of imaginative leadership and involvement in national issues without getting too far out in front before they are sure of the political impact of recommendations. Reports from commissions and consultants are frequently effective as levers to move skeptical congressional committees, special interest groups, and the President's own bureaucracy in the wanted direction, and they also serve as buffers when the administration must deal with the same groups.

The acknowledged prestige and tactical advantages provided by commissions and consultants assure their continued role in the government's decision-making process, but they have not been a major factor in shaping public policies. Even when their contributions are used, the executive branch and Congress usually eliminate objectionable or controversial suggestions before developing their own legislative and administrative proposals. This screening procedure is necessary because the differences in the perspectives, and particularly in the political sensitivities of outside groups, are too great for them to directly influence policy decisions. Independence and objectivity are generally cited as the major strengths of public commissions and consultants, but even so their influence on the inner circle of advisers around the President or on the powerful congressional leaders who dominate the fragmented committee system is inevitably limited.

Special interest groups

Special interest groups have always been an integral part of the American system because they represent particular viewpoints, provide information, and debate policy proposals. Pluralism depends upon a representation of diverse interests, and there is nothing invidious about such groups' activities so long as the methods they use to exert pressure are legal and ethical. The temporary alliances formed by special interest groups are the chief means of communicating electoral preferences when legislation is considered.

Mounting criticism of the influence that powerful groups bring to bear on the legislative and regulatory activities of government has created concern and cynicism about how decisions are made. The average citizen often believes that he is excluded, while small cliques holding extensive economic power or able to influence large numbers of voters have easy access to government officials. The news services frequently publicize disturbing examples of political favors and occasional illegal behavior in governmental affairs. These scandals undermine public support, but they also increase the interest of some in gaining preferential advantages. Such problems pose serious challenges to the system of representative government. Instead of blaming pressure groups, however, the decision-making process itself should be examined. It need not be so slow, so fragmented, so complicated, and so dominated by political considerations. These defects could be improved without changing the strength of representative government.

For example, it should not take three years of congressional hearings to consider the views of a small number of special interest groups, particularly after the subject has been extensively researched for the preceding fifteen years by academic experts, the Executive Office, and various congressional committees. Votes on important legislation should not be stonewalled by protocol maneuvers until the congressional calendar expires, particularly when the issues are well known and can be summarized in a few pages. Over ten thousand pages of verbal and written testimonies should not have to be collected before a vote occurs. There are much better ways for congressmen and senior government officials to spend their valuable time than listening to endless verbal testimony which is entirely predictable and could easily be summarized in a few pages. The largely qualitative, emotional, and anecdotal testimony of special interest groups does not have to be accepted when more rigorous analytical evidence could be developed by objective research methods. Congressional leaders should not have to be deluged with overwhelming details about such legislative and regulatory issues as NOW accounts, the percentage of assets required to be committed to mortgages, the sliding scale of tax relief, conversion of charters, and types of savings accounts, when many more urgent national issues need attention. Congressional votes should not depend upon the scheduling preferred by a few leaders and then be subject to filibusters, questionable amendments, and abbreviated work schedules. Final legislative decisions should not be controlled by a handful of congressmen meeting in conference.

The disappointing failure of comprehensive financial reform did not occur because the issues were too difficult to understand. The final outcome came about because academic experts, special interest groups, the Executive Office, and congressional committees converged on a controversial issue and failed to make a decision. Subsequent events in the marketplace fortunately accomplished many of the goals included in the neglected legislative package, but progress has not been forthcoming on even more important national issues, such as the development and conservation of energy resources, tax reform, welfare reform, social security, capital investment, preservation of an open and competitive international trading system, productivity, and structural unemployment.

Partly to blame are the tactics of the special interest groups. Most of them play to avoid losing, as we have said, rather than to win new powers and benefits. That is, they mainly wish to keep from giving up existing advantages, even though a compromise might provide offsetting, or even increased, benefits in the future. Most special interest groups evidently prefer to work directly with congressional committees, regulatory agencies, and the executive branch rather than combining to promote comprehensive legislative and regulatory reform efforts that normally require extensive trade-offs.

The wisdom of this approach, from their point of view, was once again demonstrated in April 1977 when deposit interest rate controls were extended without difficulty, and the credit unions were successful in getting favorable congressional action on their specific legislative package of reforms. The example reviewed in this study once again demonstrates that most business firms do not want competition and often aggressively seek the security of government controls, even though rhetoric about free enterprise and competition is popular and our economic system is supposedly based on these concepts. The theoretical economic arguments about the values of competition and efficiency are paid lip service, but each group claims its situation is unique and deserves special government assistance and protection when specific legislation and regulation are reviewed.

This problem of fragmented interests continues to prevent fundamental reform of financial institutions as indicated by the appraisal of the Federal Reserve Board by Governor Philip E. Coldwell.

> Over the past few months the Federal Reserve, the Banking Committees of Congress and the financial industry have been seeking an accommodation to solve the various problems associated with monetary control, membership, equity in reserves, and pricing and access. By narrow votes various alternatives failed to pass in a House Banking Committee markup session and the search for an acceptable alternative continues. What have we learned in this experience?
>
> First, it is unfortunately more difficult to sponsor new legislation than to block legislation someone else is proposing. The banking industry and its regulators have staved off a number of pieces of unwise legislation over the past 20 years, but we have sponsored very little new structural reform and much of it failed. Obviously the "turf protection" syndrome is alive and well, and financial statesmanship is not yet the order of the day.
>
> Second, we have learned that there is a politically practical dimension

to new legislation. The lack of sufficient votes to pass uniform universal reserve requirements mandatory to all depository institutions is a clear reflection of the political power of various groups. Without a demonstrated crisis, there is a notable lack of urgency to the participants. Perhaps it is testimony to our inability to communicate the serious nature of the problem and the need for prompt relief, but perhaps it may also be a lack of recognition of the political feasibility by some groups.[1]

Increasing government involvement

The case of financial institution reform provides a clear example of the familiar pattern of escalating government involvement in the private economy. Such intervention usually stems from well-intentioned efforts to promote competition, protect public health and safety, maintain public confidence, protect and assure sound allocation of national resources, and promote equal employment opportunities. These are all positive goals, and government agencies often make significant contributions to their attainment.

In some situations, however, government involvement is harmful and frustrates the marketplace forces which allocate resources and determine wage and price developments on the basis of decentralized decisions by the people actually affected. Once begun, government intervention tends to grow, whether the results are positive or negative. An unfortunate cycle often develops in which private-sector adjustments to public policies result in additional government regulations, creating continuous rounds of excessive reactions. Unfortunately, when it is clear that government intervention is unnecessarily restrictive and inefficient, the usual solution is to recommend even more regulation to make the original policies work better. Those who believe in the market approach wind up supporting existing government controls as the only means of avoiding even greater future intervention. The final irony is that as the government increases its involvement in the private economy it is less and less able to respond to particularly controversial issues. A power vacuum is created because the powerful marketplace forces of competition have been restricted.

The aim of the comprehensive reforms recommended by the President's Commission on Financial Structure and Regulation was to make controls more flexible and permissive so that each financial institution could develop operating policies that would be more re-

1. Philip E. Coldwell, "The Ball Is in Your Court," remarks before the American Bankers Association's Senior Correspondent Banking Forum, March 29, 1979, p. 1.

sponsive to the interests of its customers—both borrowers and savers. The philosophy was that competitive forces are more effective than government regulation in creating a more stable and efficient financial system. This approach was not politically acceptable, however, because of fears that actions by financial institutions might not conform to various social goals mandated by Congress, and because the proposals were opposed by powerful special interest groups who were unwilling to accept the uncertainties of change and the competitive risks created by the reforms.

Government officials have a natural tendency to believe that they are unique in recognizing the real public interest and that they can force the private markets to adapt to the specific goals and operating procedures that they decree. This elitist approach to decision making may or may not accord with the actual preferences of the people, particularly when special interest groups exercise unusual influence. In a free society individuals are able to make their own choices. The cumulative total of their decisions constitutes the public interest—in economic terminology, the marketplace forces. This concept underlies the theme of this chapter: that as long as individual choice is permitted by a representative form of government, marketplace forces will ultimately work out to express the real preferences of the people, even though decisive legislative and administrative actions are not forthcoming. In situations where government intervention has created problems, there are serious costs of inefficiency and misallocation of national resources, but private individuals and firms will find ways of adapting to the system, including circumvention of onerous regulations if that is necessary to achieve their desired goals.

In a free society the people and the institutions that serve them cannot be permanently forced to act against their personal interests. Even in totalitarian regimes there is constant pressure from the people to advance their common interests. Markets are effective, not because of any mystic ideology, but because they enable individuals to pursue their personal goals more efficiently. Government regulations which further these interests are accepted; obstructive rules are initially evaded and eventually formally revoked or simply ignored. The difficulty is that such adjustment is often long and costly. Nevertheless, the competitive forces of the markets, reflecting the cumulative individual interests, eventually become the dominant variable in developing economic policy. During the 1970s the combined pressures of severe inflation and rapid technological change have forced legislative and regulatory responses to developments in the marketplace.

Adapting to Change in the Marketplace

The dominant characteristic of private financial markets is their constant adaptation to change as borrowers and savers strive to satisfy their needs and as legislative and regulatory guidelines shift. Despite increasing government intervention in the details of the U.S. economy, particularly in recent years, the financial markets are still basically independent and able to adjust to changing competitive conditions. This independence will continue as long as financial institutions are responsive to the real interests of consumers and businesses. Marketplace developments will continue to dominate policies, barring any major shift toward arbitrary government control of the entire economy and credit allocation requirements within the financial markets.

A number of important developments have occurred in the marketplace in lieu of the legislative and regulatory changes unsuccessfully proposed in the comprehensive packages of financial institution reforms. The motive for these marketplace responses was summarized by Senator McIntyre when he began the Senate hearings on the Financial Institutions Act of 1975:

> At that time, I also noted that: Resistance to change has been a recognizable characteristic of man throughout recorded history. However, change based upon need is inevitable, and there can be no doubt of the clear and recognizable need to implement substantial changes in the present regulation and structure of our financial system.
>
> While reasonable men may differ on the type and degree of change required, it has become apparent that the need for restructuring our financial system is an idea for which the time has come.[2]

State legislative and regulatory changes

Although the Financial Institutions Acts and Financial Reform Act involved only amendments to federal laws, the major sources of change have been the various reforms instigated at the state level. Some of these financial and banking adjustments have resulted from the efforts of state officials to keep pace with the increasing services offered by federally chartered institutions competing against state-chartered organizations. For example, several states passed wild-card laws permitting state-chartered depository institutions to issue long-

2. U.S., Congress, Senate, Committee on Banking, Housing, and Urban Affairs, *Financial Institutions Act of 1975*, May 14–16 and June 11, 1975, p. 1.

term savings certificates exempt from the maximum deposit interest rate ceilings.

Most experiments with new legislative and regulatory guidelines, however, have been directly initiated by state governments. Giving state-chartered thrift institutions permission to provide customers with third-party payment services, thus enabling these firms to compete with commercial banks, is a classic example. In fact, much of the original impetus for overall financial reform was the direct result of growing dissatisfaction with the competitive disparities created by the dual-chartering system. A major advantage of the dual financial system created in this country is that it has resulted in innovation that would probably not have occurred otherwise. Even the failure of comprehensive reform at the national level has been partially offset by aggressive state actions to liberalize the asset investment and depository powers of thrift institutions and credit unions, to expand their third-party payment powers, and to enable them to handle retirement accounts and offer various consumer and business services.

In December of 1978, the Federal Home Loan Bank Board proposed that federally chartered savings and loan associations be given authority to offer Payment Order Accounts in those areas where state-chartered institutions have such powers. It is interesting that the U.S. League of Savings Associations joined the American Bankers Association in opposing the granting of this authority while the other major trade association, the National Savings and Loan League, favored the idea.

The Federal Home Loan Bank Board decision was a direct response to the regulatory change promulgated by the Federal Reserve Board of Governors to permit commercial banks to offer automatic transfer of funds from the savings accounts into the checking accounts of their customers. The automatic transfer systems enable commercial banks to pay interest on accounts even though the funds may be used for writing checks. This procedure is a means of evading the historical prohibition against paying interest on demand deposits. The U.S. League of Savings Associations immediately filed for a court injunction against the new rules. Their request was first rejected in May of 1978, but a U.S. district court in Washington, D.C., ruled on April 21, 1979, that the various automatic transfer accounts and credit union share drafts are illegal. The court then directed Congress to decide the issue of paying interest on demand deposits by January 1, 1980. This sequence of events is another classic example of the market's efforts to adapt to consumer pressures within the restrictions of a government regulatory system. This charade—of switching savings deposits into checking accounts of the same depositor by means of a computer—is an example of superfluous adjustment of procedures in an effort to conform to outmoded regulations.

In an effort to resolve the problem directly, Congressman St Germain in early May of 1979 scheduled hearings on his bill that would permit payment of interest on checking accounts in all types of federally insured financial institutions. In announcing these hearings he emphasized that it was time to "stop all the gimmickry that has surrounded efforts to back-door interest on checking accounts and give the consumer a straightforward freedom of choice in handling his checking accounts." He also pointed out that this change would enable institutions to eliminate many of the "costly giveaways and other gimmicks now employed to attract deposits."[3] Despite the straightforward approach of his proposal, the strong opposition of various financial institutions will make it difficult to pass such legislation.

As federally chartered institutions have recognized their competitive disadvantages they have applied pressure on the federal regulatory agencies to issue new rules in the absence of enabling legislative action by Congress, and they have even resorted to changing over to state charters. This unnecessary concern for organizational status based on artificial distinctions between financial institutions should be a persuasive argument in favor of comprehensive reform at the national level, but that long effort has evidently expired, leaving state governments to approve most of the innovations in the financial markets.

Electronic funds transfer systems

The major goal of the comprehensive reforms included in the Financial Institutions Acts and the Financial Reform Act was to diversify the services provided by all types of financial institutions and stabilize the availability of credit. To improve efficiency and competition the proposals emphasized increased flexibility and more freedom for managements to determine their lending and savings specialization at their own discretion. The strong impetus of advancing technology has moved the entire system of financial intermediaries in those directions despite the rejection of overall legislative reforms.

3. Nancy L. Ross, "Early May Hearings Set on Checking Interest Bill," *Washington Post* (April 24, 1979), p. E1.

The development of electronic funds transfer systems (EFTS) now makes it possible to transfer funds quickly between institutions and into different accounts through sophisticated computer technology. Electronic machine terminals, known as automatic tellers, located on the premises of financial institutions and in various other locations, such as retail stores, airports, hotels, and other public places, can instantly provide many services twenty-four hours a day at little cost. Prearranged programs or individual identity cards instruct off-premise terminals connected to a central computer. Customers can complete individual transactions in this way; they can shift their deposits between checking and savings deposits, withdraw funds automatically using special debit cards, receive loan advances, pay bills instantly, and even transfer funds between different financial institutions. Point-of-sales terminals are being placed in retail stores to enable consumers to pay for goods and services by an immediate transfer of funds, triggered when a personal identification card is inserted into the automated teller computer terminal. Despite many of the early claims, exotic technology has not yet eliminated the need for currency and for traditional checking and savings accounts, but modern financial institutions can now provide most of their consumer services around the clock through the automatic teller computer terminals. Progress in the evolution of these new financial services will continue as customers become more familiar with the systems.

Much of the controversy surrounding financial institution reform arose from the recommendation to eliminate controls like regulation Q, which determine the maximum interest payments permitted for time and savings deposits and permit thrift institutions to pay a higher rate, thus partially offsetting the competitive advantages of commercial banks, which can offer more diversified services. Banking groups were equally upset by the amendment permitting the future payment of interest on demand deposits and the proliferation of third-party payment instruments comparable to their checking accounts. The development of electronic transfers largely eliminates the arbitrary distinction between deposit accounts and the role of interest rate controls. For example, customers can keep their funds in interest-earning savings accounts until they need to pay bills, at which time they can instantly transfer the necessary amount from their deposits into their checking account. This can be done through prearranged agreements or by sending specific instructions to the electronic transfer system. When payments are received the system can transfer the funds directly into savings accounts. The same system can also easily transfer funds into and out of open-market financial instruments at the direction of customers able to respond to fluctuating yields in the financial markets. In such an environment all deposits can be regarded as transactions balances, and artificial distinctions as well as the prohibition against interest payments on demand deposits become largely irrelevant. The Federal Reserve Board of Governors finally gave explicit recognition to this marketplace development on November 1, 1978, when it authorized commercial banks to offer customers automatic transfer accounts. These special accounts permit customers to hold interest-earning savings deposits from which funds can be transferred automatically into demand deposits to cover checks. On April 21, 1979, a federal court decided that these accounts represent an illegal evasion of the law prohibiting the payment of interest on demand deposits. Congress must now decide the issue by January 1, 1980.

The gradual evolution of electronic transfers of funds has created additional controversies, and Congress has consequently turned to a familiar decision-making procedure: the establishment of a National Commission on Electronic Funds Transfers. Many financial institutions have been upset because the increased use of the systems has diminished their previous advantages of convenience, since rival organizations that operate automated teller computer terminals can provide competing consumer services. Although the final report of the public commission examining the many competitive and legal issues created by electronic transfer systems is still to be evaluated by Congress, there has been considerable activity in the regulatory sector and among state governments. The Federal Reserve Board of Governors has issued proposed regulations covering such systems and invited public comment, and other federal agencies have attempted to develop appropriate rules for this new application of technology.

A particularly complex problem involves the actions of some financial institutions to limit the expansion of funds transfer systems making branch banking regulations applicable to off-premise automated teller terminals proposed by commercial banks. All federally chartered institutions must, of course, conform to the branching laws of the state where they are located. In 1974 the Comptroller of the Currency ruled that off-premise bank terminals were not branches under the National Bank Act and could be established without regard to individual state branching laws. Federal courts subsequently overruled the Comptroller's decision, and the automated teller facilities established by national banks must satisfy state laws covering branching as well as capital and surplus requirements.

By the end of 1976 twenty-six states had passed legislation related to the electronic transfer of funds. Seven states leave the branching question up to the discretion of the state regulatory officials; thirteen states have decided that off-premise computer terminals are not branches, while four have ruled that they are; and two states permit facilities for such transfers to be established under special arrangements with state financial officials. There is also uncertainty over the sharing arrangements specified in each state. Sixteen states have ruled that electronic transfer facilities must be shared by banks; in some states they must be shared by all financial institutions operating in the state. Four states even permit out-of-state organizations to share the same terminals, while eleven states prohibit institutions from crossing geographical boundaries even though metropolitan areas frequently spread beyond such arbitrary limits.

The evolution of these systems is clearly a major factor in the competitive balance of financial institutions. Throughout the congressional hearings on financial institution reform it was emphasized that future survival would depend upon guaranteed access to developing technology. Even though heavy capital investments are required to establish facilities for electronic transfers, and customers' reservations about shifting to new automated services have restrained the expansion of automated teller terminals to date, it is clear that future legislative and regulatory actions will increasingly involve their use. The pattern of government decisions, including the use of the final report of the public commission, is also likely to parallel the example of comprehensive financial institution reform, since the basic issues of competition and specialization are the same.

Deposit interest rate controls

Since 1933 the Federal Reserve Board of Governors has had authority to set maximum interest rate ceilings on deposits at commercial banks that belong to the Federal Reserve System, and since 1966 the Federal Deposit Insurance Corporation has exercised similar control over nonmember commercial banks that have federal deposit insurance. The 1966 legislation also authorized the Federal Home Loan Bank Board to establish interest rate controls for its members and all associations that are federally insured. States are left with discretionary control in setting maximum ceilings for only a few state-chartered institutions that are not federally insured.

In 1976 the banking commissioners from New England states jointly petitioned Congress to remove interest rate controls for all financial intermediaries in their region, on the grounds that parity of operating powers between commercial banks and thrift institutions had already been achieved. Congress rejected their request, but the general trend has been clear for many years. Such restrictions will continue to be eroded as the expansion of electronic funds transfer systems and the presence of open-market investment alternatives break down barriers to competition. As future financial disintermediation occurs, electronic transfers of funds will make portfolio changes simple and inexpensive. Because of these developments and a growing awareness about relative yields, savers will become even more responsive to swings in short-term interest rates. The flow of funds into savings certificates with specific long-term maturities, rather than into passbook accounts, will partly offset disintermediation pressures, but the new technology should enable all savers to react more quickly to marketplace developments.

Diversification of lending and investment powers

A major section of the Financial Institutions Acts and Financial Reform Act provided for broadened lending and investment powers for federally chartered financial intermediaries, including liberalized powers for national banks to make more real estate loans. It was assumed that comparable regulatory changes would be made to maintain the competitive position of state-chartered institutions. Despite the failure of the comprehensive recommendations to become law, many of the proposed reforms have since been adopted.

At the federal level, the various regulatory agencies have selectively approved changes, and congressional oversight reviews have validated the liberalization of powers. Reform efforts have been even more vigorous at the state level, although the pace of change and types of powers granted have been irregular, since each jurisdiction has followed an independent path in its response to marketplace innovations. Particular emphasis has been placed on increasing consumer loans as part of the "family financial centers" approach desired by thrift institutions and credit unions, and as a result of the continued expansion of commercial banks into this profitable financial service. The growth of consumer credit has been aided by other regulatory changes in some states, permitting revolving lines of credit and overdraft arrangements, credit cards, new debit cards (which provide for deposit withdrawals and advances against loans), and the spread of third-party payment powers which are directly linked to credit purchases.

An interesting example of marketplace innovation was provided in mid-1977 by Merrill Lynch, Pierce, Fenner and Smith, the giant investment banking firm that has diversified its operations to cover the entire securities industry, and gained a dominant position among firms offering brokerage services to individuals. It introduced a plan to provide its customers with consumer credit services that would compete with those of other financial institutions. This was truly a departure, since the Glass-Steagall Act of 1933 had split investment banking and commercial banking into two separate functions. But marketplace competition and the development of electronic funds transfer systems have blurred that distinction. Securities firms have long complained that commercial banks encroach into their sphere of activities by undertaking the private placement sales of corporate securities, conducting mergers and acquisitions, underwriting state and local government bond issues, and arranging individual stock purchase plans. For this reason the Merrill Lynch entry into consumer lending represented an ironic reversal of competition.

According to the initial proposal, an experimental program in three cities would permit Merrill Lynch customers to establish a line of credit against their brokerage accounts equal to 50 percent of the value of securities held. Customers could borrow against their line of credit, using credit cards or special checks. The special checks are cleared through a regular commercial bank. The cash balances left with the brokerage firm are invested in a money market fund administered by Merrill Lynch. By mid-1978 the service had been introduced in Atlanta, Denver, San Diego, and Columbus, Ohio. Merrill Lynch consistently emphasized that the service was intended to strengthen its competitive position rather than as a substitute for regular deposit savings services.

Commercial bank representatives sharply criticized the initial proposal and argued that such plans should be subject to commercial bank regulations, including those specifying legal reserves. In Colorado, the state board that regulates banks decided in May of 1978 that the Merrill Lynch accounts should be prohibited, but the controversy was later settled out of court when the brokerage firm agreed to enforce a minimum figure of $200 for any checks written against the customer reserves and promised that the minimum deposit of $20,000 would not be reduced. Although the issue remains controversial, it appears that the Glass-Steagall Act does not apply unless deposits are accepted. Individual credit is already available to brokerage customers purchasing securities on margin, and this new program is similar to existing borrowing arrangements.

A second example of how overlapping competition spreads throughout the financial markets is the new tax law adopted in Massachusetts, which will provide tax relief from net income taxes levied against insurance companies if they make loans to small and medium-sized companies to create more job opportunities. The law includes a penalty clause that will withdraw the tax relief if the insurance companies fail to make the required loans.

On the investment side, state laws have been changed so that depository institutions can increase and diversify their holdings of commercial paper; bankers acceptances, and federal funds with short-term maturities and in U.S. government and agency securities; corporate bonds; loan syndications; unsecured property loans; variable rate mortgages; and ownership of financial services corporations. For example, state-chartered savings and loan associations in Oregon are now permitted to invest up to 25 percent of their assets in liquid assets and U.S. government debt.

Federal and state-chartered banks, thrift institutions, and credit unions have aggressively solicited deposits from individuals establishing personal pension programs for their retirement under the Individual Retirement Account (IRA) and Keogh legislation. The creation of new retirement and annuity programs is comparable to the trust powers previously available only through insurance companies, commercial banks, and specialized trust management institutions; depository intermediaries have therefore opened up an entirely new area of services.

Thrift institutions have also become more aggressive in soliciting longer-term deposits with fixed maturities to stabilize their accounts and prevent disintermediation. Since early 1973, federal savings and loan associations have been authorized to issue subordinated debenture bonds to tap new sources of funds. They have also turned to sales of bonds secured by specific pools of mortgages. These mortgage-backed bonds provide long-term sources of funds for the savings institutions and high-quality securities for investors. If more people can be interested in these new instruments, it would help to make the mortgage portfolios more liquid and enable thrift institutions to react to shifting interest rates.

The newness of these bonds will probably require them to be sold through private placements until the public bond markets become more familiar with them. Nevertheless, the new liability management techniques and liberalized lending and investment powers clearly indicate that financial institutions are evolving rapidly as a result of changes in the marketplace that force them to adapt to the borrowing and saving interests of customers if they are to keep up with the competition.

Third-party payment services

Commercial banks have been unique in offering checking accounts and other financial services and hence have had major competitive advantages. In fact, checking accounts are generally considered the most important consumer service provided by depository institutions. The Financial Institutions Act of 1975 included provisions that would have granted authority to federally chartered savings and loan associations and mutual savings banks to offer checking accounts, NOW accounts (negotiable orders for withdrawal of funds from interest-bearing deposits to make third-party payments), and credit cards.

Despite the failure of comprehensive reform in Congress, individual states have acted independently to expand the powers of state-chartered financial institutions. As a result, competition within the marketplace has rapidly changed. Various states now allow thrift institutions and credit unions to provide credit card services. By the end of 1976 most mutual savings banks offered checking account services.

Many states also permit savings and loan associations to make third-party payments for customers using telephone transfers or preauthorized "bill-payer" programs, and some jurisdictions have approved regular checking account services. Since 1972 the new NOW accounts have spread throughout the New England states as a result of a special exemption from a federal law prohibiting the payment of interest on any deposit which can be used for third-party payments. The current administration has supported new legislation which would expand the geographical availability of NOW accounts. This evolution continued when NOW accounts were approved for issue by all depository institutions in the crucial state of New York through the passage in October of 1978 of the Financial Institutions Regulatory Act of 1978. It is also believed that the competitive pressures created by the new automatic transfer system, whereby customers of commercial banks can shift funds from their savings accounts to cover checks, will eventually force serious consideration of nationwide NOW accounts.

Credit unions in several states have been allowed to offer share-draft services which are, in effect, interest-bearing checking accounts. In December 1977 the National Credit Union Administration announced final regulations that would authorize credit unions to provide share drafts beginning in February 1978. The American Bankers Association immediately went to court to seek a restraining injunction to prevent this expansion of third-party payment powers. However, the apparent success of an experimental program over the last several years indicates that credit unions will move ahead on their diversification efforts unless legal barriers are imposed. In fact, an agreement with Sears Roebuck and Company, the world's largest retailer, to use share drafts as payment for consumer purchases has already been announced.

In Rhode Island, state-chartered savings and loan associations and mutual savings banks can even own commercial banks and operate their traditional services, including checking accounts, out of the same premises. Many other specific examples of the more liberal powers that have been made available to state-chartered financial institutions could be added, but this list of marketplace innovations is enough to illustrate the trend.

Because the rapid expansion of new powers has been selective, competitive pressures have been created among the commercial banks and federally chartered thrift institutions which lost the chance to obtain comparable powers when the comprehensive legislative reforms collapsed. The resulting petitions for equal treatment will eventually force a response from federal regulatory agencies and Congress to protect the interests of federally chartered financial institutions. This piecemeal approach to structural and regulatory change ultimately accomplishes the same goals as comprehensive plans, but the pace is irregular and the resulting competitive imbalances during the transition periods are often costly.

An interesting example of marketplace adjustments occurred early in 1977 when officials representing federally chartered savings and loan associations in New York asked Congress for more flexible powers.

> With respect to the transaction account issue, our League is grateful for your recognition that the action taken by the New York State Legislature last year in granting checking account and overdraft privilege authority to state-chartered thrift institutions has created a potentially serious and destructive competitive disparity between similar financial institutions. As a matter of fact, with state-chartered savings and loans and mutual savings banks having checking account authority under state law, and credit unions offering share drafts, the Federal savings and loans, representing two-thirds of the industry's assets in New York, are the only financial institutions lacking some form of transaction account power.

The savings and loans of New York would not be asking Congress for transaction account authority at this time were it not for the action of the Legislature last year—and that action was not taken at the instance of the savings and loan business. While we recognize that third-party payment authority will be both desirable and necessary as funds transfer systems develop and direct deposit programs, both in the public and the private sector, are expanded, our primary legislative priorities have been geared more to improving and strengthening those lending and investment functions which relate directly to housing and home finance. Enactment of economically realistic ceilings for home loans and authority to develop new forms of mortgage instruments are two examples.

However, the action of the Legislature left this League with no choice but to seek transaction account authority for Federal associations that would parallel, as closely as possible, the authority granted their state-chartered counterparts.[4]

The lag in the response of federal legislation and regulation to marketplace developments is clearly evident in the brief history of NOW accounts in the New England states. Special service fees may be charged for these accounts, and financial institutions have a legal right to require a thirty-day notice prior to withdrawal, but the service actually amounts to a checking account that earns interest.

In 1972 mutual savings banks in Massachusetts found that there was no law prohibiting such accounts and began promoting this new consumer service after overcoming the challenge of legal actions initiated by commercial banks. New Hampshire thrift institutions found a similar legislative loophole. The new hybrid accounts quickly became popular among customers interested in both interest on their savings deposits and the convenience of checks. After first attacking the innovation, commercial banks in the two states responded to the competition by offering their own NOW accounts. These proved to be attractive to customers as a substitute for both checking and savings accounts. Although the transfer of funds turned out to be an expensive switch for banks, since it required a 5 percent interest payment compared with the zero return normally paid on demand deposits, pressures from customers forced the marketplace adjustments despite the extra costs.

The reaction of Congress to these developments was predictably negative, and Public Law 93-100 was passed in 1974 to prohibit the payment of interest on any deposit accounts used for third-party

---

4. U.S., Congress, House, Committee on Banking, Finance, and Urban Affairs, *Extension of Regulation Q Controls, Hearing on H.R. 1901*, 95th Cong. 1st sess., Feb. 7, 1977, pp. 123–24.

payments by federally and state-chartered commercial banks, savings and loan associations, and mutual savings banks. Massachusetts and New Hampshire were given a special exemption to continue NOW accounts on an "experimental" basis. In early 1976 the exemption was extended to Vermont, Maine, Connecticut, and Rhode Island. It is now estimated that two-thirds of the financial institutions in New England offer NOW accounts.

The legislation enacted early in 1977 to extend deposit interest rate controls and approve the detailed package of reforms proposed by the credit unions originally included a section granting new authority to federal savings and loan associations in New York, New Jersey, and Pennsylvania to issue NOW accounts (state-chartered thrift institutions already had third-party payment powers). In introducing the legislative hearings in February 1977 Congressman St Germain made the following positive statement:

> Certainly, the NOW account issue is not a new one for this committee. Since 1973, on at least five separate occasions this subcommittee has reviewed the NOW account, with affirmative legislation resulting to first conduct a NOW account experiment in Massachusetts and New Hampshire and later to extend NOW accounts to all six New England States.
>
> Today, after 4 years of exhaustive research by the Fed, the FDIC and numerous others, we know for a fact that this popular consumer account has successfully provided a needed and long overdue service and has not caused major disruptions in the banking climate or caused any banks to fail.
>
> It has, however, caused many banks to conduct their operations in a more cost-efficient manner. I personally believe that consumers should no longer be asked to await the fruits of comprehensive financial reform and, therefore, would firmly support the extension of NOW accounts nationwide for all financial institutions desiring to respond to an obvious consumer demand.[5]

Despite this glowing endorsement, strong opposition to the spread of NOW accounts into three more important commercial states forced the House subcommittee to limit its proposal, simply allowing federal savings and loan associations in New York to provide non-interest-bearing checking account services to restore competitive parity with state-chartered thrift institutions. Even that modified proposal was deleted during the conference session with Senate representatives before the final bill became a public law.

Although NOW accounts historically have been restricted to the six New England states, the issue was revived by the administration

5. Ibid., p. 2.

when it recommended two specific regulatory changes to Congress in mid-1977 in lieu of the comprehensive reform proposals considered by the previous Congress (see Chapter 10). Congress eventually approved an exemption for New York in 1978, and the combination of consumer interest in NOW accounts and the spread of electronic funds transfer systems should eventually force Congress to make an explicit decision about how to solve this controversial problem.

Chartering and branching issues

Increased flexibility in the chartering of new depository institutions and limited conversions back and forth between federal and state charters were proposed in the Financial Institution Act of 1975. In the absence of federal legislation many state governments have acted independently to pass laws permitting charter conversions. Congress has also allowed a few mutual savings and loan associations to convert to a stock form of organization without losing their federal charters, as part of an experimental program. In March of 1979 the Federal Home Loan Bank Board adopted proposed rules to regulate the conversion of mutual savings and loan associations into stock associations. These regulations are intended to control the amount of stock that can be purchased by officers and directors to prevent alleged windfall profits resulting from conversions. This issue remains controversial, and Senator Proxmire continues to request that the Federal Home Loan Bank Board stop authorizing the conversions.

It is also interesting that the controversial issue involving the granting of federal charters to mutual savings banks was resolved by the passage of the Financial Institutions Regulatory Act of 1978. Federal charters may now be issued to mutual savings banks in states where such institutions are permitted to operate.

A related issue, which was not covered in either of the Financial Institutions Acts or the Financial Reform Act, involves the controversial subject of state laws that control the branching of financial institutions. Some states, particularly along the east and west coasts, permit branching throughout the entire jurisdiction. In the plains area several unit banking states permit only one office to be established. Other states have compromised by allowing limited branching within the county where the main office is located or in contiguous counties. Under the provisions of the McFadden Act all national banks, as well as state-chartered banks, must conform to the branching laws of the state where they are located. There is no comparable federal law covering savings and loan associations, but the Federal Home Loan Bank Board usually follows the state laws, which tend to allow some form of branching or affiliate operations.

In the past, state branching laws have tended to restrict the geographical expansion of financial institutions. This statutory limitation has been frustrating to the more aggressive firms interested in adding facilities and customers to increase their volume of business and strengthen their competitive position. The President's Commission on Financial Structure and Regulation recommended that state governments be encouraged to liberalize their laws to allow statewide branching, but federal legislation cannot address this issue directly.

Nevertheless, three developments have caused a persistent trend toward reducing restrictions. First, states that limit branching have tended to approve the opening of new "limited services" facilities which can accept deposits, honor withdrawal requests, and handle loan payments. For example, in Illinois a limited services facility may be located within two miles of the main office. These often evolve into full-service centers as the branching laws are gradually eased. Second, the growth of multibank holding companies enables a central headquarters office to coordinate the activities of related banks in different areas—essentially the same thing as operating a branch network. Third, the growth of electronic funds transfer systems has created a rapid expansion of the off-premise computer terminals for automated tellers which can substitute in some ways for regular branch offices.

Twenty-six states had passed legislation by the end of 1976 to allow free or restricted authority to establish electronic transfer systems in accordance with branching laws. The increasing flexibility of branching laws and chartering regulations are additional examples of how the financial system adapts to changing customer interests.

Credit unions

The fifth section of the Financial Institutions Act of 1975 proposed that the powers of federally chartered credit unions be expanded. A detailed set of credit union reforms was approved by Congress in April 1977, and numerous state laws have been adapted to accommodate the growth and diversification of credit unions. Many states now allow state-chartered institutions to offer variable-rate savings certificates and to handle regular passbook savings accounts on which the interest rate is fixed, as distinguished from the older share accounts where the dividend is determined at the end of each quarter.

By the end of 1976 thirty-five states had approved these diversified deposit accounts, and twenty-two states had authorized the use of share drafts, which are basically the same thing as checking accounts. The National Credit Union Administration approved the unlimited expansion of share-draft powers to all federal credit unions in December 1977, and the courts originally upheld the legality of the new power. Many credit unions responded by offering this important consumer service. However, the Iowa Supreme Court reacted in June of 1978 to prevent credit unions from using share drafts and a U.S. federal district court ruled on April 21, 1979, that such accounts are illegal. In both cases the courts emphasized that legislation is needed to make such accounts legal. Given the marketplace pressures, it is likely that such permissive legislation will be passed by the January 1, 1980, deadline.

Rhode Island has also authorized credit unions to provide NOW accounts, thus giving them competitive equality with commercial banks and thrift institutions with regard to this popular type of account. Credit unions continue to make aggressive use of electronic funds transfer systems and new point-of-sale credit clearing and withdrawal services. Credit unions at the state level are clearly expanding their operations, and other financial institutions are particularly aware of the increasing intensity of competition. Another step in this evolution occurred in October 1978 when a central liquidity facility for credit unions was approved as part of the Financial Institutions Regulatory Act of 1978.

Mortgage loan incentives

Housing issues were a dominant concern throughout the legislative evaluation of financial institution reform. The last two sections of the Financial Institutions Act of 1975 focused on improving the flows of funds into mortgage markets by eliminating the interest rate ceilings on FHA and VA mortgage loans and by providing a mortgage interest tax credit for mortgage lenders. Both proposals failed because of the opposition of interest groups in favor of housing construction, but marketplace pressures have led to continuous change in the mortgage markets. Various states have recently liberalized their laws to permit higher loan-to-value mortgage loans which effectively reduce the down payments in purchasing a home, and on September 12, 1977, the Federal Home Loan Bank Board proposed a "major policy change" affecting savings and loan associations. It would enable them to make more mortgage loans calling for low down payments and to extend the rules to make more types of housing eligible for the new loans.

Six state governments had also acted by the end of 1976 to make variable-rate mortgages legal within their jurisdictions. There are a variety of different plans, but variable-rate mortgages are primarily intended to permit the interest rate charged by lenders to fluctuate according to some index of the cost of money in the short-term financial markets. The change in the interest rate can be accommodated either by shifting the maturity of the loan to leave the monthly payment the same or by adjusting the actual interest payments required. Borrowers are usually protected by statutory requirements: a maximum ceiling must be established; the number and size of the interest rate adjustments permitted each year must be specified; any changes must be linked to a public index of interest rates; borrowers may refinance their loan without any penalty; fixed-rate mortgages must be still available to borrowers; truth-in-lending regulations must be enforced; and decreases in the variable rate become mandatory, but increases are discretionary according to the decisions of lenders. The purpose of variable-interest-rate mortgages is to make the overall yield to lenders more responsive to pervasive financial market developments so that mortgage lenders can stabilize the flow of mortgage funds and avoid disintermediation.

Although variable-rate mortgages have received theoretical support from housing experts, their use has been restricted by legislation and opposition from special interest groups. Actually they have been used only in California, where the Bank of America has offered both fixed- and variable-rate options to its customers since October 1976. By May 1977 the variable-rate mortgages accounted for 16 percent of the mortgage loans being made by Bank of America.

It is significant, however, that Congress refused in 1975 to allow federal savings and loan associations to offer this new mortgage option to customers despite the support of the Federal Home Loan Bank Board. Nevertheless, state-chartered savings and loan associations, mutual savings banks, and a few commercial banks have moved ahead with this innovation, and the marketplace responded favorably to the additional flexibility with the rapid rise in the price of homes and required down payments.

Support for some federal action continued to mount and the Federal Home Loan Bank Board again announced its intention to permit federally chartered savings and loan associations to issue variable rate mortgages in its regulations issued on December 15, 1978. As of April 1979 only federal savings and loan associations in California have been given the necessary approval but it is anticipated that institutions in other states will successfully apply to the Federal Home Loan Bank Board for similar authority. At this time state-chartered savings and loan associations in more than twenty states may offer flexible rate mortgages, although most of the activity is still concentrated in California.

The Federal Home Loan Bank Board also announced two other mortgage innovations in its regulations published on December 15, 1978. For young families with limited incomes they proposed a graduated-payment mortgage. This type of contract provides for mortgage payments that start at a lower level than for a standard mortgage and then gradually rise for several years to a higher level that is sustained until the final maturity. This arrangement matches the prospective earnings pattern of younger families. A second innovation calls for offering reverse annuity mortgages to older home owners in which periodic payments would be made to them. The accumulated equity in the home would provide the security for these annuity payments.

All three of these innovative mortgage payment plans are currently being tested in various states. The National Association of Home Builders, organized labor groups, and consumer organizations continue to criticize the variable rate mortgage contracts being proposed, but the added flexibility provided to buyers is attracting interest. The variable contracts also provide a good match for the new flexible-rate savings certificates that have been authorized since June 1, 1978, to help offset the familiar disintermediation pressures that hurt depository institutions during periods of rising interest rates.

The experience with variable-rate mortgages has followed a familiar pattern in which the marketplace presses for innovations while legislative responses lag. The human reluctance to change and the risks of disturbing powerful special interest groups have delayed the widespread use of variable-rate mortgages. As economic history clearly indicates, however, the interests of customers and the innovations developed by financial institutions cannot be permanently frustrated.

Marketplace adjustment to financial disintermediation

The central point in much of the debate about financial institution reform has involved the arbitrary restrictions placed on the amount of interest that can be paid on deposits. From the fact that Congress has voted thirteen times since 1966 to temporarily extend these regulations for periods of six months to two years, it is clear that this issue remains extremely controversial. The latest test of regulation Q controls occurred in October of 1978 when authority to set ceiling rates was extended for another two years as part of the omnibus Financial Institutions Regulatory Act of 1978. The usual interagency task force of Executive Office and regulatory agency representatives was also appointed by the President to study financial institution reform in general and regulation Q controls specifically.

The results of that study were made public on May 22, 1979, when the President sent a message to Congress calling for an orderly transition period in which to phase out all deposit interest rate controls, leaving only the authority to respond to emergency conditions. That brief message also called for granting authority to all federally chartered savings institutions to offer variable rate mortgages and to invest up to 10 percent of their assets in consumer loans, and instituted a basic legal change which permits all federally insured institutions to offer interest-bearing transaction accounts to individuals. It is difficult to imagine any subject that has received more detailed study during the last twenty years. The issues are clear and the intransigent positions of various groups are well known. Political controversies, rather than economic uncertainties, prevent Congress and the regulatory agencies from acting.

While Congress avoids coming to terms with the political controversies by means of periodical extensions of regulation Q powers, at the same time that investment, lending, and savings powers are gradually liberalized in response to marketplace pressures, the risks of financial disintermediation continue. Such pressure again developed in late 1977; interest rates continued to rise rapidly while the deposit interest rate controls prevented any upward adjustment of returns paid on passbook savings accounts. For example, the average interest rate on Treasury bills in 1977 was 5.26 percent; by September of 1978 that rate had jumped to 7.84 percent and continued upward to a level of 9.65 percent by May of 1979. As returns on Treasury bills and other money market instruments moved above the rates fixed by the deposit interest rate controls, 5 percent at commercial banks and $5\frac{1}{4}$ percent at thrift institutions, the expected slowdown of savings inflows occurred. During late 1977 and early 1978 there was renewed concern about the prospects for mortgage financing and the potential impact of restricted housing activity on the general economy.

The response of the regulatory authorities to the renewed threat of financial disintermediation was to authorize depository institutions to issue new six-month savings certificates with flexible interest rates tied to the yield on six-month Treasury bills. Banks and thrift institutions were allowed to sell these new money market certificates beginning June 1, 1978, and credit unions were granted similar authority in November of 1978.

The new savings certificates have enabled depository institutions to compete for savings during periods of rising interest rates. The six-month instruments are sold in minimum denominations of $10,000 and offer a set return over the entire six months. Each week the financial institutions set their interest rate by linking it to the average rate on Treasury bills with twenty-six-week maturities as determined by the weekly auction. The thrift institutions have been allowed to preserve their traditional advantage of paying rates one-fourth of 1 percent higher than returns offered by commercial banks. By September of 1978 commercial banks and thrift institutions had accumulated $36.8 billion in deposits and by February of 1979 an estimated $116 billion had been placed in these new money market instruments. It is estimated that about one-half of the total represents transfers out of regular passbook savings accounts.

A second new savings instrument was also authorized on June 1, 1978, providing an 8 percent return ($7\frac{3}{4}$ percent for commercial banks) on certificates with maturities of eight years. It was hoped that these longer-term certificates would stabilize the flows of savings to depository institutions, but buyer response has been restricted by the surge of interest rates to double-digit levels.

The results of the sale of money market certificates by depository institutions have been mixed. On the positive side, the new authority has permitted them to compete effectively for savings at a time when financial disintermediation would normally be occurring. During the first half of 1978, for example, prior to the sale of the new six-month certificates, the inflows of deposits to savings and loan associations and mutual savings banks increased at a seasonally adjusted annual rate of only 7 percent. During the next three months savings increased at an adjusted annual rate of 16 percent. The inflow of savings to depository institutions has again moderated in recent months, but the trauma of renewed financial disintermediation has not returned as of May 1979. As a result, mortgage financing has remained readily available, although at historically high interest rates, and housing activity has been much stronger than most economists anticipated.

On the negative side, the payment of much higher interest rates on a growing share of their total deposits has created a major cost problem for most thrift institutions. Since there is no quick way for them to increase their average earnings, which result largely from their holdings of mortgages accumulated over many years, the sharp increase in payments to depositors has created a real squeeze on their earnings. While widespread financial disintermediation has been avoided so far, the extra costs have become a major problem.

The new six-month certificates have also created problems in judging the effectiveness of national monetary policies. In the past, as monetary policies were tightened and the flow of funds to various borrowers was restricted by the cost and reduced availability of credit, the first effect of financial disintermediation was a curtailment of housing activity. The restriction of housing activity, in turn, helped to slow down the entire economy. This rationing process created specific groups of winners and losers but the overall tightening of monetary policy was accomplished. The introduction of the new certificates has significantly changed this general pattern. The housing industry is no longer the first loser as monetary policy tightens. As a result, it is difficult to determine the extent of adjustment in the cost and availability of credit necessary to achieve general economic policy goals. As the overall pace of economic activity continues to erode in 1979, it now appears that the rate of new home building is beginning to slow down, but the transition is much more gradual than in earlier periods when financial disintermediation was more severe.

A closely related development is the recent rapid growth in specialized open-end mutual funds that invest in money market instruments such as large certificates of deposit sold by commercial banks which are not restricted to the maximum interest rate limits set by regulation Q controls. These money market mutual funds are generally very liquid and represent a close substitute for normal savings deposits. It is estimated that over $10 billion were added to these funds during the last three months of 1978 and the first three months of 1979. Once again, the ingenuity of the marketplace in adapting to the interests of the general public is impressive. It is likely that such innovations will continue to proliferate as long as artificial government regulations try to restrict the free flows of savings and investments.

Bank reform legislation

The dramatic action of Congress in passing the Financial Institutions Regulatory Act of 1978 is the latest step in the long history of financial institution reform efforts. The story of how Congressman St Germain shepherded this bill through the legislative process is a classic example of how the rules of the game can be used by a skillful player to achieve legislative goals. This action, however, did not constitute the comprehensive financial institution reform envisioned by the various legislative initiatives described in the preceding chapters.

In 1975 the bank regulatory authorities asked for additional surveillance powers following the shocking failure of two large banks, one in San Diego and one in New York City. In both instances a number of questionable banking practices contributed to the ultimate failure. There was little reaction to the requests for surveillance until the fall of 1977, when the resignation of Bert Lance as Director of the Office of Management and the Budget gave extensive unfavorable publicity to a variety of insider banking transactions. In light of public reaction to the disclosures, Congress moved rapidly to hold hearings and to conduct field surveys to determine the scope and prevalence of such preferential insider arrangements. Nevertheless, it appeared that the bills prepared by the House and Senate differed too widely to be reconciled before the conclusion of the first session of the ninety-fifth Congress in October of 1978. As the session entered its last few days, and long after most people had given up on the possibility that Congress would pass any financial reform legislation, Congressman St Germain set about preparing a comprehensive bill by deleting several controversial points and adding an array of provisions designed to attract the support of various special interest groups. Inclusion of the authority to once again extend regulation Q, scheduled to expire on December 15, 1978, was also a vital part of his strategy.

In the midst of a hectic closing session that lasted thirty-four hours, Congressman St Germain introduced his heavily revised package of proposals during the final hours under a special rule that prohibits any amendments during the discussion on the floor of the House of Representatives. The House eventually passed the reform act at 2:30 Sunday morning by a vote of 341 to 32. Congressman St Germain immediately carried the bill to the Senate and continued to push for passage until the House version was finally approved by a voice vote at 7:05 A.M. This dramatic example is an ironic ending to the long years of academic research, congressional hearings, and interagency studies on many of the provisions included in the bill.

The twenty-one sections of the Financial Institutions Regulatory Act of 1978 are briefly summarized below.

Title I would provide the financial institution supervisory agencies with improved and additional powers over depository institutions (civil money penalties, cease-and-desist orders, removal and suspension of insiders) and place limits on loans by commercial banks to "insiders"—i.e., executive officers, directors and 10% shareholders.

Title II would prohibit interlocking directors among depository institutions in the same geographic area and for large financial institutions regardless of geographic area.

Title III would improve the Federal Deposit Insurance Act (i.e., FDIC approval of foreign branches of state nonmember banks, subpoena power of supervisory agencies, protection for examiners and other supervisory personnel).

Title IV provides for striking and public sale of gold medallions commemorating outstanding individuals in the American arts.

Title V would create a three-member board to supervise insured credit unions.

Title VI would require that Federal banking agencies be given prior notice of proposed change in control of insured bank or holding company and gives agencies authority to disapprove the acquisition on criteria specified in title.

Title VII would require that Federal Home Loan Bank Board be given prior notice of proposed change in control of insured savings and loan or holding company and gives FHLBB authority to disapprove the acquisition on criteria specified in title.

Title VIII would prohibit preferential treatment in loans to insiders by correspondent banks and require reporting of such loans by insiders and banks.

Title IX would require banks to report a list of major stockholders and aggregate amount of insider loans to agencies and public.

Title X establishes a Federal Financial Institutions Examination Council.

Title XI, Right to Financial Privacy Act, would give individuals notice of, and a chance to challenge, Federal agency requests for an individual's bank records and establish five procedures to govern access to individual bank records. Information may be used or retained only for the purpose for which it was obtained and may be transferred to another agency only with statutory authorization, but supervisory agencies may share information.

Title XII would provide mutual savings banks the option of FHLBB charter.

Title XIII amends Public Law 93-100 to allow negotiable order of withdrawal accounts in the State of New York.

Title XIV increases the deposit insurance for individual retirement account and Keogh accounts.

Title XV extends the prohibition on merchant credit card surcharges for two years, extends the Federal Housing Administration experimental mortgage program to Massachusetts, and defines "community" for depository institutions serving military personnel.

Title XVI extends Regulation Q for two years and eliminates the differential on savings accounts linked to a transaction account through an automatic transfer of funds.

Title XVII simplies the investment authority for Federal savings and loan associations, gives such associations more authority to invest in urban areas, and creates a secondary market for rehabilitation loans through the Federal Home Loan Mortgage Corp.

Title XVIII creates in the National Credit Union Administration a Central Liquidity-Facility for credit unions.

Title XIX makes amendments to the Export-Import Act.

Title XX provides for consumer rights and safeguards in electronic fund transfer systems and creates a framework defining the liabilities and responsibilities of all participants in electronic fund transfers.

Title XXI provides the effective date for the legislation.[6]

Most of the publicity given to the bill focused on the prohibition of preferential insider loans given by banks to executive officers, directors, and major stockholders and on the new powers given to regulatory agencies to remove bank officers whose incompetent management might cause a failure. In addition, even though the comprehensive set of recommendations discussed in this study has not been accepted, the bill took specific action on several other proposals put forward in the original Financial Institutions Act:

1. Regulation Q authority was extended for two years.

2. A three-member board to supervise credit unions was created.

3. A new Federal Financial Institutions Council was established to improve the coordination of federal agencies involved in the regulation and supervision of commercial banks.

4. The Federal Home Loan Bank Board was authorized to grant federal charters to mutual savings banks.

5. A central liquidity facility for credit unions was established.

6. Authority for depository institutions in the state of New York to offer NOW accounts for the first time was approved.

7. The power of federal savings and loan associations to make loans in urban areas was improved.

Conclusion

In this study the government's complicated procedures have been analyzed through a specific case which demonstrates the relative roles of various groups, including the Executive Office, Congress, regulatory agencies, public commissions and consultants, academic experts, special interest groups, and the general public. It evaluates

6. "Summary of Financial Package," *American Banker* (Oct. 17, 1978), p. 15.

the legislative and regulatory efforts, lasting from 1970 through 1976, to reform the system of financial institutions that serve as intermediaries in matching savers and borrowers. The need for such efforts has become more significant in recent years. The cumulative strains of inflation and marketplace innovation have created serious distortions in a regulatory framework that was created over forty years ago and designed to meet a financial crisis existing at that time.

The comprehensive package of reforms recommended by the President's Commission on Financial Structure and Regulation, the Executive Order task force led by Treasury officials, and congressional staff studies called for more flexible lending and investment powers and diversified customer services to increase competition and allow each institution to develop its own degree of specialization. The rejection of these suggestions frustrated the effort to rationalize public policies in line with changing marketplace conditions despite widespread recognition that basic reforms are needed.

Internal procedural difficulties and external opposition from special interest groups combined to prevent positive legislative action on the comprehensive set of recommendations. Public opinion did not strongly support the proposals and force the federal government to act, because this issue is not a matter of popular concern and because gradual changes in the marketplace are slowly satisfying customers' needs.

The failure to accept comprehensive reform, however, has compelled financial institutions to resort to what some have called superfluous innovation, aimed at keeping one step ahead of legislative and regulatory rules. Important structural changes have already occurred and more are expected, but the "salami" approach of relying on piecemeal adjustments to avoid triggering a negative reaction from Congress and the regulatory agencies will be slow and expensive. Most reforms will continue to be defensive reactions to changing competitive relationships. State governments may provide some flexibility, however, and federally chartered institutions can be expected to apply pressure on Congress and regulatory authorities to preserve competitive parity with state-chartered intermediaries.

Looking to the future of the government's decision-making processes, they will probably continue to function as they have done in the past. Delays and fragmentation of decisions result from the form of organization and the operating procedures. These are often frustrating for those who believe the system should be efficient, more open to the views of expert advisers, and sensitive to general as well as special interests, but the political domination of the process is not likely to change in a representative government. Inefficiency and legislative failures are evidently a necessary price for the unequaled advantages of democratic institutions.

Following the existing rules of the game does provide for broad analysis and continuity in the decision-making process and helps prevent impetuous reactions to specific problems. National issues are rarely simple enough to create an overwhelming consensus; they must be attacked through the political expedients of compromise and exchanging votes. Parliamentarian strategy and protocol make the system work and enable minority views to be represented. The great strength of our democratic system is that people can eventually express their views through the electoral process.

While it is clear that the representative form of government used in the United States provides many benefits for the general public, it obviously fails many times to fulfill its great potential. In conforming to the political rules of the game, decision making often becomes too much like a game in which strategy and tactics dominate substance, and the divisive efforts of special interests manipulate the system to the neglect of the general interest. The arcane operating procedures and protocol—the club rules—and the ponderous pace of legislative and regulatory actions justify the popular skepticism about the efficiency and equity of the entire system. Important decisions do not need to wait several years until additional studies are prepared on issues that are relatively easy to understand, even if they are extremely controversial. When the Senate passes a bill by a vote of 79 to 14, the House should make a serious effort at least to formally vote on comparable legislation, rather than simply waiting for the congressional calendar to expire.

It is true that issues like financial institution reform have only narrow public appeal and that they entail serious political risks because of the intense controversy they arouse, but when government officials intervene in the markets they create the need for difficult decisions on their part. By failing to act, the government causes confusion in the private sector and makes competitive adjustments not only more expensive but unnecessarily slow. Unwanted and wasteful "innovation" occurs as institutions attempt to evade rules or create artificial advantages to replace the real price and service competition which is unfortunately prevented by arbitrary government intervention.

Instead of allowing the chairmen and important members of committees to dominate the timing and progress of specific legislation, the work schedule should be predetermined; and Congress should vote yes or no on issues, rather than rely on operating procedures and protocol to avoid difficult decisions.

Most of all, it would be helpful to improve the quality of the analyses on which the final decisions are based to some extent, even though political factors will still dominate. Most descriptive and statistical information, inadequate as it is, is now supplied by groups whose special interests are at stake, and they can hardly be expected to be an objective source. Academic experts are generally ignored, and the views of the Executive Office are heavily discounted by suspicious congressional committees. It is a disheartening personal experience to observe the dominating role that special interest groups play in decisions that directly affect the entire society. Political scientists can describe the process clinically in terms of the use of power, but the actuality is difficult for government officials to reconcile with their duty to serve the general public.

Since every important public policy decision is largely shaped by political considerations, the private sector must adapt to the system because it is unlikely that the process will be changed. This simple reality is particularly difficult for economists to accept because of their concentration on questions of national priorities, competition, efficient allocation of resources, and the distribution of income and wealth. To explain how the economy should work, they rely on sophisticated models based on historical relationships and assumptions about the future. Congressional committees, however, must focus on the pragmatic issues of who wins and who loses if change occurs and how to get from the current situation to the idealistic goals. Economists rarely suggest public policies that will answer the real problems of allocation and transition that Congress must deal with. The unfortunate result is that independent economists have little impact on public policy, and their potentially valuable analytical and persuasive skills are rejected as being too theoretical or uncertain to have much value in the "real" world.

To make themselves heard economists must clearly distinguish between the rigorous process of reaching a decision and the political framework within which this occurs. Since the existing arrangements are unlikely to change it is up to professional experts to work for greater recognition and acceptance of their recommendations in the political process of decision making.

Most of all, it is up to the general public to demand a significantly higher standard of performance from government officials if they wish policy decisions to be more responsive to their interests rather than to those of special groups. In athletic contests sportsmanship may count for more than victory. In policy making the results of the process are more important than how well the rules of the game have been followed. Judged against this standard, the eight-year effort to legislate a comprehensive set of reforms for financial institutions has been disappointing, despite the many changes that have occurred in the marketplace.

APPENDIX

Acronyms

ABA	American Bankers Association
CB	commercial bank(s)
CFA	Consumers Federation of America
CUFIAA	Credit Union Financial Institutions Act Amendments
CUNA	Credit Union National Association
EFTS	electronic funds transfer system(s)
FHA	Federal Housing Authority
FHLBB	Federal Home Loan Bank Board
FIA	Financial Institutions Act
FINE	*Financial Institutions and the Nation's Economy* (a study)
FRA	Financial Reform Act
FSLIC	Federal Savings and Loan Insurance Corporation
GAO	General Accounting Office
IBAA	Independent Bankers Association of America
IRA	individual retirement accounts
MSB	mutual savings bank(s)
NAHB	National Association of Home Builders
NAMSB	National Association of Mutual Savings Banks
NOW	negotiable order(s) of withdrawal
NSLL	National Savings and Loan League
USLSA	United States League of Savings Associations
VA	Veterans Administration

BIBLIOGRAPHY

Books

American Bankers Association. *Summary and Interpretive Analysis of the President's Commission on Financial Structure and Regulation.* Washington, D.C.: American Bankers Association, 1972.

Bailey, Stephen K. *Congress Makes a Law.* New York: Columbia University Press, 1950.

Biederman, Kenneth. *Federal Income Taxation of the Savings and Loan and Commercial Banking Industries.* Washington, D.C.: 1973. Prepared for the League of Insured Savings Associations.

Brookings Institution. *Economics and the Policy Maker: Brookings Lectures, 1958–59.* Washington, D.C.: Brookings Institution, 1959.

Cronin, Thomas, and Greenberg, Sanford, eds. *The Presidential Advisory Systems.* New York: Harper and Row, 1969.

Dougall, Herbert E., and Gaumitz, Jack E. *Capital Markets and Institutions.* Englewood Cliffs, N.J.: Prentice-Hall, 1965.

Fair, Ray C., and Jaffee, Dwight M. *The Implications of the Proposals of the Hunt Commission for the Mortgage and Housing Markets: An Empirical Study.* Revision of "Policies for a More Competitive Financial System." Boston: Federal Reserve Bank of Boston, June 1972, pp. 99–148. Conference series no. 8.

Federal Home Loan Bank Board. *A Financial Institution for the Future—Savings, Housing Finance, Consumer Services—An Examination of the Savings and Loan Industry.* Washington, D.C.: Federal Home Loan Bank Board, 1975.

Freeman, J. Leiper. *The Political Process: Executive Bureau–Legislative Committee Relations.* New York: Random House, 1965.

Friend, Irwin. *Study of the Savings and Loan Industry.* Philadelphia: University of Pennsylvania Press, 1969.

Goldsmith, Raymond W. *Financial Institutions.* New York: Random House, 1968.

Grebler, Leo. *The Future of Thrift Institutions: A Study of Diversification versus Specialization*. Danville, Ill.: Joint Savings and Loan Mutual Savings Bank Exchange Groups, 1969.

Horvitz, Paul M., et al. *Private Financial Institutions*. Englewood Cliffs, N.J.: Prentice-Hall, 1963. Sponsored by Commission on Money and Credit.

Key, V. O., Jr. *Politics, Parties, and Pressure Groups*. New York: Thomas Y. Crowell Co., 1958.

Leiserson, Avery. *Administrative Regulation: A Study in Representation of Interests*. Chicago: University of Chicago Press, 1942.

Lindblom, Charles E. *The Policy-Making Process*. Englewood Cliffs, N.J.: Prentice-Hall, 1968.

Marcy, Carl M. *Presidential Commissions*. New York: King's Crown Press, 1945.

Popper, Frank. *The President's Commission*. New York: Twentieth Century Fund, 1970.

Seidman, Harold. *Politics, Position and Power*. New York: Oxford University Press, 1970.

Sorenson, Theodore C. *Decision Making in the White House: The Olive Branch and the Arrows*. New York: Columbia University Press, 1963.

Truman, David B. *The Governmental Process*. New York: Alfred A. Knopf, 1960.

Wolanin, Thomas R. *Presidential Advisory Commissions*. Madison, Wis.: University of Wisconsin Press, 1975.

Articles

Anderson, Clay J. "Diversification, Supervision and the Public Interest." *Federal Reserve Bank of Philadelphia Business Review,* Jan. 1968, pp. 3–11.

Avio, Kenneth L. "Economic Rationale for Statutory Interest Rate Ceilings." *Quarterly Review of Economics and Business* 13 (Autumn 1973): 61–72.

Benston, George J. "Savings Banking and the Public Interest." *Journal of Money, Credit, and Banking* 4 (Feb. 1972): 133–226. A study commissioned by the Savings Bank Association of New York State, Dec. 14, 1971.

Board of Governors of the Federal Reserve System. "Ways to Moderate Fluctuations in the Construction of Housing." *Federal Reserve Bulletin* 58 (March 1972): 215–25.

Bratter, Herbert. "Nixon-Hunt Proposals—Pro and Con." *Bankers Monthly* 90 (Oct. 1973): 20.

Brill, Daniel H., and Ulrey, Ann P. "The Role of Financial Intermediaries in U.S. Capital Markets." *Federal Reserve Bulletin* 53 (Jan. 1967): 18–31.

Brown, M. V. "Prospects for Banking Reform, FINE Study." *Financial Analysts Journal* 32 (March 1976): 14–18.

Burke, J. "Preparing for FINE Testimony: The Road to Washington." *Banking* 68 (Feb. 1976): 24–31.

Burns, Arthur F. "Maintaining the Soundness of Our Banking System." *Federal Reserve Bank of New York Quarterly Review* 56 (Nov. 1974): 263–67.

Chase, Samuel B., Jr. "Financial Structure and Regulation: Some Knotty Problems." *Journal of Finance* 26 (May 1971): 585–97. *See also* entry for Mayne, Lucille S.

"Don't Count Credit Allocation Out Yet." *Bankers Magazine* 158 (Sept. 1975): 19–21. Interview with Congressman Henry Reuss.

"Drive for Sweeping Financial Reform." *Business Week,* May 26, 1975, p. 83.

Ensley, Grover W. "Need for Modernizing Our Financial Structure." *Commercial and Financial Chronicle* 215 (April 6, 1972): 1103.

Ettin, Edward C. "The Development of American Financial Institutions." *Quarterly Review of Economics and Business* 3 (Summer 1963): 51–69.

Garn, E. Jacob. "Legislating in Washington." *Federal Home Loan Bank Board Journal* 9 (July 1976): 14–17.

Golub, Sheldon D. "Regulatory Reform Gets Top Billing in House Banking Committee's New Legislation Package." *Banking* 68 (March 1976): 6.

Guenther, Harry, and Meyer, Philip. "Banking Control: New Hands at the Helm." *The Banker* 125 (Sept. 1975): 1069–77.

Guthmann, Harry G. "Prospects for Financial Institutions: Critical Evaluation as Seen by the Commission on Money and Credit." *Harvard Business Review* 40 (March–April 1962): 151–56.

Horvitz, Paul M. "Hunt Commission Report—A Search for Politically Feasible Solutions to the Problems of Financial Structures." *Journal of Finance* 29 (March 1974): 267–69.

"House Group's 'Reform' Plan Draws Few All-Out Supporters." *Banking* 68 (April 1976): 42.

"House Study Stuns the Banking Industry." *Business Week,* Nov. 17, 1975, pp. 44–45.

"How Newcomers to the House Banking Committee See Their Role." *Banking* 68 (Jan. 1976): 31.

"How Reuss Fumbled Financial Reform." *Business Week,* June 14, 1976, pp. 26–27.

"Hunt Commission Theme: Let Freedom Ring." *Banking* 64 (Jan. 1972): 15.

"Hunt Report—An Agenda for Counterreformation." *First National City Bank,* July 1972, pp. 7–12.

Jackson, William. "Commercial Bank Regulation, Structure, and Performance." *Journal of Finance* 30 (June 1975): 917–20.

Jacobs, Donald P., and Phillips, Almarin. "Commission on Financial Structure and Regulation: Its Organization and Recommendations." *Journal of Finance* 27 (May 1972): 319–41.

Jaffee, Dwight M. "The Extended Lending, Borrowing, and Service Function Proposals of the Hunt Commission Report." *Journal of Money, Credit, and Banking* 4 (Nov. 1972): 990–1000.

Kichline, James L. "Prospects for Institutional Reforms of the Major Depository Intermediaries." In *Ways to Moderate Fluctuation in Housing Construction*, a Federal Reserve staff study, pp. 282–99. Board of Governors of the Federal Reserve System, Dec. 1972.

Klamon, Saul B. "Savings Banks Must Gear Up to Imaginative Financing." *Commercial and Financial Chronicle* 213 (Jan. 21, 1971): 212–14.

Lindblom, Charles E. "The Science of Muddling Through." *Public Administration Review* 19 (Spring 1959): 79–88.

McConnell, Richard M. M. "Treasury Officials Assess the Reaction to Structure Package." *Banking* 66 (Oct. 1973): 100–104. An interview with W. E. Simon and W. H. Beasley.

Mayne, Lucille S. "Discussion." *Journal of Finance* 26 (May 1971): 647–49. *See also* entry for Chase, Samuel B., Jr.

Meltzer, Allan H. "Public and Private Financial Institutions: A Review of Reports from Two Presidential Committees." *Review of Economics and Statistics* 46 (Aug. 1964): 269–78.

"Mr. Proxmire and Mr. Reuss Talk about Banking." *Bankers Magazine* 158 (Autumn 1975): 36–42.

"Mutuals Are Bigger Competition than S & L's." *Banking* 63 (Sept. 1970): 76.

Nadler, Paul S. "Nixon-Hunt Proposals—An Appraisal." *Bankers Magazine* 90 (Sept. 1973): 9–10.

"New Momentum in Banking Reform." *Business Week*, Oct. 13, 1975, p. 41.

Randall, Kay. "Hunt Commission—A Delayed Response." *Journal of Commercial Bank Lending* 56 (Dec. 1973): 38–45.

"Retail Banking Loses Its Great Allure." *Business Week,* June 28, 1976, pp. 45–46.

Reuss, Henry S. "Fair Deal for the Small Saver." *Money* 5 (Sept. 1976): 100–102.

———. "Shaping Banking's Future." *Credit and Financial Management* 77 (Sept. 1975): 12–13.

Ritter, Lawrence S. "Nixon's Commission on Finance: Pious Hopes and No Teeth." *The Banker* 122 (Feb. 1972): 147–50.

Robertson, J. L. "Yes, Banks Need More Freedom to Compete with Each Other." *Fortune* 82 (Nov. 1970): 66. *See also* entry for Wallich, Henry C.

Rousselot, John H. "Congressman Speaks Candidly." *Credit and Financial Management* 78 (March 1976): 12–13.

Sametz, Arnold W. "Cyclical Problems Facing S & L's in the Next Decade and Suggested Reforms." In *Cyclical and Growth Problems Facing the Savings and Loan Industry—Policy Implications and Suggested Reform*, edited by Arnold W. Sametz. New York: New York University Graduate School of Business Administration, 1968.

Schott, Francis H. "Qualified Yes to the Hunt Commission Report." *Bankers Magazine* 155 (Summer 1972): 91–95.

Strachan, Stan. "U.S. Banking Regulations and Competition." *The Banker* 122 (Dec. 1972): 1671–79.

"Studies in the Economics of Bank Regulation—A Symposium." *Journal of Finance* 31 (May 1976): 215–55.

"The Commission: How to Create a Blue Chip Consensus." *Time* 95 (Jan. 19, 1970): 22–23.

"The President's Commission on Financial Structure and Regulation—A Symposium." *Journal of Money, Credit, and Banking* 3 (Feb. 1971): 1–34.

"Treasury's Simon Wants Financial Reform." *Commercial and Financial Chronicle* 219 (May 20, 1974): 32.

Walker, Charls E. "Why Banking Reform Is Coming." *Business Week*, Sept. 15, 1973, p. 39.

Wallich, Henry C. "Banks Need More Freedom to Compete." *Fortune* 81 (March 1970): 114–15. *See also* entry for Robertson, J. L.

"What Went Wrong with Financial Reform." *Business Week*, Nov. 3, 1973, pp. 83–84.

Wilson, Stanley. "Housing Lobby Wrecks Financial Reform." *Business Week*, April 26, 1976, p. 36.

Public Documents

U.S., Congress, House. *Proposed Legislation: Financial Institutions—Message from the President.* H.D., 94th Cong., 1st sess., March 19, 1975.

————, Committee on Banking and Currency. *The Crunch and Reform of Financial Institutions, Parts 1 and 2.* Hearing before a subcommittee on Banking Supervision and Insurance, 93d Cong., 1st sess., Sept. 10–14 (Part 1) and 17–20 (Part 2), 1973.

————. *Federal Savings Institutions.* Report on H.R. 13718, 90th Cong., 1st sess., 1967.

————. *Financial Institutions: Reform and the Public Interest.* Staff report of the subcommittee on Domestic Finance, 93d Cong., 1st sess., 1973.

————. *Regulation Q, NOW Accounts, Investment in State Housing Corporations.* Hearing before a subcommittee on Bank Supervision and Insurance, 93d Cong., 1st sess., March 13–15, 1973.

U.S., Congress, House, Committee on Banking, Currency, and Housing. *Explanation of Proposed Financial Institutions Act of 1976.* 94th Cong., 2d sess., Feb. 1976.

————. *Financial Institutions and the Nation's Economy (FINE) "Discussion Principles."* Part 1, 94th Cong., 1st sess., Dec. 2–10, 1975. *Part 2*, 94th Cong., 1st sess., Dec. 11–17, 1975. *Part 3*, 94th Cong., 1st and 2d sess., Dec. 18, 1975–Jan. 29, 1976. *Part 4, Appendixes A and B*, 94th cong., 2d sess., 1976.

———. *Financial Reform Act of 1976.* Hearing before a subcommittee on Financial Institutions, Supervision, Regulation, and Insurance. *Part 1,* 94th Cong., 2d sess., March 4, 9, 11, 16, 1976. *Part 2,* 94th Cong., 2d sess., March 17, 18, 23, 1976.

———. *FINE: Financial Institutions and the Nation's Economy—Compendium of Papers Prepared for the FINE Study: Books 1 and 2.* 94th Cong., 1st sess., June 1976.

———. *Regulation Q, Part 4.* Hearing before a subcommittee on Financial Institutions, Supervision, Regulation, and Insurance, 94th Cong., 1st sess., Sept. 9–11, 1975.

U.S., Congress, Senate, Committee on Banking, Housing, and Urban Affairs. *Extension of Regulation Q and NOW Accounts.* Hearing before a subcommittee on Financial Institutions, 93d Cong., 1st sess., March 20–22, 1973.

———. *Federal Bank Commission Act, 1976.* Hearing, 94th Cong., 2d sess., Feb. 3, March 1, 19, 1976.

———. *Financial Institutions Act, 1973.* Hearing before a subcommittee on Housing and Urban Affairs, 93d Cong., 2d sess., May 13–17, 1974.

———. *Financial Institutions Act of 1975.* Hearing before a subcommittee on Financial Institutions. 94th Cong., 1st sess., May 14–16, June 11, 1975.

———. *Financial Institutions Act of 1975.* S.R., 94th Cong., 1st sess., Nov. 20, 1975.

———. *Financial Structure and Regulation.* Hearing before a subcommittee on Financial Institutions. 93d Cong., 1st sess. Nov. 6–8, 1973.

———. *Housing and Financial Reform.* Hearing before a subcommittee on Financial Institutions. 93d Cong., 2d sess., Dec. 11, 1974.

———. *Housing Goals and Mortgage Credit 1975–80.* Hearing before a subcommittee on Housing and Urban Affairs. 94th Cong., 1st sess., Sept. 22–25, 1975.

———, Subcommittee on Financial Institutions. *International Banking Act of 1976.* 94th Cong., 2d sess., Aug. 31, 1976.

———. *Reform of Financial Institutions: 1973.* 93d Cong., 2d sess., Sept. 11, 12, 25, 1974.

U.S., Department of the Treasury. *The Financial Institutions Act of 1975.* Washington, D.C.: U.S. Government Printing Office, 1975.

———. *Recommendations for Change in the U.S. Financial System.* Washington, D.C.: U.S. Government Printing Office, 1973.

U.S., National Commission on Consumer Finance. *Consumer Credit in the United States.* Washington, D.C.: U.S. Government Printing Office, 1972.

U.S., *Report of the President's Commission on Financial Structure and Regulation.* Washington, D.C.: U.S. Government Printing Office, 1971.

INDEX